Growing Public
Social Spending and Economic Growth
Since the Eighteenth Century

Growing Public explores the links between economic growth and social policies that redistribute income. Taxes and transfers have been debated for centuries, but only now can we get a clear view of the whole evolution of social spending. What kept prospering nations from using taxes for social programs until the end of the nineteenth century? Why did taxes and spending then grow so much, and what are the prospects for social spending in this century? Why did North America become a leader in public education in some ways and not others? Lindert finds answers in the economic history and logic of political voice, population aging, and income growth. Contrary to traditional beliefs, the net national costs of government social programs are virtually zero. This book not only shows that no Darwinian mechanism has punished the welfare states, but, it uses history to explain why this surprising result makes sense. Contrary to the intuition of many economists and the ideology of many politicians, social spending has contributed to, rather than inhibited, economic growth.

Peter H. Lindert is Distinguished Professor of Economics at the University of California, Davis, and a research associate of the National Bureau of Economic Research. His writings have touched on a wide range of economic and historical topics relating to Europe, the United States, China, Indonesia, and the global economy. His textbooks in international economics have been translated into eight other languages.

Advance praise for *Growing Public*

"Peter Lindert has written a dazzling book. He takes on one of the grand topics of economics – the rise of social spending – and offers us a remarkable combination of new data, historical insight, political analysis, and economic assessment. Amazingly, Lindert comes up with fresh, convincing, and important insights on issues that have been debated for decades. Two of Lindert's major conclusions are that the spread of democracy has historically played a pivotal role in the rise of social expenditures; and that social spending has not gravely weakened economic incentives and long-term economic growth, despite the drumbeat of criticisms from free-market devotees. Indeed Lindert concludes that 'the net national costs of social transfers, and of the taxes that finance them, are essentially zero.' This powerful book will be widely read and debated for many years to come."

– Jeffrey D. Sachs, Director, The Earth Institute at Columbia University

"What determines social spending, also known as public education, also known as social security, also known as taking from the rich and giving to the poor? This question is the subject of much theoretical and empirical speculation and some moderately detailed previous work. Yet this magnificent summa by Peter Lindert blows away the field. He probes the historical and comparative rise of social spending in today's OECD countries and derives many new insights into the classic themes of social spending and elite behavior, democracy, inequality, religion, and ethnic divisions. He draws out the implications of his careful analysis for the future of the Third World and First alike. A must-read for anyone interested in big government, political economy, helping the poor, or simply the fate of human societies."

– William Easterly, New York University

"Peter Lindert has given us a treatise on the economic and political forces driving social spending and of the effects of the welfare state that sweeps over time, over nations, and over disciplines. It is simultaneously comparative–political–economic history, demography, applied econometrics, political theory, and political economy. While few will agree with all of the often-surprising answers he gives to the most fundamental questions regarding the existence and the effects of public social welfare policies, no one will suggest that they are not bold and provocative. *Growing Public* is a most readable and insightful and, yes, irreverent volume that will be discussed by all concerned with these front-page issues."

– Robert Haveman, John Bascom Emeritus Professor of Economics and Public Affairs, University of Wisconsin-Madison

"*Growing Public* offers economic historians, policy analysts, development gurus, and the general public – all of whom have reason to be deeply concerned about the growth implications of fiscal policy – the most comprehensive historical and econometric examination of the essential value of public expenditures I have seen anywhere. His lens of inquiry encompasses everything from early modern European charitable activities to the apex of the late-twentieth-century welfare state, from the 'Old Poor Law' to the rise of public schooling, from old-age pensions in the west to social transfers in the developing world. By the conclusion of this tour, the reader is left with a clear view of a world in which public expenditures on human welfare not only do no harm to national growth trajectories, but one in which investment in the infrastructure of human capital formation is itself growth-enhancing. This core finding of Lindert's exhaustive research will appear radical, perhaps even heretical, to a generation trained in neo-classical economics, but he arrives at it by employing the best of the theory and methodology of that discipline. As such it will be hard to refute."

– Anne E. C. McCants, Associate Professor of History, Massachusetts Institute of Technology

"What determines how much governments spend on health, welfare, education, and social security? What effect does this social spending have on economic growth? Peter Lindert gives new answers to these big questions, in a lucid and engagingly written book that ranges across the globe and from the eighteenth century up to the current day. His surprising finding is that social spending does not slow growth, at least in western democracies, and his gem of a book will be essential reading for historians, economists, political scientists, and modern-day policy makers."

– Philip T. Hoffman, Richard and Barbara Rosenberg Professor of History and Social Science, California Institute of Technology

Growing Public

*Social Spending and Economic Growth
Since the Eighteenth Century*

Volume 1
The Story

PETER H. LINDERT
University of California, Davis

CAMBRIDGE
UNIVERSITY PRESS

PUBLISHED BY THE PRESS SYNDICATE OF THE UNIVERSITY OF CAMBRIDGE
The Pitt Building, Trumpington Street, Cambridge, United Kingdom

CAMBRIDGE UNIVERSITY PRESS
The Edinburgh Building, Cambridge CB2 2RU, UK
40 West 20th Street, New York, NY 10011-4211, USA
477 Williamstown Road, Port Melbourne, VIC 3207, Australia
Ruiz de Alarcón 13, 28014 Madrid, Spain
Dock House, The Waterfront, Cape Town 8001, South Africa

http://www.cambridge.org

First published 2004

Printed in the United States of America

Typeface Sabon 10/12 pt.   System LaTeX 2ε   [TB]

A catalog record for this book is available from the British Library.

Library of Congress Cataloging in Publication Data
Lindert, Peter H.
Growing public : social spending and economic growth since the eighteenth century /
Peter H. Londert.
p. cm.
Includes bibliographical references and index.
ISBN 0-521-82174-6 – ISBN 0-521-52916-6 (pbk.)
1. Government spending policy – History – Case studies.   2. Income distribution – History –
Case studies.   3. Transfer payments – History – Case studies.   4. Welfare economics –
History – Case studies.   I. Title.
HJ2005.L565   2004
339.5'22 – dc22   2003061672

ISBN 0 521 82174 6 hardback
ISBN 0 521 52916 6 paperback

To Lin, Kathy, Alex, and Nick

Contents

Preface to Volume 1

The main issue dividing political parties today divided their predecessors two decades, two centuries, and two millennia ago: What role should redistribution through government play in our lives? While the issue is eternal, the facts are recent. More than two millennia ago, Aristotle foresaw that the poor could use their political voice to get transfers from the rich, yet through most of history the poor never gained either the voice or the transfers. Only in the past 200 years has government social spending grown large. Only in the past two decades have scholars and government agencies put together the information needed to explain why the growth of social spending has been so recent and to judge what impact it has had on economic growth.

Telling the story of social spending and economic growth requires weaving together a wide variety of materials. Most of the key ideas and displays of evidence can serve a very wide audience, but some are statistical. To address different audiences, I have divided the book into two volumes. Volume 1 is written for human beings and Volume 2 for social scientists. Here is a quick tour of the contents of Volume 2, which carries the subtitle *Further Evidence:*

PART FIVE: THE UNDERLYING FRAMEWORK

13. A Minimal Theory of Social Transfers
    Sketches a simple unified theory that predicts many of the key findings of the whole book.

14. A Guide to the Tests
    Sets up the procedures and conducting tests and judging impacts in Chapters 15–19.

E. Regressions Predicting Social Spending, Growth, and
   Employment, OECD 1962–1995
   Displays the detailed postwar regression results used in
      Chapters 7 and 17.

F. Social Transfers circa 1990 versus History
   Gives the numbers behind Figures 9.2–9.5 in Chapter 9.

G. Postregression Accounting Formulas
   Derives the algebra for Chapter 17's decomposition of
      international differences in social transfers into explained
      and unexplained parts.

Bibliography for Volume 2

For readers wishing to dig deeper into the evidence of these two volumes, the main underlying data sets are available online at either (http://www.cup.org/0521821746) or the author's home page (http://www.econ.ucdavis.edu/faculty/fzlinder).

Permissions for Both Volumes

Portions of Chapters 7 (Volume 1) and 16 (Volume 2) first appeared, in different form, in Peter H. Lindert, "The Rise of Social Spending, 1880–1930." *Explorations in Economic History* 31, 1 (January 1994): 1–37.

Portions of Chapters 7 (Volume 1) and 17 (Volume 2) first appeared, in different form, in Peter H. Lindert, "What Limits Social Spending?" *Explorations in Economic History* 33, 1 (January 1996): 1–34.

A portion of Chapter 13 of Volume 2 first appeared, in different form, in Lorenzo Kristov, Peter Lindert, and Robert McClelland, "Pressure Groups and Redistribution." *Journal of Public Economics* 48, 2 (June 1992): 135–163.

PART ONE

OVERVIEW

I

Patterns and Puzzles

Over the next one hundred years, there will be waves of intense debate over using taxes for social programs. Defenders will package such programs as high-return investments that benefit most of society and tax only those people whose share of income and wealth could stand to come down. Opponents will decry the two-sided stifling of initiatives that invites both the taxed and the subsidized to be less productive. Both sides will invest in studies showing that they are right.

This future debate seems to follow naturally from the flow of history, the logic of self-interest, and the inevitable help-versus-incentives quandary.

The two opposing sets of arguments have been rediscovered and repeated for centuries, mainly in debates over social transfers to the poor. Any reading of the social history of early modern Europe turns up all the arguments we hear today. Long before the Fabians, there was a Left argument that the poor, elderly, and uneducated were people who needed help through no fault of their own. Many of these unfortunates could never be self-supporting, so that harsh work incentives would be cruel and unproductive. Others were the "able–bodied" whose productive potential could handsomely repay any society that wisely invested in them.

And long before Malthus there was a conservative argument that any combination of taxes and transfers is doubly costly. It erodes incentives to work, to take risks, and to accumulate, both for those being taxed and for those receiving benefits based on their low incomes. Such a system makes the poor, the elderly, and the uneducated worse off in the long run, by shrinking the size of the whole economy and by trapping them into dependence on public largesse. Self-help is the key to getting out of poverty and having enough saved up for old age. Accordingly, traditional conservatism keeps rediscovering the efficiency of the marketplace and the value of tough work incentives.

Aside from any simple projection of past history into the future, one can forecast that the same debate will continue if only by the logic of self-interest. Humans' self-interests will differ because their earning-power endowments will always differ. They are sure to take opposing sides in any discussion of the merits of using some people's tax money to help others with insurance or human development. In fact, the whole history of debate over social programs is just a shifting back and forth between two poles of self-interest. Newly popular arguments in the debate reflect shifts in the balance of power between the two long-fixed poles, not new ideas.

New facts cannot end the debate. This is partly because the equilibrium between self-interests will prevent resolution. People have different self-interests, and these are still the dominant force governing how people vote.[1] There will always be a political tug-of-war between those who are more likely to benefit from redistribution and those who would be taxed by it.

More fundamentally, the debate cannot have a clear resolution because there is no escape from the conflicts involving the desire to help others and the desire to give them incentives for self-help. We are most familiar with this conflict in debates over helping the poor. In any debate over public assistance, or what the Americans call welfare, we are caught within a triangle where the three corners represent three social goals: helping people in a given state, giving them an incentive to avoid that state, and keeping down the program budget. Any movement within this triangle must move away from at least one corner, one goal. No new facts can alter this.

Yet new facts can raise the level of the debate. They arm all sides with an awareness of how tax-based social spending would affect collective goods that all profess to care about – social peace and the size of the economy. The competitiveness of the intellectual marketplace, and of the political marketplace in electoral democracies, allows new facts to exert pressure toward these collective goods. At the very least, new facts can speed up society's rejection of bad arguments.

THE ROAD FROM HERE

Most of the facts we need come from a history dating back to the late eighteenth century. Back then, in the age of Adam Smith and the dawn of classical economics, governments hardly imposed any taxes at all, and there were practically no social programs, by today's standards. The facts are not easy to assemble, because the early facts are so scattered among the archives and because today's large social programs are so complex in their effects. Yet they do yield answers to the big historical questions about tax-based social spending:

- Why so late in history? That is, why did no country before the end of the eighteenth century have even 3 percent of its national product devoted to redistributive social programs?

- Why so big? That is, why did social spending expand to claim over one-third of national product in so many countries?
- Why was this rise so much greater in some countries than in others?
- Why no sunset? That is, why did social spending as a share of national product stop growing, yet not decline, after about 1980 in the leading countries?
- How much has the rise of social spending cost us in terms of lost economic growth? Why hasn't its rising cost brought social spending to its sunset?
- Will today's developing countries and transition economies go through the same history?

The scope of this story will keep widening as this volume progresses. Our view is narrow at first, because social spending was so limited before the twentieth century. Geographically, Part Two begins in Western Europe and North America alone in the eighteenth and nineteenth centuries. In the dawn of social spending, there were only two kinds of redistributive tax-based social spending to discuss: poor relief and public schools. Chapters 3 through 6 grapple with the puzzle that England and Holland led in poor relief, but first the German states and then North America led in the support for public schooling. By the period 1880–1930, social programs had spread enough that we can widen our focus to twenty-one countries. For this period we can also survey several government-budget categories – a few kinds of taxes and several social-spending categories, now including unemployment compensation, public health, and housing subsidies, as well as poor relief and public schooling. By this point, in Chapter 7, we can draw on statistical patterns as well as on institutional and budgetary history. It turns out that the differential rise of social spending is best explained by international differences in democracy, aging, income, and religion.

The real boom in social spending came in the latter half of the twentieth century. Chapter 7 finds that a few forces again suffice to explain most of the differences in the social-spending boom, with some countries developing true welfare states while others stick with minimal government social programs.

Population aging will bring social budget crises for a few highly industrialized countries, but not for the rest of the world, as Chapters 8 and 9 will show. Social spending patterns in developing countries have much in common with the earlier history of the core set of industrialized countries belonging to the Organization for Economic Cooperation and Development (OECD). Asia is not as different as we thought, either from the OECD core or from Latin America, once the same explanatory variables are introduced. What had passed for a wholly different approach to pensions and other social programs turned out to be explainable in terms of democracy, income levels, and the aging of the population. The transition economies of Eastern Europe and the former Soviet Union also fit the same broad patterns, though they have been dealt a particularly difficult hand by the collapse of previous regimes that had promised more growth, and even more social security, than they delivered.

Chapters 10 through 12 tackle the most controversial part of the topic: What about those rising costs of the welfare state? They prove surprisingly elusive. Volume 2 will statistically confirm a puzzle posed later in this chapter: There *is* *no* clear net economic cost to the welfare state, either in our first glance at the raw numbers or in deeper statistical analyses that hold many other things equal. To avoid accepting a statistical mirage, Chapters 10 through 12 take a deeper look into the underlying institutional mechanisms. It turns out that there are good reasons why radically different approaches to the welfare state have little or no net difference in their economic costs. Those reasons are many, in terms of an institutional list, but they boil down to a unified logic: Electoral democracy, for all its messiness and clumsiness, keeps the costs of either too much welfare state or too little under control. This interpretation is also consistent with the disturbing rise of European unemployment from the 1970s through the 1990s.

To keep this complex and widening topic under control, an initial clarification about social spending and transfers is in order. As our focus shifts back and forth between different programs, a reader may well wonder, "Is this a book about redistribution? Don't the various social programs differ greatly in the extent to which they redistribute between rich and poor? For what purpose can you add different types of social spending together?"

Social programs do differ greatly in how much they redistribute between rich and poor, and just adding their expenditures together is not a measure of redistribution. In fact, as we shall see, as social spending redistributed more and more overall, the average redistribution of each extra dollar dropped. That is, programs drifted from being help-the-poor programs to being broad social safety nets that gave many benefits back to the income classes who paid the taxes. Still, there is a definite redistributive element to all social spending, and this is what makes it so controversial. To deal with the continuum of degrees of progressivity in a study focusing on explaining society's demand for social programs, we shall use these two definitions:

Social spending consists of these kinds of tax-based government spending:

- basic assistance to poor families, alias "poor relief" (before 1930), "family assistance," "welfare" (in America), or "supplemental income";
- unemployment compensation, alias "the dole";
- public noncontributory pensions, in which the funds come from persons other than the recipient and his or her employer;[2]
- public health expenditures;
- housing subsidies; and
- public expenditures on education.

The distinct term *social transfers* shall be reserved for all of the social spending above *minus* government expenditures on education.

These terms, and the list above, are designed to bring order to the blurry differences in redistributive "progressivity" – the rate of transferring income from rich to poor. In general, social spending categories are ranked as follows in terms of their progressivity:

> Basic assistance and
> unemployment compensation
> > pensions and   > housing
> > public health   subsidies
> > > primary   > secondary   > higher
> > > public   public   education
> > > education   education

Since the controversy of these programs, and the fear that they damage the economy, runs in this order of their progressivity, this book will focus a bit more heavily on social transfers than on education. It will also concentrate more on basic aid to the poor, the most controversial program of all, than on other social transfers.

We begin with an age in which almost none of this existed.

TAXING, SPENDING, AND GIVING IN THE LATE EIGHTEENTH CENTURY

In 1776, when Adam Smith's classic *Inquiry into the Nature and Causes of the Wealth of Nations* was published and the American colonies declared their independence from Britain, the modern age of social spending had not yet dawned. People paid hardly any taxes for the social programs that take such a large tax bite from paychecks today. Most poor people received negligible help from anybody. The elderly received no public pensions, mainly because few people survived to be elderly and average working incomes were too low to support many dependents. Most children did not go to school, and parents had to pay for those who did.

Poor Relief, Public and Private

In the late eighteenth century the payment of taxpayers' money to the poor, or "poor relief" as it was called before the 1930s, was just becoming noticeable as a share of the average wage or the average income anywhere in the world. As Table 1.1 suggests, it exceeded one percent of national income only in the Netherlands and in England and Wales. By the 1820s England and Wales had become the world's center of poor relief, both in fact and in public debate, the Netherlands having cut back its commitments in the wake of the damage

Growing Public

TABLE I.I. *The Low Levels of Tax-Based Social Spending in the Late Eighteenth Century and Early Nineteenth*

| Country | Year | Percent Shares of Gross National Product | |
		Relief for the Poor	Public Education, Primary through University
Belgium	1820	1.03	
	1850	0.28[a]	0.38
England and Wales	1776	1.59	0
	1820–1821	2.66	0
	1850	1.07	0.07
France	1833	0.63	0.13
Netherlands	1790	1.70	
	1822	1.36	
	1850	1.38	0.29
Sweden	1829	0.02	
United States	1850	0.13	0.33
All other countries	1776–1815	Zero or negligible	Zero or negligible

Note: The poor relief estimates are from Lindert (1998), and the estimates of public education expenditure estimates are from Lindert (2001).

[a] The poor relief figure is for 1840–47.

its economy suffered in the wars of 1792–1815. Yet even in England and Wales around 1820, as Table 1.1 shows, poor relief was still less than 3 percent of the income, and this was as high as its share got in any country before 1930.

Yet even this amount of transfers – tiny by today's standards – was enough to spark great controversy at the end of the eighteenth century and into the early nineteenth. Reverend Malthus wrote his famous *Essay on Population* in 1798 largely to criticize England's rising practice of local poor relief. He argued that helping the poor just invited them to have too many children. Giving birth to extra laborers would eventually force wages back down to the bare subsistence level. David Ricardo agreed with Malthus' criticisms on this point. So did Parliament, when it passed the famous Poor Law Reform in 1834, cutting taxpayers' commitment to the poor. Even Karl Marx agreed that English poor relief was degrading in the late eighteenth and early nineteenth centuries, both when that relief was condescendingly given and when it was cut in the 1834 reform. He viewed both the giving and the taking away as parts of the internal contradictions of capitalism. Even today emotions continue to run strong on the issue of using tax money to help the poor.

One might think that the churches and other private donors supplied the help that the poor failed to get from tax-based public relief. But this conventional wisdom is probably wrong. As we shall see in Chapter 3, the rich variety of early charities gave the poor very little in Europe and the United States, even when church giving is included.[3] Private charity was not a substitute for taxed-based poor relief and was not crowded out by the later rise of that public aid. It was a complement, and the two rose, and occasionally fell, together. Back in the eighteenth century, both public and private aid were withheld from the poor.

The Elderly

There were no public pensions for the elderly in the late eighteenth century.[4] Rather the elderly had to rely on their own assets, family help, and any self-insurance groups they had joined – unless they were truly poor. If they were truly poor in their old age, then they qualified for ordinary poor relief. What they received from local governments is already included in the meager poor-relief totals shown in Table 1.1.

The elderly poor may have been better supported than other paupers, since they fell into the "deserving" category by being less able–bodied, less fit for work. Some have even argued that before 1840 they were supported as well as pensioners in the late twentieth century.[5] Yet there were limits to what they were given, both as a share of national product and as a ratio of recipients' support to an average adult income. The elderly received a much smaller share of national income than their share of the whole population, meaning that the average money received by the average elderly person must have been well below the average income of the whole country, even if it compared well with the aid to younger paupers.[6]

Public Education

While the elderly poor may have received their share of that small poor relief budget in the later eighteenth century, schools received only negligible aid. Table 1.1 lists some shares of national product going to public support of all levels of education in the leading countries in 1833 or 1850. No country collected even as much as one-half of 1 percent of national income in taxes for education. Small as these shares were, the shares back in the late eighteenth century were much smaller. Taxpayers had hardly begun to support education, especially the education of the poor, in the late eighteenth century, as Chapter 5 will show.

Why didn't the political leaders of the late eighteenth century believe in public education? This book will argue that the real reason was the unequal distribution of political voice, not a lack of intellectual leaders who saw a case for public schooling. In fact, both Adam Smith in Britain and Thomas

Jefferson in colonial America spoke out for using taxpayers' money to pay for the education of other people's children. Their view is worth noting, even though it was overruled by the self-interests of powerful persons opposed to taxes for schools.

Even though Adam Smith is best known for arguing in favor of free markets, he saw a case for having taxes and government spending provide useful things that individuals would not provide adequately themselves. National defense, justice, commercial infrastructure, and public education should be funded by taxes, or even directly provided as state services. The case arises from the same basic point, both in the *Wealth of Nations* and in today's economics: If individuals failed to capture all the social gains from providing these things, then individuals could not be relied upon to provide enough of them:

[An essential] duty of the sovereign or commonwealth is that of erecting and maintaining those publick institutions and those publick works, which, though they may be in the highest degree advantageous to a great society, are, however, of such a nature that the [social] profit could never repay the expence to any individual or small number of individuals, and which it, therefore, cannot be expected that any individual or small number of individuals should erect or maintain....

When the institutions or publick works which are beneficial to the whole society, either cannot be maintained altogether, or are not maintained altogether by the contribution of such members of the society as are most immediately benefited by them, the deficiency must in most cases be made up by the general contribution of the whole society.[7]

This is not to say that Smith liked taxes and big government for their own sake. On the contrary, he saw waste in much of the government spending of his day, especially in the subsidy to unproductive high offices. He railed at length against tariffs on imported goods, such as England's infamous Corn Laws. And even where he approved of taxes as the basis for those "publick institutions and publick works," he approved of some kinds of taxes and not others. He preferred either user charges or proportional direct taxes on income. He disliked most indirect taxes (sales taxes, tariffs, excise taxes) and would probably not have approved of today's highly progressive income taxes.

Still, Smith did approve of charging taxpayers for some things, and one kind of social spending seemed to rank with national defense at the top of his list of tax-worthy public improvements. Smith favored tax support for public education at all levels, especially if the taxes were borne by the local beneficiaries of educating other people's children.[8]

Thomas Jefferson agreed with Adam Smith about public schooling. In 1779 Jefferson introduced his *Bill for the More General Diffusion of Knowledge* in the Virginia assembly, calling for a statewide system of free public elementary schools to be paid for by local taxpayers. Like Adam Smith, the main author of the Declaration of Independence felt that everybody, and not just the parents of school-age children, was better off if all (white) persons had an equal maximum chance to achieve a liberal education at public expense. At the secondary level, he proposed, the burden should be shifted more to parents and away from taxpayers, though he called for full tax-based aid to the top-scoring students from elementary school. At the university level, Jefferson again saw a case for tax-based education. Unhappy with the performance of the private College of William and Mary, he called for state administration, state taxpayer funding, and secularization.[9] His bill was a harbinger of America's early leadership in public schooling, as we shall see in Chapter 5. Yet each time he introduced it in Virginia – in 1779, in the 1790s, and again in 1817 – it was defeated by those whose self-interest would be compromised by property taxes that would pay for common schools.[10] The same kind of political opposition was also characteristic of the British society that Adam Smith was trying to educate in the *Wealth of Nations*.

THE LONG RISE OF SOCIAL SPENDING

Starting from that negligible base in the late eighteenth century, social spending as a share of the national economy rose haltingly over the next one hundred years, then accelerated between 1880 and World War II, and boomed between World War II and about 1980. Since 1980 its share of national product has risen very little. Table 1.2 and Figure 1.1 show the progress of total social transfers (thus excluding public education) for several countries.[11]

The most obvious pattern in the rise of social transfers is that it happened to every OECD country sooner or later, mainly in the twentieth century. By 1980 all of them took more than 10 percent from taxpayers on behalf of the poor, the elderly, and the sick, even without including public educational spending. The loud message here is that the history of taxing and transferring is not just a miscellany of separate and unique national histories. There is an obvious common pattern, and later chapters will show that it is spreading to still other countries as their incomes grow. Is this a diffusion process, in which some countries learn from others the wisdom and technique of setting up social programs? Probably not. As we shall see, some basic common forces were at work in all countries, evoking similar responses that probably owed little to any diffusion of knowledge about tax-based social programs.

Within this impressive upward trend in all countries, there were some intriguing changes in leadership, as suggested by the boldface entries in Table 1.2 and the top national paths in Figure 1.1. In the late nineteenth century, the social-transfer pioneers were the Scandinavian countries, especially Denmark and Norway, followed by Britain. Around 1900, these leaders were joined by Australia and New Zealand, which suddenly instituted generous public pension and health care programs. Before 1930, no leading role was assumed by North America or Japan or any Continental European country below Scandinavia.[12]

TABLE 1.2. *Social Transfers in OECD Countries, 1880–1995, as Percentages of Gross Domestic Product at Current Prices*

(1880–1930: Welfare, unemployment, pensions, health, and housing subsidies)
(1960–1980: OECD old series; 1980–1990: OECD new series)

	1880	1890	1900	1910	1920	1930	OECD Old			OECD New		
							1960	1970	1980	1980	1990	1995
Australia	0	0	0	1.12	1.66	2.11	7.39	7.37	12.79	10.90	13.57	14.84
Austria	0	0	0	0	0	1.20	15.88	18.90	23.27	23.43	24.54	21.39
Belgium	0.17	0.22	0.26	0.43	0.52	0.56	13.14	19.26	30.38	22.45	23.11	27.13
Canada	0	0	0	0	0.06	0.31	9.12	11.80	14.96	12.91	17.38	18.09
Denmark	0.96	1.11	1.41	1.75	2.71	3.11	12.26	19.13	27.45	26.44	26.97	30.86
Finland	0.66	0.76	0.78	0.90	0.85	2.97	8.81	13.56	19.19	18.32	24.66	31.65
France	0.46	0.54	0.57	0.81	0.64	1.05	13.42	16.68	22.55	22.95	23.70	26.93
Germany[a]	0.50	0.53	0.59			4.82	18.10	19.53	25.66	20.42	19.85	24.92
Greece[b]	0	0	0	0		0.07	10.44	9.03	11.06	8.67	13.95	14.43
Ireland	0					3.74	8.70	11.89	19.19	16.20	18.05	18.30

Italy	0	0	0	0	0.08		**13.10**	**16.94**	21.24	17.10	21.34	23.71
Japan	0.05	0.11	0.17	0.18	0.21		4.05	5.72	11.94	10.48	11.57	12.24
Netherlands	0.29	0.30	0.39	0.39	0.99	1.03	**11.70**	**22.45**	**28.34**	**26.94**	**27.59**	**25.70**
New Zealand	0.17	0.39	1.09	**1.35**	**1.84**	**2.43**	10.37	9.22	15.22	16.22	22.12	18.64
Norway	**1.07**	**0.95**	**1.24**	1.18	1.09	**2.39**	7.85	16.13	20.99	18.50	**26.44**	**27.55**
Portugal	0	0	0	0	0			..	..	10.10	12.62	15.23
Spain	0	0	0.02	0.04	0.07		..	..	..	12.97	17.01	19.01
Sweden	**0.72**	**0.85**	**0.85**	**1.03**	**1.14**	**2.59**	**10.83**	**16.76**	**25.94**	**29.78**	**32.18**	**33.01**
Switzerland	..	..	..	..	1.17	**4.92**	8.49	14.33			..	18.87
U.K.	**0.86**	0.83	1.00	**1.38**	**1.39**	**2.24**	10.21	13.20	16.42	16.94	18.05	22.52
U.S.	0.29	0.45	0.55	0.56	0.70	0.56	7.26	10.38	15.03	11.43	11.68	13.67
Median	0.29	0.39	0.55	0.69	0.78	1.66	10.41	14.84	20.09	21.36	24.00	22.52

Sources: Lindert (1994), OECD (1985), *OECD Social Expenditure Database 1980–1996* (CD Rom). For a similar chronology, with different detail, see Tanzi and Schuknecht (2000, Chapter 2).

Note: o = known to be zero; blank = not yet a sovereign state; .. = known to be positive, but number unavailable. **Boldface** = leaders. These exceeded the median-country share by 0.5 prior to 1930 or by 2.0 after 1960.

a Germany = West Germany only for 1960–1990.
b "1995" is actually 1993.

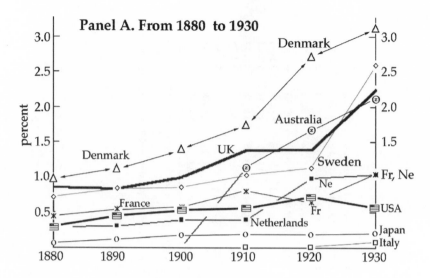

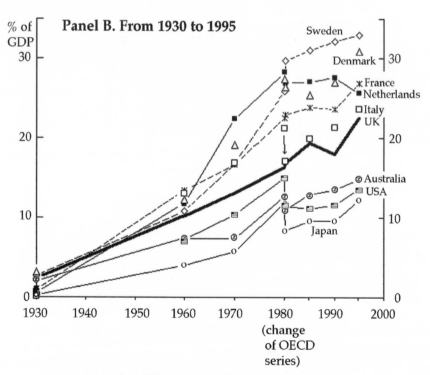

FIGURE I.I. Social Transfers as a Share of GDP, 1880–1995.

The ranks had been reshuffled by 1960, however. The upheavals of the World Wars and the Great Depression caused Continental Europe to shift dramatically toward progressive taxation and expanding social programs. One underlying reason, to be discussed again in Chapter 7, was a shift in the attitude of the Roman Catholic Church and Catholic political parties in favor of redistribution as a means to bring social justice and counter the threat of Communism. Thus in the postwar era, Scandinavians were joined in their welfare-state leadership by several other Continental countries – Austria, Belgium, France, Germany, Italy, and the Netherlands. Through it all, Japan, Switzerland, and the United States firmly resisted the rise of taxing and transferring, and they still have some of the lowest OECD transfer rates today. Chapter 7 will take up the challenge of explaining these international differences.

The Robin Hood Paradox

A useful way to summarize the global history of social spending takes the form of a puzzle that prods us to think hard about the underlying political forces. The puzzle is this: *History reveals a "Robin Hood paradox," in which redistribution from rich to poor is least present when and where it seems most needed.* Poverty policy within any one polity or jurisdiction is supposed to aid the poor more, the lower the average income and the greater the income inequality. Yet over time and space, the pattern is usually the opposite.

While there are exceptions to this general tendency, the underlying tendency itself is unmistakable, both across the globe and across the past three centuries. A global tour of nations shows stark contrast in the shares of gross domestic product (GDP) devoted to social security or social insurance programs of central governments. For example, in 1985–1990, such programs absorbed about 16.3 percent of GDP in the rich OECD countries and only 2.7 percent in developing countries, where poverty and inequality are greater.[13] Similarly among states in the United States, support for the poor takes a lower share of income in states with worse poverty and pre-fisc income inequality.[14] What Table 1.2 and Figure 1.1 are adding is the reminder that this is also a basic paradox of history. It was in the poorer and more unequal national settings before World War II that the least was given to the poor – or, equivalently, it is in today's prosperous world with lower pre-fisc income inequalities that the poor get the most generous support by historical standards. Why should the pattern across polities be the opposite of the pattern of redistribution that is typically desired and designed within a polity? And why should governments provide less (more) social insurance where private insurance is less (more) available?

That policy paradox probably has been inefficient, in that aid to the poor probably has the most positive effect on labor supply and GDP where it is least given. To underline the paradox further, consider the traditional concern that social programs subsidize leisure and therefore cut labor supply, hurting employers (and GDP) as well as taxpayers. This concern is reasonable today, even though a vast empirical literature has taught us not to expect a great response of labor supply to changes in average-tax wage rates.[15] Yet in the more distant past, and in the poorest countries today, there are important countertendencies. Granted, even in those poor settings it is plausible to believe that extra leisure was taken when funded, as Malthus and Britain's poor-law reformers of 1834 famously believed. But nutritional status and housing conditions were then so poor that extra poor relief almost surely had the effect of keeping more of the poor alive and working. Could the extra labor supply implied by this mortality response have outweighed the reduction in labor supply from subsidizing nonwork?[16]

In addition, Malthus' classic complaint about poor relief has an odd labor-supply implication: The more it encouraged fertility, the more extra labor it supplied a generation or two later. One should take George Boyer's demonstration that Malthus was right about poor relief and extra babies,[17] and amplify it by the extra labor supply they would bring even if they remained as welfare-dependent as the average person who received some relief.

If the net effect on labor supply was in fact positive, then poor relief could have promoted economic growth. As the extra workers entered the labor force, they would raise national product. In fact, their extra labor supply would have raised even the incomes of the propertied taxpayers who failed to give that relief when lives were at stake. It could have done this because having a greater supply of labor meant higher rents for landlords. If this was a distinct possibility, why was the relief not given to the poor, except in the interlude of England's Old Poor Law before 1834? We explore the determinants of early poor relief in Chapters 3 and 4.

Is the Welfare State a Free Lunch?

Another puzzle that beckons is related to, but larger and more controversial than, the Robin Hood paradox.

Knowing that higher tax rates and higher subsidies to people who don't produce could discourage productivity, many of us naturally suspect that taxes and transfers should reduce the productivity of the whole economy. When we give to the poor, don't we subsidize their staying in poverty? When we give to the unemployed, don't we subsidize not getting a job? When we give to the retired, don't we subsidize early retirement? And so forth. These natural suspicions pose a sobering question when combined with the rise of social transfer programs shown in Table 1.2 and Figure 1.1. If the welfare-state countries of Europe are now spending between 25 and 35 percent of their national product on less productive people, and are taxing the more productive to pay for it, doesn't this damage economic growth?

Here arises the puzzle of a potentially free lunch. If the antiproductive taxing and spending are as big as 25–35 percent of national product, why

TABLE 1.3. *How Social Transfers as a Share of GDP Correlate with Growth and Prosperity in 19 Countries, 1880–2000*

Time Period	The Coefficient of Correlation between the Initial Share of Social Transfers in GDP and	
	(a) the Growth of GDP/capita	(b) the Level of GDP/capita
1880s	0.10	−0.18
1890s	0.34	−0.05
1900s	−0.23	0.09
1910s	0.12	0.31
1920s	−0.24	0.49
1960s	−0.17	−0.07
1970s	0.14	0.00
1980s	−0.07	0.12
1990s (to 2000)	0.01	0.12
simple average of these	0.00	0.09
From 1880 to 1910	−0.02	−0.18
From 1960 to 2000	−0.11	−0.07

Notes and Sources: Social transfers/GDP for 1880–1930: Welfare, unemployment, pensions, health, and housing subsidies, as given in Lindert (1994, Table 1).

Social transfers/GDP for 1960–1980: OECD old series (OECD 1985); 1980–1990: OECD new series (OECD 1998).

Real GDP per capita: Penn World Table 5.6, supplemented by Penn World Table 6.1 (Heston et al 2002) for 1990–2000.

The 19 countries are Australia, Austria, Belgium, Canada, Denmark, Finland, France, Germany, Greece (1960s, on) Ireland (1960s on), Italy, Japan, Netherlands, New Zealand, Norway, Sweden, Switzerland, the United Kingdom, and the United States.

The same lack of any strong negative correlation was noted, in postwar data, by Slemrod (1995, 375–379).

don't we see a big negative effect on the level and growth of GDP per capita? Even if one grants that GDP is the result of many forces, the negative effect of social transfers should have been visible to the naked eye if each dollar transferred caused, say, a loss of $0.60 per dollar transferred. That rate of output loss times 25–35 percent of GDP should have put a dent of 15–21 percent in the size of the economy. And if the antiproductive programs have arisen almost entirely since 1960, shouldn't we see slow growth in those welfare-state countries since 1960?

Yet the history of economic growth is unkind to this natural suspicion. Neither simple raw correlations nor a careful weighing of the apparent sources of growth shows any clearly negative net effect of all that redistribution. Table 1.3 dramatizes the overall puzzle. Nine decades of historical experience fail to show that transferring a larger share of GDP from taxpayers to transfer recipients has a negative correlation with either the level or the rate of growth of GDP per person. The average correlation is essentially zero. If we pooled all the decades of international experience, instead of just averaging them, we could find that social transfers had *positive* correlations with both the level and the growth of GDP per person. The strongly positive correlation with the level of GDP per person underlines the Robin Hood paradox: Taking all historical experiences as a single experiment, the richer the country, the more it tends to transfer to the poor, the sick, the elderly, and the unemployed.[18] So far, any negative feedback from social programs to productivity levels, or productivity growth, remains well hidden.

The puzzle deepens a bit when we switch from GDP per person, the usual measure of income and productivity, to GDP per hour worked, a better measure of labor productivity. If higher social spending dampens incentives to invest and to raise labor productivity, this should make the higher-spending countries fall further behind the lower-spending leaders like the United States and Japan. Yet as others have noted, countries like the Netherlands, France, and Germany have caught up with the United States in output per labor hour. In fact, in GDP per hour worked, the United States ranked below eight other countries in 1992. Six of these eight countries with higher output per hour worked were continental welfare states.[19]

Since we care more about well-being than about labor productivity alone, the free lunch puzzle is even deeper. Along with their near-American productivity levels, people in the countries with higher social budgets get to enjoy more free time every year and retire earlier. They work fewer hours per employed person. In 1997, for example, the average employed American put in 1,966 hours and the average employed person in Japan about 1,900 hours. By contrast, their counterparts worked only about 1,550 hours in West Germany and Sweden and only 1,400 in Norway.[20] The extra free time is valuable, as are the extra years of leisure enjoyed by elderly West Europeans because they retire earlier and live longer.

Nor is the puzzle strictly international. Within the United States since the 1960s, social transfers have taken a rising share of state product, and the variance in their generosity has also risen – and has been positively, not negatively, correlated with the level and growth of state product per capita. How can the generous states, like Connecticut, New Jersey, and California, get away with giving out more generous welfare and other transfers year after year? Why haven't they grown more slowly than other states? Why hasn't business deserted them, leaving them with fewer firms and more welfare families?[21]

By themselves, near-zero correlations and brief charts cannot prove or disprove any argument, nor can one win the debate about social spending and growth just by choosing a favorite contrast between two countries.[22] The only way out of the puzzle posed by the historical correlations is not a retreat into selective journalistic contrasts, but a determined march into multivariate analysis and institutional history to see what the cost of social transfers might have been after other explanatory forces have been given their due. This difficult task is the subject of Part Three.

An Educational Puzzle

A third leading puzzle in the history of social spending is the identity of the leaders in public education. The nineteenth-century leaders in providing mass schooling at taxpayer expense were not the leaders in poor relief. Britain, the Netherlands, and Scandinavia led in poor relief, even though they spent only tiny amounts by today's standards. Yet in providing tax money for mass primary schooling, the lead was taken by Prussia, a few other German states, and North America. Why were the identities so different? What made some countries tilt toward maintaining the poor while others opted for taxes to pay for schools?

The nations that led in tax-based mass schooling were themselves an odd combination. What did the autocratic German states have in common with laissez-faire North America? What attribute did either set of countries have that would bias it toward taxes for schools? Surely no historical law dictates that undemocratic German monarchies should have wanted all children schooled. It is equally strange that Upper Canada and the non-Southern states of the United States should having voted so early and spontaneously for higher local taxes. What forces promoted mass public education in these countries and not in Britain, the Workshop of the World, in the nineteenth century? Chapter 5 offers some answers.

Then, in the twentieth century, leadership in education changed again, in a way that demands an explanation in Chapter 6. Across the century, by most measures of educational inputs and achievements, the United States fell back into the middle of the ranks and Germany fell into the lower half, among the top twenty OECD countries. The fallback is not uniform, in that Americans continue to excel in the numbers of years spent in school. Yet in expenditures as a share of GDP, teachers per one hundred students, and test scores, these two leaders definitely fell back. For Germany, the usual one-word explanation for educational decline (Hitler) fails to explain why German children have a lackluster education even in the early twenty-first century. And why should U.S. education look so unimpressive at the primary and secondary levels, when U.S. higher education still leads the world in its job payoffs and its exports of educational services to the rest of the world?

Puzzles like these call for a deeper historical inquiry.

2

Findings

Since the eighteenth century, the rise of tax-based social spending has been at the heart of government growth. It was social spending, not national defense, public transportation, or government enterprises, that accounted for most of the rise in governments' taxing and spending as a share of GDP over the last two centuries.

The increasing role of social spending in our lives has been linked to three other great social transformations: the transition to fuller democracy, the demographic transition toward fewer births and longer life, and the onset of sustained economic growth. Social spending's share of national product derives its permanence from the likely permanence (we hope) of these three great transformations – that is, of democracy, of human longevity, and of prosperity.

NINE CONCLUSIONS

Exploring these themes leads to a set of varied but logically consistent results. The rest of this chapter offers a guide to the whole set of arguments of the entire book, grouping most of them around these nine conclusions:

(#1) There was so little social spending of any kind before the twentieth century primarily because political voice was so restricted.

(#2) The central role of political voice is shown by an exceptional early case. Both Britain's relatively high poor relief in 1782–1834 and its cutbacks in 1834 and 1870 fit the changing self-interest of those with voice.

(#3) Similarly, just noting the interests of those with voice helps to explain Chapter 1's education puzzles: Why did Germany and laissez-faire North America lead the way in tax-based public schooling, and why did Britain lag behind in the nineteenth century? How did the United States remain a leader in educational attainment, yet end up ranked about fourteenth in students' test scores? Again, the concentration of voice was the enemy of education.

(#4) The great advance of social spending since 1880 is explained partly by the same political-voice motif, partly by population aging, and partly by income growth. Roman Catholicism was a negative influence on taxes and transfers before, but not after, World War II.

(#5) Postwar welfare states developed more fully in countries where the middle and bottom ranks traded places more and were ethnically homogenous.

(#6) The same forces that explain the growth of social spending until the 1990s carry implications for the future of social spending in all regions – in the affluent OECD countries, in the transition countries, and in Third World countries. In Western Europe, the political power of the elderly and the generosity of their public pensions have already matured and will fade. The social transfers that aging societies have supported will not decline as shares of *GDP*, but the generosity of pensions per elderly person will decline. Support for the elderly will also be under pressure in the formerly communist countries. Among prospering countries in the Third World, however, pensions will probably become more generous as income grows.

(#7) The net national costs of social transfers, and of the taxes that finance them, are essentially zero. They do not bring the GDP costs that much of the Anglo-American literature has imagined. Accordingly, differences in these costs play almost no role in either the rise or the deceleration in social spending's share. No Darwinian mechanism has punished the bigger spenders.

(#8) That large social programs have cost little in practice is consistent with the rise of European unemployment since 1970. Differences in social insurance did play a role in the OECD differences in unemployment over time and space, but only a partial role. Furthermore, the loss in output was less severe because those who remained out of work tended to be less productive workers anyway. Therefore any percentage loss of output tends to be much smaller than the percentage of jobs lost.

(#9) Two general principles seem to explain why the welfare state does no net damage to GDP per capita and why welfare states will not collapse. The first is that high-budget democracies show more care in choosing the design of taxes and transfers so as to avoid compromising growth. The second is that broad universalism in taxes and entitlements fosters growth better than the low-budget countries' preference for strict means testing and complicated tax compromises.

As of about 1780 hardly any taxes went into social spending in Western Europe or the United States, as Chapter 1 noted. The main kind of social spending was the modest poor-relief system, which was stretched thin to cover the poor and disabled of all ages. There were no mass public school systems, no tax-based health insurance, and no unemployment compensation beyond seasonal poor relief. Things stayed that way for the next one hundred years, except for the rise of mass public schooling, an interesting early rise and fall of Britain's poor-relief tax effort, and a slow upward creep in tax-based poor relief on the Continent.

The stirrings of a movement toward comprehensive social insurance programs were more evident after 1880. The real social-transfer pioneer from the 1880s on was Denmark, followed by the early pension schemes of Germany, Britain, Australia, and New Zealand.

The real boom in all sorts of social programs did not come until after World War II. Interestingly, the overall data make the rise of social spending look more monotonic than one would have thought from the tone of public discourse after 1980. For all the often-reported "crisis" or "demise" of the welfare state, all one really sees after 1980 is a slowdown, not a decline, in the shares of GDP that welfare-state taxpayers put into such programs.[1]

Familiar as the broad rise of social transfers may look, it should also seem curious. Why should it have been delayed for so long? Why did it march so far by 1980? Why has it stabilized since, neither retreating nor advancing? And what difference did it make to economic growth?

HOW SOCIAL SPENDING EMERGED BEFORE WORLD WAR II

Conclusion #1. There was so little social spending of any kind before the twentieth century mainly because political voice was so restricted.

If all residents had equal vote, and if the only way one could influence a political outcome was by using that single vote, the rich would be heavily taxed to support redistributive social programs. This seems likely as long as the middling (median) incomes are much closer to the bottom of the income ranks than to the top.[2] That is the way it is in most less-developed countries, just as it was in the earlier history of the most advanced countries. The distribution of before-tax income and wealth has been highly skewed, with the median income well below the mean income,[3] creating a golden opportunity for a Robin Hood. That he failed to show up in such settings must relate to a concentration of power in the hands of the rich.

Political power was indeed concentrated in the past. The only people allowed to vote were men who owned some minimum land value, earned some minimum income, or paid some minimum value of direct taxes. It was the retreat of such restrictions in nineteenth-century Europe that opened the initial door for a shift toward progressive taxation and social spending.

The spread of voting rights had nonlinear effects on social spending before World War II. Chapters 4, 5, and 7 trace the effects of switching from non-democracies to elite democracies and then to full democracies, with both genders and all economic classes permitted to vote. Part of that history comes from written accounts and part from a systematic statistical analysis of twenty-one countries in the periods 1880–1930 and 1962–1995. For social transfers, such as aid to the poor, the elderly, and the sick, elite democracies tended to offer no more than the average nondemocracy, when other things are held equal. The elite democracies, in which fewer than 40 percent of men had the vote, were actually more opposed to overall social transfers, and to public pensions, than the average authoritarian nondemocracy. Only basic poor relief was given out as much in the elite democracies as in the average nondemocratic monarchy of that time. More dramatic were the effects of spreading the vote from an elite to nearly all adults. Once the right to vote was extended to poorer men, the stage was set for Lloyd George's assault on Britain's rich just before World War I and for corresponding political transitions in other countries. When that happened toward the end of the nineteenth century and the start of the twentieth, comprehensive nationwide social insurance programs began to emerge. Extending political voice to all adults raised spending on public schools as well.

Conclusion #2. The central role of political voice is shown by an exceptional early case. Both Britain's relatively high poor relief in 1782–1834 and its cutbacks in 1834 and 1870 fit the changing self-interest of those with voice.

The importance of historical shifts in who had voting power transcends the simple idea that the rich fight redistribution and lose that fight when voting rights march down the income ranks. Political historians rightly insist that the issue is much more complex. Even in a full democracy people lack the right to vote on each issue separately. Rather, they must elect representatives that trade influence on multiple issues.

Yet the link between economic self-interest and political voice is still there, even in cases that may seem to deny the link. A good illustration is the strange rise of English poor relief after about 1780, when only a small landed elite could vote. Why should such a society vote to tax itself 2 percent of GDP to support the poor, when it had not done so earlier? Why did Britain move back toward toughness after the Reform Act of 1832 had extended the franchise?

The whole pattern makes good sense, in time and in space, once one understands the self-interest of Southeast England's farmers and wealthy rural landlords and combines it with George Boyer's model of their approach to poor relief.[4] As seasonal hirers of farm labor in an industrializing and urbanizing economy, they had strong incentive to make sure that laborers stayed in their area across the low-income winter months instead of emigrating to cities and industrial centers. The richer the farmer or landlord, the more he or she hired labor. Local poor relief became a way of making the less landed households pay a share of local "poor rates" to retain a seasonal labor force they used little. The Reform Act of 1832 shifted voting rights toward rich industrialists in the rising centers, who saw little merit in a system that kept workers in the stagnating rural Southeast.[5] The spatial pattern of generous poor relief in the rural Southeast and greater toughness[6] in prospering cities and the Northwest fits the same model of self-interest (though it is an exception to the Robin Hood paradox). Chapter 4 argues that England exhibited this pattern, while other countries gave more poor relief in cities, because of the peculiar political power of labor-hiring landlords and farmers in England.

Exploring the puzzles of early English and Continental poor relief in Chapters 3 and 4 turns up another striking conclusion that later chapters will rediscover for the postwar era. There was no "race to the bottom," in which governments compete in trying to attract investors and skilled migrants by slashing their social transfers. The rural parishes of southeastern England, and the cities of other countries, managed to levy higher local taxes and to give more to the local poor than other areas without seeming to suffer loss of business as a result of the aid. In fact they explicitly used such relief, decade after decade, to retain their local labor supplies. In the political fights over poor relief, it was typically the central government that tried to impose limits on local taxes and transfers and the local governments that tried to find ways to keep giving relief. The notion that local governments would race to the bottom in their taxes and transfers was not true in the nineteenth century, just as it is not true today. The reason seems to be that taxes and transfers had their benefits for some who had local political voice.

Conclusion #3. Similarly, just noting the interests of those with voice helps to explain Chapter 1's education puzzles: Why did Germany and laissez-faire North America lead the way in tax-based public schooling, and why did Britain lag behind in the nineteenth century? How did the United States remain a leader in educational attainment, yet end up ranked about fourteenth in students' test scores? Again, the concentration of voice was the enemy of education.

Similar reasoning about voice and economic interests helps to explain a curious pattern in the rise of tax-based mass public schooling. In the first half of the nineteenth century, the wave of mass schooling started in some of the German states, most visibly in Prussia. After 1860, the leadership shifted to North America and Australasia. England and Wales, the Workshop of the World, lagged behind, before catching up quickly in the period 1891–1914.

While every nation's educational history has its unique elements, two systematic causal forces emerge from the comparative political economy of mass schooling before 1914 (see Chapter 5 in Volume 1 and Chapter 15 in Volume 2).

The first causal force was the spread of voting rights. Abstracting from the specific character of ruling elites, we find a systematic influence of the spread of voting rights upon primary-school enrollments. Other things equal, countries where a majority of adults voted had significantly more children in school than either nondemocracies or elite democracies where only a propertied minority could vote. Thus North America and Australia and even France were ahead of Britain in school enrollments between 1850 and 1900 in part because they were more democratic. Within North America, broad democracy had the same effect, in that the educational backwaters were those regions still controlled by a landed elite or by a single religion. The backwaters were the U.S. South, Quebec, and Canada's Maritime Provinces, whereas Upper Canada and the U.S. non-South were world leaders in schooling.

The second causal force seems to have been decentralization. Germany and North America, unlike Britain, left the decision of how much tax to pay for schools up to the localities. In Germany's case, one could even say that primary education was a matter left to local democracy, even though the national government was relatively undemocratic. Localities raised most of the taxes for schools, and locally elected and appointed officials ran the schools. The landed Junker elite could, and did, keep down the level of schooling, but only in its own localities. Similarly, plantation owners in the U.S. South could keep down education spending and taxes only in their own states. A decentralized approach to school finance, as in most of Germany and most of North America, brought a world in which localities competed for migrants and business by providing attractive tax-based schools. The effect of decentralization on public schools does not always run in the same direction, however. There seems to be a systematic reversing relationship between decentralization and the long rise in demand for public goods that comes with economic development, as Chapter 5 explains.

Although the public funding of schools remains a positive influence, public provision and control of most schools can either help or hinder education, depending on who has voice and who can exit. In twentieth-century United States the rise of centralized power may have raised the quantity of schooling, but it seems to have lowered its quality, as suggested in Chapter 6. Throughout the twentieth century, the United States continued to be a leader in the quantity of education, measured by educational attainment. Yet in all the international test score comparisons from 1964 through 2000, U.S. teenagers have never finished in the upper half of the ranks among OECD nations.

Chapter 6 shows that several common suspicions about the sources of this student performance shortfall are *not* true. Though it is natural to say that quality should be stressed over quantity, the emphasis in the United States on schooling quantity (years) over quality (as reflected in achievement tests scores) may have served U.S. growth well. Furthermore, the U.S. test score shortfall is not the result of inferior home backgrounds relative to those experienced by children in other countries. U.S. children are not behind as of ages nine or ten. Something detracts from their education in later grades. Nor are the shortcomings of U.S. education due to too much private education, too little pay for teachers, low teacher quality, or even to a simple story of decentralization versus centralization. The shortcomings were not even due to a rigid flat pay scale that failed to pay according to teacher merit, for the simple reason that *all* OECD countries have failed to develop enough rewards for teacher performance.

Two defects of the U.S. system of primary and secondary education seem to explain its low performance on test scores. One defect takes the form of insufficient centralization, and the other takes the form of excessive centralization. The United States places too little stock in centralized achievement tests, making its students and teachers insufficiently accountable for curriculum learning. On the other hand, the United States gives too little voice to students and local teachers and too much voice to giant school administrations and to teacher unions. Ironically, Milton Friedman's call for school choice for individual students has been answered better in some European welfare states than in the United States.

Conclusion #4. The great advance of social transfers since 1880 is explained partly by the same political-voice motif, partly by population aging, and partly by income growth. Roman Catholicism was a negative influence on taxes and transfers before, but not after, World War II.

The changes in total social transfers from 1880 to 1930 are partly explained by three main sets of systematic forces (see Chapter 7 in Volume 1 and Chapter 16 in Volume 2). In all countries, part of the rise was explained by income. Of similar importance was the aging of the population: An older population was apparently one that preferred more social insurance. The third force was a set of voting-rights variables, which had a strong positive effect on the rise of social transfers (and taxes). Other things equal, heavily voting democracies taxed more and spent more on social insurance, especially those democracies that had granted women the vote.

LESSONS FROM THE POSTWAR BOOM

The great postwar rise in social transfers brought the same explanatory forces to center stage, but this time with different shares of the limelight. Electoral democracy is less important for explaining differences in nineteen OECD countries after World War II than in 1880–1930, for the simple reason that the OECD countries now differ less in their degrees of democracy. Population aging, however, continued to play a starring role. An older society seems to be one that wants higher tax-based social insurance.[7]

The age effect has some important dimensions that need emphasis. First, we must remember that at the moment it is a reliable statistical result in search of an underlying mechanism. Is it gray power that demands more social insurance (and, implicitly, taxes)? What share of that power has arisen, as lives lengthen, because younger voters either want government help in handling their parents or foresee that they too face a long retirement? Is the aging effect getting credit for other forces that happen to be correlated with aging? A second point to emphasize is that the underlying analysis shows that (up to a point) an older population seems to be one that prefers higher social spending of all kinds and not just the more age-targeted higher public pensions and health care. Finally, the effect of an older population on the budget share of social transfers, or on their generosity per recipient, is not linear. Being a larger share of the population does not keep helping your redistributive fight forever. We return to this point shortly.

Conclusion #5. Postwar welfare states developed more fully in countries where the middle and bottom ranks traded places more and were ethnically homogenous.

It makes sense that social transfers and public education derived much of their political success from the willingness of swing voters, presumably middle-income voters, to identify with the need for such tax-based programs. The economic stake of middle-income voters is likely to depend on their social affinities.[8] For which group do middle-income voters say "That could be me" – the tax-burdened rich or the poor to be caught in safety nets? There is no easy way to measure such affinities, aside from being alert to whether middle-income voters share the same language, religion, and race with those at the top or bottom.

One way of measuring such affinities reveals robust effects, and one yields fragile effects. Ethnic homogeneity strongly promotes every kind of social transfer program through government. Stated the other way around, ethnic fractionalization is a strong negative influence on the political will to raise taxes for social spending and related public investments. This result stands out in global data sets as well as in recent studies of African and U.S. local governments.[9] There is some fragile support for the prediction that the pre-fisc income gap between middle and low incomes is also a negative influence on social transfers. That gap between middle and low incomes is wider in the United States than in any other OECD country, a fact that may have stifled redistribution to the poor in the United States.

SINCE 1980, AGING HAS BROUGHT NEW BUDGET PRESSURES

What happened to social spending since 1980 is not a simple story of retreat from the welfare state, despite the ideological wave ushered in by the Reagan–Thatcher era. As we have seen in Chapter 1, the shares of social transfers in GDP merely stagnated and did not decline. Would we expect the early twenty-first century to bring the rollback that did not come in the last two decades of the twentieth?

Some continue to predict a retreat. The most careful basis for such a prediction sets aside any journalism about a bold swing to the right in favor of a more plausible forecast based on incremental learning from past mistakes in the public sector. Vito Tanzi and Ludger Schuknecht predict that such a new sobriety will strongly outweigh the pressure to spend more on an aging population:

Governments will become more efficient and public spending (and taxation) will decline in the future in spite of demographic trends that will tend, under existing policies, to increase public spending. Spending will not decline to the levels seen 100 or 70 years ago, but it can be rolled back to levels closer to those experienced around 1960.[10]

The analysis of this book does not make the same prediction, at least not about social transfers. Rather, it foresees little change in government efficiency and a compromised response to the rising elderly share.

Conclusion #6. The same forces that explain the growth of social spending until the 1990s carry implications for the future of social spending in all regions – in the affluent OECD countries, in the transition countries, and in Third World countries. In Western Europe, the political power of the elderly and the generosity of their public pensions have already matured and will fade. The social transfers that aging societies have supported will not decline as shares of GDP, but the generosity of pensions per elderly person will decline. Support for the elderly will also be under pressure in the formerly communist countries. Among prospering countries in the Third World, however, pensions will probably become more generous as income grows.

Given the apparent roles of aging, income, and other forces in explaining countries' levels of social transfers since 1880, we can explore what the statistical analysis revealing these effects would predict about the near future. Some extrapolation is possible, since the results seem to give a large role to the age distribution of the population, which can be projected into the future with fair confidence.

Looking ahead to the older world of the year 2020 suggests where aging will strain public pension systems and all social transfer programs most over the early twenty-first century. That strain will be greatest in countries that are already committed to generous support ratios for the elderly and are older than the average OECD country. Which countries fit this description? Thanks to the relative predictability of age distributions, Chapters 8 offers suggestions. The strongest pressure within our OECD sample will be felt by Italy, with Austria, Belgium, Finland, France, Germany, Greece, Netherlands, and Spain not far behind. Japan, Norway, and Sweden have forestalled deep pension trouble by already raising the average retirement age well up into the 60s. The pension crisis should also be less severe in countries like the United States, which are aging more slowly.

In Third World countries that actually succeed in developing, the political process will probably raise social transfers as a share of GDP, as suggested in Chapter 9. Their transfers to the elderly will probably rise even per elderly person, at least until those over the age of sixty-five reach 8 percent of their populations. Convergence toward the OECD standard of high social transfers will probably occur even in East Asia, contrary to the frequent rhetoric about antistatist "Asian values." As their populations age, even those countries where official dogma espouses Confucian traditions of reliance on family support will experience a rise in public pensions and other social transfers as a share of GDP. When an East Asian country passes the demographic threshold where persons older than sixty-five are more than 20 percent of the population, it will face new pressures on its public budget – just like Japan, which many had considered a country where people turn to family, not government, for help.

The extrapolations to 2020, based on statistical patterns in tax and transfer policy up to 1995, predict that the elderly will bear most or all of the burden of the OECD countries' pension crisis, in the form of reduced pensions per elderly person. The behavior of OECD countries until 1995 predicts no decline in the GDP shares of transfers or of nonpension transfers. There will be no race to the bottom, in which countries compete against each other to cut social-spending budgets.

What drives social spending in the long run, then, is the shifting balance of political power between income groups, age groups, and ethnic groups. For the world as a whole, no demise of social programs is imminent. The share of product that transferred through government social programs will probably not shrink, despite all the rhetoric predicting a rollback of the welfare state.

UNLOCKING THE FREE-LUNCH PUZZLE

Conclusion #7. The net national costs of social transfers, and of the taxes that finance them, are essentially zero. They do not bring the GDP costs that much of the Anglo-American literature has imagined. Accordingly, differences in these costs play almost no role in either the rise or the deceleration in social spending's share. No Darwinian mechanism has punished the bigger spenders.

It might seem as though a central explanation of countries' social-spending trends has been missed. Doesn't a large welfare-state establishment drag down growth and doesn't this loss of income tend to choke off the advance of the social spending itself?

Such intuition draws on a standard economic imagination that most economists share. We imagine an experiment in which Country A wisely holds down social spending while Country B raises it to a third of GDP, raising marginal tax rates on both the taxpayers and the recipients. Both the taxpayers and the recipients respond by working less and taking less productive risk, thus lowering GDP.

The problem with this consensus is that the data refuse to confess that things work out that way. The basic empirical problem stares at us in the raw data, just as it did in Chapter 1. Across countries or over time, the coefficients linking growth to total government size are not negative, even in sophisticated multivariate statistical analysis. In the global cross-section, richer countries do not tax and spend less. Similar results were obtained among past studies that limited themselves to the effects of social transfers.[11] The longer sweep of history also refuses to cooperate. Among the advanced OECD countries, the period with the fastest-growing welfare states – between 1950 and 1980 – included history's best-ever golden age of growth (1950–1973), even though it also included the oil shocks that hit in 1973 and 1979. Whether one looks at levels or at rates of change, one cannot show any clear negative relationship between social spending and GDP per capita.

Those convinced that tax-based social programs must have large negative effects on GDP have tried two strategies. Some have doggedly tortured the data further, to get the right confession. But the preferred negative relationship to social spending remains elusive. Thus others have used the second strategy of retreating to computer simulations on imagined data, or imagining macro-extrapolations of a micro-study labor-supply slope, to get out the truth we know is there.

Manipulating statistical techniques may yet unlock the puzzle and show large negative effects of taxes and social spending on growth. So far, though, no negative effects look robust in international perspective or even in interstate contrasts within the United States.

Why not? The fundamental answer is that *the real world has never performed the extreme and simple tax-transfer experiment that economists and the public keep imagining*. Governments that spend an extra twenty percent of GDP on social programs do not simply raise the direct tax rate on productive people and turn over that 20 percent of GDP to people who choose not to work. They dare not do so, since the high marginal costs of mishandling huge programs could throw them out of office.

What exactly do the high-spending countries do instead? Chapter 10 shows a multitude of institutional facts that have been left off the blackboards, at least in North American classrooms.

How Welfare States Control the Disincentives

When taxes, transfers, and subsidies abound, marginal incentives are far more complex than the blackboard diagram of a tax imposed in an otherwise perfect economy. The effects of changing any one marginal rate, such as raising the corporate income tax rate, often cannot be judged without extensive study of its interactions with a host of other taxes and subsidies, and with private market power. James Meade and other economists have called this distortion-filled world the world of the "second best," to distinguish it from that first-best Garden of Eden so often portrayed in textbooks and in classrooms. To get reliable comparisons of welfare states versus free-market economies, one must wander through this second-best world. The kinds of policies carried further by welfare-state governments than by free-market-oriented markets might either raise or lower national product.

We now know several reasons why the damage from tax-and-transfer programs is offset or even completely reversed by other features of the welfare states.

On the taxation front, the high-spending welfare states have developed a style of taxation that few have noticed when debating the effects of the welfare state. In general, high-budget welfare states have a *more pro-growth and regressive mix of taxes*. The European high-budget countries do not have higher average rates of taxation on capital income. They have been cautious about the double taxation of dividends. Rather, they rely more heavily on labor income taxes and on flat consumption (or value-added) taxes. They also tax addiction goods (e.g., alcohol and tobacco) more heavily, thus taxing complements to health-compromising leisure. Granted, the rates of overall taxation are still higher in the high-budget countries, yet their attention to the side-effects on economic growth seems to have led them to choose types of taxes that minimize or eliminate any damage to growth, relative to the types of taxes levied in the lower-spending countries such as the United States, Japan, or Switzerland. Chapter 11 illustrates this point from Chapter 10 by taking a closer look at the Swedish experience.

The high-spending countries have *fine-tuned the work incentives* of their welfare and unemployment compensation programs to limit welfare dependency among young adults. Their "transfers" to the unemployed and poor are in effect purchases of behavior and investments in job qualifications. It has never been the case that welfare and unemployment compensation offer young adults a lifetime of near-full pay regardless of the recipients' behavior. In fact, some of the highest marginal tax rates on work have been those faced by the poor in the tougher means-tested environments like Britain and the United States. Only in the last decade of the twentieth century did these countries wisely offer tax breaks tied to work by low-income workers. This was a helpful, though belated, step toward the universalism of the welfare states, where the poor can often take home a larger share of the pay they gain by getting a job.

The higher-spending countries are also more open economies, with *lower import barriers*.[12] By subjecting more of their economy to the discipline of international competition, they have made producers operate more efficiently.

Early Retirement: A True, but Limited, Cost

The most prominently costly part of social transfer policy in many Western European countries, including some of the welfare states, is their elaborate set of early-retirement incentives at taxpayer expense. Many men in the fifty-five to sixty-four age range retire earlier in the countries that heavily subsidize early retirement – Belgium, France, Germany, Italy, and the Netherlands – than in countries that spend less on the elderly. Since many of the earlier retirees would have been employed without the policy encouragement to retire early, surely that must have lowered GDP. This is one kind of intuitive skepticism that does carry weight. There must have been a GDP cost of this policy-induced earlier retirement.

The output cost of government subsidies to early retirement is limited, however, by several factors explained in Chapter 10. First, it is tied to international differences, not levels, in the employment rate of people aged fifty-five to sixty-four. Second, the fifty-five to sixty-four age group is only a small part of the total work force. Third, the extra retirement effect shows up clearly only for males. Finally, the average laid-off person of ages fifty-five to sixty-four was less productive at work than the average employee. It should not be surprising, then, that the statistical analysis of GDP per capita shows only a small effect of early-retirement policies on GDP.

The Pro-Growth Side of High Social Spending

The welfare-state package to which the higher-spending countries are more committed includes certain *social-spending programs that make people more productive*. The best-known example is, of course, public education. While many studies find that private schools produce higher-achieving students, this quality differential is partly the result of self-selection in mixed public–private systems. The quality differential is also outweighed by the quantity effect, the fact that tax-based public schools raise total educational attainment.

A second example is their better fiscal and legal support for child care and parental leave. These supports for new parents' career continuity cut their human capital losses from being forced off their career paths.[13] For example, such social investments in careers have given Sweden one of the world's highest rates of relative earnings by women.

A third example is welfare states' greater reliance on public health programs. Chapter 10 reports that more public health expenditures significantly avert deaths relative to private spending of the same magnitude, and presumably also reduce morbidity, within the OECD countries.[14] Government investments in health have an even greater impact in countries that are still developing. Numerous studies have found that basic public health facilities not only lengthen life, but actually raise peoples' productivity within each year of their adult lives. The United States is an unhealthy outlier partly because its history and ideology have blocked the shift to public health care and health insurance for all.

Reconciling Europe's Unemployment with Its Satisfactory Growth

Conclusion #8. That large social programs have cost little in practice is consistent with the rise of European unemployment since 1970. Differences in the generosity of social insurance did play a role in the OECD differences in unemployment over time and space, but only a partial role. Furthermore, the loss in output was less severe because those who remained out of work tended to be less productive workers anyway. Therefore any percentage loss of output tends to be much smaller than the percentage of jobs lost.

The tentative finding that larger social spending entails little net cost in terms of GDP must confront the fact that unemployment has indeed risen to deplorable heights in OECD Europe since the 1970s. The possibility remains that social-insurance programs have caused many of those job losses. Indeed, the extensive OECD literature finds that more generous unemployment compensation and family support does raise the unemployment rate.[15]

Yet programs such as welfare and unemployment benefits are not the only leading suspects in the literature seeking to explain why so many Europeans are out of work. One other leading suspect is the set of workers' rights laws in several countries (Italy, France, Spain, Belgium, Britain, Ireland, and Germany), which seems to have created a firing-and-hiring problem in which few can lose their jobs from layoffs, so that few are hired.[16] A second is an official minimum wage rate that crowds up against the average wage rate of all production workers. Minimum wage rates need not generate much unemployment if they remain well below the average market wage rate for, say, semiskilled workers. But those in France, and in Italy before 1988, were high enough to destroy a noticeable fraction of jobs. The third leading suspect is a general background of politicized class antagonisms. Many authors have noted that labor markets can preserve full employment, even in the face of what may look like elaborate institutional rigidities, if there is relative cooperation and peace in labor-management bargaining.[17] By contrast, countries where labor-market rigidities are accompanied by antagonisms and high rates of work disruption have higher rates of unemployment, other things equal. Such antagonisms, inherited from history, cost jobs, partly because they are the reasons why those first two suspects – job protection laws and particularly high minimum wage rates – have so much more effect in some countries than in others.

In addition, the persons who end up being unemployed, when a less generous support system might have made them work, tend to be persons with lower productivity. Thus preventing or delaying their reentry into paid work does not cut national product by much at all, even though it cuts the number of jobs.

Two Cost-Cutting Principles in Democratic Welfare States

Conclusion #9. Two general principles seem to explain why the welfare state does no net damage to GDP per capita and why welfare states will not collapse. The first is that high budget democracies show more care in choosing the design of taxes and transfers so as to avoid compromising growth. The second is that broad universalism in taxes and entitlements fosters growth better than the low-budget countries' preference for strict means testing and complicated tax compromises.

There are good reasons why the statistical tests reveal no clear net cost of massive social programs in developed democracies. In all likelihood, one underlying force behind these cost-cutting mechanisms is democracy itself, which arms whistle-blowers in the fights against either public waste or public underinvestment. Electoral democracy does not achieve finely tuned efficiency, but it has ways to limit the costs.

One principle limiting the cost of the welfare state is the budget–stakes principle. The higher the budget, the greater the stakes in designing social programs in ways that minimize the unit costs of the extra taxes and transfers. The high-budget welfare states have done more to address the dangers of getting taxes and transfers wrong than have low-spending countries like the United States. There is some evidence that political debates over expanding the welfare state were aware of the high cost of getting the design wrong. This seems to be a basic reason why they drifted toward relatively growth-promoting consumption taxes.

The other cost-cutting principle has been revealed over the centuries in countries that became both richer and more democratic. The universalism of today's high-budget welfare states, in which both entitlements and marginal tax rates are similar for the whole population, involves lower deadweight costs per dollar taxed and transferred than the older and narrower systems it is replacing.

Two main kinds of net national ("deadweight") costs associated with government budgets are their administrative cost percentage and the percent ratio of their incentive costs to the amounts taxed and spent. We can measure trends in the first of these and conjecture plausibly about the second.

Administrative cost percentages have historically declined, both in tax collection and in the administration of welfare and pension programs. Britain's tax-collection system, which was already a recognized model of efficiency by 1780, became increasingly cheap to administer, per pound collected, across the nineteenth and early twentieth centuries. So did the U.S. Internal Revenue

Service. These cost savings implicitly reduced the cost of any programs the tax revenues were spent on, such as the social programs that are our focus here.

The cost of administering poor-relief programs also dropped, especially in the great twentieth-century welfare-state expansion, but its cheapening was less a price drop, and more a shift in "quality," than on the tax-collecting side of the budget. In the age in which it was called "poor relief" and not "welfare" it was very expensive to administer. Administrative costs often ate up 25 percent of the budget, unlike today's welfare and social security programs, which can use as little as 2–3 percent of their budgets for administration. The old way of helping the poor, the sick, and the elderly was so much more expensive in those days because taxpayers wanted so much more monitoring of the behavior of the poor than today. The role of monitoring costs shows up as a strong contrast between the administrative cost shares on indoor (poorhouse, workhouse) and outdoor (at-home) relief. Wherever the share of outdoor aid given to persons in their own homes was higher, costs were lower and more of the budget was at the disposal of the poor themselves. By contrast, the tougher indoor relief was very expensive, because the poor had to be supervised so intensely, in an attempt to reform their behavior and keep them out of public view. Interestingly, both England and New York moved *toward* that tough and costly regime across the nineteenth century, raising the administrative cost share. Only since World War I, with welfare support given to the poor more abundantly and with fewer strings, did the welfare costs drop to today's rates.

Like administrative costs, the incentive cost of social programs probably also came down. On the tax collection side, the prevailing historical shift in tax collections was the same one we observe when scanning from lower-income to higher-income countries in today's global cross-section – a shift from (a) arbitrary and narrow taxes, to (b) customs and excise taxes, to (c) direct taxation on income and wealth, and finally to (d) broad-based consumption and labor taxes in the high-budget welfare state. The famous incentive costs of any tax rise with the elasticities of the behavior being taxed. These elasticities declined as the taxes evolved from (a) to (b) to (c) to (d) during the growth of government and the economy. Accordingly, the deadweight costs of the tax system also declined as the tax base became broader and more universal.

The switch to universalist welfare states, in which entitlements to basic income, to public health care, and to other services are shared by all, has also reduced at least some work incentive problems. By abandoning the strict means testing practiced in low-budget countries, welfare states allowed a poor person to keep a larger share of his or her pay when getting a job. Perhaps even more important was the universal access to public health care, which has performed better than the United States' complicated and bureaucratic health care and health insurance.

The two principles, the budget-stakes principle and the efficiency of universalism, are probably linked politically. Having committed themselves to universal entitlements, social democrats have had both the political need and the political chance to favor pro-growth tax mixes. It is easier to pass pro-growth, relatively regressive changes in the tax structure if the left opposition can be calmed by a commitment to spend tax proceeds on universalist safety net transfers. Such political bargains seem to have tied the postwar emergence of the welfare state to the rise of broad consumption taxes rather than taxes aimed at businesses and the wealthy. By contrast, conservatives in low-budget countries like the United States have lacked such protective political clothing for their preferred tax reforms. Having rejected the welfare state with its broad transfers and public health care, conservatives have looked like blatant redistributive grabbers when they have called for consumption taxes and tax relief for capitalists.

PART TWO

THE RISE OF SOCIAL SPENDING

3

Poor Relief before 1880

The first kind of social spending to exceed 1 percent of national product was, and still is, the most controversial kind: direct assistance to the poor. The eighteenth and nineteenth centuries had as much trouble with policies toward the poor as we do today. In fact, they had the same troubles, and the same opposing arguments came up.

The early debates were as intense as today's debates, the main difference being that the poor faced a much harsher world before the late eighteenth century. Many with power and voice held the poor in contempt, so that governments were more active in punishing beggars and vagabonds than they were in helping them. Private giving did little to offset this harshness. Contrary to a long tradition of imagining that churches and philanthropists were generous toward the poor before government moved into the charity business, there was never much private charity for the government to displace.[1]

How was poor relief, the ancestor of today's public assistance and welfare programs, born and nurtured in such a harsh climate? Where did significant tax-based poor relief emerge, and where did it remain negligible as late as World War I? How did they handle the welfare trilemma, that unavoidable tradeoff between guaranteeing a bottom income, giving incentives to work more, and protecting the government budget? How did their approach differ from city to countryside, from region to region, and from nation to nation? In charting the broad contours of poor relief, we will find some patterns that seem easy to explain and some that pose genuine puzzles. The task of explaining the early rise of poor relief will be tackled here in Part Two.[2]

We will discover a main pattern for all countries and an outstanding early exception to that pattern. The main pattern is that the poor got help from taxpayers when some combination of three things happened: people who cared about them got political voice and voting rights, the adult population got older, and average income rose. For most countries, this came extremely late in history – not until the late nineteenth century or the twentieth.

The outstanding early exception is England, one of the two pioneers in raising over 1 percent of national income in taxes to help the poor.[3] England's poor-relief history is puzzling. There was an initial rise to unprecedented levels in the 1795–1834 era of the "Old Poor Law," and two episodes of declining relief, before a permanent political shift raised public assistance across the twentieth century. Why the shifts in English policy? Why would the early landed elite have acquiesced in a pioneering rise in paying "poor rates" (taxes for the local poor) before 1834, and why was that policy reversed thereafter? Why was early English relief largely given from taxes in the countryside, when most of Europe and the United States concentrated their taxes and aid in the cities?

This chapter explores how poor relief really worked before 1880, to clear the way for Chapter 4 to offer a political-economic explanation of some of the twists and turns in how several countries treated their poor. In Chapter 4's interpretation, the peculiarity of England will turn out to be explainable by combining a global theme – the key role of knowing who had political voice – with England's distinctive evolution of group self-interests.

HOW MUCH DID EUROPE GIVE THE POOR BEFORE 1880?[4]

Private Charity in Early Modern Europe: A Miscellany of Pittances

Long before tax money was turned over to the poor, private and church charity was ubiquitous and elaborate. In each country there were at least tens of thousands of organized charities with freedom to design their activities as they saw fit. There were many churches, and charity practices were not even uniform within any one church. Wealthy individuals seeking salvation went beyond almsgiving and set up their own trusts, just as many do today. The private imagination knew few bounds and set up an array of institutions that defies summary. Most charities were not for the poor, but for supporting general worship, apprenticeships, higher education, and general hospitals. Some, such as mutual aid societies, were more like contributory insurance pools or savings institutions than charities. Those that were aimed at giving to the poor covered a miscellany of contingencies. Some paid for burying the anonymous. Others targeted widows of husbands in specific occupations. The mainstays either struggled to limit the mortality of abandoned children or wisely defended female honor, such as "the dowry of the pauper girl, that ubiquitous symbol of *ancien régime* charity."[5] The task of understanding these institutions is vast and ongoing.[6]

In the early modern struggle to cope with mass poverty, government did the whipping and left the giving primarily to churches and private donors. True, some laws were passed giving local governments the duty (but usually not the money) to deal with poverty. England's oft-cited Elizabethan Poor Law was an example. It is also true that governments intervened aggressively to keep food affordable during famines, but their use of requisition and price controls may have made food crises more severe in the long run. Yet as late as the mid-eighteenth century these gestures were still eclipsed by laws ordering the persecution of beggars, vagabonds, rogues, and idlers. In 1740, for example, England passed another law fine-tuning the use of whipping and imprisonment for "Rogues, Vagabonds, and other idle and disorderly Persons."[7]

Church aid and government aid were both controversial. Some approved of the church's generosity or at least felt that whatever was given should be given by the churches and not the state, as in this nineteenth-century Dutch view:

The state...must prohibit beggary...But the state can never alleviate poverty. As far as relief of the poor is concerned, the best institution is the church rather than the state. Because of the church's familiarity with the domestic circumstances of the poor, it can combine living assistance with remedial instruction. The church never humiliates the indigents by providing poor relief in public. The church maintains the voluntary nature of charity and leaves room for the altruistic compassion of the giver and the warm gratitude of the receiver.[8]

Others felt that nobody should give to the poor and faulted the churches for being so generous, as in this nineteenth-century German view:

[Due to the] excessive Charities of the Church...a ruinous course was entered upon which turned comfort into destitution, and where it found destitution made it twofold....It was the natural result of the ecclesiastical method that the number of poor greatly increased....In France, as in England,...pauperism...had grown to a plague through the excessive almsgiving of the Church.[9]

How much did the churches and other private charities actually give to the poor in the eighteenth and nineteenth centuries? Our tour of what these institutions gave in the late eighteenth century and in the nineteenth proceeds in four stages. We turn first to England. Second, we will try to blaze a trail through the thicket of the Low Countries and France, where donors, churches, and taxpayers were intertwined by law. Next, we will turn to other Continental countries, where church and private giving, while still elaborate in its form, was simpler in its revenue base and negligible in amount. Much the same was true in the United States, our final destination in this chapter.

In England and Wales tens of thousands of private charities were monitored by the Charities Commission in the eighteenth and nineteenth centuries. Some were for the poor, some for education, some for apprenticeships, and others for miscellaneous religious purposes. How much did they give? The first exhibit in Table 3.1 suggests that this recorded charity amounted to only 0.4 percent of national product early in the nineteenth century and fell to 0.1 percent by 1861–1876. Poor relief in Scotland, still dominated by the churches and charity until the 1840s, was even more meager than charity in England.[10]

TABLE 3.1. *Church and Private Charity for the Poor, as Shares of National Product in the Eighteenth and Nineteenth Centuries*

(1) Charities in England and Wales 1819–1837 ≤ 0.40%, 1861–1876 ≤ 0.10% of GNP.

In England and Wales tens of thousands of private charities were monitored by the Charities Commission in the eighteenth and nineteenth centuries. Some were for the poor, some for education, some for apprenticeships, and others for miscellaneous religious purposes. In 1819–1837, these endowments yielded £1.2 million in annual income, or about 0.40 percent of the annual national income of England and Wales. In 1861–1876, when the charities were next surveyed, they yielded £2.2 million, or about 0.24 percent of national income. But of this only £0.9 million, or only 0.10 percent of the national income, was aimed more or less at the poor. Poor relief in Scotland, still dominated by the churches and charity until the 1840s, was even more meager than charity in England.

(2) Netherlands 1790, private, church, and government aid combined = 1.46–1.93%.

In the complex Dutch system they were mixed together in the same institutions. So it's hard to say how much was charity, versus the taxpayers' contribution. Looking at the accounts of Amsterdam charities for 1829–1854, Marco van Leeuwen (2000, Chapter 5) estimates that 23 percent of the funds came from municipal taxpayers and another 31 percent from properties owned by the charities. Depending on how much the municipal government contributed to the latter properties, the share paid by private donations would be between 46 and 77 percent of the total. If this held for the Netherlands as a whole, then private and church aid = 0.67–1.49% of GNP. That's still the largest measured charity rate before the twentieth century.

(3) Churches in France, 1790 = 0.17% of GNP.

French charity at the onset of the French Revolution was given an upper-bound estimate by the Committee on Mendicity in 1790. The committee's reports reckoned what ecclesiastical charity should be if the tithe (*dîme*) were faithfully paid and if all of it were spent on helping the poor and sick. That amount of 10 million livres, or a mere 0.17 percent of GNP, was more than the church actually delivered, since the tithe was never fully paid by parishioners and the church channeled part of the funds into noncharity uses. Even the committee's own unfulfilled revolutionary demand was only to raise total relief to 51.5 million livres, or 0.87 percent of GNP, from all sources.

(4) Church and private charity in France 1880 ≤ 0.50% of GNP.

(5) Charities in Italy 1868 also ≤ 0.50%.

In Italy in 1868 there were 17,718 data-providing charities in Italy outside Venice giving out Lit. 69,987,291. Adding another three million for Venice yields a figure that was 0.73 percent of national income in 1868 (Maestri 1868, pp. 155–156). Ten years later 16,881 reporting charities gave out Lit. 82,644,006, or 0.79 percent of national income (Italy 1881, pp. 566–12 and 566–13). These figures cover all kinds of charities, however, not just those targeted at the poor. Again, as with France, it seems unlikely that these institutions gave the poor half a percent of national income, though one must allow for additional giving not covered here.

Sources: Lindert (1998), Van Leeuwen (2000, Ch. 5).

Figures on charity to the poor are, of course, subject to great errors. The most likely cause of underestimation is that no statistical source can include the countless individual acts of giving, of which no record is ever kept. David Owen has argued that

aggregate statistics for charitable giving almost inevitably understate the reality. Even apart from the individual almsgiving which leaves no record, a large volume of benevolence was comprehended in *ad hoc* collections, both local and nationwide...the kind of generosity which responded to appeals in *The Times*, as when in the winter of 1859 the Reverend H. Douglas raised £15,000 for his starving parishioners in the Victoria Dock district, does not figure in the totals.[11]

Yet the amounts involved in such unrecorded charity seem so low that the unknown total was probably not a great multiple of the aggregate data. And, again, the numbers typically *over*state charitable giving to the poor by including charities not targeted at the poor.

The role of church and private charity was more complex in the Low Countries and France. Here government typically shared funds, control, and personnel with churches and private philanthropies in the running of poor-relief institutions. Even before the 1790s the government–private institutional marriage was complex in the Dutch Republic,[12] and the French-revolutionary system of *bureaux de bienfaisance* (welfare bureaus) continued the marriage in all three countries. The complexity is evident in any statement of accounts. What was spent on the poor came from a mixture of three sources: direct government subsidies, direct spending by private charities, and the agency's own asset incomes. The asset-income flows in turn mixed originally public and originally private funds in unknown proportions.

The complexity and the giving were both greatest in the Netherlands. In general, the Dutch system had a peculiar intertwining of church and government. Unlike England, the parishes had not become local government agencies. Yet the two were joined in poor relief by tradition and, after 1814, by royal decree. Local governments expected the various church denominations to raise donations for their own members. Where this fell short, supplements by government could be negotiated. On the other hand, church charity revenues were sometimes turned over to local governments for distribution to the poor. The roles of church members and taxpayers were thus blended together.

If we are forced to study a public–private aggregate in the Netherlands, how much did that aggregate give to the poor? For the Dutch Republic around 1790, Table 3.1 suggests shares that were large for that time, though not so impressive by today's standards. Again, an unknown part of that came from private sources. Across the middle third of the nineteenth century perhaps a third of funds went directly from church donations to the poor, a quarter went directly from taxpayers to the poor, and the remaining two-fifths were administered though government, but with a blending of public and church and secular-private funds.

French charity was apparently less generous. Its magnitude at the onset of the French Revolution is judged by Table 3.1's entry for France in 1790 – less than 0.17 percent of national product. After France introduced its *bureaux de bienfaisance* in 1797, private and government moneys were mixed together. We can judge the limits to private giving by looking at the whole mixture as of 1880, the end-year for this chapter. As of 1880, charities gave 7.04 million francs (only 0.03 percent of a GDP of 25,409 million francs) through the *bureaux de bienfaisance*, which was less than the direct subsidies from government. If charities similarly supplied less than half the prior accumulation of the bureaus' own asset-income revenue, then they gave less than 0.13 percent of GDP through the bureaus.[13] To this should be added the private part of the 0.41 percent of GDP spent by hospices and hospitals and the 0.05 percent for abandoned children – but only the part that was both privately funded and actually given to the poor. Overall, private charity, including the part channeled through the churches, probably did not account for half a percent of French GDP in 1880, as shown in Table 3.1.

For the other Catholic countries, as for France, our few clues suggest that church and private giving probably offered the poor a plethora of moral instruction and a pittance of material aid. Table 3.1 sketches the likely shares for Italy around the time of national unification. Again, as with France, it seems unlikely that charitable institutions gave the poor half a percent of national income, though one must allow for additional giving not covered here.

Our few quantitative clues about church and philanthropic giving to the poor hint at two conclusions to be tested further: (1) Such nongovernment flows of poor relief were probably below a half of a percent of national product in all cases except in the Netherlands, where charity was mandated by, and chained to, government relief administration. (2) In general, the best working hypothesis on charity and religion is to agree with Stuart Woolf that

Only in the Protestant countries, such as England, Holland and Denmark, was the wealthy minority forced by law more or less continuously to maintain the poor majority.... In eighteenth-century Denmark [for example] poor relief was financed by town rates and, at the end of the century by excise and income tax. There could hardly be a greater contrast with the Catholic Continent, where in the Napoleonic years outdoor relief agencies were dependent on alms and a tax on theatre ticket sales.[14]

There is probably more private social expenditure today, with all the public programs in place, than before the rise of the public programs. At face value, some of the complementary increase in private giving might look large as a share of national income. In 1995, for instance, the United States, perhaps the world's leader in private giving, seemed to give as much as 7.0 percent of GDP privately, while ten other OECD countries gave from 0.6 percent to 3.7 percent privately.[15] We should subtract out the large part, probably over half, of these recent sums that went to such nonpoor recipients as universities and cancer research foundations. Still, the part left is still likely to be larger today than in those past centuries when churches and philanthropists were thought to have given so much.

By the late eighteenth century, then, the stage was set in several countries for a resort to nonvoluntary poor relief through government. That step was taken in the wake of food crises, wars, religious feuds, and revolutions.

The Amounts of Public Poor Relief to 1880

Soon after governments took the permanent step into controlling poor relief, numbers began to be published. The main numbers available at the time were the numbers of people on relief and the amounts spent, supplemented by the price of grain and by total population counts from the early censuses of population. Publishing these few indicators, scholars could calculate three ratios to summarize the extent of poor relief and pauperism:

(1) $Nr/N =$ the share of poor-relief recipients (Nr) in the population (N),
(2) $B/Nr =$ poor-relief benefits (B) per recipient, and
(3) $B/N =$ poor relief per capita.

None of these can capture the generosity or penury of society. The first two suffer from the defect that merely adding more recipients who were given low amounts of aid because of low need could greatly inflate Nr. In fact, that happened often. Whenever it did, from year to year or from place to place, it invited the false inference that society had cut the aid to each recipient (since B/Nr dropped). The third of these is also ambiguous, since a high level of it could mean either very generous benefits to a few recipients (a caring affluent society) or meager benefits for many of them (a stingy impoverished society). But writers made do with the materials at hand, so they used measures like these.

Thanks to the efforts of postwar economic historians, we now have rough measures of nominal national product (Y). We can now study the historical movements in two more indicators:

(1) $B/Y =$ the share of poor-relief spending in national product, and
(2) the support ratio $R = (B/Nr)/(Y/(N - Nr)) =$ the ratio of (benefits per recipient) to (national income per nonrecipient).

Both of these indicators have their uses. It might seem that the support ratio R is closer to being a measure of the generosity of support. Yet it falls short of capturing the set of society's offers to poor people in different situations. For example, it can be raised – making society look more generous – just by denying aid to people who would have individually received small amounts of it and giving aid only to higher-cost paupers. As we shall see, that also happened in several countries. The larger point here is that R, like the first

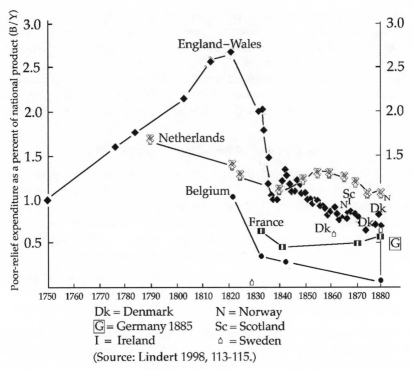

FIGURE 3.1. Poor-Relief Expenditures as a Share of National Product, Europe 1750–1880.

three measures, is sensitive to the trickiest of the measures used here, the number of recipients (*Nr*).[16]

More reliable and more available is *B/Y*, the share of poor relief in national product. While it cannot distinguish small amounts of aid to many people from large amounts of aid to a few, it is relatively available and has the virtue of portraying the average tax rate that society is paying for the poor. So we turn to *B/Y* measures when we can, both for private relief and for tax-based public relief.

How much did taxpayers actually have to pay for the poor, and when? The first step toward getting the magnitudes right is to set aside most of the histories of European poor laws written before, say, 1980. Such histories are literally histories of the passage of national laws, not histories of how the poor were treated in their villages.[17] Unfortunately, the passage of laws is often a misleading clue about the timing of movements in actual policy. In the histories of English poor relief, for example, most accounts have talked as though the passage of the Elizabethan Poor Law of 1597 and 1601 set up a national system of relieving the poor. In fact, all that law did was to instruct local parish governments to deal with the problem of poor relief somehow,

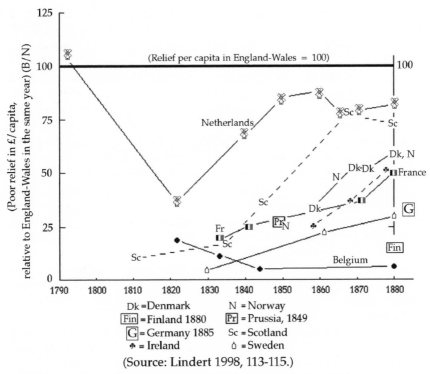

(Source: Lindert 1998, 113-115.)

FIGURE 3.2. Poor-Relief Expenditures per Capita of National Population, Relative to Relief per Capita in England–Wales.

without any money from the Royal treasury. While it probably did help the eventual emergence of poor relief at the local level – for example, by telling parishes to appoint overseers of the poor – there was neither a system nor noteworthy amounts of aid until well into the eighteenth century.

To follow the contours of tax-based relief from the eighteenth century to the late nineteenth, let us concentrate on two of the five measures listed earlier. The two are the share-of-income measure (B/Y) that resembles a societal tax rate on behalf of the poor and the crude measure of real relief per capita (B/N), which is available for additional places. Studying the movements of these two indicators in Figures 3.1 and 3.2 reveals that England and Wales were different from the rest of Europe in the level and timing of their public aid. The best way to view the international contrasts is to divide the 1750–1880 history into three periods: (1) 1750–1795, (2) the 1795–1834 heyday of England's Old Poor Law, and (3) the cutback era 1834–1880.

In the first phase, before England raised its relief so markedly in the 1790s and tied it to the price of bread in 1795, there was not a clear contrast with the Continent. Dutch taxpayers probably paid something close to the English as a share of income, perhaps about 1.75 percent in the early 1790s. Most other countries had little or no relief.

The second phase in the Anglo–Continental contrast could be equated with the 1795–1834 heyday of England's classic Old Poor Law even though the rise in English poor relief dates back to the mid-eighteenth century and 1795 was not a sharp watershed for England.[18] After 1795 the Dutch were paying less than half as much per capita as the English, due to events in both countries. The French takeover and retreat left Dutch poor-relief institutions with fewer assets, partly because they suffered default on some government bonds. England, meanwhile, had raised its poor relief to unprecedented levels, in response to the near-famine and food riots of the 1790s and the sound of the guillotine from across the Channel. In this era England–Wales stood alone. Its poor-relief share stayed over 2 percent of national product, versus under 1.5 percent for Netherlands, Belgium, or France, even though these three countries' figures include private as well as government funds. That primacy as a payer of taxes for the poor did not go unnoticed, and intense controversy set the stage for history's most famous cut in poor relief in England's Poor Law Reform of 1834.

The Reform of 1834 slashed English relief greatly, though not so fully as the champions of the cuts had hoped.[19] Relief in most other countries rose toward the English standard, the exception being Belgium.[20] Whether the Continental countries after 1834 actually raised their relief per capita in real terms cannot be determined here, given the difficulties of measuring the cost of living in so many countries, with or without the use of exchange rates. Still, it is clear that over the half century after 1834, with English relief dropping, there was a tendency for the levels of poor relief per capita to converge.

The puzzle about the English commitment of resources to poor relief is why it rose so much and then fell so much in England and Wales, with little echo of this movement in other countries. The puzzling rise and fall of English relief were not due to any mere substitution of state for private giving. On the contrary, English private charity rose soon after the poor taxes rose and fell when they fell, as Table 3.1 suggested. The 0.40 percent of national income given to all charitable purposes in 1816–1837, around the peak time of poor-tax burdens, was higher than before the rise in the poor rates.[21] Then, when taxpayer support for the poor was cut back by the Poor Law Reform, total private charity also declined, from about 0.40 percent to 0.24 percent of national income in 1861–1876, as noted above, with only 0.10 percent ending up in the hands of the poor. Chapter 4 tackles the task of interpreting this puzzle.

HOW EUROPE GAVE RELIEF AND FOR WHAT

The Eternal Search for the Worthy and Unworthy Poor

The history of poverty policy is not a voyage of fresh discovery, but an oscillation back and forth between two long-familiar poles of opinion. We have always known that laziness and bad luck are two sources of poverty, but we have swung between believing that one or the other source dominates. We swing to the left in moments like the 1960s in the United States, when the deserving poor were "discovered" by Michael Harrington's *The Other America* (1962), as if the deserving poor had been ignored for centuries. We swing to the right with new visions of "workfare," as if the need to provide strong work incentives had been ignored for centuries. Neither discovery is authentic. As historians of poverty have long known, the political pendulum of opinion merely swings back and forth between those two fixed poles. That will surely continue.

Throughout the eighteenth and nineteenth centuries, and probably earlier, those in charge of the poor tried to monitor their behavior.[22] In general, poor relief was not a gift and not an entitlement, except perhaps for the well-respected elderly poor. Rather, local taxpayers used the relief to purchase, or demand, certain kinds of behavior from the poor. In giving or denying aid, they were engaged in that eternal struggle to distinguish the deserving dependent poor from the undeserving ones, especially from the able–bodied, who could and should support themselves.

The kinds of behavior demanded of the poor are illustrated, in negative mirror image, by Table 3.2's listing of some of the reasons why the village of Great Burstead (in Essex, England) denied weekly relief to certain paupers between 1823 and 1828. Topping the list of infractions that would cause the overseer of the poor to withdraw aid was a pauper's failure to attend church the preceding Sunday. After all, poor relief was administered by the parish, which continued to be a Church of England entity as well as a tax-collecting unit of local government. Next on the list of top pauper sins in Great Burstead was failure to report one's labor earnings accurately to the parish overseer. Third was refusal to work for low pay for a local farmer. Even having a pet as a companion was a transgression, as when poor Widow Tyler had to get rid of her pet dog before the parish would continue supporting her. Conspicuously absent from this list of sins was a kind of welfare-recipient behavior that today's administrators would be most insistent on stopping: absence of one's children from school. School was still not seen as a primary road out of poverty in England in the 1820s. But they did insist that you work for the local farmers if you were able–bodied.

The Battle over Putting the Poor to Work

Today's enthusiasm for getting the poor to work cannot exceed that shown by those in power in the eighteenth and nineteenth centuries. At no time were the able–bodied encouraged to remain unemployed for long, even though they did qualify for seasonal or cyclical outdoor relief in many instances. The unemployed and able–bodied were pushed toward work by the lingering beggar-punishment laws and by the fact that so much outdoor aid was conditional on job-search and work.

TABLE 3.2. *Reasons Given for Denying Relief to Poor Persons in the Village of Great Burstead, Essex, 1823–1828*

---

(1) Failing to attend *worship* last Sunday, 17 cases recorded. Example:
  • "October 6th [1823] Burrell, Jno For not attending Divine Worship on Sunday last agreeable to former orders."

(2) Failing to provide an accurate report of family labor *earnings*, or known to earn too much for the relief they requested, 16 cases. Example:
  • "April 12th [1824] Burrel John For not giving a true account of his wife's earnings and swearing several oaths in presence of the Committee."

(3) Refusing to *work* for a local farmer, 10 cases. Examples:
  • "October 6th [1823] Marsh, Jas. Not allowed a pair of shoes for refusing to work with Mr. Barnard at 1/6 per day."
  • "Dec. 17th [1827] ___ Nash Not relieved because he was saucy, and would not work for Mr. Gates if ordered."
  • "May 10th [1825] [Name of person] Not allowed because will not allow his daughter to go into service."

(4) Keeping a *dog* as a pet, 5 cases. Example:
  • "Oct. 24th [1824] Tyler Widow Not relieved for keeping a dog in the house." "Reconsidered, the dog to be got rid of by Nov. 1st."

(5) Using a *doctor* other than the one designated by the parish, 3 cases. Example:
  • "Oct. 31st [1824] Garnish, Thos Not allowed, having employed another medical man for his wife enstead of the parish Surgeon."

(6) Miscellaneous other reasons, such as
  • "Nov. 24th [1823] Taylor, Jas: not relieved, on account of his wife's appearing in unbecoming dress on Sundays and other days and children likewise."
  • "Feb. 9th, 1824 Kirby, Saml Not relieved for being saucy."
  • "Nov. 29th [1824] Collins Wm labourer Not relieved being forward in liquor."

Sources: Legible entries in the 1823–1828 book listing reasons for not relieving certain paupers at weekly meetings, Great Burstead, Essex. Essex Record Office Ex, D/P 139/8. Note: Some of the cases were repeated incidents involving the same person, such as the persistent Jonathan Burrell cited twice here.

This work requirement took many forms. In agricultural England before 1834 its most famous forms were the roundsman system, the labor rate, and the infamous workhouse test.[23] These had their counterparts on the Continent. For indoor relief, there were various experiments in trying to make workhouses and work colonies pay for themselves. That these had already failed to run without subsidy in the eighteenth century did not stop nineteenth century officials from trying again. The French and Dutch long maintained workshops for women (*ataliers*).[24] The most famous experiment was the Dutch system of agricultural work colonies dating from the founding of the *Maatschappij van Weldadigheid* in 1818, which was imitated in Belgium and much discussed elsewhere. These work farms, physically outdoor but indoor in the sense of work-team incarceration, survived and even expanded for many decades. They never shed their dependence on government subsidies, however. Thus a nineteenth-century economist felt it necessary to spend three pages describing the meagerness of the prospects for these colonies to cool "the sanguine expectations formed by many persons in England of their success."[25] Even Colonel Forsell of Sweden, who railed against entitlements as an invitation to laziness, was not sanguine about the Dutch forced-work colonies:

As to Holland, the poor colonies there established since the year 1818, have attracted the attention of all of Europe. Many able authors have stated, that these colonies are not only able to support themselves, but even to pay both the interest and capital of their establishment within a period of 16 years. Mr. Gyllenhall (a Swede) having lately visited them, has proved, that these settlements, though enjoying many hundreds of thousand florins as annual revenue, both from the state and from many towns and corporations, nevertheless cannot succeed.[26]

Another device for maintaining work incentives while giving aid was to assist the able–bodied only in the winter, when work was less available. As George Boyer has emphasized, seasonality of relief was a key to English rural relief in the classic 1795–1834 era. In fact, rural relief for the able–bodied was already seasonal in the seventeenth and eighteenth centuries in the Netherlands, in England, and probably in most countries.[27]

Thus even an age when the well-off fully believed in the distinction between the deserving and the undeserving poor (a distinction dating back at least to the Justinian Code), and were fully convinced that the latter needed to be prodded to work, they kept doing what we do today: They mixed work incentives with at least some outdoor relief for the able–bodied unemployed, while forever tinkering with the details.

Indoor versus Outdoor Relief

To what extent were the poor were allowed to remain in their own homes, instead of being forced to enter a workhouse or asylum to receive indoor aid? Indoor relief was designed to be unpleasant in most cases. Outdoor relief meant the limited dignity and privacy of being able to keep one's own residence.

If you never saw any numbers about poor relief, and you read only its legal history, you might think that all paupers were kept indoors like Oliver Twist. Law after law decreed that outdoor relief should be either rare or prohibited altogether, and funds were repeatedly approved for the building of new poor houses. Yet the repetition of decrees against outdoor relief betrays officials' inability to resist it, as a look at the numbers reveals. Table 3.3 shows the share of outdoor (*à domicile, a domicilio, huiszittende*) relief in the pauper counts and the amounts spent on the poor for England–Wales, Ireland, France, and the Netherlands. With the exception of Ireland, the figures come from countries whose governments probably had a high willingness to give

TABLE 3.3. *Administrative Costs and Places of Poor Relief, Various Countries and Years up to 1911*

	Administrative Costs as a % of Poor Relief Expenditures	Outdoor Relief as a % of		Sources and Notes
		the Number of Paupers Relieved	the Value of Transfers to the Poor	
English parish workhouses, 1772–1774:				
Rural East Anglia	29.2		10.5	House of Commons,
London	23.6		27.4	*Sessional Papers*, 1775.
Towns	15.6		32.8	"
cities (excl. London)	10.1		47.5	"
All reporting parishes	19.4		32.5	"
England and Wales				
1840		85.2	77.1	Williams (1981, Tables 4.5, 4.6), year
1850		87.9	78.4	starting April 1st, outrelief as a share
1860	11.4	86.8	74.4	of itself plus in-maintenance;
1870	10.6	85.8	70.6	administrative here = salaries and
1880	13.2	77.7	58.9	rations of officers as a share of total
1887	20.1	76.5	38.9	expenditures.
1895	22.0	74.1	33.4	
1905	22.1	68.9	30.8	
1911	24.7	60.4	22.6	
Ireland				
1858	21.3		1.2	House of Commons, *Sessional Papers*,
1871	17.2		15.4	1878–79, xxx, p. 20; administrative is
1878	15.7		19.7	again salaries and rations of officers.

| | Administrative Costs as a % of Poor Relief Expenditures | | | Outdoor Relief as a % of | | |
	Poorhouse	Outdoor	Total	no. of Paupers Relieved	Value Transferred to the Poor	Source
France						
1846			73.0			Gouda (1995, p. 228). *Annuaire Statistique*.
1871		15.1				"
1880		15.8				
Netherlands						
1822			89.3			De Bosch Kemper (1851).
1848			94.8	60.1		Netherlands statistical yearbooks.
1864			87.9	57.1		"
Sweden						
1829			87.6			Great Britain, *First Report of Poor Law Commissioners* (1834), App. F, p. 370F.
New York State (excl. New York City)						
1840–44	21.2	14.7	18.3	63.1	47.4	Hannon (1984, 1986).
1846–50	20.6	14.2	17.5	69.6	49.9	
1851–55	12.9	10.0	11.6	73.0	46.0	
1856–60	18.4	8.9	13.8	78.9	50.8	
1870–74	25.7	3.8	16.0	74.8	50.7	
1875–79	25.6	9.4	17.7	81.3	53.7	
1880–84	25.3	8.3	17.8	73.4	49.3	
1885–89	27.0	8.3	20.0	64.8	43.2	
1891–95	32.0	9.1	24.7	69.6	38.6	

outdoor relief in the nineteenth century – a willingness that we are told was not mirrored in other countries.[28] Yet in all of the countries for which we can get information, outdoor relief was the rule for most paupers and took more than half the relief budget in England and the Netherlands. France seemed to induce a greater share of paupers to live in hospices, but here again more paupers received their aid in their own homes.[29]

Most reliant on the workhouse test was British policy toward Ireland. In the wake of the Irish Poor Law of 1838, most relief had to be taken in the indoor institutions, or at least was administered by them, so that by the late 1870s outdoor relief was still much less prevalent in Ireland than in England and Wales.

British policy continued to treat English paupers more gently than Irish paupers across the mid-nineteenth century. From the laws of the time and most subsequent literature, one would think that English paupers would have been driven indoors, or into work, between 1834 and 1880. Outdoor relief in England and Wales was targeted for severe reduction in the original Poor Law Reform of 1834, again in the Outdoor Relief Prohibitory Order of 1844, again in the Outdoor Relief Regulation Order of 1852 (extending the 1884 order to urban poor-relief unions), and again in the major campaign against outdoor relief in the 1870s.[30] Yet as late as 1880 outdoor relief still accounted for 78 percent of the pauper counts and 59 percent of what the poor received in England and Wales. For all the campaign against outdoor relief in England and Wales, the net drop from 1840 to 1880 was not much greater than the shift *toward* outdoor relief in Ireland 1858–1878. England's Poor Law Union workhouse, which was intended to be the locus of virtually all relief after 1834, was "relegated to the status of a general asylum for the very old, the very young, and the infirm," who remained a minority of those relieved.[31] Perhaps two of the forces holding back the expansion of English indoor relief were (1) the unwillingness of policy to make indoor relief at all pleasant except, gradually, for the aged, and (2) the fact that indoor relief cost so much more per pauper – about four times as much in England and Wales in 1856–1857.[32]

Administrative Costs

What share of the tax money spent on the poor was lost to administrative costs? The left-hand column in Table 3.3 offers some initial clues about how big these costs could have been in England–Wales, Ireland, and France. The administrative costs, as measured by remuneration to poor-relief officers, ran between 10 and 30 percent of total expenditures on poor relief, with no clear average differences among the shares for England–Wales, Ireland, and France (for given shares of outdoor relief). All of these administrative-cost percentages seem to be above today's rates, which are typically as low as 2–3 percent of the amounts transferred for social-security programs, though a bit higher for welfare programs.[33] Nineteenth-century taxpayers paid a higher administrative cost for aid to the poor, largely because they insisted even more strongly than we that the poor be heavily supervised.

There are hints of trends in each country's cost share, and the trends seem to be linked to changes in the outdoor share of all poor relief. In England, the administrative cost share was lower by 1840 than it was in a poorhouse-related sample of places in 1772–1774. It crept up from 1840 to 1880 and continued to rise until it peaked in 1920.[34] One likely source of these contrasts was the fact that the share of outdoor relief grew in the eighteenth century and fell back after 1834. Since outdoor relief was cheaper to administer, as well as requiring that each outdoor pauper should receive less, the fall-and-rise in administrative costs could be related to the rise-and-fall in outdoor relief. Ireland's contrasting movement fits the same pattern: A likely source of the decline in the administrative-cost share for Irish relief between 1858 and 1878 was the rise of outdoor relief. Officials and taxpayers faced the same kind of choice that we face: spend even more to supervise the poor carefully and seek ways of finding work for them or save on administrative costs by guiding them less.

What They Gave: Cash versus Aid in Kind

Another of today's poor-relief dilemmas that was evident throughout western Europe in centuries past was the tough choice between giving cash and giving aid in kind. Long before twentieth-century economists said so, officials knew there was a case for giving the poor cash and letting them decide what they needed. Yet they also knew the opposing "merit goods" argument that twentieth-century economists have also sharpened: The taxpayers can reasonably insist that the poor consume a bundle biased toward good health and child development. Today's critics of welfare as a support for substance abuse are no more blunt than predecessors like this Dutch critic in 1846:

Doling out money and alms publicly, at the doors of houses or in the open streets, is a bad habit. Such charity is not benevolent: it is a destructive activity that encourages sloth, idleness, and inebriation. However, when we give food and the necessary cloth we incur the smallest risk because, after all, we cannot allow the indigent to be personally responsible for spending his or her charitable support freely.[35]

In this spirit, the new Dutch Poor Law of 1854 reaffirmed that "as much as possible" relief should not be cash, but rather food, fuel, clothes, bedding, and housing. Data for France show that relief from the *bureaux de bienfaisance* was always a mixture. These shares of the value of aid in 1860 were typical of those recorded in France for the rest of the century: 21 percent in cash, 55 percent food, 6 percent clothing, 5 percent fuel, 6 percent medical care and drugs, and 7 percent other.[36]

Who Received It

Who were the paupers? The easiest pattern to document and understand was the general age–sex mixture of recipients. The age–sex pattern followed dependency rates: the higher any group's rate of dependency on the incomes earned by other family members, the greater that same group's likelihood of being on relief. Thus the high participation rates, in dependency either among self-supporting families or among poor-relief recipients, were those of the elderly, of the infirm, of children, and of women without husbands. Females were always the majority of the pauper host – for example, 60–68 percent of all recipients in Sweden between 1810 and 1870 and 71–74 percent of all recipients in Scotland between 1870 and 1880.[37] The share of able–bodied adult males on relief was probably always low. For England and Wales, we know they made up less than 0.6 percent of paupers, or less than 0.1 percent of adult males, from 1851 on.[38] More controversial are their shares of recipients and of adult males in the higher-spending era 1795–1834, but we unfortunately lack numbers on the relief rates for men in that era.

Town versus Country

England–Wales stood out more sharply in its relative relief-giving between town and country than in its reliance on outdoor relief or its administrative costs. The English gave relatively more relief in the poor and declining countryside, whereas the rest of the world gave more relief in the towns and cities.

Our best map of the English pattern is afforded by the 1802–1803 poor relief returns to Parliament. The 1802–1803 returns make it clear that the rising centers, especially London, had these attributes relative to heavily agricultural counties: (a) lower poor taxes as a percentage of income, (b) lower shares of the population on relief, (c) greater emphasis on indoor relief in workhouses, and (d) frequent denial of relief to immigrants.[39] In other words, the English pattern was for toughness in the growing cities and relative generosity in agricultural parishes and counties. The urban toughness took the form of allowing fewer people onto the relief rolls and forcing a greater share of them indoors. It did not take the form of lower relief per recipient, however, partly because indoor relief cost more.[40]

The peculiarity of the spatial pattern of relief in England and Wales was long-standing, as Peter Solar has noted.[41] The revolutions in poor relief between the late eighteenth century and the mid-nineteenth century changed the positions of cities and regions, but only moderately. Before 1795 the prevailing pattern was regional: Relief was greater in the Southeast and less in the Northwest, either on the relief-per-capita measure (B/N) shown here or as a share of income (B/Y). Between 1795 and 1834, the regional pattern

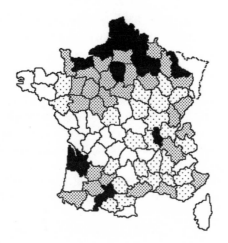

■ = 1.00 - 2.86 francs/capita (top 13 départements)
▦ = 0.60 - 0.94 francs/capita (next 27)
⬚ = 0.40 - 0.38 francs/capita (next 24)
☐ = 0.07 - 0.38 francs/capita (bottom 23)

Source: France, Ministère du Commerce, *Annuaire Statistique de la France, 1883.*
Notes: The averages cover expenditures by the *bureaux de bienfaisance.*
The three over-1-franc départements in the south include the cities of Bourdeaux, Toulouse, and Lyon.

FIGURE 3.3. French Poor Relief per Capita in 1880: The Cities and the Far North Gave Most.

became less sharp in the countryside, and the English countryside as a whole stood out more clearly as Western Europe's area of greatest poor relief, now in contrast to urban-industrial England. After the 1834 Poor Law Reform had centralized poor relief, there was some convergence in relief per capita, but the countryside still spent more than the urban and industrial centers and the Southeast still spent more than the Northwest.

The Continental contrast in rural and urban relief was the opposite. In France in 1833, the use of charitable funds (as distinct from the funds of the *bureaux de bienfaisance*) was highly tilted toward major towns. Their receipts per capita (of total population) were 9.5 times as great as those of the rural and small-town population. And in the rural areas, the aid was channeled toward the towns and not the countryside, leaving Porter to ponder at length how the agricultural population got so little.[42] The geography of French poor relief shows up clearly in Figure 3.3. Those top thirteen departments in terms of poor relief per capita in 1880 fell into two geographic categories. Some were in the far North of France, the part of France closest to the countries that then led the world in poor relief, namely England, Denmark, and the Netherlands. Aside from this relatively generous far North, each of the others was dominated by a large city – Paris, Lyon, Toulouse, and Bordeaux.

In other Continental countries, as in France, relief was given much more in the cities than in the countryside. In Belgium in the 1840s, the pauper shares of population were similar between town/city and country, but aid per pauper was higher in the towns/cities. In Sweden between 1860 and 1870 relief per recipient in the towns and cities was between two and three times its level in the countryside. In the German states, too, cities paid more per capita for poor relief, and each pauper received more, than in the countryside.[43] According to Stuart Woolf, the Continental tilt toward relief in cities and towns was a pattern already established centuries before.[44] Why was poor relief so rural in England and Wales, and so urban on the Continent and – as we shall see – in the United States? Here is another puzzle to be tackled in Chapter 4.

AMERICAN PRIVATE AND PUBLIC RELIEF BEFORE THE NEW DEAL

Compared with Northwestern Europe – say, England and Wales, France, Belgium, and the Netherlands – U.S. poor relief showed these main features before the 1930s:

(1) *Americans gave less from taxes.* U.S. government poor relief never exceeded 0.2 percent of national product anytime before the Great Depression of the 1930s.

(2) *Americans gave less from private charity.* Organized philanthropy in the United States was equally limited before the Great Depression. Since the 1930s the recorded delivery of charity to the poor has stayed below half a percent of national product, far below the level of assistance from government. Such was the case even in the early 1980s, when charitable contributions were generously deductible against the income tax, leaving a strong incentive to report all giving. One half of 1 percent of national income thus seems like a generous upper bound on the extent of private American giving in any era.

(3) *There was no "crowding out," over time or space.* U.S. history, like Western European history, rejects the perennial notion that governmental support for the poor crowds out private aid. Both the temporal and the spatial patterns from the past reveal that when government gave nothing, private charity also gave virtually nothing to the poor. If there is any partial correlation between public and private aid, it is more likely positive, not negative.

(4) *Waves of reform revealed the cost of monitoring.* As in Western Europe, so too in the leading U.S. cities, poor relief waxed and waned through recurring campaigns of reform. In New York State, as in

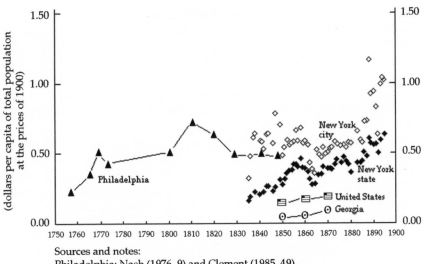

Sources and notes:
Philadelphia: Nash (1976, 9) and Clement (1985, 49).
New York city and New York state: Hannon (1986, Appendix A,
   using the David–Solar (1977) consumer price index.
United States and Georgia: U.S. Superintendent of the Census (1872),
   again combined with the David–Solar consumer price index.

FIGURE 3.4. Government Expenditures on Poor Relief per Capita, America 1757–1895.

England, local governments favored more generosity than state or national governments seemed to show. And in the United States, as in Western Europe, getting tougher on the poor raised administrative costs as a share of the amounts spent.

How Much Public Relief Was Given

One would imagine that a young and frontier America would be a harsher climate for generous poor relief, and what few numbers we have on relief in the United States seem to support that intuition. Figure 3.4 plots what little we know about U.S. tax-based relief before 1895, using the relief per capita (B/N) measure that is available. In the colonial and early federal period, relief was a local affair and only cities gave much. Thanks to the research on Philadelphia's early poverty and poor relief, and to the David–Solar consumer price index, we know the levels of real relief expenditures per capita in Philadelphia from 1757 on. By 1835, we have returns for the city and state of New York from already-published sources. Then, in the censuses of 1850, 1860, and 1870, the federal government tried to collate nationwide returns on poor relief.[45]

U.S. public relief levels have always been below the relief given in England and Wales, which oscillated between one dollar and two dollars per capita.[46] They have also been below the relief levels in the Netherlands, except that during the French War era and the 1820s Dutch relief may have fallen temporarily below that of Philadelphia and one or two other U.S. cities. As of 1823 only 1.13 percent of the population in New York State got any relief at all. If the amount they received were one-sixth of average income per adult, as in England's relatively generous system, then poor relief in New York State was less than 0.2 percent of state income in 1823. When regular data on New York began in 1835, it is evident that the city and especially the countryside paid less in poor relief than the average resident of England or the Netherlands. By 1850, when the federal census made its first unsteady attempt to measure poor relief over the whole nation, the national average poor tax revenues per capita look lower than those in France and Scotland as well as England and the Netherlands. That national average was dragged down by near-zero rates in the South, as illustrated by Figure 3.4's early returns for Georgia.

From 1850 on, we can follow the level of tax-based relief as a share of national income (Figure 3.5 and Table 3.4) in addition to charting the amounts paid per capita (Figure 3.3). There are signs of a slight rise in the level of relief across the second half of the nineteenth century, though Figure 3.4 shows that the rise did not continue in the first three decades of the twentieth. Thus by the time the Great Depression hit, the United States was still a country that paid far less in taxes for the poor than most countries in Western Europe. Among the nations of the world at the end of the 1920s, the United States would have ranked about fifteenth in taxes for poor relief as a share of national product.[47] U.S. aid had an urban bias, like the aid in Continental Europe, and it was also greater in New England and the eastern seaboard than in places further west.

Private Charity in the United States and the Crowding Out Issue

In the United States, as in Europe, many insisted that aiding the poor was the business of churches and philanthropies, not of governments. The private approach has survived in U.S. political rhetoric to this day. Unlike the European political climate, which embraced comprehensive state aid to the poor, the United States' powerful conservatism continues to conjure up the image of church giving as more generous, more efficient, and more in tune with the needs of the local poor.

A fundamental assumption underlying the preference for private aid is that government transfer of taxpayers' money to the poor will "merely crowd out" private giving, leaving the poor with little or no net gain. A complete dollar-for-dollar crowding out has been imagined in the 1980s wave of

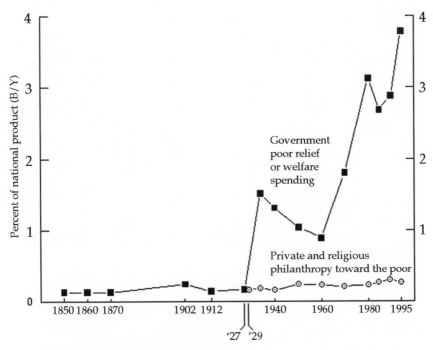

(Sources: See notes to Table 3.4.)

FIGURE 3.5. Public and Private Assistance to the Poor in the United States, 1850–1995.

enthusiasm for privatizing aid to the poor.[48] If that were true, then trying to have the government help the poor would seem truly futile.

Yet history clearly rejects the notion that government aid to the poor just crowds out private aid. The easiest way to see this is to look again at Figure 3.5 and Table 3.4. Back in the late 1920s, when government aid to the poor was still only one-sixth of 1 percent of national product, private charity to the poor was the same. The subsequent rise of government "welfare" aid to around 4 percent of gross national product (GNP) by 1995 could not just crowd out private charity, because there was only one-sixth of 1 percent of GNP in private philanthropy that could have been crowded out in the first place. In fact, private charity to the poor rose slightly as a share of donor's incomes during the expansion of the United States' tax-based government welfare spending.

Before the late 1920s private charity toward the poor had always been negligible, though we lack systematic national figures. It could hardly have been otherwise, so strong was the U.S. opposition to charity. There were actually two strong branches to the conservative campaign against poor relief in the United States. Many condemned any significant amount of aid,

TABLE 3.4. *Public and Private Assistance to the Poor in the United States, Approximate Measures as Shares of GNP, 1850–1995*

	(% of GNP through 1970, then % of GDP)									Category used for 1980 and 1995
	1850	1860	1870	1902	1913	1927	1970	1980	1995	
Public expenditures:										
Public poor relief, welfare	0.13	0.13	0.13	0.24	0.14	0.17	1.79	3.12	3.85	Public aid, other soc. welfare
Unemployment compensation							0.29	0.66	0.36	Unempl. insurance, empl. services
Old age survivors and disabil.							3.67	7.60	9.34	Social insur. minus unempl. insur.
Hospitals and health				0.29	0.29	0.45	1.39	0.97	1.18	Health & medical n.e.c.
Housing and urban renewal							0.33	0.25	0.40	Housing
Memoranda: Public education	0.33	0.48	0.73	1.19	1.47	2.36	5.71	4.35	5.03	Education
Philanthropy revenue of recipients:										
Total						1.43	1.85	1.75	1.71	Total
Youth serv's, welfare, race rel.						0.16	0.21	0.23	0.26	Human services, public/societal benefit
Hospitals and health						0.09	0.25	0.19	0.17	Health
Other						0.06	0.29	0.23		Unclassified
Memo.: paroch. & higher educ.						0.35	0.40	0.18	0.24	Education

	($ billions, current prices)									Category used for 1980 and 1993
	1850	1860	1870	1902	1913	1927	1970	1980	1995	
Public poor relief, welfare	0.003	0.005	0.011	0.05	0.06	0.16	17.52	87	280	Public aid, other soc. welfare
Unemployment compensation				0	0	0	2.82	18	26	Unempl. insurance and empl. services

						1929/30	1970	1980	1995	
Old age survivors and disabil.				0	0	0	35.83	212	679	Social insurance minus unempl. insur.
Hospitals and health				0.06	0.11	0.43	13.59	27	86	Health & medical n.e.c.
Housing and urban renewal				0	0	0	3.19	7	29	Housing
GNP	2.32	4.17	8.41	21.65	39.56	94.90	977.1	2784	7270	GDP
Memorandum: Public education	0.01	0.02	0.06	0.26	0.58	2.24	55.77	121	366	Education
						1929/30	**1970**	**1980**	**1995**	**Charitable Bequests**

Philanthropy revenue of recipients:

						1929/30	1970	1980	1995	
Total						1.47	18.05	49	124	Total
Youth serv's, welfare, race rel.						0.17	2.05	6	19	Human services, public/societal benefit
Hospitals and health						0.10	2.40	5	13	Health
Other						0.06	2.84	7	7	Unclassified
GNP	2.32	4.17	8.21	21.65	39.56	94.90	977.1	2784	7270	GDP
Memo.: paroch. & higher educ.						0.36	3.91	5	18	Education

Notes and Sources: Poor relief, 1850–1870: U.S. Superintendent of the Census, *Compendium of the Ninth Census* (1872), pp. 530–537. These figures probably include some public subsidies to private charities. All public expenditures (federal, state, and local), 1902–1970: *Historical Statistics*, Series Y533–Y566. Philanthropy, 1929/30 and 1970: *Historical Statistics*, Series H405–H411. GNP: U.S. Census Bureau, *Historical Statistics*, Series F1, and *Statistical Abstract* 1999. All data for 1980, 1995: U.S. Census Bureau, *Statistical Abstract* 1999. For alternative estimates of public welfare, health–sanitation, and education for 1890, 1902, 1913, and later dates, see Musgrave and Culbertson (1953, pp. 114). The Musgrave–Culbertson estimates were used in Lindert (1994). Public education expenditures, 1850–1870: Albert Fishlow (1966b). Figure 3.5's "philanthropy toward the poor" graphs the series on "youth services, welfare, race relations" up through 1970.

from any source, on the classic grounds that most of the poor had themselves and their drinking to blame and needed to be taught by a tough society to take care of themselves. Even Josephine Shaw Lowell, founder and director of the New York Charity Organization Society, blamed the poor in 1896:

Their distress is due to inherent faults, either physical, mental, or moral.... [R]elief is an evil – always. Even when necessary, I believe it is still an evil. One reason that it is an evil is because energy, independence, industry, and self-reliance are undermined by it.[49]

Equally sweeping in his opposition to any kind of transfer to the poor was Nathaniel Ware, pamphleteer, trade protectionist, and slave owner in 1844:

Better, if it came to the worst, let a few perish in the streets, than have one-twentieth part of mankind degraded, rendering worthless, & what is worse, eating the substance of the industrious and valuable portion of the community.[50]

Others objected only to using taxes to aid the poor, and strongly preferred private giving:[51]

"Charity is heaven-born, and ceases to be a virtue, when made compulsory by a tax." – Editorial in the *Newark Daily Advertiser*, 1857.
"[If ever America lost its freedom, it would be] by the slow and insidious growth in large cities of claims for subsistence upon the public treasury." – A committee of the Boston city council, 1859.
"[By replacing the tenderness of private giving, the cold poor law] eclipses half the loveliness of the character of woman, by interposing its opaque form, between the shivering child of want, and the sun-shine of her soul." – Samuel Young, Schenectady, 1826.

This latter group was the one that emphasized the crowding out of worthy private aid by tax-based relief.

If wealthier countries tend to offer their own citizens more public assistance, other things equal, why did the United States offer so little? A traditional way of disposing of this question is to say that U.S. culture is different, partly because the United States is a frontier nation. That explanation is a plausible part of the story. Yet even it is linked to another explanation, a demographic one, that seems to add to our understanding. To see the demographic effect, note that all the opinions just quoted focused on the work incentives facing able–bodied young adults. The frequent European discussion of widows and orphans seems to have figured less prominently in the U.S. debate.[52] It was crowded out, so to speak, by imagery of drunken working-age males. Behind this imagery lies the United States' demography. It was indeed a young-adult nation, meaning not only that paupers were often imagined to be able–bodied persons of working age, but also that the social critics were themselves young. It was a demographic context in which belief in self-help could thrive. As we shall see in Chapter 7, the age of the adult population is a force that has consistently shaped public preferences about social spending. The same tendency helps explain why the United States, still younger than Europe, remains more critical of safety net programs today.

Two Attacks on Outdoor Relief in New York

A good illustration of how the United States discussed poor relief, and how poverty failed to vanish when ordered to, is the experience of New York State, a relative leader in poor relief in the U.S. context. New York had poor relief relating back to the Dutch era and as early as 1683 had passed a colony-wide poor law. The problem of poor relief remained under control, essentially because there were so few poor and because local officials were prepared to dispel newcomers who looked poor. The pauper ranks slowly expanded with succeeding cyclical downturns and population growth. A true crisis by the standards of the day came in the downturns during and after the War of 1812.[53] By 1823 paupers were 1.13 percent of the state population, as already noted.

Responding to the expanding poor rolls, the state legislature passed a new state poor law of 1824. This law slightly centralized relief, shifting responsibility from towns to counties, in a manner similar to England's shifting of responsibility from parishes to poor law unions a decade later. Each county was ordered to build and maintain a county poorhouse. Counties were prohibited from removing paupers, but had the right to order them to the county poorhouse. The legislators intended that outdoor relief was to be phased out, but were immediately compelled to give thirty-eight of the state's fifty-four counties exemptions from the poorhouse requirement. The main hope was that the poorhouse offer would drive many applicants back to work, and to this end expenditures per pauper within the poorhouse were cut. Yet the 1824 law failed in its attempt to cut what was then known as the pauper rate, or the "welfare caseload" in today's terms. In fact the pauper share of the state population went on growing, and the share of paupers getting outdoor relief failed to fall. By the early 1860s the share of paupers sent to the poorhouse had fallen to less than 15 percent.[54]

The state gave it a second try in 1875, with a new campaign against outdoor relief, one contemporaneous with England's similar campaign. Yet the relief rolls continued to expand, in part because of the depressions of 1873–1879 and 1891–1894. The end result was a buildup of state statutes restricting outdoor relief – and a rise in outdoor relief at the local level. As in England, tension continued between local needs, transmitted by local officials, and the collective state-level campaigns to tighten up.[55]

SUMMARY

Now that the contours of poor relief policy before 1880 are coming into view, we can see some familiar objects and four puzzles.

The familiar objects are those eternal arguments on the two sides of the debate over what to do about the poor. The ardent humanitarian appeals on one side were matched then, as they are today, but arguments stressing that relief discourages productivity effort and rewards irresponsible behavior.

The four challenging puzzles are:

- Why did England have such an extraordinary early rise of poor relief and a major drop in that relief in the Poor Law Reform of 1834?
- Why did England give its relief a bit more generously in the countryside than in the cities, when practically every other country had an urban bias in its giving?
- Why did the rate of poor relief, either as a tax or as a benefit relative to average income, stagnate or decline over most of the nineteenth century? The twentieth-century experience made it look normal that rising national incomes meant rising support for the poor. Why didn't that happen in the nineteenth century?
- Finally, why was it that central governments intervened to cut relief and local governments were more willing to let it drift upward over time? Very plausible economic theories predict the opposite, yet in centuries past, as in the United States in 1996, it fell to the national government to put limits on what local governments could give the poor.

4

Interpreting the Puzzles of Early Poor Relief

The four puzzles just distilled from a survey of poor relief before 1880 deserve answers. Why did England have a dramatic early rise of poor relief? Why was poor relief a rural and regional outcome in England, when it was heavily urban in the rest of the world? Why did poor relief stagnate as a share of national income in many countries between 1820 and 1880? Why did it fall to central governments to *limit* relief, when theory suggests that central governments might be more efficient than local governments in providing it?

A few key factors help to resolve all four puzzles. The comparative history of poor relief becomes somewhat less mysterious if we follow the roles of *electoral democracy, decentralization in government*, and *changes in economic self-interest*. The same forces that push back the veil of mystery about early poor relief, it will turn out, will also help to explain some puzzles about the rise of public schooling in Chapter 5.

THE RISE AND FALL OF ENGLAND'S OLD POOR LAW, 1780–1834

The first puzzle to be addressed in the pre-1880 experience is the peculiarity of English poor relief movements.[1] Why did England lead so early in poor relief in the eighteenth century? Why did it then cut relief, yet remain one of the top-spending nations? Did the same powerful interests change their minds on this issue, or was it the arrival of new interest groups that led to the relief-slashing Poor Law Reform of 1834?

Who Supported England's Old Poor Law?

Before 1832 power was concentrated into the hands of landowners, both in Parliament and in local government and local courts. To vote in parliamentary elections, one had to own property and pay property taxes. Very few did. As best one can estimate, only about one household in seven owned any real estate in England and Wales between the late seventeenth and the late nineteenth centuries. England had a landed elite as entrenched as that of most Latin American countries.[2] Accordingly, less than one man in seven had the right to vote in England and Wales, and less than one man in ten in the United Kingdom as a whole. Membership in Parliament reflected this strong bias toward landowners. Why did landowners either sponsor or acquiesce in the world's most generous tax-based poor relief before 1834? Was it narrow self-interest or some larger sense of paternalistic social mission? The narrower interpretation seems to fit the facts of that setting, and it offers better explanatory power when carried beyond that setting.

Substantial landowners dominated poor-relief policy in local parish vestries as well as in Parliament before the 1834 reform centralized poor relief. The progressive decision to raise outdoor relief in the late eighteenth century and up to Waterloo needed the approval of the rate-paying owners and tenants of large holdings. This group had reason to worry about the poor. All the real-wage indicators for 1770–1815 suggest a rise in rural poverty in that era.[3] The French War era included the hasty parliamentary sanction of relief scales that protected the poor against rises in the price of bread, probably in part because of the sound of the guillotine from across the Channel and the sight of food riots at home. At the same time, the accelerating rise of London and the new industrial centers was siphoning off agricultural laborers, whom labor-hiring farmers and landlords tried to induce to stay in the countryside by offering more relief in the wintertime, especially in the declining rural South and East. They succeeded in getting those who did not hire farm laborers to share in the local tax burdens of keeping the laborers nearby.[4]

Landlords' and large tenants' grip on local political power was actually reinforced slightly up to 1830. Landlords and farmers were often magistrates and controlled key votes where property holding was the main voting requirement and ballots were not secret. The Sturges Bourne Act (Vestries Act) of 1818, while professing to bring local waste under control, actually reinforced the power of the more landed by proportioning votes in vestry to the *value* of rates paid on real estate.[5] This seemed to tip the scales in favor of those who had more self-interest in continued spending on poor relief.[6]

The willingness of the landed to share in taxes for poor relief seems to have accorded with their direct self-interest. The main competing explanation for this landed concern with the poor goes under the vague name "paternalism." The term suggests a wider vision on the part of the landed, a vision in which they were the stewards of the poor and the preservers of social order. Yet as a departure from the view that they simply followed their narrow self-interest, paternalism lacks any explanatory power. Its shortcomings are particularly obvious at the parliamentary level. At this level the dominant landed interest maintained another policy relevant to the poor, one that obviously lowered the living standards of the poor. That additional policy is England's infamous

Corn Laws, which had a major impact on the cost of staple foods in the peacetime years between 1765 and 1843.

In fact, a closer look at the timing of the Corn Laws' impact on food costs helps us better understand when it was that Parliament actually redistributed income toward the poor before 1834, all policies taken together. Around 1765, England became a permanent net importer of grain, and the import duties stipulated by the Corn Laws began to bind. The gap between English and Dutch wheat prices was significant from 1765 until extreme food scarcity forced suspension of the Corn Laws between 1793 and 1815. It was even wider in the 1820s and still existed on the eve of the 1846 repeal. During the French War interim (1792–1815), the price gap gyrated and was sometimes substantial, but for reasons other than the Corn Laws, which were quickly suspended in the food crisis of 1795–1796 and not effectively reactivated until 1815.

To make wheat expensive was to make rural land expensive. The Corn Laws probably bid up land rents, to the advantage of landlords. To make wheat expensive was also to make bread expensive, raising the cost of living for the landless masses. Statistical regressions suggest that a 10 percent increase in the English price of wheat tended to raise the London price of bread by 6–8 percent.[7] The rough effects of the Corn Laws on the prices of wheat, bread, and a poor worker's cost of living were:

			Approximate% effect of the Corn Laws on the price of
Period	Wheat	Bread	Cost-of-living bundle (if breads = 40%)
1770s	26%	18%	7%
1780s	25%	18%	7%
1820s	44%	36%	14%
1830s	29%	23%	9%
1840–45	24%	19%	8%

Any reckoning of the fiscal treatment of the poor by the politically powerful in Georgian and Victorian England must weigh these episodes of policy-induced food scarcity, plus the effects of other trade barriers and excises, against the direct poor relief. In the decades shown here, the only poor being subsidized were those low-income households receiving more in relief than they paid in higher prices and taxes. The label "paternalism" does not seem to fit, at least at the national level.

The rest of the laboring classes, those not getting as much in poor relief as policy added to their cost of living were thus pushed down toward the same level of subsistence to which those on relief were being raised. It is as if Parliament shared Mandeville's belief in the social utility of keeping the lower orders up to, but also down to, the subsistence level, since they "have nothing to stir them up to be serviceable but their wants, which it is Prudence to relieve but Folly to cure."[8] Perhaps England's policy combination of poor relief and the Corn Laws helped to produce an "iron law of wages" *by policy design*, not just from the workings of demography and the free market that Malthus and Ricardo believed in. While the labor-force effects of this mix were dynamic and complex, there is at least something classical in the look of a policy that pulled the most destitute up toward subsistence (mainly before 1834) and pushed other workers down toward it (Corn Laws 1765–1793, 1815–1846).

Before the middle of the nineteenth century, the only time period of significant net relief to the poor, and of significant direct taxation of the rich, was the French War Period. It was primarily during the French Revolution that the Corn Laws were suspended, though they were also eased in a few years of food crisis before 1793. Similarly, the top strata paid income tax only in the 1799–1815 part of the wars. Few direct taxes were paid by high-income households during peacetime until a small income tax reappeared in 1842. The land taxes of 1688–1832 were fixed at levels low enough to be outweighed, for landlords, by the Corn Law aid to rents, at least in the periods 1765–1792 and 1816–1846.

There is a pattern here. Progressivity and relief were limited to the most destitute and rose and fell with the share of the destitute in the population. The wartime period may have been the nadir of real living standards for unskilled workers. It was an era of food riots, of poor health for the workers, and of upper-class fears that the French Revolution might cross the Channel. The repeal of the Corn Laws, too, came in an era when (Irish) famine raised mortality and emigration. In their combination of fiscal tools and their timing, Parliament and parish authorities behaved as if they were price-discriminators exploiting the unfranchised masses. Price discriminators tax those who will not exit from exchanges and spare those who will. Whenever the threat of exit loomed, in the form of rebellion or high mortality, they delivered more than enough aid to offset the effects of their trade barriers on the group posing the greatest threat. At other times, and from other groups, they took taxes.

This kind of price discrimination is akin to something that economists call the "Ramsey tax problem," in which government efficiently taxes price-inelastic demands more than elastic ones.[9] The switch to more generous poor relief in emergencies in fact fits the Ramsey pattern. Below some poverty-level threshold of subsistence and peaceful labor supply, the poor may respond more elastically, dropping out of peacefully supplying labor if there is any further reduction in their real disposable incomes. Elite fears of famine and revolution may have sensed as much, especially in the hardest times between the famine of 1795 and Waterloo. However complex the inner politics may have been, they fit this broad pattern.

The Reform Acts, Voice, and the Poor

Soon after the Reform Act of 1832 Parliament passed the historic Poor Law Reform of 1834, which called for a new regime of toughness toward the poor. Control of poor relief was taken away from parishes and lodged in new multiparish Poor Law Unions, which were to operate under strict national rules. Able–bodied adults were not to be given relief in their homes. If they really needed help, they were to report to the local poorhouse. As Chapter 3 showed, the share of national income paid in taxes for poor relief was cut in half, even though local resistance limited the cuts in practice.

Why would a landed English aristocracy still in control at the start of the 1830s try to overthrow its own poor-relief system, mobilizing the economic liberalism of the day? The rich literature on the politics of the New Poor Law, while still characterized by debate, does have what appears to be a majority view. By the early 1830s, the landed interest – still firmly in control of Parliament – had switched its own view on the threat of revolution and the causes of poverty in the countryside. Gone were the French threat and food scarcity, replaced by declining food prices and rents, high real burdens of poor relief, and the Swing Riots of 1830–1831, which seemed to show that generous poor-relief entitlements bred insolence and rebellion. Even without invoking any urban interest's political ascent after 1832, then, the usual explanation is well armed with reasons why the landed first raised and then slashed poor relief.

Surely everything in this prevailing tale is a valid part of a fuller explanation. But its incompleteness is severe. Indeed, some earlier ideas rejected by the usual view deserve revival. The explanation of 1830–1834 in terms of landlord interests wears temporal and spatial blinders. Above all, it focuses too much on the 1830–1834 short run, without enough comparison of this short period with what came before it or what came later. Comparing 1830–1834 with earlier years, several authors have questioned whether events had really changed enough by 1830 to turn the landlord interest 180 degrees.[10]

To compare 1830–1834 with later years, why did the English poor-relief rates decline slowly between 1834 and 1880? As landlords became eclipsed enough to bring Corn Law repeal, why did the Poor Law Reform of 1834 continue so much longer? Should we not return to the Webbs' and others' view that this long-sustained toughness must owe something to the spread of political voice to the industrial and commercial interests in the Reform Acts of 1832 and 1867?[11] Perhaps the 1834 reformers' insistence on centralization of poor-relief administration was aimed at local landed control over spending.

To underline this point, consider the march of voting rights summarized for the English income ranks in Table 4.1. In Britain, as in other countries, the nineteenth century brought increasing shares of adult males into the voting place.[12] And as the century wore on, the ballot became secret and the property qualification faded away.

TABLE 4.1. *The Exclusiveness of the British Franchise, 1688–1918*

	Estimated Percent of Household Heads (HH's), or of Men, having the Right to Vote	Franchised Voters' Relative Income (Median Household Income of the Franchised/Median Income of All Households)
1688, England–Wales HH's	15.3	2.75
1759, England–Wales HH's	20.0	2.40
1803, England–Wales HH's	13.5	2.73
1831, United Kingdom men	8.6	
First Reform Act, 1832		
1835, United Kingdom men	13.4	
1866, United Kingdom men	18.0	
1867, United Kingdom HH's	17.8	1.46
1867, England–Wales HH's	19.0	1.37
Second Reform Act, 1867–1868		
1868, United Kingdom men	31.4	
1883, United Kingdom men	36.0	
Third Reform Act, 1883–1884		
1886, United Kingdom men	63.0	
1910, United Kingdom men	62.4	
1911, United Kingdom HH's	74.2	1.13
1918, United Kingdom men	88.6	

Sources: (a) For the estimates relating to household heads (HH's): The author's rough estimates, using the sources cited in Lindert and Williamson (1982, 1983) and the House of Commons historical volumes. Unpublished revisions have been used to improve the 1867 and 1911 estimates to put them on the same household, or "family," basis as the estimates for earlier benchmark years.

(b) For the estimates of United Kingdom men: The estimated electorate share of males over 20, from Flora (1983, vol. 1, 149).

It seems plausible that as the vote spread from the top propertied elite to include more industrial interests seeking additional labor supply from the countryside, it lowered poor relief, before the further spread of the franchise to the lower classes raised poor relief and other social spending after 1880. Table 4.1 suggests that this historic reversal linking the vote to social spending is a real possibility for England and Wales. On the eve of the Second Reform Act in 1867 the vote still just extended to 19 percent of household heads, with a franchised median household income still above the middle-class ranks. Such an economic profile of voters would include many less-landed taxpaying hirers of migrants from the countryside, with little interest in rural income supports that would keep the poor where they were. Even after that Second Reform Act had raised the voting share to nearly a third of all men, the electorate still consisted predominantly of self-employed men, with landowners in a minority. And it was in the wake of that Second Reform Act that Parliament renewed its attack on outdoor relief in the 1870s.

As further indirect testimony that the Reform Act of 1832 reshaped British economic policy toward the masses, consider the tax changes ushered in by the 1840s.[13] The direct tax on top incomes was reinstated in 1842, and the Corn Laws were repealed, making bread cheaper for workers and workers cheaper for capitalists. Even here one could interject that the crucial change was a change in Tory attitude, rather than just the arrival of new voters. One particular Tory, Peal, played a crucial role by switching to the side of Corn Law repeal. His conversion was apparently not due to any larger conversion to liberal political economy. Rather he had come to perceive by the 1840s that real wages had indeed been rising for some time, a fact that refuted the view of Malthus, Ricardo, and others who thought that cheaper grain would only accelerate population growth and drive the wage back down to subsistence.[14] While he may have reached this conclusion independently, it is what the free traders of the Anti-Corn Law League had been arguing for some time, and they in turn represented classes who did not have the vote before 1832.

By itself, this rough association of legal changes with changes in the electorate can easily be challenged as a casual *post hoc ergo propter hoc* argument. Yet, as we shall see, the same association shows up for other countries and for other kinds of social spending. The spread of the franchise is not a sufficient explanation for the policy changes, but it may be a necessary one, in the sense that it will become increasingly difficult to explain the broader patterns without assigning any significant role to the changes in political voice.

THE RURAL–URBAN PUZZLE

If England Were Invisible: The Urban Bias in Poor Relief

England was also exceptional in the locus of its poor relief, as Peter Solar and Chapter 3 have pointed out.[15] The English gave heavily in the countryside, at least as heavily as in the city. The opposite pattern held in all the other countries for which we have sufficient information.

The first step toward explaining this rural–urban puzzle in the eighteenth and nineteenth centuries is to hide England from our view for a moment and note the ways we can make good sense of the pattern that prevailed elsewhere. That is not hard to do. We have at least three forces that should have explained why more support was given in the cities – whether we measure it per capita, per full-time-equivalent recipient, or as a percentage of local income. First, cities were richer than the surrounding countryside, and richer populations have higher standards for a minimum acceptable quality of local life. As Chapter 7 will confirm, higher incomes usually mean higher social spending even as a share of local income. As long as the widespread settlement laws and social barriers kept the flow of the poorest immigrants under control, urban authorities could offer higher relief *per recipient*. Second, the fear of the disorderly poor as fuel for riot and insurrection should have been stronger in the cities. Malcontents can organize more easily there. Third, cities had a turnover-cost reason for worrying about the exodus of impoverished workers. If their workers were not supported in bad times or in slack seasons, those workers would emigrate (or retire or die) and be unavailable the next time they were needed. True, rural employers had the same fear. Yet it is at least possible that the cities' labor demands involved greater skills requirements or greater experience requirements on the average. Perhaps their turnover costs were higher.

For Amsterdam in the early nineteenth century, the fear of losing labor in seasonal or cyclical downturns was explicit. Marco Van Leeuwen offers an example from a debate among the businessmen and professionals serving as regents of the Amsterdam Municipal Charity in 1826. Like their counterparts in London, New York, and elsewhere in the 1820s, some Amsterdam mayors and aldermen suggested that the regents could withdraw relief from able–bodied workers. They could send them off to the northern farm work colonies run by the *Maatschappij van Weldadigheid* since 1818. The regents rejected this on labor-supply grounds:

Artisans of all kinds, bricklayers, hod carriers, joiners, carpenters, painters, cobblers and the like...earn by their manual labour all or part of their family's keep in the summer. However, their earnings are not sufficient to put aside enough for the winter – when...all these trades or occupations grind to an almost complete halt – enough, that is, to enable them to come through this harsh season without relief or support. For them, this charitable institution is of the utmost benefit, indeed one might say almost indispensable.... Suppose many of them left the city and settled elsewhere, what effect would this have on the city and on society? *What other effect than to create in summer a shortage of hands able to work in at least some of the trades?* Real harm would thus be caused, which could not be made good except perhaps to a small degree by the arrival of a few wholly unknown persons from outside.

The mayors and aldermen immediately retreated, apologizing for not making clear their support of relief, and their conviction that "once trade or demand for their labour picked up again at the end of the winter, these men would have to be replaced with others from outside, who would need just as much relief, especially in winter."[16]

Any of these three forces – cities' higher incomes, their greater fear of organized insurrection, or labor turnover fears – or any combination of them, could account for the general tendency of cities to give more relief, even though unique factors affect each city or region. As long as we can ignore

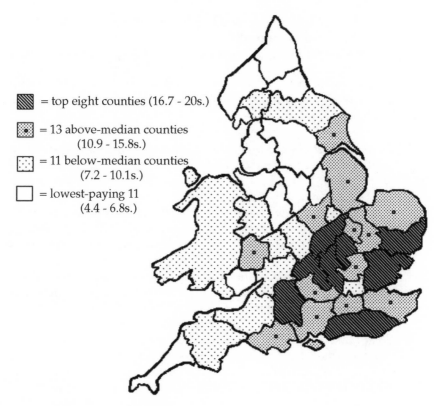

= top eight counties (16.7 - 20s.)

= 13 above-median counties
(10.9 - 15.8s.)

= 11 below-median counties
(7.2 - 10.1s.)

= lowest-paying 11
(4.4 - 6.8s.)

Source: Blaug (1963, 178-179).
Note: For 1821, when rates were higher than the 1831 rates shown here,
   Manchester paid only 3.8 shillings, Liverpool 6.2, Birmingham 7.2,
   and Bristol 9.7 -- all below even the 1831 median. Thus these cities
   gave low relief per capita.

FIGURE 4.1. Poor Relief Payments per Capita, Counties of England and Wales, 1831.

England and study Amsterdam, Stockholm, Lyon, Pisa, and New York, all is
well. We have good reasons to expect more generous poor relief in the cities.

England's Rural Southeastern Bias and the Boyer Model

But in England, the pattern was dramatically different. Relief was greater,
per capita or per pound of local income, in the rural southeast than in the
countryside to the north and west. It was greater in southeastern cities than
cities of the north and west. Figure 4.1 offers a county-level snapshot of relief
per capita in the England and Wales of 1831. Even Middlesex, representing
London to a large extent, did not stand out. Yet London's relief per capita
was probably as high as that of most Continental cities, and higher than

that of any U.S. city. It was the southeastern countryside that stood out, internationally as well as nationally.

To explain this peculiarity of southeastern rural England, George Boyer developed an ingenious implicit-contracts model and tested it extensively on English data. The model is based on a set of four conditions sufficient for successful intervention by the rich on behalf of the poor, in a setting where the poor have no political voice:

(a) *Dominant elite:* A particular elite group has such a large share of all political voice and representation that its most strongly held views shape policy. It could get the rest of society to share in the cost of policies it favors.

(b) *The elite worries about the poor:* The elite does not want the poor to exit from local economic life because it hires them, because its property values depend on their staying in the area, or because it fears the spread of political unrest from the bottom ranks.

(c) *The poor could exit:* There is no way that the elite can compel the poor to stay and work. Serfdom, prohibitions on emigration, and intimidation are not options.

(d) *Economical transfers can prevent exit:* With transfers to the poor that do not cost the wealthy very much, the poor could be induced to stay. In Boyer's model of England, the seasonality of labor demand allowed part-time (winter) support to keep some of the poor from leaving the locality before the next (summer) period of high labor demand.

In its main version, aimed squarely at the peculiarity of the rural southeast, Boyer's model is a tale of agriculture, and of labor-hiring landlords and farmers in a relatively stagnant countryside. They do not want their farm workers to become so destitute across the winter season that they would emigrate to rising cities or to the rising industry of the rural north. The problem was more acute in the highly seasonal grain-based agriculture of the southeast than in the less seasonal emphasis on animal products to the north and west. If the labor-hiring landlords and farmers had to pay for all poor relief themselves, Boyer reasons, it is not clear that they would have supplied so much more poor relief than the rest of the country. But their local political power allowed them to pass a large share of the tax burden onto others who did not hire much labor – onto family farmers, shopkeepers, and the holders of tithes. They voted for higher poor rates (taxes) in the knowledge that others were paying for part of their labor-supply insurance. Also convenient was the fact that relief given in the winter was not in workers' pockets at harvest time, when they were supposed to work.

If the Boyer model is equated with its archetype, one might think that it would not apply outside of the world of seasonal agriculture and powerful landlords in the countryside. Yet the model is more usefully viewed in a broader form, where it is stripped of the agricultural imagery. It is more useful when equated only with those four key conditions: (a) a politically dominant elite, (b) an elite worried about the poor, (c) the danger that the poor could exit from the locality or from labor, and (d) an economical way of subsidizing loyal labor services.

To apply the Boyer model to that larger world where cities gave more relief, let us begin by remembering the example of the Amsterdam regents in 1826. All four elements of the broad Boyer model were in place. Employers of labor were collectively powerful enough to force other property owners to share in the tax burden of poor relief. They feared labor turnover. The poor could and did migrate. And making the relief seasonal confined its expense to the period of low labor demand.

Boyer himself extended his model to the case of powerful urban-industrial interests in the north of England. Urban manufacturers hiring large numbers of workers used the Poor Law as a system of local unemployment insurance. Where the Poor Law Reform of 1834 constrained their right to share the burden of extra support with other taxpayers, they circumvented the Reform and the extra support was provided anyway. Yet the same industrialists that resisted the application of the harsh Reform in their own cities "supported its implementation in the agricultural south and east of England," where the Reform could dislodge more poor workers for migration to the north. Again, in this urban and industrial setting, the elements of the broad Boyer model seem to have been in place.[17]

An Extension to Scandinavia

As a further test of the usefulness of the Boyer model, let us turn to another set of countries with significant poor relief and a strong seasonality to its labor demand. Did Scandinavia, like England, have more noticeable poor relief before 1880 because it fit the Boyer model? That is, did it have a disproportionately powerful labor-hiring elite, the possibility of exit by laborers, and an economical mechanism of preventing worker exit with partial relief? While the available information is generally consistent with this view, that information is meager, at least in the English-language literature. We know only the distribution of political power, the policy outcomes, and little else. This is enough for a prima facie case that a bias in political power preserved poor relief against the opposition of those who hired little labor, until the poor were fully franchised and could demand even more.

Among Scandinavian countries in the nineteenth century, Denmark may have been the extreme case of an atavistic distribution of political power, in which conservatism held a firm grip long after its proponents had been eclipsed economically. The inequality of property ownership and economic power was transformed radically between the late eighteenth century and the mid-nineteenth century. As of the 1780s, Denmark was still abolishing serfdom and may have had the most unequal distribution of wealth in all of Europe.[18] By the 1860s, the large estates had declined greatly, and most of the land was worked by independent family farmers, with emphasis on dairy and other animal products. Of all the classes in Denmark, only the urban bourgeoisie was in greater ascendance than the farmers.[19]

Given their rising share of the economy, the farmers should have had considerable voice. They would have used that voice in the nineteenth century to slash their tax burden, which was apparently heavier than the tax percentage on urban or aristocratic incomes. They would have cut poor relief as well, because its beneficiaries consisted of the urban poor and crofters who labored for the estates. They would also have won an educational system that was useful and emphasized primary education, instead of the stultifying Latinist classical higher education maintained at the wishes of the urban bureaucracy, the remaining estate owners, and the Lutheran church. They demanded all these things throughout the nineteenth century.[20]

Political power in Denmark, however, remained firmly in the hands of the throne, the church, the bureaucracy, and the estate holders. The period 1815–1830 was marked by continued absolutism, as in many other countries. In 1834, the king set up an estate system of representation in the national legislature and the new provincial assemblies. The three class estates – owners of city property, owners of rural estates, and owners of small properties (which the king insisted had to include tenants holding seven acres or more) – were all strictly subordinate to the throne. Furthermore, local government was highly constrained and the rights of provincial representation were further restrained in 1855 so as to favor the richest 20 percent.[21] So if farmers, for example, had wanted to push for useful public schooling, they could not raise local taxes to do so, nor could they rid themselves locally of the taxes that supported poor relief.

Thus power in Denmark remained much more concentrated than one would have thought by glancing at the mid-century statistics on the share of men who voted. The system of unequal representation remained more or less in place throughout the century, and the ballot was not secret until 1901. Absent a revolution, Danish farmers could only complain a lot and seek alliances that finally won them some tax relief in 1874 and the universalist and progressive pension system of 1891.[22]

Does nineteenth-century Denmark fit the Boyer model of poor relief supported (and schools discouraged) by a powerful interest that got others to share in the cost of their relief? For Denmark, as for the Netherlands and other Continental countries, the broader Boyer model fits well enough, once one sets aside the image of labor-hiring landowners in the countryside. Denmark did have that same look of an overly powerful conservative alliance that was quite content with a system in which family farms had to pay a large share of the tax burden for poor relief.

Sweden, like Denmark, spent much of the nineteenth century in political conflict over a system of unequal representation that lagged behind economic realities. Both the economic realities and the atavistic politics, however, took slightly different forms. On the economic front Sweden's farmers were not as fully independent or as safely specialized in animal-product production as their Danish counterparts. Landed estates retained more visibility in the countryside, and a majority of farmers continued to grow rye, under increasing threat from foreign competition.[23]

The system of electoral voting and legislative representation lagged far behind. Until 1865 the king remained the supreme authority and the legislature (*riksdag*) was divided into an estates system, with separate and unequal estates for the nobility, clergy, urban propertied, and peasants. Local government was very constrained and rigged with unequal representation, as in Denmark. Even occupational mobility was blocked by special laws that were not reformed until mid-century. The share of men who voted remained extremely low throughout the century, because even the reform of 1865 imposed high property and income requirements for voting. Sweden, like the rest of Scandinavia, was basically not a democracy before the end of the nineteenth century.[24]

The tension between the economy and political institutions affected policies relevant to Sweden's farmers and the poor. The split in farmers' self-interests brought a more conservative and protectionist outcome. After mid-century there was some protection against imported grains, to the disadvantage of the poor, and a split over whether new systems of social security should be noncontributory (i.e., redistributive). The more independent farmers, as possible employers, resisted contributory pensions, for example, preferring the more redistributive kind of system pioneered by Denmark in 1891. But the more dependent and conservative farmers were willing to have a less redistributive system, with greater employer contributions, as part of their alliance with conservative protectionists (Baldwin 1990, 83–93).[25] On the poor relief front, the political balance was again favorable to the continuation of some poor relief. Part of the peasantry, like the farmers of Denmark, grumbled about having to pay for poor relief that helped only the crofters and those landlords that hired them. But King Oscar's new poor law of 1847 kept the system intact.

Norway's farm sector was more like Denmark's, in that it had few grain producers and farmers became quite independent of landlords. Its political system, however, shared the same atavistic inequalities as the other two countries, not least because its political union with Sweden lasted throughout the nineteenth century. Until 1885 not only representation, but even suffrage, was based on an unequal system of occupational estates, and the ballot was not secret.

Within this setting, the large farm population won some victories, but with the effect of creating a solid opposing alliance of the upper bourgeoisie and the bureaucracy. It won a seeming commitment to universal elementary schools in 1842, but the subsequent decades produced inadequate funding. For much of the century peasant energies were spent in fighting the regressivity of the tax system. It fought in particular against having to bear a disproportionate share of the burden of poor relief.[26]

Thus the nineteenth-century experience in all three Scandinavian countries has some outward similarity to the broader version of the Boyer model of poor relief, even though the English-language literature does not afford a clear view of the labor-market mechanisms.

THE INTERNATIONAL STAGNATION OF RELIEF, 1820–1880

The third puzzle of early poor relief is that it failed to rise, and even fell in some countries, as a share of national product from around 1820 to around 1880. As we saw in Chapter 3, this happened not only in Britain, but also in the Netherlands, Belgium, France, and the United States. Granted, the growth in income per capita was accompanied by a slow rise in relief per capita. To judge a nation's effort and commitment, however, one seeks a measure of the share of their incomes they were willing to pay in taxes, and that is the share that stagnated before 1880.

One plausible hunch is that relief failed to rise any faster than national income because the need for it was dropping. Since real wages began to rise in all the leading counties after about 1820, maybe relief stagnated simply because the poor were becoming less needy in some absolute sense. The premise about real wage improvement is correct. Yet the inference missed the mark. Real wages have continued to rise in most industrializing countries in every decade since the 1880s, and taxes to assist the poor have risen even faster than national income. If real wages were also rising from 1820 to 1880, why did assistance not rise as a share of income?

The Predicted Effects of Extending the Franchise

A simple balance-of-power framework, plus the likely attitudes of the landed aristocracy toward tax-based poor relief and schooling, yields different predictions about the political progress of doles and schools as political voice spreads down the economic ranks across the nineteenth century. Table 4.2 summarizes the predictions that follow from the simple ideas just introduced, using hypothetical numbers to illustrate realistic voting preferences.

On the poor-relief front, Panel A of Table 4.2 predicts a reversal in poor-relief policy as the franchise spreads to more and more classes, starting on the left and moving rightward across the table. The reversal comes because the labor-hiring landed aristocracy is imagined to have more sympathy for poor relief than the next class to gain political voice, the "self-employed males." This mixture of capitalists, professionals, shopkeepers, and yeoman farmers sees little danger that they would need poor relief and are averse to being taxed for it. Some of them, as prospective employers, are also averse to supporting those who choose to remain unemployed. Then, as the adult

TABLE 4.2. *How Extending the Franchise Might Affect Poor Relief and Other Social Spending, with Fixed Group Preferences*

	Labor-Hiring Landed Aristocracy	Self-Employed Males	Well-Paid Male Workers	Low-Paid Men and the Poor	Women of All Classes
Panel A. Issue = taxes for generous poor relief?					
Voters in favor:	55	25	120	180	400
Out of these total voters:	100	100	200	200	600
Percent in favor:	55	25	60	90	67

Stages of franchise, and vote outcome:
Pre-Reform (e.g. England 1800)　　　　　　yes (55%)
After First Reform (England 1834)　　　　　no (80/200 = 40%)
After Third Reform (England 1891)　　　　　indecisive (200/400 = 50%)
Full male suffrage (England 1914)　　　　　yes (380/600 = 63%)
Full adult suffrage (England 1929)　　　　　yes (780/1,200 = 65%)

	Labor-Hiring Landed Aristocracy	Self-Employed Males	Well-Paid Male Workers	Low-Paid Men and the Poor	Women of All Classes
Panel B. Issue = taxes for public pensions or public schooling?					
Voters in favor:	25	55	140	120	360
Out of these total voters:	100	100	200	200	600
Percent in favor:	25	55	70	60	60

Stages of franchise, and vote outcome:
Pre-Reform (e.g. England 1800)　　　　　　no (25%)
After First Reform (England 1834)　　　　　no (80/200 = 40%)
After Third Reform (England 1891)　　　　　yes (220/400 = 55%)
Full male suffrage (England 1914)　　　　　yes (340/600 = 57%)
Full adult suffrage (England 1929)　　　　　yes (780/1,200 = 58%)

male franchise spreads to lower and lower income groups, the support for poor relief rises sharply on the popular assumption that the higher-income groups will pay the lion's share of the extra taxes. Finally, when women are granted the vote, the case for poor relief is strengthened slightly, since societies recognizing women's right to vote are predicted to a higher probability of wanting safety nets (a prediction borne out in Chapter 7). The net movement predicted for poor relief is thus a reversal. First comes an initial phase in which the landed get others to share their tax burden to keep the poor available for labor. This is followed by a liberal break, in which self-employed males demand that society stop subsidizing unemployment. Thereafter, the stage is set for the return of Robin Hood, as the increasingly powerful lower-income groups demand progressive redistribution.

For other forms of social spending, such as public pensions or public schools, no reversal is predicted. As illustrated in Panel B of Table 4.2, voter approval of taxes for pensions or schools rises monotonically as males of

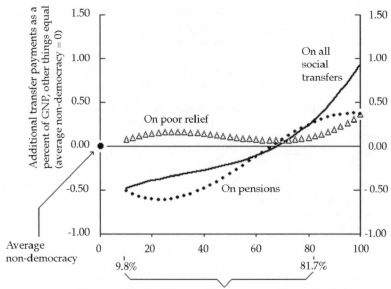

Range of voter turnout as a percentage of adults,
from 5th to 95th percentiles among democracies, 1880-1930

Notes: (1) For sources, see Appendix D in Volume 2.
      (2) These estimates hold constant the age distribution,
          income per capita, and religion.
      (3) The effects shown here are only the same-decade effects,
          without the additional feedback through lagged enrollments.

FIGURE 4.2. The Voting Share of Adults as an Influence on Poor Relief and Other Social Transfers, 21 Countries in 1880–1930.

ever-lower income ranks gain the vote. If there is any bend in this relationship to votes, it comes from the likelihood that the demand for pensions, schools, and the like might be greater among the middle classes and well-paid workers than among the lowest paid.

The General Pre-1930 Pattern of Votes and Social Spending

The earliest measurable history for a large number of countries supports the hypothetical scenario sketched in Table 4.2. Here I report on statistical patterns estimated on a sample of twenty-one countries in the six decennial years 1880, 1890, 1900, 1910, 1920, and 1930.[27] This makes a good laboratory for exploring the influences of voting power, since countries differed greatly in their commitment to democracy between 1880 and 1930.

The effects of the spread of voting rights on social spending when other forces are held equal are shown in Figure 4.2. An initial distinction is between nondemocracies (the dot at the left origin) and democracies, following guidelines given by Arthur Banks.[28] The independent variable on the horizontal axis is the percentage of adult males who actually voted. It is a convenient proxy for how far political power has spread down the ranks, even though a fuller analysis should weigh such additional factors as the unequal representation of different groups of franchised voters. In the democracies among those countries in the 1880–1930 sample, the share of men voting was usually between 10 and 82 percent. The vertical axis shows the social-transfer results of changing the voting share. Chapter 5 will plot the corresponding electoral effects on public schooling, and Chapter 7 will explore the influence of nonpolitical variables.

For public pensions and for social transfer payments in general, there are clear contrasts between nondemocracies and elite democracies, in which only the most propertied 10–40 percent of men voted in national elections, and between elite democracies and fuller democracies. Elite democracies, like the United Kingdom, the Netherlands, Norway, and Sweden in the late nineteenth century, were the least likely to have any commitment of general taxes to public pensions and to social transfers in general.[29] They were even less likely to have such programs than the average nondemocracy, a variegated group including the Austro-Hungarian Empire, Finland under Russian rule, Japan, Latin America, Portugal, and Spain. Some nondemocracies felt pressure to provide social programs; some did not. Comparing elite democracies with fuller democracies (more than half of men voting) yields an even sharper contrast. Extending the franchise so that even poor households had a vote opened the door for redistribution-minded politicians like Lloyd George.

Poor-relief policies had a quite different political pattern, however. Here elite democracies, with votes for only the most propertied, were likely to give as much tax money to the poor as any other group of countries, for given levels of income and other variables. The elite-democracy prototypes represented in the 1880–1930 sample were, again, the United Kingdom, the Netherlands, Norway, and Sweden, with Denmark in a transitional political condition in 1880–1890. Thus the march of the franchise from elite democracy toward full democracy did not seem to imply any change in poor relief as a share of national product.

The stagnation of poor relief's share of the economy between about 1820 and 1880 seems to have reflected this franchise pattern. Extending the vote, and fairer representation in legislatures, to the self-employed middle classes would not bring any new enthusiasm for poor relief. It was accompanied by an actual retreat from poor relief in a few cases in the 1820s and 1830s, and by stagnation thereafter. The motif of a middle-class attack on poor relief policies, policies that some of the most propertied groups favored, thus stands out rather clearly in 1820–1880 histories and in the predictions of Table 4.2, even though its statistical embodiment in the 1880–1930 experience, and Figure 4.2 was only a stagnation, not a reversal.

LOCAL VERSUS CENTRAL GOVERNMENT: WHAT HAPPENED TO THE "RACE TO THE BOTTOM?"

The fourth poor-relief puzzle touches on the larger theme of centralization versus decentralization in government. There is a plausible economic argument that local autonomy in poor relief would lead to a "race to the bottom," in which localities competed with each other to attract productive people, and to shed the dependent, by slashing the taxes for poor relief. What localities want from poor relief is good support for those already permanently settled there. The greater the chance that generous relief would attract less productive persons as immigrants, the less enthused is the electorate about relief. Charles Brown and Wallace Oates have plausibly argued that the only way to uphold high standards of relief is to have it done by the central government, to minimize the migration problem.[30]

Yet the reverse happened. In England, it was the central government that imposed toughness, first in the famous 1834 Poor Law Reform and then in the campaign against outdoor relief in the 1870s. It was the localities that quietly fought the new laws, in an attempt to give more generous local support.[31] In the United States, the New York State legislature twice passed tough reforms telling local governments to cut outdoor relief and cut what we would now call "welfare caseloads." So did other states. Yet the share of the population receiving outdoor relief did not decline. In Prussia, the central government passed laws saying that poor relief should be supported from local taxes only if endowments, charities, and tuition could not do the job. Why were central governments tougher than local governments?

The answer is twofold. The first part of the answer is a general historical observation not fully captured by Table 4.2. The historical accounts repeatedly note that local governments, at the level of the village, township, or parish, knew their poor people personally. They had the best chance to separate the deserving from the undeserving poor and the best chance to tailor their aid or punishment to fit the individual. Did this relatively personal knowledge lead to more or to less aid? As we saw in Chapter 3, it meant less local aid in the countries dominated by Roman Catholicism and more aid in mixed and Protestant countries.

The second part of the answer is that those countries where central authority tried to be tougher than the locals were in a certain early phase in the historical cycle of a public good, a phase to be described at greater length in Chapter 5. In this early phase a rising minority of local governments who want to give relatively generous support to the poor already settled there will do so unless blocked from above.[32] The advocates of toughness still retained strength at the national level. The pro- toughness camp included those wanting to force the able–bodied to migrate toward work in the expanding parts of the economy. Only much later in the process of expanding democracy, where those wanting a tough denial of tax-based relief were in the national minority, would central government take the side of raising taxes and relief over local objection.[33] Thus the world in which local governments wanted more of this public good than national governments was an early phase in the growth of the demand for poor relief, the phase where we would predict that decentralization would yield more taxes for the local public good.

SUMMARY: POLITICAL VOICE AND POOR RELIEF

Just as all politics is local, one could insist that all political history is unique to its time and place. Yet respect for the unique elements in each history is overdone if it leads to the nihilistic denial that any explanation works well across historical settings. This chapter has emphasized that voting rights and the degree of local autonomy are useful as partial explanations in a wide range of settings. Even when other historical forces have been given their due, the twin themes of democracy and decentralization played roles in shaping poor relief, that predecessor to modern social spending programs. The roles they played in resolving the four poor-relief puzzles were as follows:

First, the extraordinary early rise of English poor relief under the Old Poor Law (c. 1780 to 1834) was explained in large part by the self-interest of labor-hiring property owners. They had disproportionate political power, both in local government and in Parliament, and used it to get others to share the tax burden of insuring their local labor force. A main use of the poor relief was to offset some of the worst effects of their defense of Britain's Corn Laws, which were designed to make food and land more expensive. The combination of poor relief and peacetime Corn Laws allowed labor-hiring landlords and farmers to maximize their labor supply, by raising paupers up to subsistence while pushing less impoverished workers down toward it.

Second, the paradox of strong rural relief in England and an urban bias in relief elsewhere seems to fit a broader version of the Boyer model. Outside of England, urban authorities in slow-growing cities had strong Boyer-type motives for using poor relief to retain their labor force, as well as to prevent urban disorder. In England, the part of the slower-growing region threatened with labor loss was played primarily by the rural southeast. While a single model cannot explain all differences in practice, these are at least reconcilable with the Boyer model.

Third, the long international stagnation in poor relief between 1820 and 1880 is explained in part by differences in the interest of economic classes in an era when political power was extending down through the self-employed middle income ranks. This group had less interest in poor relief relative to public pensions and other programs. Thus at the same time that the expansion of voting rights pushed countries toward instituting other social programs, poor relief stagnated for several decades.

Fourth, the puzzle of having central governments assume a tougher stance toward the poor than did local governments in England, the United States, and Prussia probably owed something to the fact that this was still an early phase in the rise of demand for safety-net programs. In such an early phase, freedom and discretion for local governments produce more taxes for social spending, such as poor relief, than would the balance of power in the central-government arena. There was no race to the bottom among local governments' policies toward the poor. Only much later, when most localities wanted support for the poor, would central government become a force pulling up the least enthused regions into a national tax-based poverty program.

5

The Rise of Mass Public Schooling
before 1914

OVERVIEW

The second kind of social spending emerged in the nineteenth century. Country after country turned toward tax revenues as a basis for launching or expanding schools, especially primary schools. Yet some countries took far longer than others to develop universal primary schooling – and most countries have deficient primary education even today. These differences in basic schooling have long been recognized as one of the keys to global income inequalities.[1] Of all the kinds of public spending considered in this book, expenditures on public schooling are the most positively productive in the sense of raising national product per capita. Here we concentrate on primary public education, the kind of education that involves the greatest shift of resources from upper income groups to the poor.

What holds back primary and secondary education in so many societies, and what forces promoted it in the history of today's high-income countries?

How some nations came to promote mass schooling through taxation, capturing its external benefits for growth and democracy, while most others lagged behind before 1914, is the central issue in this chapter. As with poor relief, so too with early schooling, the roles of elite self-interest, democracy, and decentralization will help us interpret the rich variety of national experiences. The main arguments are as follows:

(1) *Global leadership:* German states led the way in elementary education from 1815 until about 1860. In terms of enrollment rates, it was then overtaken not only by the United States, but also by several other countries. By 1882 France had become an enrollments leader in Europe. In the share of national product spent on education, Germany retained leadership throughout the nineteenth century, though other countries were not far behind.

(2) *England lagged:* An anomaly in nineteenth-century educational effort was the low level of English primary and secondary schooling before

1891. Oddly enough, the English had been leaders in literacy and education *before* the era of England's world economic leadership, but temporarily fell behind *during* it.

(3) *Self-interest at the top:* Most theories of early mass schooling are cynical theories about the self-interests of elites and autocrats. This emphasis seems valid, but the competing elite-interest theories need to be tested, and they need to be supplemented with a rethinking of the role of centralization versus decentralization in government.

(4) *Democracy and decentralization:* Recasting the link between political voice and school policy allows us to reinterpret some leading national histories. Britain was an educational laggard in the nineteenth century largely because educational reform was blocked by suffrage restrictions and by government centralization. By contrast Prussia, long viewed as a central autocracy, left its schooling more to local forces than has been realized, and the notorious Junker dominance in national politics was largely irrelevant to the provision of schooling. The themes of democracy and decentralization also help explain how the United States, as well as Germany, led in mass primary education despite having strong regional landed interests.

(5) *Public education drives total education:* The history of mass primary and secondary schooling is dominated by the rise of public, not private, supply. No high-income OECD country has relied solely on private demand and supply in education, least of all in primary schooling.

TO BE EXPLAINED: PATTERNS IN THE INPUTS INTO MASS SCHOOLING

This chapter focuses on explaining society's inputs of time and money into schooling, not on the outputs of true learning. Even with this restriction of focus, there are many educational input measures to choose from. Any input measure could relate to public education alone or to private and public combined. It could measure money inputs, inputs of the child's time, or both. It could be a measure of inputs per student, per child of school age, per capita of total population, or as a share of GDP. The measure could relate to any level of schooling, from kindergarten through advanced degrees. These dimensions alone imply twenty-four different kinds of input measure for each level of education.

Of the many kinds of measures to choose from, let us use just four that together shed the most light on the extent of useful school participation and its potential for progressive redistribution:[2]

(1) *enrollment rates for primary education*, public plus private, which show what share of children are benefiting from society's efforts to raise the bottom level of learning;[3]

(2) *public spending for primary education,* as a share of GNP, which gives a sense of how much tax effort goes into egalitarian mass schooling;

(3) *total public education spending,* again as a share of income, which suggests the average tax rates being borne to educate others' children; and

(4) the *public-education support ratio,* or the average subsidy per school-age child divided by the average income per adult, a measure of society's effort to raise the knowledge of individual children relative to society's ability to pay.

The global view reveals wide nineteenth-century gaps in school enrollment rates and in society's educational efforts. By 1914, some nations were well into their secondary-school revolution, led by the United States and Germany.[4] Most nations and colonies had no schooling at all beyond that privately provided for the children of a powerful elite.

These striking differences in nations' education in the nineteenth century were noticed at the time, as were differences in curriculum and teaching technique. Educational leaders traveled abroad to study other countries' innovations in public education. Many of the pioneering international observers were French and American, and the systems they studied most closely were those of the German states (and, to a lesser extent, Switzerland and the Netherlands). France sent Victor Cousin to study the educational system of the German states in 1831, and Eugéne Rendu followed in 1854. At least three American experts, including Horace Mann, went to Germany and made reports between 1837 and 1843. The Scandinavian countries sent official missions to study Prussian education in the 1840s.[5] The first official British tours of Continental educational systems came only in 1859–1861, when the Reverend Mark Pattison reported on Germany and Matthew Arnold reported on France, Netherlands, and Switzerland.[6] Yet the 1861 Report of the Newcastle Commission, which had sent them across the channel, brushed aside Continental experience as lacking in lessons for Britain.[7] By the end of the century, the leading compendia on education around the world still emanated from the United States and France, laying a statistical cornerstone for this study.[8] The governments of China and Japan also gathered numerous reports on education in the advanced countries. Their goal was not pure imitation, however, and both countries went to some effort to check the direct importation of Western schooling, especially as taught in missionary schools.[9]

Who led and who lagged behind? For the most global perspective, let us begin with the primary enrollment rates in Figure 5.1 and Table 5.1.[10] The leadership role changed at least once, and by 1910 several countries vied for the top enrollment rate. For a half-century before 1860, Prussia was known the world over for its high enrollment rates, though North America[11] and Norway were not far behind. From 1860 to 1900, the clearest leaders were

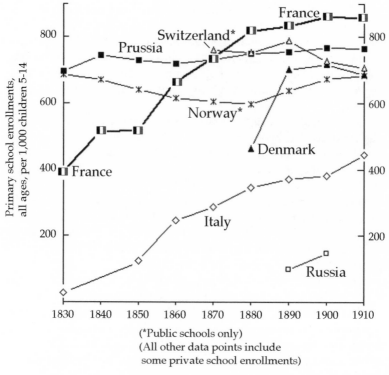

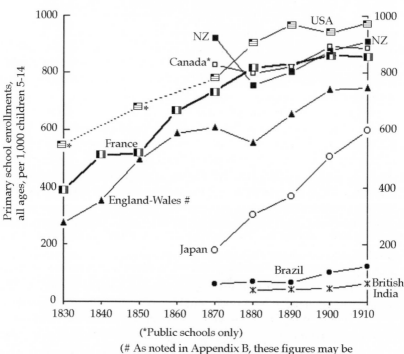

FIGURE 5.1. Enrollment Rates for Primary Schools, 1830–1910.

TABLE 5.1. *Student Enrollment Rates in Primary Schools, Selected Countries, 1830–1930*

	Students Enrolled in Primary Schools, per 1,000 Children of Ages 5–14										
	1830	1840	1850	1860	1870	1880	1890	1900	1910	1920	1930
Austria, pub + priv		367	389	417	426	562	633	670	746	917	839
Austria, pub only					412	543	612	647	680	805	704*
Belgium, pub + priv	346	526	549	557	582	522	434	592	618	757	701*
Belgium, public only					427	371	312	358	339	757	701*
Bulgaria, pub + priv							238	332	412	444	472
Denmark						462	701	717	687	648	674*
Finland, pub + priv							105	188	274	400	582
Finland, public						68			260	400	582*
France, pub + priv	388	513	515	665	737	816	832	859	857	704	803
France, public enr.		398	367	418	424	545	584	625	848	565	653
France, pub. subsid.		359	351	469	515	780	800	820	850	697	796*
Germany, pub only				719		711	742	732	720	758	699
Prussia, pub only	687	736	722	698	717	741	747	763	757		
Prussia, pub + priv	695	714	730	719	732	749	755	768	764		
Greece	28				253	293	312	324	408	589	617*
Hungary					334	457	513	542	526	484	495
Italy, pub + priv			124	247	286	346	370	382	446	506	594
Italy, public only				219	260	324	350	362	422	479	563*
Neth., pub + priv			541	591	639	628	647	663	703	706	780
Neth., public			417	466	491	473	458	456	438	706	780*
Norway, pub + priv					658		637				
Norway, pub only	685	671	640	616	606	596		674	685	694	717*
Portugal, pub only			52		132	178	220	194	200	219	300*

(continued)

TABLE 5.1 (continued)

	1830	1840	1850	1860	1870	1880	1890	1900	1910	1920	1930
Students Enrolled in Primary Schools, per 1,000 Children of Ages 5–14											
Romania, pub only								256	354	293	588
Russia								149			
Serbia							99				
Spain				285	401	517	506	475	473	566	717*
Sweden, public					589	705	683	689	699	640	779*
Switzerland, pub only					759	753	789	727	707	710	701
U.K., mostly public											
England–Wales, pub + priv	274	351	498	588	609	555	657	742	748	725	755
Scotland, priv + pub			592	643	697	776	802	765	729	648	675
Scotland, public only			572	620	673	749	774	748	724	648	675
Ireland, pub + priv				294	384	443	508	525	574	559	751
Ireland, public only				218	285	379	462	525	574	559	751
N. Ireland (these seem low)										272	316
Canada, pub w/sec					835	808	831	901	917	992	1000*
Canada, pub, elem only					827	800	822	892	886	949	966*
USA, pub only	546		681		779	800	857	884	896	857	835*
USA, pub + priv						906	971	939	975	924	921
Mexico						187	181	185	186	231	374*
Australia, elem + sec				453	601	891	762	872	892	883	923*
Australia, elem only				453	598	882	751	855	870	856	890*
New Zealand, pub + priv					923	756	803	879	912	887	962
New Zealand, public					775	654	706	769	793	778	835*
Argentina							266	324	409	548	613*
Bolivia								136			
Brazil					61	70	69	102	123	147	215*

	1	2	3	4	5	6	7
Chile		111	192	245	431	422	556
Colombia					306	250	
Costa Rica		271	142	259		329	405
Cuba, w/sec, pub only to '22				373	354	414	516
El Salvador							119
Guatemala			453			218	
Jamaica, w/sec to 1895		333	509	506	449	442	554
Nicaragua						174	
Trinidad & Tobago			444	517	690	663	688
Uruguay				207	292		
Egypt				7	74	108	178
India (British)		42	44	47	65	80	113
Japan	182	306	370	507	599	602	609*
Philippines, pub only							364
Sri Lanka, w/sec						352	
Thailand					59	78	242

Notes: w/sec = primary plus secondary enrollments together. pub only = just public (government-run) schools. pub + pr = public plus private schools together. (blank after country name) = secondary source does not state whether the estimates include private schools. * = series used in the 1880–1930 sample, Chapter 7 and Appendix D, in Volume 2.

For sources and further notes, see Appendix Table A1.

For secondary-school enrollments, and for numbers of primary and secondary school teachers, see Appendix Tables A2–A4.

outside Europe – North America and New Zealand, with Australia's position less consistent. From 1882 on, France may have been the European leader. Not until 1900 did Great Britain approach the top ranks.[12]

That France may have led Europe in primary-school enrollments after 1882 was not noted at the time and has not been noticed by the postwar scholarly literature.[13] The reason relates to the choice of a population denominator for Figure 5.1 and Table 5.1: it is the population in the five to fourteen age range, not the total population. This contrasts with common practice. Both nineteenth-century observers and postwar historians have used the more available ratio of enrollments to total population.[14] While there are more data on total population than on any age group, the usual convention misses the mark. We are interested in what share of *children* were in school each year, not the share of adults plus children, and using the available data on the five to fourteen age group corrects for this basic point. The distinction does matter quantitatively if a country has an unusual age distribution.

That is where France comes in. France was the leader in voluntary fertility reduction and had a population older than any other country in the nineteenth century, with postfamine Ireland in second place. The usual ratio of primary-school students to total population gives France a deceivingly low rank. Adjusting this ratio for the age distribution reveals that France was a leading country in enrollments per child of school age.

While this chapter focuses on the average primary-school enrollments of both boys and girls, there was a strong correlation between the overall enrollment rate and the share of all students who were girls, as shown in Table 5.2 and Figure 5.2. Among the top countries, the gender differences in primary-school enrollments were small. A sure sign of a country with a backward educational system was a wide gap between male and female enrollments. Thus in the 1890s, a country like England and Wales, which was catching up to the leaders in total enrollments, was also finally bringing its female share of students close to 50 percent. But deficiencies in the schooling of girls were a main reason why Switzerland was falling behind by the turn of the century. And as one shifted attention toward countries with lower and lower average schooling, as in the Mediterranean countries and the whole underdeveloped world, the female share dropped off faster. Girls were less than a third of all primary-school students in Greece, Portugal, and Japan and less than a tenth in India. The same close link between gender equity and overall educational progress is still very visible in late-twentieth-century global data on education and literacy.[15]

While the enrollments are a key outcome of the educational system, we also want to know which nations were trying hardest, devoting the most resources to schooling. A first step is to look at educational expenditures as a share of GDP,[16] starting again with primary school and starting with public funds alone. Using expenditures as a share of GDP allows our measure to imitate a rate of income taxation for the benefit of schools.[17] Using the historical expenditure shares available, we know who the global expenditure

TABLE 5.2. *Female Shares of Primary School Enrollments, Selected Countries and Years*

Country	Years	Females as a % or Primary Enroll.	Source
Europe			
Austria	1898	49.8	(b)
France	1890–94	49.5	(a)
Hungary	1899	49.2	(b)
6 German States	1890–94	49.2	(a)
Netherlands	1899–00	48.0	(b)
England–Wales	1850	45.7	(c)
Italy	1890–94	45.6	(a)
Belgium	1890–94	45.6	(a)
Switzerland	1898	44.5	(b)
Spain	1890–94	42.9	(a)
Bulgaria	1898–99	32.6	(b)
Portugal	1890–94	31.9	(a)
Greece	1900	23.1	(b)
Serbia	1890–94	14.6	(a)
North America			
Canada, 7 prov's	1901	49.0	(b)
Unites States	1880	48.5	(c)
Non-South	1880	48.8	(c)
Southern states	1880	47.7	(c)
Latin America			
Chile	1900	51.6	(b)
Cuba	1901–02	46.8	(b)
Argentina	1900	46.1	(b)
Uruguay	1890–94	45.1	(a)
El Salvador	1893	43.4	(a)
Guatemala	1890–94	32.8	(a)
Australia and Asia			
3 Australian states	1890–94	48.3	(a)
Japan	1892	30.9	(a)
Mysore	1900–01	17.8	(b)
Bombay	1900–01	14.2	(b)
Burma	1900–01	7.8	(b)
Punjab	1897–98	7.6	(b)
Madras	1899–00	6.2	(b)
Ceylon	1898	5.0	(b)
NW prov's & Oudh	1897–98	4.9	(b)

Sources: (a) E. Levasseur (1897, 560–561), citing "Report on Education," 1893–1894; (b) U.S. Commissioner of Education, *Report* 1900–1901, pp. 2480–2482; (c) U.S. Censuses 1850–1900.

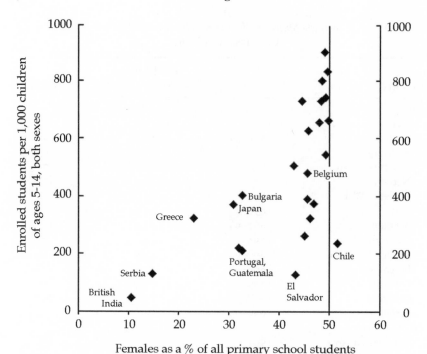

Main sources: Levasseur (1897), U.S. Commissioner of Education (1900, 1903), and the Brian Mitchell volumes for age distributions.

FIGURE 5.2. Female Share of Enrollments, as a Source of Differences in Overall Primary Schooling, around the 1890s.

leaders were, since leadership in the good-data club of countries probably also meant global leadership. Germany stood out consistently in the share of national product given to education, whether private expenditures are included or excluded, though Canada and other countries were close. Germany's lead was especially clear in the totals for all levels of education, since its university and top-vocational systems were the envy of the world.[18] As we shall note in Chapter 6, Germany fell behind in its educational commitment under Hitler and has never caught up to the leaders since.

Aside from world leadership, what we know about educational expenditures also confirms that the rise of tax-based public schooling did not displace private schooling. The estimates of spending in Germany, France, or the United States suggest that the share of income spent on private education did not change, despite the sharp rise in the share spent on public education. This lack of massive "crowding out" mirrors the history of poor relief, for which the rise of public support has not been accompanied by any decline in private charity in Europe or the United States, as we saw in Chapter 3.

While the oft-used expenditure shares of GDP are our best imitation of a rate of tax on income, they represent a step backward in that they do not

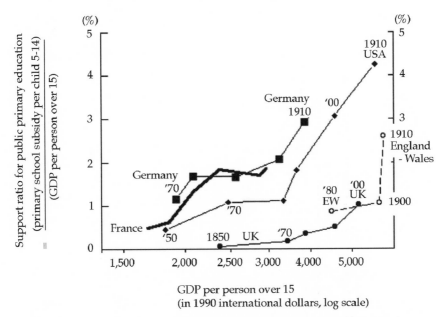

FIGURE 5.3. Support Ratios for Public Elementary Education, in Relations to Average Adult Incomes, Selected Countries, 1850–1910.

keep the age distribution in focus, as the enrollment rates did. To put the expenditure data into per-child perspective, while also affording a quick view of their relationship to income, Figure 5.3 and Table 5.3 look at a support ratio in relationship to adult income levels:

Support ratio for education = (expenditures per child)/(GNP per adult)

Which countries' education efforts really stood out, given their age distribution and level of income? Figure 5.3 and Table 5.3 sharpen our perspective by comparing the support ratio to the level of real income per adult, in the knowledge that even this refined support ratio drifts upward with income. To ease comparison, among leading countries, Figure 5.3 compares some other countries' paths with the thick-line path followed by prewar France. France itself looks relatively advanced once again, as it did in the enrollment rate, though not in the shares of expenditure in GNP. There was no clear global leader in the education support ratio, once one expects higher-income countries to spend more on education. Even the support ratios of Italy and Japan were respectable given the low average incomes of these countries.

If there is a standout among the countries shown here, it is the lagging education of English children before 1900. Figure 5.3 dramatizes this lag by showing England–Wales advancing in the lower right-hand corner, with

TABLE 5.3 *Public Elementary Education Support per Child, as a Share of Average Adult Income, Selected Countries 1830–1910*

Support Ratio for Primary Education = (Elementary School Subsidy per Child 5–14)/(GDP per Person over 15), as a Percent

	1830	1840	1850	1860	1870	1880	1890	1900	1910
United States		0.28	0.45	0.67	1.08	1.12	1.82		
United Kingdom			0.06	0.18	0.17	0.36	0.51	1.01	
England–Wales						0.87		1.05	2.60
France	0.19	0.53	0.48	0.52	0.62	1.36	1.84	1.70	1.87
Germany				0.91	1.15	1.68	1.65	2.07	2.83
Belgium			0.56		0.95	1.36			2.01
Italy						1.03			
Netherlands				0.56	0.78	1.22	1.49	1.96	2.72
Norway						0.84	0.85	1.17	1.20
Sweden					0.76	1.47	1.80	2.14	2.72
Japan						0.14	1.17		

Source: The data sets cited in Appendix C of Volume 2.

strikingly little commitment to education for so rich a country. The English lag did not go unnoticed at the time. In 1839, Dean Henry Alford of the Church of England rightly complained that

Prussia is before us; Switzerland is before us; France is before us. There is no record of any people on earth so highly civilized, so abounding in arts and comforts, and so grossly generally ignorant as the English.[19]

England and Wales especially lagged behind in the period between mid-century and 1891.[20] Only thereafter did they begin to catch up rapidly, catching the global leaders by 1910 in primary-school enrollments, though not yet in expenditures per pupil.

This brief review of global differences yields some clear results that demand a systematic explanation:

- Above all, why did education march upward almost monotonically, with only a few countries stagnating in enrollments or expenditures once they had raised them?
- Why did this happen in the nineteenth century and not earlier?
- Why did most of the world remain uneducated in the early twentieth century?
- Why should those two leaders in mass schooling, Germany and the United States, have been countries we traditionally view as having extremely opposing philosophies of government's role?
- Why was England, the "Workshop of the World," so far behind Germany, North America, France, and others as late as 1880?

COMPETING THEORIES

Cynicism dominates the leading explanations of the stark differences in educational history. Scholars have focused on interpreting the motives of powerful elite groups in fighting or shaping public education. Having spotlighted an elite self-interest, many writers have given little attention to other environmental factors in the background on that stage where the self-interest acts to block, control, or promote the education of the masses.

The cynical interpretations of early mass schooling are on the right track. In their haste, however, they have developed three limitations:

(1) Satisfied with just finding the smoking gun of powerful self-interest, scholars have not bothered to establish whether those self-interests raised or lowered the amount of schooling and its usefulness to children.

(2) Environmental influences on the amount of schooling need to be given their due. That correction is feasible if one is aided by multivariate statistical analysis.

(3) The focus on elite motives alone has diverted attention from the important role of the degree of centralization or decentralization of control over school finance.

Updating the Elite-Pressure Theories

Which powerful lobbies actually favored more schooling for the masses and which favored less? Many of the pressure groups themselves were ambivalent on how much schooling they wanted the masses to have. Fortunately, what threatens to be an unruly diversity of hard-to-test possibilities yields to testing with simple measures of democracy and the spread of political voice. To see how, let us examine the leading elite pressure groups that are thought to have played major roles in advancing, retarding, or distorting the progress of primary education, in search of testable hypotheses.

Landlords and Toryism

A powerful landed interest could either favor or oppose the spread of education down the ranks of society, as Carl Kaestle has reminded us.[21] As guardians of the social order, top landlords – or any other privileged elite – might conclude that schooling the masses was the only way to control crime, sedition, and revolutionary chaos. On the other hand, they might conclude that schooled masses were more trouble and burden.

The latter view, called Tory opposition here, was probably more prevalent. Its basic case against mass schooling was given a classic English expression in Parliament in 1807, when a parochial school bill to provide tax-based elementary schools was introduced by Samuel Whitbread. Among those who successfully opposed it in the House of Commons was Davies Giddy, who later became president of the Royal Society:

[G]iving education to the labouring classes of the poor . . . would . . . be prejudicial to their morals and happiness; it would teach them to despise their lot in life, instead of making them good servants in agriculture, and other laborious employment to which their rank in society had destined them; instead of teaching them subordination, it would render them factious and refractory, as was evident in the manufacturing counties; it would enable them to read seditious pamphlets, vicious books, and publications against Christianity; it would render them insolent to their superiors. . . . Beside, . . . it would go to burden the country with a most enormous expence, and to load the industrious orders of society with still heavier imposts.[22]

Three premises behind this classic statement were all correct. Yes, education would cause laborers to leave agriculture for better jobs.[23] Yes, education was seditious, in the sense that it would raise public opposition to landed Tory supremacy. And yes, paying for mass education would mean more taxes – even though the proposed tax rates that horrified Giddy would have looked negligible today.

Such attitudes were not an invention of English Tories alone. Indeed, the same could be found on the part of propertied conservatives in practically any country and century. Writing in 1800, a landed conservative in German Silesia also emphasized the landlords' stake in preventing education:

> Our forefathers never had occasion to quarrel with their illiterate serfs: an illiteracy which did not prevent fields from being cultivated at least as well as they are today, and manners being unquestionably purer.... And [is it not true that] the lords experience far more difficulty in maintaining authority over their serfs than they did when the latter were still illiterate? ... The most uncouth and ignorant peasant will invariably make the best soldier. He can be treated as if he were a machine, and when he is so treated one can rely on him absolutely.[24]

A quarter century earlier, the Bavarian official J.G. Schlosser even called for *de*-educating the masses:

> The vocations of men are in most cases so incompatible with the all-around development of their faculties that I would almost say that one cannot start soon enough to encourage the atrophy of those faculties; for most men are destined for vocations where they cannot use them in later life. Why do you castrate oxen and colts when you prepare them for the yoke and cart, yet wish to develop the totality of human powers in men similarly condemned to the yoke and cart?[25]

The fruits of this view depended on the social terrain on which it was cast, as Carl Kaestle has pointed out. On less fertile ground, such landed conservatism would bear less fruit. While landed conservatives in, say, Kansas might echo the same arguments, they were compelled by their different social environment to yield to that opposing argument that mass schooling was needed to keep the peace.[26] The theory that Tory opposition determined the pace of progress in schooling thus makes a conditional political prediction, namely that landed Tory opposition would block education only where it had the power to do so. In what follows, we relate its share of power inversely to the share of men who voted.

Capitalist Social Control

The interests of an industrial capitalist elite are featured in the social control interpretation of nineteenth-century educational reform.[27] This view focuses less on the amount of schooling being provided, in money or years, and more on the curriculum content, seeing in it a type of brainwashing to create obedient factory hands. In most variants, it sees this elite as favoring a centralized and mandatory school system for all, though in others the industrial elite shares the Tory preference for ignorant masses. Either variant is a testable theory featuring an elite interest.[28] In what follows, we will identify this interest group as a significant share of those who gained the vote when it spread from the top 20 percent or less to the top 50–70 percent of adult males.

Domineering Government

Sometime in the last 50,000 years, the secret slipped out: Governments have their own self-interest and can pursue it aggressively. A study of primary education should confront at least three variations on this theme: the self-enriching autocrat, the state-building central government, and the control-hungry bureaucracy.

The self-enriching autocrat is cleverly modeled by McGuire and Olson, who build an attractive simple model of how both public goods and transfers respond to autocracy and democracy. Their model is an optimal-exploitation model, similar to the predator–prey models of biology or the optimal-taxation models of economics.[29]

What their model predicts about schooling expenditures (and enrollments) depends on whether schooling is viewed as a transfer to a favored group or as a public good that raises national product. If schooling is viewed as a transfer, then McGuire and Olson predict that the more "encompassing" is the democracy, with greater shares of the populace having a voice, then the lower will be the tax rate and the transfer to those the rulers want to favor. If schooling is viewed as a productive public good, their prediction is that the degree of democracy will not matter. All that will matter is the tug-of-war between the inherent productive merits of education and the deadweight cost of discouraging production with a higher tax rate to pay for the schools. So McGuire and Olson imply that the effect of a greater voting share on the level of schooling is either negative or zero, depending on the interpretation.

State-building by central governments has been linked to education.[30] To forge national obedience and military might, the absolutist state seeks full state control over education. It does so on behalf of one elite or another, such as "Junker hegemony" in the case of Germany or "bourgeois hegemony" in the cases of France, Britain, or the United States. Its drive for uniform and mandatory schooling implies educational growth as well as control.

In a third take on government control of education, a faceless bureaucracy seeks control for its own sake. In the tradition of Parkinson and Niskanen, E.G. West argues that a central bureaucracy, allied with vested interests in the public education sector, pushes relentlessly for expanding budgets and the suppression of independent private education. John Lott sees in all public school provision an attempt by central authorities to indoctrinate children with a centrally approved set of teachings. In West's version, at least, the prediction is that the total amount of schooling does not rise. Any extra public schooling would just crowd out private schooling. In a stronger version of the argument, West uses a model once advanced by Samuel Peltzman to suggest that growing government supply of a uniform grade of education would *lower* the quality of education.[31]

Dominant Religions

In every country of Europe and the Americas, the early history of education was plagued with fights about religious control over the content and the amount of schooling. Where one religious establishment reigned supreme, would it lobby for more, or for less, primary schooling? Theory is ambivalent on this question. While an established church would naturally seek to universalize its message, preferably at the expense of all taxpayers, it might also fear that a system of universal education would get out of control and undermine religion. Their fear of secularization was well based. Since the global rise of schooling has been driven by growing economic demand for secular knowledge, there has always been a powerful lobby for secular education, no matter how strong the official religion. As we shall see, the actual history is also ambivalent about the role of religion in the overall supply of primary schooling.

Vested Interests within the Educational Sector

An educational establishment, like the other elites, could either favor or oppose the spread of primary education at public expense. As a champion of education, it would naturally seek universal mandatory tax-based schooling under its own control. This mission could easily lead it to expand the total amount of schooling, or it might just displace private schools, as West insisted.[32]

Two kinds of direct self-interest could lead educational elites to *oppose* mass schooling. First, recipients of a lucrative higher education could wish to have the whole educational base restricted so as to enhance their privilege and wealth, especially if the top educational slots could be passed on within the family. Second, protectionist suppliers of education might wish to suppress competition. In the nineteenth-century struggles over universal mass education, both of these conservative interests were well represented among university faculties, classicists, and central boards of education. Classical education was staunchly defended in most countries in Europe and the Americas, even in Lutheran countries that might have been expected to shed Latin much earlier.[33] Reformers in many countries had to fight long and hard for "bifurcation" that would allow a useful-education track to take its place alongside the classical track.

With so many competing interest groups that could have raised or lowered schooling, and with so many countries and decades to study, how can one sort out these groups' systematic influences on the early history of mass education? In each case, there is a fingerprint to examine. The landed aristocracy's preferences were revealed in the early settings when they dominated a very restricted franchise. Capitalists' traces are more hidden, though they would tend to appear when urban and industrial interests became a large share of total political voice. The heavy hand of a ruling government class is clearest when the nation is not a democracy. The influence of a religion will show up in settings where it has clear dominance.

As a whole the elite-pressure emphasis will receive support in this chapter and in the statistical analysis of Volume 2's Chapter 15. It will turn out, though, that some of these theories fare better than others. Landlord

TABLE 5.4. *Decentralization and the Rise of Public Schooling:*
A Simple Example

Suppose that there are two adjacent local governments with equal numbers of voters, who face an all-or-nothing choice between setting up uniform tax-based public schooling for all children or having no public schools. Let's imagine a pro-school North and a less enthused South. Decisions are made by majority rule.

Would public schooling advance faster if the two local governments were merged into one or if they remained separate? That should change over time, as economic development raises the share of people wanting public schools:

	Share of Voters in Favor of Taxes & Public Schools			Whose Children get Public Schools?	
				with	with
Era	North	South	Both	Decentralization	Centralization
(1) Backward era	30%	10%	20%	none	none
(2) Early rise	55	25	40	North only	none
(3) Middle era	70	40	55	North only	all
(4) Advanced era	85	55	70	all	all

self-interest and Toryism will play a central role. Capitalist social control theories are kept offstage, because they have no clear prediction about the amount of school support. The McGuire–Olson version of dominant government will be rejected by the statistical analysis in Volume 2. The state-building and absolutism theories will be set aside as lacking in explanatory power. Lobbying by the educational suppliers themselves is set aside here, because it did not seem prominent in most nineteenth-century settings. It will return, however, in Chapter 6's look at the power of the educational establishment in the twentieth century.

The Role of Decentralization

The emergence of mass primary schooling also depended on whether school finance and curriculum were decided locally or by the central government. This influence has been omitted from most accounts, perhaps because it could work in either direction. Local control could either accelerate or prevent the rise of schooling. Yet as the total demand for tax-funded schooling, or any other public good, advances with economic development, local autonomy should have clearly positive effects in some settings and clearly negative effects in others.

Table 5.4 sketches how the long rise of demand for public schooling is likely to interact with government centralization or local autonomy. In the most backward and most advanced eras, represented by the first row, the locus of government hardly matters. In a poor and backward setting, there is no mandate for public schooling in any locality, whereas in a rich and advanced setting all localities want it. Yet the locus of government matters greatly during the transition from the least developed to the most developed settings. To understand which countries became the early leaders in public schooling, let us focus on the second row's portrayal of political possibilities in the "early rise" era, when a slight mandate for public schooling has emerged only in one region. Decentralization of government allows that region to vote for its own taxes and schools. If it were forced to put the same issue to a national government, the taxes and schools would not happen, because the balance of power is still against them at the national level. As we shall see, this simple prediction looks powerful in explaining international differences in the nineteenth century. The early leaders were those countries where local governments were free to choose their own levels of commitment to tax-based schools. The middle era, in which centralization could raise schooling in the least-schooled localities, also has its counterparts in the later history of mass schooling, though it gets less attention in this chapter.

POPULAR VOTES, PUBLIC SCHOOLS

The blessing and burden of having so many countries to compare, and so many explanatory forces to weigh, call for two kinds of explanation, one narrative and one statistical. The rest of this chapter will take on the narrative task of highlighting those institutional forces that do the most to explain the differences in national educational histories before World War I. The systematic statistical approach is only summarized here, with detailed analysis deferred to Volume 2's Chapter 15.

The spread of democratic voting rights plays a leading role in explaining why some nations forged ahead in education and others fell behind. So we learn from the experiences of twenty-one countries in the 1880–1930 era, which reveal some of the forces behind patterns in public school enrollment rates, a clue to the level of political commitment to education.[34]

The rise of voting rights apparently accelerated the rise of primary schooling, according to the historical patterns revealed in Figure 5.4. The solid line in Figure 5.4 traces out such a democratic picture, based on analysis in Volume 2. There is a positive relationship between voting rights and schooling, but it has a curvature with respect to voting that sheds new light on some of those theories about the role of elite self-interest. "Democratic voting" here combines whether this country was a democracy at the time (1 = yes, 0 = no) and the share of all persons over twenty who actually voted.[35] Focusing on the world before 1914, when women still did not vote, we set aside the role of later female suffrage, whichChapter 7 will show was an important influence on other kinds of social spending.[36]

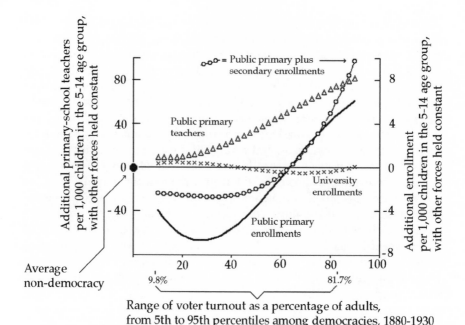

FIGURE 5.4. The Voting Share of Adults as an Influence on Enrollments and Teachers per 1,000 Children, 1880–1930.

Figure 5.4's electoral spectrum starts with nondemocracies, in which nobody voted effectively, at the origin. Prewar nondemocracies included the Austro-Hungarian Empire, Japan, the Mediterranean, and Latin America.[37] Creating an elite democracy in which fewer than 40 percent of adult men voted brought no more schooling than the average nondemocracy. Examples of such elite democracies in the late nineteenth century were the United Kingdom, the Netherlands, and Sweden. But countries where most men voted had significantly more primary schooling than in the average nondemocracy, other things equal. The same significant response to widespread voting is evident in the total number of teachers hired and in primary plus secondary enrollments. There was no such democracy effect, however, for enrollments at the university level. Nondemocracies, elite democracies, and broad democracies all had similar average commitments to higher education once income, religion, and other influences are held constant.

Democracy and active voter participation, then, seem to have left a deep footprint. Figure 5.4 thus confirms the link between unequal political power and underdeveloped human capital recently emphasized by Engerman, Mariscal, and Sokoloff.[38] It adds a twist relating the concentration of power to the distribution of public funding (enrollments) across levels of education. What fuller democracies delivered, relative to nondemocracies or elite democracies, was *primary* education, the kind of tax-based education that redistributed the most from rich to poor.

BUT WHAT CAUSED DEMOCRACY?

The finding that democratic voting seemed to explain much of the differences in schooling is subject to an immediate challenge: Couldn't it be that the other forces featured here are the true underlying sources of differences in democracy itself? This suspicion has two variants that must be addressed here: (1) Wasn't mass schooling itself an influence on the extension of voting rights? (2) Couldn't religious diversity be the historical source of differences in *both* democracy *and* schooling? These challenges must be addressed before we can go on to offer fresh reinterpretations of the education histories of individual nations.

Reverse Causation from Schooling to Democracy?

One could posit that it was more schooled societies that became more democratic. This suspicion emerges naturally from a cross-sectional look around the world at a particular date.

The best way to see the limits to the possibility of reverse causation is to look at the historical sequences rather than at a global cross-section. Most countries with high voting shares got them long before they attained anything like the schooling levels they had reached in, say, 1880. In fact, the rise of primary schooling came from public funding, which in turn came from critical votes. In most cases those critical votes took place within a context of widespread suffrage. The great rise of French enrollments in the 1870s and 1880s was preceded by the jump to near-universal adult male suffrage in 1848. England's catch-up after 1891 was preceded not only by the Fees Act of 1891 and the Forster Education Act of 1870, but also by the extension of suffrage in the first three reform acts. Nearly universal white male suffrage in the United States and Canada set the stage for local tax-based funding of a heavily public school system, and similarly in Australia and New Zealand.

Religious Diversity and the Rise of Democracy and Schooling

Placing religion and democracy side by side, we find an intellectual opportunity and an econometric challenge. A closer look at the international patterns shows that electoral democracy correlates strongly with *diversity* of religion – not with the dominance of any one religion. The correlation is so strong that it suggests that the absence of a dominating religion may have contributed both to the rise of democracy and to the rise of schooling.

To see how religious diversity may have played such a role, consider Table 5.5's international snapshot. In the twenty-one-country sample every single

TABLE 5.5. *Religious Mix and Electoral Democracy in 1880*

| | Religion — Shares of All Religious Declarants: | | | Democracy | | | Schooling, 1880–82 — Primary School Enrollments per 1,000 Children of Ages 5–14 | |
| | | | | 1880 | Was this an Electoral Democracy – | | | |
	Catholic	Protestant	Other Religions	Voter Turnout	by 1910?	by 1930?	Total	Public
Electoral democracies as of 1880 (ranked by public schooling)								
United States	0.35	0.57	0.08	0.690	yes	yes	906	800
Canada	0.42	0.56	0.02	0.509	yes	yes		800
Australia	0.23	0.74	0.03	0.464	yes	yes	882	780
France	0.82	0.02	0.16	0.680	yes	yes	816	654
New Zealand	0.15	0.79	0.06	0.424	yes	yes	756	537
U.K.	0.20	0.79*	0.01	0.367	yes	yes		473
Netherlands	0.36	0.62	0.02	0.098	yes	yes	628	462
Denmark	0	1.00	0	0.225	yes	yes		
Nondemocracies as of 1880 (ranked by public schooling)								
Sweden**	0	1.00	0	0	yes	yes		737
Norway**	0	1.00	0	0	yes	yes	646	564
Austria	0.91	0.02	0.07	0	no	yes	562	543
Spain	1.00	0	0	0	no	no		517
Belgium**	0.98	0.02	0	0	no**	yes	522	371

Italy**	1.00	0	0	0	no**	no	346	324
Japan	0.02	0.02	0.96	0	no	no		306
Greece	0.01	0	0.99	0	no	yes		293
Mexico	1.00	0	0	0	no	no		187
Portugal	1.00	0	0	0	no	no		178
Argentina	0.99	0.01	0	0	no	no		143
Finland	0	0.98	0.02	0	yes	yes		78
Brazil	0.99	0.01	0	0	no	no		70

Notes and Sources:

* Of which, the Anglican Church represented about 66 percent of total declarants for 1880–1910 and about 60 percent after the separation of Ireland.

** Belgium and Italy were rated by Banks (1971) as having a nonelective chief executive before World War I, presumably because the king had some power in both cases. One could choose to discount that royal power and count both countries as democracies. Similar ambiguities arise for Sweden and Norway in 1880.

Here, as elsewhere, voter turnout is the share of national-election voters in the adult (over 20) population for the enfranchised gender(s). Thus for all these countries before 1914, it was a share of adult males.

The sources are those described in Appendix D.

It is not clear whether the enrollments for Argentina, Brazil, Denmark, Greece, Japan, Mexico, and Spain include enrollments in private schools.

Germany is omitted from this table. As noted in the text, it was clearly not a democracy in terms of voting and representation at the national level, but allowed locally chosen authorities to raise tax money for, and to manage, local schools.

See Chapter 15 for multivariate regression analysis.

nondemocracy was dominated by a single major religion, Catholic, Lutheran, Eastern Orthodox, or Japan's Shinto–Buddhist mixture. By contrast, the democracies of 1880 had a more diverse mix of religions. Most of those with Protestant majorities were fragmented in their Protestantism. The only dominant-religion case among the democracies was France, at 82 percent Catholic (though one might call single-religion Norway, Sweden, Belgium, and Italy democracies as of 1880).

Democracy and voting out-performed religion as directly competing influences on schooling, if we may judge from the statistical evidence in Chapter 15 of Volume 2. Still, religious diversity might have been a historical *parent*, rather than a competitor, of democracy as an influence on schooling. Most countries with diverse religions in the nineteenth century had reached an uneasy balance that often guaranteed freedoms of religion and local political voice. The whole nexus of relative tolerance helped both democracy and schooling to blossom in the nineteenth century, when the economic demand for schooling was becoming obvious. Religious diversity, democracy, and schooling were probably intertwined.

REINTERPRETING NATIONAL HISTORIES OF MASS SCHOOLING

Combining the systematic effect of widespread democracy with other historical influences allows us to reinterpret some national education histories for the century before World War I.

France, the Baseline Case

France developed an above-average commitment to schooling in the nineteenth century, in a way that illustrates not only the role of democracy but also the role of military defeat and some of the subtle decentralization pattern. While revolutionary France was a professed leader in the cause of an educated citizenry, French reality lagged behind until mid-century. France's experience mirrors that of many other countries. There were early lofty proclamations that led to nothing. There was a constant fight over religion in the schools. Classicists fought with secular scientists. And nationalistic arguments were used to buttress the case for mass schooling. If France shared so much educational history with other countries in the nineteenth century, why the early lag behind the world leaders, and why did France rise to the top of the European schooling ranks by the 1880s?

The progress of French school funding followed the changes in political regime across the century after Waterloo. The transitions stand out clearly enough in Figure 5.5's history of revenues for primary education, thanks to France's superior educational data as recently distilled by Alain Carry.[39] Under the backward-looking Bourbon restoration, spending was as low and as private as one might expect. The July Revolution of 1830 was followed by the Guizot Law of 1833, which among other things required local commune

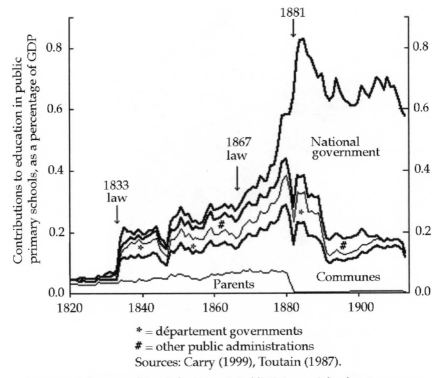

* = département governments
# = other public administrations
Sources: Carry (1999), Toutain (1987).

FIGURE 5.5. Sources of Funds for France's Public Primary Schools, 1820–1913.

governments to set up at least one elementary school and required the eighty-plus departments to establish normal schools for teacher training. The results were immediate, though modest, as shown in Figure 5.5. The national government provided controlling legislation, but the money was local.

Once the 1848 Revolution had led to voting rights for all men, one would have expected a mid-century jump in French educational spending and enrollments. Yet the period 1848–1870 was one of ambivalent educational politics. True, all men could vote, but Emperor Napoleon III's takeover denied the democracy that voting might have implied. The emperor equivocated on the educational front, balancing the strong conservative lobbying by the Church and the university elites against the generally secular and democratic reformers. While proclaiming in 1865 that "in the country of universal suffrage, every citizen should be able to read and write," he immediately repudiated a plan for universal primary education drawn up by his minister of education Victor Duruy. What emerged was the law of 10 April 1867, which merely liberated communes to raise more local taxes if they wished and mandated more local schools for girls.[40] Figure 5.5 shows that the communes accelerated their raising of local revenues in apparent response to this encouragement. The 1860s thus represented a midpoint, with

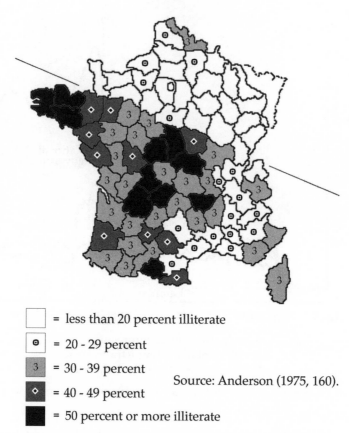

= less than 20 percent illiterate

= 20 - 29 percent

= 30 - 39 percent

= 40 - 49 percent

= 50 percent or more illiterate

Source: Anderson (1975, 160).

FIGURE 5.6. Illiteracy among French Army Conscripts in 1862.

French expenditures making gains, but still lagging well behind Prussia and other leaders.

The 1860s were also a midpoint in the nineteenth-century equalization of education among regions and between sexes. A snapshot of the illiteracy rates in 1862 (Figure 5.6) shows the characteristic regional split between an advanced France to the northeast of the line from St. Malo to Geneva and a less educated, more Patois-speaking, south and west. Such were the lingering inequalities and the partial progress under decentralized school funding as of the 1860s. The same inequalities in literacy had been even more dramatic back in the 1830s and date back to the seventeenth century.[41]

The resounding defeat by Prussia tipped the scales in favor of the educational reformers. Enrollments and expenditures accelerated across the 1870s, with local taxation leading the way. The real victory of universal tax-based education came with Jules Ferry's Laic Laws of the 1880s, especially the 1881 law abolishing all fees and tuition charges in public elementary schools. The national government took over the payment of all teacher salaries, while the local governments provided and maintained the schools and teachers' lodging. The regional differentials in literacy and primary education began to fade.

Thus both the march of democracy and the reversing effects of decentralization were evident in nineteenth-century France. More votes eventually brought universal primary schooling at taxpayer expense. And as predicted, France's decentralization served well enough in the early phase, allowing the Northeast and cities to push ahead. While national politics could not deliver a centralized victory for universal schooling before the military defeat of 1870, the localities that wanted the taxes and schools went ahead. After 1881 centralization performed the mopping-up role predicted by the sketch in Table 5.4.

The English Delay

England's lag in primary and secondary education between the 1850s and the 1890s looks odd at first glance. Wasn't England always a leader in literacy and science, from the Middle Ages through the nineteenth century? The answer appears to be that England was indeed one of the leaders in basic education *before* the era of her economic world leadership, but not *during* it. England had been one of the leaders in literacy, along with the Netherlands, between 1540 and 1700, when schooling was still mainly private – and meager – all over the world. But across the eighteenth century, English literacy diffused less rapidly than literacy in the North American colonies, Scotland, the Netherlands, northern France, Switzerland, and Italy's Piedmont. The advance of all these regions relative to England was partly due to their more rapid development of public schools. Within England's relatively slow advance in literacy across the eighteenth century, the differences by occupation and region give hints about the barriers to more rapid progress. Literacy was already nearly universal among men in the clergy, the other professions, and the commercial classes, all of whom paid privately for their children's basic education. Yet among the masses, literacy actually retreated from mid-century to the 1785–1814 period. The retreat was southern and rural and was partly offset by a rise in literacy in the north.[42]

England's lag in the Industrial Revolution era and the mid-nineteenth century was real and can be explained at least in part. So can the speed with which England nearly caught up with the leaders by World War I.

Aside from the delay in British democracy, what flow of history produced that educational lag, and what changed the picture after the 1890s? Parliament debated education bills over the entire century, so that there was no one defining moment of Britain's conversion to universal tax-financed public education.[43] The opposition included a strong defense of private "voluntary" education, along with the usual established-church fears that public education meant secular education. The core problem was what to do about educating the poorest children. The Church felt it had the sole right to educate them, yet delivered little education. Legislating small grants to the voluntary societies for the purpose of teaching poor children resulted in more controversy than education. Similarly, local authorities delivered little schooling. Education bills and commissions came and went.

There was at least some relationship of the rise of schooling to the rise of electoral democracy in nineteenth-century Britain, as Figure 5.4 would have predicted. In particular, the extension of voting rights under the Second Reform Act (1867/8), the passage of the secret ballot (1872), and the Third Reform Act (1884/5) were followed by the greatest educational breakthroughs of the century. After the Second Reform Act had extended voting rights from 19 percent of men to about 31 percent, touching the upper artisan occupations, Forster's Elementary Education Act finally passed in 1870.[44] The 1870 Act, however, was a convoluted compromise, moving in steps toward compulsory education without having solved the basic problem of public school finance. After the Third Reform Act extended the franchise from about 31 percent up to about 63 percent of men in the United Kingdom, Tory and Church opposition began to retreat. After further complicated maneuvers, the Fees Act of 1891 finally produced the momentum needed for universal free primary education.[45] At that time British educational progress still lagged behind the French by about a decade, but the gap was closed over the next two decades.

Another source of the British lag is suggested by the decentralization motif already introduced. If the delay in electoral reform held back universal education at the national level, why didn't education-minded local governments step forward and supply their own schools based on local taxes? That worked moderately well for education-minded communes in France and even better for Prussian and North American school districts. Here is the curious episode of the dog that did not bark in English educational history.

Parliament had quietly erected barriers to local government initiative that effectively blocked the creation of local tax-based schools. True, in the early nineteenth century Parliament had set up templates for local organizations to petition Parliament at low expense, in the form of permissive legislation and model-clause acts. But there were still high hurdles in the way of a locality that wanted to set up a new institution. First, a locality would still have to get a Parliament stacked in favor of landed and church interests to approve new local taxes for schools. Second, the initiative had to come from a local group according to a weighted-voting scheme. Even at the local level, voting rights on bills to be submitted to Parliament were in proportion to property held, with a high minimum property ownership for having any local vote at all, in imitation of the property-biased requirements of the Sturges–Bourne Acts of 1818. Third, this weighted-voting provision was reformalized in the new poor law unions set up by the Poor Law Reform of 1834. Fourth, those poor law unions, a potential fresh departure in local government, were not allowed to deal with education and health.[46] Thus did Parliament keep hold of the reins of local government.

Britain's dependence on central government and wholly private sources for school funding departed from the typical practice of the nations that led in early mass schooling. As Table 5.6 shows, central government played a smaller role, and local taxes a greater role, in the nations that led in primary schooling and in Italy, a nation that provided higher support per child than its low per-capita income would have suggested. Table 5.6 also leaves another clue to the role of local autonomy in the growth of schooling within the United Kingdom. Scotland, which was allowed to rely more on local taxation as far back as the late seventeenth century, slightly surpassed England in schooling enrollments. As of the 1870s Scotland resembled France, both in its sources of school finance and in its enrollment rates.

Rethinking German Education[47]

Of all the national experiences, none cries out more loudly for reinterpretation than that of the German states and, after 1870, the German Empire. Before 1870 Prussia already led the world in the quantity of schooling, as reflected in enrollments and expenditures, and drew admiring foreign visitors. It gave girls more equal primary schooling than in England and most other countries and it mixed the social classes in primary schools more than English reformers dared to try.[48] What made that possible? Does German primary-school experience fit the causal stories sketched here on the basis of an 1880–1930 sample that excluded Germany?

A prevalent error in the comparative history of education is the tendency to view Prussian and German pioneering in nineteenth-century education as something imposed from the top down by state-building emperors and by Chancellor Bismarck in alliance with the famous Junker landlords of the Prussian East. A fairer examination of the historical record reveals that German educational leadership was built from the bottom up. Its three main origins lay in (1) the strong latent local demand for education as of the late eighteenth century, (2) the key liberal opportunity created by Napoleon's victories over the German states, and (3) the decentralized nature of German government when it came to education.

The error in the top-down story should be evident once one reflects on how the realities of Germany's imperial governments should have caused *lower* education in the nineteenth century. The political structure of the Prussian state and the German Empire was as elite-biased as that of England and Wales, and some differences between the two should have hindered public mass schooling even more in Prussia than in England. Prussia's Byzantine rules giving social classes unequal representation in the national bicameral legislature (*Herrenhaus* and *Abgeordnetenhaus*) made a mockery of the

TABLE 5.6. *Central versus Local Sources of Primary School Funds: Britain in International Perspective, 1860s–1870s*

Years and Countries, Ranked by National-Government Share	Percentage Contributed by				Source	Notes
	National Government	Provincial Government	Local Gov't	Private & Other		
1873–74 United States	0.0	16.6	78.0	5.4	e	reporting schools in 16 states
1863 Upper Canada	0.0	12.6	78.4		f	common schools
c.1870 Switzerland	0.0	55.0	45.0		a	
c.1870 Italy	1.0		95.8	3.2	a	
c.1870 Saxony	1.6		98.4		a	
1876 West Prussia	8.5	0.0	75.9	13.2	g	From Brandenburg and Silesia east.
1876 East Prussia	10.8	0.0	71.2	18.0	g	
1870 France	13.7	13.6	34.6	39.5	c	état, départ's, communes, ménages, other
1879–80 Netherlands	14.5	4.0	81.5		d	
c.1870 Bavaria	39.6		60.4		a	
c.1870 Württemberg	40.8		59.2		a	
1869 Belgium	42.5	3.9	37.4	16.2	b	state, prov's communes, other

Percentage Contributed by

		National Government	Local Gov't	Private & Other	
c.1870	England–Wales	17.3	5.2	77.5	a
1874–75	England–Wales	35.5	15.4	49.0	h
1874–75	Scotland	30.0	33.2	36.8	h
1874–75	Ireland	85.0	3.6	11.4	h
1874–75	United Kingdom	42.1	16.0	41.9	h

Notes and Sources: "National government = imperial, federal, central "state." "Provincial" government = province, canton, U.S. state, département. "Local" government = commune, municipality, township, county, school district.

In France in 1870, private households paid 23.5% and other administrations paid 16.0%.

a = U.S. Commissioner's *Report* 1857 (pp. cxxvi–cxxvii), citing "Allgemeine Deutsche Lehrerzeitung," published in Leipzig.

b = Pirard (1985), pp. 1,196, 1,202, and 1,210.

c = Carry (1999).

d = U.S. Commissioner *Report* 1880, p. ccxxii.

e = U.S. Commissioner *Report* 1873–1875, per Adams (1875, pp. 66–71).

f = Fraser (1866, p. 230).

g = Herrfurth (1878).

h = "Return of the Cost of Public Elementary Education and Sources from which Defrayed in Great Britain and Ireland 1874–85," House of Commons, *Sessional Papers* 1876 (284.) lix, 149.

ostensible right of almost all men to vote in national elections after 1848. In response, less than a third of the Class III voters – the masses – bothered to vote in any national elections of the 1850s and 1860s. These biases were upheld in the larger national politics of the Empire.[49] These inequities should have lowered public funding and sanction for mass primary education, and so should the power of rural landlords, especially the famous eastern Junkers, and the heavy claims of the military on the national budget.

The traditional way of reconciling these contradictions does not work. Most treatments of Prussian and German educational history have been content to cover what should have been glaring contradictions under the single cloak of conservative Prussian "absolutism," the same cloak that has been thrown over all of German history from the eighteenth century to World War I.[50] The usual reconciliation involves the content and quantity of education, a reconciliation that somehow spilled over to other German states. The absolutist state kept firm control over the content of education, suppressing free thought and promoting loyalty. At the same time, it pioneered in universalizing education in order to keep the entire population in line. The path was supposedly blazed by imperial edicts calling for mandatory community provision of universal education as far back as the 1760s, though progress awaited the Stein–Hardenberg reforms of the Napoleonic era. Thus was the world's leading system of primary education imposed and administered from above.

Revisionists have exposed several flaws in the usual top-down absolutist tale.[51] First, it relies excessively on official pronouncements and not enough on "the actual day-to-day functioning – that is, the concrete reality of the schools."[52] Second, those foreign visitors were impressed not with the centrality of the successful Prussian system so much as with its flexibility and democracy and its responsiveness to local demand.

Contrary to the usual top-down story, Prussia's kings did as much, and said as much, to *block* schooling and free thought as to spread it. Their occasional decrees calling for universal education were merely attempts to order localities to educate at their own expense, without effective enforcement from above. Frederick William II, despite some waves of enthusiasm for mass education, often yielded to more reactionary instincts. He felt that any retired army sergeant who knew a little about reading and writing could serve as a suitable teacher and therefore set aside a proposal by his minister K.A. von Zedlitz calling for a state-funded teacher training program. In another revealing test case in 1787, no sooner had Zedlitz and the new State Board of Education called for a general land tax that was needed to fund badly needed schools than Zedlitz was sacked by Frederick William II and replaced with a conservative who buried all progressive recommendations.

Frederick William III was no more progressive than his father. In 1803 he rejected the introduction of the relatively progressive Pestalozzi method into primary schools because it would give young minds ideas not fitting their inherited social station:

> One must not forget that, with few exceptions, we are dealing with our precious lower class (*schatzbare Volksklasse*). . . . the children of this hard-working *Volksklasse* should not become lecturers, not chancellery officials, not mathematicians, not religion professors. They should learn to read their catechism, Bible, and hymnal, to write and calculate in accordance to their limited circumstances, to love and fear God and behave accordingly.[53]

Only after the humiliating defeat by Napoleon at Jena in 1806 did Frederick William III commit to educational reforms, and up to his death in 1840 he remained ambivalent on whether mass schooling helped or hurt national security.[54]

Almost a half century later, after a surge in local provision of education, his son, Frederick William IV, still wanted education to be restricted in content and reportedly castigated educators in the wake of the 1848 revolution.[55] The king did succeed in causing a brief retreat in curricula from freer education back to classical rigidity. But neither before nor after his outburst were the expansion of mass education budgets and the shift in curriculum toward sciences really checked. Even though the Prussian monarchy was never noted for its generosity in funding education, education continued to receive more local funding than in other countries.[56]

To rebuild the more plausible bottom-up story of German education in the nineteenth century, we should begin with the strong local demand for schooling as of the late eighteenth century, a demand that was growing despite indecision and debate around the throne. Part of that strong demand arose from the urbanization and economic development of the northwestern half of the Germanies. Part came from the Pietism embraced by an increasing minority of Germans starting in the late seventeenth century. The Pietist movement argued forcefully for universal literacy, so that all could read the Scriptures. While neither urbanization nor Pietism was victorious in the eighteenth century, they contributed to agitation for more universal education.[57]

The second key to the bottom-up pressure for universal primary education was the crucial liberal moment created by Napoleon's defeats of German armies and French influence in western Germany during the occupation. Indeed, Napoleon Bonaparte was probably the person who did the most for German education. His resounding defeat of the German states, culminating with his humiliating Prussia at Jena in 1806, sparked widespread reforms. This window of opportunity allowed the establishment of a reformed structure from above, modernizing the funding and administration of education. The key role of these reforms again contradicts the myth of an educational system controlled and expanded by an "absolutism" dating from the eighteenth century.

The third key is to understand that once the reformed Prussian educational framework was in place, it could not be dislodged by the subsequent waves of conservatism. This is partly because a new decentralization was promoted by the territorial changes that followed the defeat of Napoleon in 1812–1815. The postwar Congress of Vienna gave Prussia vast new territories with extremely high and extremely low demands for schooling. The new high demanders of schooling were the urbanized Rhineland and lower Saxony. The new low demanders were those landlords and officials in charge of the new Polish territories. While these differences were already pronounced in the eighteenth century, bringing these two extremes into the kingdom probably tilted Prussia's reforms toward a more decentralized system.[58]

Control remained largely local, in Prussia as well as in the separate German states.[59] By law and tradition, standards for elementary education in the Prussian state varied widely. Local communities were responsible for both administration and funding. The constitution of 1850 added the clarification that the state was to be a backup in case of need. A school district's local deputation or board consisted of one to three members of the town magistry, an equal number of town councilors, an equal number of citizens acquainted with educational affairs, and the leading pastor.[60] For the most part, these appear to have been either locally elected or appointed by local officials, some of whom were elected.

Meanwhile, the German tax system gave states a more elastic tax base than the central government, even after unification. This gave subnational governments greater discretion over the level of taxation to be devoted to expanded domestic programs, such as education. On the tax side, as well as on the school expenditure side, it is a mistake to think that the Imperial German government was all-controlling.[61]

That the funds for primary schools were raised locally, in response to local debates, seems clear from the available figures. In 1876, funds from the Prussian state accounted for only 8.9 percent of the budgets of public primary schools (*Volksschulen*), endowments for 3.2 percent, fees for 15.1 percent, and the remaining 72.8 percent came from local taxes. The eastern provinces, where the Junkers held more sway, got slightly more from the central government (10.8 percent), and the western provinces slightly less (8.5 percent).[62]

The amounts spent on each child of primary school age in different regions can shed light on Prussian educational goals and the locus of power. Table 5.7 shows the urban and rural levels of spending per child over a forty-five-year period. The patterns resemble those of almost any country. Urban children received more than rural children, as in other countries, though part of the gap might reflect differences in the local cost of living. More was spent on children in the more industrial west than in the more agricultural east. If one were to look for a broad region in which the least was spent, it would be in the countryside in the east – where the Junkers were dominant. Furthermore, since the east got greater net transfers from the central government for its primary schools, the true distinguishing feature of the Junker-dominated

TABLE 5.7. *Regional Differences in Public Primary School Expenditures per Child of School Age within Prussia, 1861–1906 (Marks per Schulkind)*

	1861	1871	1896	1901	1906
Cities and countryside together					
Nine eastern areas	9.6	12.5	30.3	39.1	44.5
Nine western areas	10.6	14.3	35.9	47.5	51.7
West/East	1.10	1.14	1.18	1.21	1.16
Countryside only					
Nine eastern areas	8.2	9.9	26.4	31.7	34.5
Nine western areas	9.7	12.8	32.2	39.7	42.4
West/East	1.19	1.29	1.22	1.25	1.23
Cities only					
Nine weastern areas	15.0	20.7	39.5	50.5	59.8
Nine eastern areas	13.5	18.2	42.6	60.6	64.7
West/East	0.90	0.88	1.09	1.20	1.08
Cities/countryside					
Nine weastern areas	1.84	2.08	1.50	1.59	1.73
Nine western areas	1.40	1.42	1.32	1.52	1.53

Notes and Sources: The nine eastern areas (*Regierungsbezirke*) are Königsberg, Gumbinnen, Danzig, Marienverder, Frankfurt Oder, Stettin, Posen, Bromberg, and Breslau.

The nine western areas are Münster, Minden, Arnsberg, Koblenz, Düsseldorf, Köln, Tier, Aachen, and Sigmaringen.

Simple averages were across the nine areas in each case, without weighting by the number of schoolchildren.

The source is Petersilie (1906), p. 147.

eastern countryside was that they paid less in taxes than the rest of the Prussian state or German empire – and their children received less. This does fit an image of Junker self-interest, but it is an image that does not reflect any educational vision for nation-building – other than avoiding taxes on Junkers.

It is hard to tell the Imperial and Junker footprints in educational history from those left by England's landed Tories or U.S. plantation owners. As Thomas Nipperdey puts it,

Expansion [of schooling] was silent and largely outside the discussions of domestic affairs, but continued inexorably.... Despite the powers of the state over the schools,... institutionally they remained schools for the community.[63]

The tentative suggestion here is that Prussia's early leadership in education received only a slight impetus from the central state. It was more the result of a spontaneous political will to levy local taxes in thousands of school districts. In fact, that political will manifested itself not only within the Prussian Empire but also in the other German states. Table 5.8's data from

TABLE 5.8. *Expenditures per Pupil, throughout the Germanies, 1900–1901 (Marks per Schulkind)*

	Expenditures per Pupil		Expenditures per Pupil
Northwest		*Northeast*	
Bremen	77.1	Lübeck	64.9 (Prussia)
Hamburg	74.2	Potsdam	59.5 (Prussia)
Sigmaringen	58.2 (Prussia)	Saxony	49.9
Düsseldorf	57.1 (Prussia)	Stettin	46.6 (Prussia)
Arnsberg	51.2 (Prussia)	Anhalt	45.1
Köln	50.4 (Prussia)	Saxe-Meining	44.6
Hesse	47.5	Saxe-Coburg-Gotha	44.6
Brunswick	44.5	Danzig	43.6 (Prussia)
Koblenz	44.2 (Prussia)	Saxe-Weimar	43.1
Oldenberg	44.0	Breslau	42.5 (Prussia)
Trier	43.1 (Prussia)	Schwz.-Sondersh.	41.6
Aachen	42.2 (Prussia)	Saxe-Altenburg	40.7
Münster	40.6 (Prussia)	Königsberg	39.3 (Prussia)
Minden	40.5 (Prussia)	Gumbinnen	38.4 (Prussia)
Waldeck	34.9	Reuss, junior	37.8
Schaumb.-Lippe	27.9	Bromberg	36.3 (Prussia)
Lippe	25.4	Posen	34.2 (Prussia)
Southwest		Marienwerder	33.9 (Prussia)
Bavaria	45.5	Meck-Strelitz	33.6
Württemberg	41.6	Schwz.-Rudol.	33.6
Baden	41.3	Reuss, senior	29.7
German Empire	44.6	*Southeast*	
Prussia	47.7	Austrian Empire	24.0

Wilhelmine Germany at the turn of the century show the spatial inequalities in German education that appear to have spanned the entire nineteenth century. It was equally strong in Saxony and the Swiss federation, for example, yet weak in the south and in the Austrian Empire. This diversity suggests a three-part explanation. First, the strong demand for education in some German states before Napoleon was probably due to a combination of urbanization and Pietism. Second, the rise and fall of Napoleon kindled a new demand for mass schooling citizens in all the German states. Finally, a key permissive role was played by Germany's (and Switzerland's) behaving like a set of local democracies when it came to primary education.

Decentralized North America

Why was it North America that most conspicuously caught up with Prussia in the mid-nineteenth century? As we have already noted, the sharing of leadership by these nations looks odd at first, in view of the well-known contrasts in their political institutions. It looks just as odd that relatively laissez-faire Canada and the United States would be leaders in raising local taxes for schools as it looks to see a conservative Junker-dominated state be the pioneer in egalitarian schooling for all.

Yet these three countries seem to have resembled each other as far as the locus of educational funding is concerned. All three countries left primary school finance to decentralized local control, unlike the British. Those localities wanting more education, with the median voter willing to pay for it, were unchecked by the hostility of elites outside their own communities. The full potential efficiency of local schools as a public good serving a local consensus was realized.

The quickest key to understanding the early rise of schooling in North America is to note where it arose, how early it arose, and who took the initiative and paid for most of it. Throughout the nineteenth century the North American leaders in school enrollments and expenditures were communities in the non-southern United States and in Upper Canada.[64] We know that the American colonies and the early United States were precocious in developing primary schools.[65] Starting in the seventeenth century, more and more localities developed their own school districts. Their funds came mainly from local property taxation, but also from tuition, donations, and occasional help from state land-sale revenues. By the 1820s school districts were prevalent in the rural North, especially in the Northeast, and "old-field schools," often with itinerant teachers, were common in the South.[66] Indeed, the much-heralded "common school" movement of the 1830s–1840s is now known to have been only a continuation, without an acceleration, of previous progress in public primary schooling.[67]

The nonpioneering nature of the common school movement carries an important message about the role of local versus state government in the early rise of public schools. Early American experience, like early experience in the German states, suggests an important role for local autonomy. The prediction from Table 5.4's early-rise era seems to fit the early federal era. The areas with strong demand, as in the northern states, were able to march ahead, relative to centralized countries with weak demand at the national level. America's common school movement of the 1830s and 1840s should be interpreted as a middle era, in which the formation of centralized state school systems was aimed at bringing the least enthusiastic localities into a uniform public school system. It was an era in which the education lobby was able to consolidate its own power and continue, but not accelerate, the advance of average schooling across the state.

The main U.S. contrast was between the South and non-South, illustrated in Figure 5.7. Within the former confederate states, public school expenditure per child aged five to nineteen was only 3.2 percent of the annual income per adult in the twenty to sixty-four age range in 1902, whereas outside the

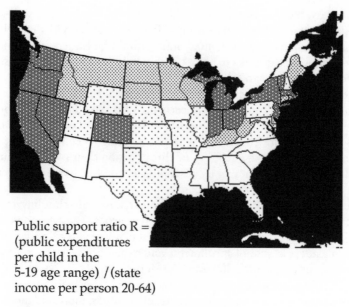

Public support ratio R =
(public expenditures
per child in the
5-19 age range) /(state
income per person 20-64)

▓ = 6.1% - 12.2% = top dozen states

▒ = 5.0% - 6.0% = second dozen states

░ = 3.7% - 4.9% = third dozen states

☐ = under 3.7% = bottom dozen states and territories

Sources: Sylla–Legler–Wallis data set on state and
        local governments, kindly supplied by John
        Wallis. Income per capita from Easterlin (1961).

FIGURE 5.7. Support for Public Education, among States of the United States, 1902.

South the same support ratio stood at 5.1 percent.[68] In the North where
suffrage and property were relatively widespread, local communities were
free to choose to tax themselves for schools, in the knowledge that the benefits
would be reflected in local land values.[69] Rural communities were often as
schooled as urban ones, where school districts became more centralized. In
the South, the disenfranchisement of blacks gave plantation owners relatively
more power. Lacking an incentive to educate blacks or even poor whites,
they created America's educational backwater.[70] The American South thus
resembled a more extreme version of eastern Prussia.

The desire to discriminate against black schooling, which was set back by
slave emancipation and by the state constitutions of the Reconstruction era
(1865–1877), returned when the rise of racial intimidation and Jim Crow

TABLE 5.9. *The Effect of Political Voice on Discrimination in School Spending in Selected Southern States, c. 1890–c1950*

Each number here = ($ spent on black school teachers per black pupil in attendance), as a % of ($ spent on white school teachers per white pupil in attendance) so that 100 = equality.

	Around 1890	The Year in which Blacks Lost the Vote	Around 1910	Around 1935	Around 1950
Alabama	99	1901	31	33	76
Georgia	67	1908	29	27	68
Louisiana	50	1895–98	17	27	62
Mississippi	50	1890	28	23	31
North Carolina	101	1900	54	64	93
South Carolina	91	1895	19	28	64

By contrast, school spending ratios in states that did not take the vote away from blacks:

Arkansas	n.a.		42	45	62
Kentucky	n.a.		100	n.a.	n.a.
Tennessee	n.a.		67	57	69
Texas	n.a.		63	50	83

Source: Margo (1900, esp. Table 2.5), except that the 1890 figures of Georgia and South Carolina, and the 1910 figure for Kentucky are from Freeman (1972).

laws disenfranchised blacks and left whites in control of school finance. The overall effect on expenditures for black schools is sketched by Table 5.9's history of interracial spending ratios in several states. Across states, and among localities within the Deep South, the degree of discrimination varied with the share of blacks in the population. Where black population dominated, in the cotton-growing "Black Belt" counties, whites took state funds allocated to schools on a per-child basis and applied most of the funding to white schools. Their degree of discrimination was constrained only by the threat that their "separate but equal" defense of segregation would be overturned by the Supreme Court if they spent virtually nothing on black schools.[71]

Even whites had lower education in the South, on average, as illustrated by Table 5.10's display of white literacy rates in 1860. In large part, this could be explained by the fact that the South had lower average incomes, presumably even for whites. In the Deep South, however, it seems to have reflected some of the lobbying force of greater landowners, who shared that Tory lack of interest in paying taxes to make their labor force leave.[72] One could rightly ask whether Southern employers would not have felt an incentive to pay taxes for schools that would keep white (and black) laborers from leaving for cities and the North. Why didn't they use schools as a magnet against

TABLE 5.10. *White Illiteracy in the United States in 1860*

Confederate South	Percent of Whites over 20 Unable to Read or Write	Non-South	Percent of Whites over 20 Unable to Read or Write
Alabama	16.6	California	7.4
Arkansas	17.7	Connecticut	3.2
Florida	15.4	Delaware	15.0
Georgia	16.9	Illinois	7.2
Kentucky	16.3	Indiana	10.2
Louisiana	9.8	Iowa	6.6
Mississippi	9.9	Kansas	5.8
North Carolina	23.1	Maine	2.3
South Carolina	10.8	Maryland	6.1
Tennessee	19.1	Massachusetts	6.5
Virginia	15.1	Michigan	17.4
		Minnesota	5.7
		Missouri	12.3
		New Hampshire	2.4
		New Jersey	5.7
United States		New York	5.6
average = 8.3%		Ohio	5.4
		Oregon	5.9
		Pennsylvania	5.2
		Rhode Island	6.0
		Vermont	5.1
		Wisconsin	4.5

Source: U.S. Census of 1860.

emigration, just as in the Northeast? The best answer seems to be that the South, through cultural gaps and intimidation of those who might try to leave, had less need for using good schools to retain workers.[73]

SUMMARY: ELITES, VOTES, AND SCHOOLS

While national educational histories contain their unique elements that cannot be forced into any simple framework, the puzzling diversity of pre-1914 educational histories does yield to systematic partial explanation. Focusing on mass primary schooling here, we have found new empirical patterns and new partial explanations:

(1) Prussia led in schooling until about 1860, when several other countries caught up. France was closer to being Europe's leader, especially after 1882, than past writings have implied.

(2) Britain lagged behind until 1891 and then caught up rapidly.

(3) The themes of elite self-interest, the spread of political voice, and central–local relations allow us to reinterpret some leading national histories. Differences in democracy and decentralization help to explain how the (non-Hapsburg) German states and North America, seemingly poles apart in their national politics, both led in mass education despite having strong regional landed interests. These themes also help to explain why Britain was still so far behind as of the 1880s.

(4) This reinterpretation is aided by a careful introduction of decentralized government as a historically conditioned influence on the advance of schooling. In the early-rise phase of the rise in demand for tax-based schools, local autonomy liberates the areas with stronger demand to go ahead with their local public schools. In a later phase, decentralization would have the opposite effect, by allowing the lowest-demand areas to lag behind. The early-rise phase seems to have fit North America and the German states in the early nineteenth century. The United States' common school movement of the 1830s and 1840s represents the middle phase, an era of centralization in which the laggards are brought into a statewide system. By contrast, one reason why England lagged behind until the 1890s was that Parliament kept a central hold on local finance.

6

Public Schooling in the Twentieth Century: What Happened to U.S. Leadership?

Having emerged as one of the world's leaders in public education by the start of the twentieth century, the United States continued to lead, at least enough to remain the world's top producer of knowledge. As Claudia Goldin has rightly emphasized, the twentieth century was the "American century" in education, first in the secondary-school wave and then in the postwar college boom.[1]

Yet over that century Americans became concerned about the quality of their children's primary and secondary schools, both when perceiving trends and when viewing international comparisons of test scores. In response to news that was mixed or worse, the United States has set up task force reports with names like *A Nation at Risk* and has passed legislation with names like *No Child Left Behind*. American writers came forth with an imaginative array of "usual suspects" in the perceived shortfall in American learning. Too much TV. Too many extracurricular activities. Bad diets and not enough exercise. Grade inflation. Fuzzy-headed liberal dilution of the curriculum with courses that do not teach the basics. Fluffy teacher-education courses. The rise of public-school bureaucracies. The rise of teacher unions and collective bargaining. Too many ill-prepared immigrant students. Urban decay. The breakdown of the traditional family. Stingy taxpayers.

Before diving for explanations deep below the surface, however, we should first take soundings from the historical and international record, to map the basic factual contours. Since the locus of concern has shifted from getting more schooling to getting better schooling, we must spend much of this chapter looking at the last quarter of the century, where the twentieth-century evidence on the quality of schooling is most abundant.

This chapter tentatively reinterprets what had happened in U.S. public schools by the end of the twentieth century. Critics of the school system argue that there is a crisis and that U.S. public education institutions are at fault. Defenders of the schools agree that there is a crisis, but the institutions are doing all that can be done to solve it. My tentative third view is that there is no crisis, *and* U.S. public education institutions are partly at fault.

Twentieth-century experience seems to confirm some hunches widely held by economists. There is a strong case for public *funding* of education, but not for public dominance in *providing* education. Where the United States has continued to lead is in the solution of the easier problem, coming up with tax revenues to subsidize extra years of schooling. The tougher problem has been the task of keeping the government-supplied schools from becoming inefficient. Publicly run schools, like nationalized industries in general, can perform well or badly depending on how they are regulated. Their efficiency depends on the flow of political history. No country has a permanent solution to this tougher problem of running public schools, and U.S. education institutions have not evolved as successfully as those in some other countries. Or so it seems from a comparison of the twentieth-century results of public primary and secondary schooling and from an emerging economic judgment on where the main flaws seem to lie.

WHO ARE THE LEADERS?

In Years of Education

In one key educational dimension, the North Americans remained world leaders until the very end of the twentieth century. From 1960 on, and probably over the whole century, both the United States and Canada ranked among the top six nations in terms of the average number of years of schooling attained by their adults. Though New Zealand was often the leader in average school years for adults, by the century's end Canada had taken the lead and the United States was second. Table 6.1's first two columns show the shares of all adults between the ages of twenty-five and sixty-four that finished secondary school and finished a tertiary education (e.g., college) degree or certificate.

This is about to change. The North Americans are already losing their leadership in the number of years of education attained by the younger generations of adults. Even though succeeding generations of North Americans are spending more and more years in schools and universities, Europe, Japan, and Korea so accelerated their own education across the 1980s and 1990s that a few countries are already overtaking the North Americans on this front. Table 6.1 shows the emergence of this catch-up in two ways. First, in the young adult age group between twenty-five and thirty-four years old, the shares that have finished secondary school and tertiary degree programs are converging globally. While Canada is still the top producer of higher education among those between twenty-five and thirty-four years old, Japan is not far behind, and Finland has caught up with the United States.

TABLE 6.1. *Educational Attainment of Adults, Current and Expected, in 1999*

	All Adults –		Young Adults –		Latest Rates –
	Ages 25–64 Percent Completed Secondary Education	Ages 25–64 Percent Completed Tertiary Education	Ages 25–34 Percent Completed Secondary Education	Ages 25–34 Percent Completed Tertiary Education	Expected Years of Full-time Education for a 5-Year-Old, at the School Continuation Rates of 1999
Australia	57.5	26.5	65.5	29.0	17.1
Austria	74.0	11.0	83.0	12.5	15.9
Belgium	56.5	25.5	73.0	34.0	17.5
Canada	79.5	39.0	87.5	47.0	15.9
Czech Republic	86.0	11.0	92.5	11.0	15.1
Denmark	79.5	26.5	87.5	28.5	17.9
Finland	71.5	31.0	85.5	37.5	18.3
France	62.0	21.5	76.5	31.0	16.5
Germany	81.0	22.5	85.5	21.5	17.2
Greece	50.0	18.0	71.0	25.0	15.5
Hungary	42.0	13.5	80.0	13.5	14.9
Iceland	56.0	23.0	64.5	27.5	16.6
Ireland	51.0	21.0	67.0	29.5	15.6
Italy	42.5	9.5	55.5	10.0	15.8
Japan	81.0	32.0	93.0	45.0	n.a.
Korea	66.5	23.0	92.5	35.0	15.8

Mexico	20.5	13.0	25.0	16.5	12.4
Netherlands	77.0	22.5	n.a.	25.0	16.8
New Zealand	73.5	27.0	79.5	26.0	16.2
Norway	84.5	27.5	94.0	32.5	17.4
Poland	54.0	10.5	62.0	12.0	15.2
Portugal	21.5	9.5	30.5	12.0	15.3
Spain	35.5	21.0	54.5	33.5	17.1
Sweden	76.5	28.5	87.5	31.5	18.5
Switzerland	82.0	24.0	89.0	26.0	16.1
Turkey	21.5	7.5	26.0	8.5	10.6
United Kingdom	61.0	25.0	65.0	28.5	16.8
United States	86.5	36.0	88.0	37.5	16.3
Simple average	61.8	21.7	72.6	26.0	16.1
U.S. rank	1st	2nd	6th	3rd–4th	14th
Canada's rank	7th–8th	1st	7th–9th	1st	19th

Notes and Sources: The source is OECD (2001, 43–47 and 133).

The completion rates are the simple averages of the male and female rates.

The expected years of schooling equal the expected full-time years plus one-half of the expected part-time years. Schooling before the fifth birthday is omitted. Japan is judged to have a schooling expectancy higher than the United States in 1999 in view of its very high rates of tertiary education for the twenty-five to thirty-five age cohort.

A more striking harbinger of things to come is revealed by the final column's report of expected years of schooling for a child starting from his or her fifth birthday and progressing through the national education system at the 1999 rates of continuation and graduation. This is one of those synthetic, but useful, current-period measures of expected survival for a cohort, just like the use of a single year's mortality rates to predict the life expectancy of newborns or the use of a single year's divorce rates to predict the survival of new marriages. The likely years of schooling that face a five-year-old in the United States and Canada work out to about sixteen full-time years at the 1999 rates. This sixteen-year expectation, roughly a college degree for the average five-year-old, is not at all unusual any more. In fact, it places the United States and Canada down in the middle of the pack, running in fourteenth place and nineteenth place, respectively. So great is the underpublicized advance of graduation rates in Europe, Japan, and Korea that a continuation of the 1999 pattern would mean that by mid-century the United States and Canada would rank only fourteenth and nineteenth even for the whole adult age range. By 2050 the world's most educated adult labor forces might be in the Nordic countries. The larger point here is that there are signs of catch-up and reshuffling in educational attainments among the top-ranked countries.

In Learning

Does the same pattern appear when we look at the productive learning that those years of education produce in different countries, rather than just at the numbers of years spent in school?

The clues to the value of what students learn in different countries consist of one abundant indicator that fails to shed light directly on the quality of education, plus some scarce and recent test scores that reflect a little more directly on what has been learned. The abundant indicator is the set of real wage and salary rates that await graduates in the different countries. To the extent that education is aimed at improving adults' productivity and earning power, the wage and salary rates for different levels of education look appropriate. But they reflect too many forces at once. The wage and salary premia for those with higher education reflect the whole general equilibrium of a national economy. They are shifted not only by the quality of what is learned in school but also by all the demand forces in the economy. To judge different countries' efforts and effectiveness in producing knowledge in their educational systems, we need more direct indicators of what is learned in schools and universities.

International Test Scores at the End of the Twentieth Century

Inevitably, we must turn to test scores as clues to what educational systems are actually delivering. The first hurdle to overcome in approaching test-score evidence is a familiar dismissal: "Test scores don't measure true learning, true knowledge, or true ability." Indeed, they are very incomplete and indirect measures of the human attributes we want the educational process to foster. We all know that adult success depends on such factors as creativity, patience, and communications skills. Tests miss these. Furthermore, some tests are not even aimed at testing the achievement of learning in school, the kind of test score we would find most useful in this chapter. IQ tests are supposed to indicate aptitude, not achievement (though we shall note evidence that school-age learning achievements do color even IQ tests). The same is true of some other widely used tests, such as the United States' SAT-I, which was originally called the Scholastic *Aptitude* Test, before the retreat to the vaguer Scholastic Assessment Test.

The best kinds of test scores for our purposes are those that try to measure the achievement of knowledge taught in the school curriculum. These achievement test scores must be internationally comparable, both in the content of the tests and in the sampling from age group populations. Critics will insist that even these international achievement tests miss the mark, because they do not test for those other skills that make a person successful and productive. True enough, but we must avoid making a negative assumption so commonly made in the test-score debates. We must avoid assuming that educational systems preparing children for national and international achievement tests do so *at the expense of* creativity, patience, or communication. This negative assumption seems unwarranted. Even if an individual student or an individual nation faces some marginal trade-off between working toward the test and developing other skills, the overall interstudent and international correlations between achievement scores and those good attributes are probably positive, not negative. Furthermore, there is evidence that better mathematics and science test scores have a positive effect on adult productivity.[2] We can use test scores as a somewhat useful, though still far from definitive, guide to the overall achievement imparted in schools up to the age of testing.

Internationally comparable test scores are now available for students ages nine through seventeen. International agencies have taken steps to make the student populations comparable, mainly by randomizing the selection of tested schools, though they still fail to test nonstudents of the same age groups. The main limitation in the international test score evidence is that it is all so recent. None of the multicountry controlled comparisons antedate 1964, except for variations on IQ tests, which are more removed from testing achievement in school. We must confine our international comparisons of the twentieth-century efficacy of primary and secondary education to very recent snapshots, just as most families lack photos of their great-grandparents.

Where the United States stands in the recent global school snapshots is summarized in Table 6.2. Looking first at test scores for preteens, at the top of the table, we see no clear danger signal flashing at the United States.

TABLE 6.2. *America's International Rank in Achievement Test Scores, 1980–2000*

Year of Test	Subject	Tested-Student Age	America's Ranking among Surveyed Countries	Top Seven Countries
		Pre-teens		
1970–71	Reading	10	7th out of 12	Italy, Swe, U.K., Fin, Bel, Neth, U.S.
"	Science	10	3rd out of 14	Japan, Swe, U.S., It, Fin, Hung, U.K.
1992	Reading	9 to 10	2nd out of 27	Fin, U.S., Swe, Fr, It, NZ, Norway
1995	Math	9 to 10	12th out of 26	Sing, Korea, Japan, Hong Kong, Neth, Czech Rep, Austria
"	Science	9 to 10	3rd–4th out of 26	Korea, Japan, U.S., Austria, Australia, Neth, Czech Rep.
		Teens		
1970–71	Reading	17	10th out of 13	NZ, U.K., Neth, Fin, Bel, Swe, Israel
"	Science	17	13th out of 17	NZ, W. Germany, Austria, Neth, U.K., Hungary, Finland
1980–82	Math	13	8th out of 10	Japan, Neth, Bel, Fr, Can, U.K., Fin
1991	"	13	8th out of 9	Switz, Fr, It, Can, U.K., Ire, Spain
1995	"	13	24th out of 39	Sing, Korea, Japan, Hong Kong, Belgium, Czech, Netherlands
"	"	14	28th out of 41	Sing, Korea, Japan, Hong Kong, Belgium, Czech, Slovakia
"	"	17–18	19th out of 21	Neth, Swe, Denmark, Switz, Iceland, Norway, France
"	Science	14	17th out of 41	Sing, Czech, Japan, Korea, Bulgaria, Netherlands, Slovenia
"	"	17–18	15th–16th out of 21	Swe, Netherlands, Iceland, Norway, Canada, NZ, Australia

1999	Math	13	9th out of 12	Singapore, Korea, Japan, Hong Kong, Belgium, Can, Australia
"	Science	13	10th out of 12	Hungary, Japan, Korea, Neth, Austral, Czech Rep, England
2000	Reading	15	14th out of 31	Fin, Can, NZ, Austral, Ire, Kor, U.K.
"	Math	15	18th out of 31	Jpn, Kor, NZ, Fin, Can, Austral, U.K.
"	Science	15	15th out of 31	Jpn, Kor, Fin, Can, NZ, Austral, U.K.

Sources and Notes: Reading and Science, 1970/71: Wolf (1977, 34–41).

Math test, 1980–1982: Second International Mathematics Study, per OECD (1992, 114–7). Average of geometry, arithmetic, and algebra scores. Canada = BC and Ontario only, U.K. = Great Britain only.

Math test, 1991: Second International Assessment of Educational Progress, per OECD (1992, 119). Switzerland = 15 cantons, Italy = Emilia-Romagna, U.K. = England and Scotland, and Spain excludes Catalonia. Reporting countries excluded here = Israel, Korea, Slovenia, Soviet Union, Taiwan.

Reading test, 1992: U.S. National Center for Education Statistics (1999, 467).

Math and science tests, 1995: Beaton et al. (1996a, 1996b) and the U.S. Department of Education's *Pursuing Excellence* volumes of 1997 and 1998. Some nations' tests were rated as not meeting international comparability guidelines, the top-ranking example being the Netherlands. The U.S. rank reported here is a point estimate within the range of statistically significant pairwise rankings. For thirteen-year-olds in math, for example, the United States was significantly below seventeen countries but significantly above the bottom nine countries out of thirty-nine.

Math and science tests, 1999, twelve main countries: Third International Mathematics and Science Study, per OECD (2001, 307–19).

Many more countries were covered in the different tests, but the four results reported here all refer to the same set of twelve countries, consisting of those mentioned here plus Italy and New Zealand.

Three tests, 2000: The Program for International Student Assessment (PISA), from http://www.pisa.oecd.org, printed March 8, 2002. The set of reporting countries excludes the Netherlands. The PISA study gives confidence intervals for its rankings. Thus the U.S. ranking was tenth to twentieth for reading literacy, sixteenth to twenty-third for math literacy, and eleventh to twenty-first for scientific literacy at the 95% confidence level.

Granted, U.S. students in the nine- to ten-year-old age range achieved only middling mathematics scores by international standards. Yet in 1992 reading tests, and again in 1995 science tests, the United States had nearly the highest average scores in the world. If there is any systematic shortfall of U.S. home environments or of U.S. schools, it has not shown up in national averages for these early years of the schooling cycle.

U.S. mediocrity shows up more clearly for teenagers, as the rest of Table 6.2 suggests. In all cases between 1970 and 2000, U.S. teenage students finished either in the middle or in the lower half of the surveyed student populations. So it has been for any testing age between thirteen and seventeen, and for any subject.[3] At least eleven countries have finished consistently higher than the United States in teenage tests, though there is no obvious cultural or institutional commonality among them. Alphabetically, these are Australia, Belgium, Canada, Czech Republic, Finland, France, Japan, Korea, Netherlands, Singapore, and the United Kingdom. If all nations' fifteen-year-old student populations were to be thoroughly tested in basic reading, mathematics, and science skills, as in the Programme for International Student Assessment (PISA) tests for 2000, then the United States would finish fourteenth at best.

What may look like a constant mediocrity of U.S. teenage performance in Table 6.2 should be viewed instead as a downward trend in U.S. relative achievement, masked by the removal of a bias against the Americans in the early tests. The bias is clear in the earliest tests shown here, the reading and science tests for 1970–1971. Those tests are taken only by *students,* not by the whole population in their age group. Back then the seventeen-year-olds in other countries were still an academically select group, unlike the Americans. In 1970, fully 75 percent of the seventeen-year-old age group was finishing high school in the United States, versus only 45–47 percent in Belgium and Sweden and below 30 percent in all other tested countries. Little wonder that U.S. students failed to shine in those international comparisons back in 1970.[4] Yet by 2000, nearly all seventeen-year-olds were in school, making the comparisons fair. Thus there was probably a decline in the relative performance of U.S. students between 1970 and 2000, holding constant the degree of selectivity.

Certain systematic variables affect test scores in all countries, as shown in an analysis of the PISA tests for the year 2000. Children of single parents score lower, other things equal, as do immigrant children and children of less educated or lower-occupation parents. Having cultural and educational resources in the home helps. Girls are significantly stronger at reading literacy than boys in every surveyed country.[5] Controlling for these differences would shrink the unexplained part of the differences between individuals, but it would have little effect on the differences between countries' average scores.

National averages can conceal a lot, of course, and it is natural to suspect that a country's average scores are being held down, or held up, by the behavior of some very special group. How do the compositions of the top-scoring countries differ from the Americans and other student populations with less impressive scores? Are the top national averages being held up, and the Americans held down, by the performance of particular groups?

The top scoring countries achieve those high average marks not so much by having better top scores as by having better middle and bottom scores. Korea, Finland, Japan, and Canada stand out as countries with such high and equal scores in the PISA2000 tests. Their combination of excellence and equality seems closely tied to equality in socioeconomic status. In all countries, the socioeconomic status of parents' occupations had a strong influence on students' test scores. This shared occupational slope translates less inequality in occupational status into more equal test scores. For example, students in the bottom quarter of the parental occupational ranks in Korea, Finland, and Canada had higher reading scores than the average for all students across the OECD nations.

On the other side of the same coin, the countries with mediocre average scores had greater variance both in test scores and in socioeconomic status. Examples are Belgium, Germany, Switzerland, and the United States. These countries had their scores held down more by lower scores at the fifth, tenth, and twenty-fifth percentiles than by any disadvantage among the top percentiles of the respective national student populations. Again, there is a link with the gaps in socioeconomic status, represented by parent's occupation. The United States in particular is a country of greater than average inequality, most famously its inequality in income and wealth, and this inequality is mirrored in the greater inequality of U.S. test scores.

Following such clues, does the disadvantage of U.S., Belgian, German, and Swiss student populations rest in their having *ethnic groups* with lower economic status, in contrast to Japan, Finland, Korea, and Canada? There is no easy answer here. Granted, the first group has had a greater recent influx of immigrant populations not filtered by high skill requirements. Even stronger suspicions surround the United States' particular tragedy of poor school performance of its predominantly black urban schools. Can the low scores of blacks and immigrants explain away the mediocre average test performance of teenagers in the United States, Belgium, Germany, and Switzerland? Can the relative ethnic homogeneity of Japan, Korea, and Finland and some selectivity in Canadian immigration policy explain their higher and more equal scores?

The answer is not as simple as it may seem from a quick glance at group difference in scores. That glance confirms that blacks and Hispanics in the United States had lower PISA scores in all subjects than did white students. Another quick glance confirms that in many countries immigrant children test lower. Yet the magnitudes of these gaps do not seem to explain away the international differences in overall averages.

Take the stark differences between (non-Hispanic) white and black test scores among U.S. fifteen-year-olds in 2000. U.S. white students had average scores in math, reading, and science that would place them about fourth in the international ranks. A quick reaction might be that the puzzle of mediocre test scores in the United States has vanished, since it is just a reflection of the well-known tragic breakdown of U.S. school districts with heavily black and Hispanic populations. But the high international ranking of white Americans is a biased comparison. By redefining the U.S. comparison group as white and non-Hispanic, one would fall into the trap of comparing a privileged group in one country with all students in another. The unfairness of such a comparison was evident to Americans when some of the earlier international comparisons judged U.S. students unfavorably because they were out-scored by elite student groups in other countries. Symmetrically, it is unfair to compare white American test scores to other countries' national averages.

If we seek clues about systematic differences in the performance of the educational system, we should at least compare student populations with the same degree of selectivity. A rough calculation that places the white American student average on the spectrum of all U.S. test scores allows us to define comparison groups in all other countries that are about as selective, about as advantaged, as are non-Hispanic whites in the United States.[6] It turns out that U.S. whites do not rank any better relative to the counterpart advantaged groups in other countries than in the international comparisons in Table 6.2. That is, U.S. whites still rank only in the fourteenth to eighteenth range relative to similar somewhat-advantaged groups in other countries. The United States' test score mediocrity seems to transcend race. Similar results seem likely in calculations of the scores of nonimmigrants. Something not confined to race or ethnicity seems to make for international differences in test scores and keeps the United States out of the top dozen countries.

When Did This Pattern Emerge?

Was the quality of U.S. learning always just respectable by international standards? Or are there historical signs that U.S. children began to be taught, and to learn, less efficiently sometime in the twentieth century? What can test scores suggest on this historical issue?

The United States and other countries have emerged from the statistical darkness on achievement test scores only very recently. We therefore can shine only a few thin rays of light back into the statistical darkness before 1967 in the United States and almost no light for other countries. What information we have does leave a hint, but only a hint, of a special historical period in which U.S. students' learning achievements may have fallen behind.

The kind of test on which we have the longest time series is one that is not meant to reflect achievement, but one that can help us with an indirect hint about what did and did not deteriorate at times in the twentieth century. IQ test scores are available back to the 1930s for the United States. A vast literature has questioned whether IQ measures intelligence. It may just represent a fair measure of abstract problem-solving ability. Certainly it was never designed to measure the achievement of learning in the schools, and the hint that it offers us about the efficiency of learning is only indirect.

To limit the range of speculations about the quality of learning in schools, let us first note the most likely time path of those IQ scores in the United States and other countries. The underlying statistical issues are complex, even after scholars have carefully adjusted for sample biases and have translated the scales of the Stanford–Benet form, the Wechsler scale, the Ravens Progressive Matrices Test, and other tests into a common IQ scale. Yet the current weighing of the evidence suggests a simple conclusion: IQ has been creeping up monotonically in all the data-supplying countries. For whites in the United States the improvement has continued in all decades since 1932 or earlier. U.S. blacks have had at least as fast a rate of gain in the postwar period. IQ scores have also marched upward in other surveyed populations since the 1930s, specifically in parts of Canada from 1956 to 1978; among eighteen-year-old males in Belgium, France, and the Netherlands from the 1950s to the 1980s; among nineteen-year-old males in Norway from 1954 to 1968; among ten- to thirteen-year olds in New Zealand from 1936 to 1968; among Austrian six- to fifteen-year-olds from 1962 to 1979; among the same age group in Japan from 1951 to 1975; among Australians between the ages of ten and fourteen, from 1936 to 1981; and among British children ages eight to fourteen, from 1938 to 1979. The only good-data exception for an extended period was that there was no clear rise in the average IQ scores of nineteen-year-old males in Norway between 1968 and 1980.[7]

The main impact of this finding is to refute the notion that IQ is something immutable. Its bearing on our search for clues to performance in the public education sector is less direct. What the rise of IQ does suggest is that the educational system has been presented with succeeding generations of children who have ever better aptitude at basic problem solving. So any shortfall in achievement after some years of schooling looks even more serious in view of this evidence that students have a rising, or at least not declining, basic aptitude at problem solving.

Test-based time series on student curriculum learning are available in the United States only for the postwar era. We discern three or four distinct periods in the postwar trends for tested American seventeen-year-olds, as marked out in Figure 6.1. The first period is the quarter century up to 1967, for which we can view only two series here. The average verbal score on the Scholastic Aptitude Test must be viewed with great caution for this early

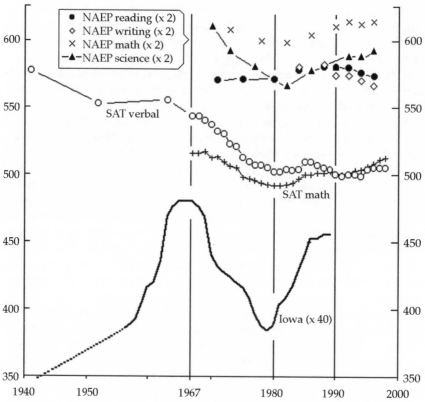

FIGURE 6.1. Some Test Score Averages for U.S. Students Around Age 17, 1941–1999.

Sources and Notes: SAT verbal and math averages: The averages, on the new scale, since 1967 come from U.S. National Center for Education Statistics (1999, 149). Verbal test average on the old scale for 1941–1963 from Flynn (1984, 37) were converted to the new scale by adding 77 points.

Iowa scores: The averages for the Iowa Test of Educational Development for twelfth-graders is extended back to 1942 and forward to 1989 with the help of John H. Bishop of Cornell and Robert A. Forsythe of the Univesity of Iowa. I have rescaled the units so that the average for 1965 = 12 (to imitate an historical twelfth-grade normal achievement). See Bishop (1989) for discussion of this series and its counterparts for the third and the eighth grades.

NAEP: The source is U.S. National Center for Education Statistics (1999, pp. 130, 136, 139, 147), which also gives results for fourth and eighth graders.

period. Its decline between 1941 and 1967 was due largely, perhaps entirely, to the transformation of the SAT from an elite test taken by less than 1 percent of seventeen-year-olds, those bound for the top universities, to one taken by over 40 percent of seventeen-year-olds. More revealing is the other early time series, the average score of seventeen-year-old students on the Iowa

Test of Educational Development. For our purposes, this series is usefully broad in one respect and usefully narrow in another. Every student in Iowa had to take the test, removing any large bias from changes in selectivity. On the other hand, the students covered by these data were all Iowans and overwhelmingly white. So for a consistent and well-understood population, we have a time series on the results of a consistent test. By 1967 Iowa twelfth graders had achieved a clear improvement over their parents' generation back in 1942, an improvement worth perhaps two years of learning in the core curriculum.

The next period, 1967–1980, is the most striking. Here the tested achievement of Iowa graduating seniors seems to have fallen by about 1.25 years of core learning, according to John Bishop's estimates.[8] The SAT scores continued to decline, even though the share of high school students taking the exam had stabilized. The mathematics and science scores of seventeen-year-olds on the National Assessment of Educational Progress (NAEP) also declined, though reading scores were stable. To interpret these declines correctly, one must note that some important groups of students did not have declining scores. Above all, students under the age of ten did not have declining scores in any documented period, either in the Iowa tests or in the NAEP tests. The 1967–1980 test-score decline, like the United States' mediocre performance at the end of the century, was apparently caused by something that happened to U.S. children *after third grade.*

The decline happened to white students. It was not due to any increase in the shortfalls in black students' test performance, which was steady or improving on the NAEP tests.[9] True, many black children were stuck in urban school systems that were breaking down in this era and later. On this, the testimony of the 1960s was already eloquent, as delivered from black schools to white readers by Herbert Kohl's *36 Children* and Jonathan Kozol's *Death at an Early Age.* Yet this tragic decay was more than offset by improvements in the schooling of most black children, for whom conditions had been even worse in the earlier segregation era,[10] nor did blacks rise enough as a share of all students to explain much of the national decline.

Any explanations of the United States' 1967–1980 decline must fit with the different trends after 1980, as sketched in Figure 6.1. Across the 1980s five out of six available scores showed improvement by seventeen-year-olds, with only the SAT verbal score lacking a clear trend. The 1990s brought a split trend for seventeen-year-olds: further improvement in mathematics and science, but a slight drop in language-related skills. Meanwhile, preteens, represented by the scores of third graders, continued their slow improvement.

What was it that made the gains in knowledge after the age of nine drop in 1967–1980, if they were improving before and after that era? And were the losses of 1967–1980 permanent, as suggested by the fact that the earlier rise in scores resumed but without any accelerated catch-up to the pre-1967 trend?

In Inputs into Education

Understanding why Americans were outstanding in their years of schooling, yet mediocre among OECD countries in their test scores at a given age, might be easier if we knew which countries put the most resources into education. It would help to distinguish countries putting more into education from countries that were more efficient at using a given resource commitment per child. Let us turn first to the implicit tax rates paid for public expenditures on education, before turning to a measure of real inputs per student or per child of school age.

Taxpayer Effort on Behalf of Education

At the end of the twentieth century, the United States ranked near the median, eleventh out of twenty countries, in terms of public education expenditures as a share of GDP. The world leaders in such taxpayer effort for public education were Denmark, Sweden, Norway, New Zealand, Austria, Finland, France, and Canada.[11] The United States was never far from its middling position in the twentieth century. Indeed, it was apparently near the middle of the ranks of the top twenty-odd countries in this tax-rate measure throughout the hundred years from the 1870s to the 1970s.[12] The only shift in our ranking came in the 1980s, when the United States scaled back its education spending during the baby bust, while other countries went on raising their tax rates on behalf of schools.

Expenditures per Student

Another common practice is to compare expenditures per student across school districts, regions, or nations. This is a staple in the "does money matter" debate over the role of resources in U.S. student achievements. Scores of studies have used measures of expenditure per student as a possible influence on achievement. Most have failed to find a significantly positive effect within one country, especially in studies at the level of the individual student.[13]

It might seem natural to contrast the expenditures per student in different countries, to see if differences in resources brought differences in student achievement. This approach would make the United States look like a big spender. As of 1998, and probably today, its expenditures per pupil were fourth highest in the world in primary schools and third highest in the world in secondary school, behind Switzerland, Austria, and (for primary school) Denmark. This extra spending fails to push these countries' tests scores to the same lofty international rank, as we have seen. A natural inference might be that extra spending just doesn't help student performance, either between nations or within nations.[14]

Yet one should avoid comparing absolute expenditures per student, without somehow scaling them to the general income levels of different countries. To see the danger here, consider two countries, the United States and

Belgium, which have different average income levels. Most occupations pay much more in the United States than in Belgium, since various sources of growth make the whole U.S. economy more productive and prosperous. For this very reason, however, teachers and other inputs into education cost more in the United States, even for the same quality. Students in the two countries could face teachers of identical quality, yet the U.S. teachers would be paid much more than the Belgian teachers. To see what students actually receive, we need to look at the real inputs, not their nominal money value.

Teaching Inputs per Student

In principle, a measure of real education inputs per student would weigh all inputs, including all supplies and facilities as well as teachers' time and skills. Yet for practical reasons we should focus just on the amount of teachers' time inputs per student and on the quality of those teachers.[15]

U.S. primary and secondary students receive a low-to-middling amount of teacher time inputs by one international standard and a rather high amount by another. The most widely reported standard is the student/teacher ratio, which we will invert, in order to look at teachers per one hundred students. By this standard the United States has a rank as undistinguished as its tests scores. The top set of rows in Table 6.3 shows that in 2000 the United States ranked tenth or worse in teachers per one hundred students. This was probably the case throughout the twentieth century.[16] Only in the nineteenth century would the United States have had one of the world's better ratios of teachers per student, presumably because this was a rich and sparsely settled country that set up schoolhouses for small local student populations. Having only a low-to-middling rank in teachers per student was not necessarily a handicap, however, for U.S. children after the middle of the twentieth century. In this country, as in all the prospering OECD countries, the ratio of teachers to students has kept improving (rising). That is, the average class size has shrunk. Studies of the effect of class size on student learning suggest that smaller class sizes – or more teachers per one hundred students – stop bringing gains once one gets to ratios better than one teacher per twenty-five students. Roughly speaking, this is a threshold that the United States and other leading countries passed around the middle of the twentieth century. Therefore having a rank of only tenth to fourteenth in the world probably did not mean that the U.S. system suffered any handicap in terms of the number of teachers per student.

Yet the number of annual hours that each teacher had contact with students, or the number of hours a student saw a teacher each year, reveals a different contrast between the Americans and most others. U.S. secondary school teachers work more hours per year than teachers in any other data-supplying country, and U.S. primary school teachers work longer hours than their counterparts in any country other than Australia and New Zealand. Combining these long hours with the low-to-middling number of teachers

TABLE 6.3. *Teachers per One Hundred Students and Teacher Pay: America's International Ranking in the Late Twentieth Century*

	America's International Ranking	
Teaching inputs per 100 students, in 1999		
Teachers per 100 students		
Elementary	10th	out of 18
Lower secondary	14th	out of 18
Upper (general) secondary	12th	out of 15
Annual teaching hours, per teacher		
Elementary	3rd	out of 23
Lower secondary	1st	out of 23
Upper (general) secondary	1st	out of 22
Annual teaching hours, per 100 students		
Elementary	5th	out of 22
Lower secondary	8th	out of 17
Upper (general) secondary	3rd	out of 17
Teachers' average annual salary		
As a percent of GDP per capita, 1984		
Elementary	9th	out of 10
Lower secondary	9th	out of 10
Upper (general) secondary	9th	out of 10
As a percent of GDP per member of the labor force, 1999, for starting teachers		
Elementary	19th–20th	out of 24
Lower secondary	21st	out of 25
Upper (general) secondary	21st	out of 24
As a percent of GDP per member of the labor force, 1999, for teachers with 15 years of experience		
Elementary	17th–18th	out of 24
Lower secondary	21st	out of 25
Upper (general) secondary	22nd	out of 24
Teachers' salary per 2000 hours of contact time, as a percent of 1999 GDP per member of labor force, for teachers with 15 years of experience		
Elementary	23rd	out of 24
Lower secondary	24th	out of 24
Upper (general) secondary	23rd	out of 23

Notes and Sources: OECD *Education at a Glance* 2001; UNESCO, *World Education Report* 1998, Tables 8, 11; Barro and Suter (1988, Table 3).

Canada and Japan are missing from the data-supplying group of countries for the year 2000.

For the study of teacher pay in 1984, the set of countries consisted of Canada, Denmark, West Germany, Japan, Korea, Netherlands, New Zealand, Sweden, the United Kingdom, and the United States.

per one hundred students yields Table 6.3's third set of rankings, those for annual teaching hours per one hundred students. On this synthetic measure, U.S. students get an above-average exposure to teaching staff, ranking third to eighth internationally at different levels of schooling.

If U.S. teachers put in more hours, without the benefit of smaller class sizes or more support staff per one hundred students, how do we evaluate the productivity contribution of those longer hours? They could either raise or lower the rate at which students learn. More hours of contact might offer students more enrichment – or less enrichment, if the long hours have a bad effect on the teachers. With longer contact hours, teachers cannot prepare as much for each hour of teaching, and their morale and enthusiasm may drop.

Teachers' Pay and Quality

What we know about the pay of primary and secondary teachers suggests that the United States might or might not have a problem. The pattern is this: Relative to teachers in other OECD countries, U.S. teachers are paid less relative to other job opportunities, even though they are paid more in absolute terms. That is, their rate of pay puts them lower on the national pay scale than their counterparts in other countries. This has led to the controversial assertion that U.S. teachers are of lower quality, because that lower pay attracts only less qualified job candidates. A recent paper by Darius Lakdawalla even said that by 1970 "teachers had become the dregs of the U.S. college population."[17]

That U.S. primary and secondary school teachers fall lower on the income scales seems clear enough. Table 6.3 ranks teachers' relative pay according to their annual salaries and their salaries per hour of contact with students. The salary itself looks low when viewed in two layers of comparison. Comparing it with the average pay per member of the labor force, and then comparing this ratio of teacher pay to general pay across countries, shows that the United States ranks near the bottom of the data-supplying countries. That was already true in 1984, and it remained true as of 1999, both for starting salaries and for the salaries of teachers with fifteen years' experience. The low relative pay of U.S. teachers stands out even more starkly if we compare salaries per hour of contact with average pay per member of the labor force. By this pay-per-hour measure, the United States ranked either last or next to last out of two dozen countries in 1999, as the bottom panel in Table 6.3 makes clear.

Is this lower relative pay a new phenomenon? U.S. scholars have tended to think so, most of them dating the relative decline of U.S. teacher pay since the 1960s or 1970s and others emphasizing the period since the late 1980s. Cohn and Geske show a decline in U.S. teacher pay in relation to personal income per capita between 1960 and 1980. Darius Lakdawalla dates the decline from the 1960s to the 1990s. He interprets the relative decline of teacher pay as something natural and not a social disgrace. It is a natural outcome of having productivity advance more rapidly outside of the teaching sector than within it, the kind of thing one should expect of an economy that has become a world leader in technology. To support this interpretation, he argues that the relative pay decline was not experienced by university professors, whose skills have kept pace with the rise of college-graduate skills in general. Caroline Hoxby also dates the relative pay decline from the late 1960s and attributes it to an increasingly negative influence of teachers' unions and the lack of school choice on pay and productivity. Peter Temin shows a decline in teachers' relative pay since 1987. He attributes this to three forces: the rise in nonteaching career opportunities for top female graduates, the negative effect of teacher unions, and the erosion of the U.S. property tax base that states and (especially) localities use to finance schools.[18]

Yet some of these attempts to capture a trend use a misleading measure. That misleading measure is the one most easily available: the ratio of teachers' pay to GDP per capita. The main flaw here is in the "per capita" part of the denominator. Why compare an employed adult's pay rate to income of a population that includes children and others who don't work? More insight comes from comparing teachers with either everybody employed, everything in the labor force, or persons in jobs that teachers might have chosen as alternatives. Choosing a better population group in the denominator, like the labor force measure used in Table 6.3, avoids misreading history. It frees the measure of teachers' relative pay from trends in the child/adult ratio and trends in the rate of labor force participation among adults. This correction *erases the decline in U.S. teachers' relative pay from around 1960 to around 1990*, a point we support again shortly.[19]

To get the story of teachers' relative pay in the right perspective, we need to reach further back into history. Concern about teachers' pay and quality is hardly new. Indeed, for at least one hundred years we have been going through cycles of declared "crises" about the pay, the supply, and the quality of U.S. teachers. The three concerns – pay, supply, and quality – have gone together in a cyclical fashion that economists would call a "cobweb." A rise in the demand for teachers makes them scarce, leading to a call for producing more teachers, raising their pay, and relaxing quality standards. This produces a surplus of teachers several years later, renewing the long-run movement to protect the existing teachers' pay by tightening up entry standards in the name of quality. When one hears that "[i]n every large city school system the provision of an adequate supply of properly prepared teachers is one of the most difficult problems with which we have to deal," it is worth remembering that exactly the same was said as far back as 1908.[20] The cycle of shortage and surplus, with attendant swings in the concern for teacher quality and salaries, was summarized by W. Timothy Weaver twenty years ago:

Three U.S. presidents (Wilson, Eisenhower, and Johnson) have made the issue of teacher shortages a matter of national urgency. Each period of "critical" shortages has been followed by a surplus, and each surplus has been followed by still another "critical" shortage. There is a sort of rhythm to this history.... There are proposals calling for cutting [teacher training] requirements and then proposals for extending them. The only consistent argument made by educators is that there never seem to be enough "well-qualified" or "superior" teachers and never enough money for decent salaries.[21]

Reaching back as far into history as the national numbers go, we find that the recent era of declining relative pay for teachers in the United States is shorter than imagined, and there is no clear trend over a century or longer. Figure 6.2 summarizes this history with a series on the annual pay for teachers in primary and secondary schools as a share of the average GDP per person in the labor force.

What should the time series show if the widespread pessimism is correct and if Lakdawalla is correct in attributing the teacher pay decline to the fact that teaching productivity growth lags behind in a high-tech economy like ours? The series should decline rather steadily over at least the second half of the twentieth century. But that did not happen, as Figure 6.2 makes clear. What teachers got paid for their eight or nine months' annual service hovered around 70 percent of GDP (or about 83 percent of average personal income) per member of the labor force from the 1950s on. Teachers made either just a bit more or just a bit less than the average income, depending on how one valued teachers' longer vacations. There were only brief periods of decline in their relative pay. The latest one dates only from 1991, not the longer period claimed by many observers. In earlier history, the only declines in teachers' relative pay were cyclical in nature, not a trend. It seems that teachers were relatively well paid during a slump, as shown for 1934, but that their relative pay took a dive in any major boom, when others got better pay gains. Looking at the past 130 years, one could not say that primary and secondary school teachers suffered any decline relative to the rest of society.[22]

In fact, there was one group of teachers that did suffer a long downward slide in relative pay. It was not the teachers of primary and secondary school, but college professors. Figure 6.2 shows that the relative pay of college teachers was (scandalously!) cut more than in half over the century. Perhaps it was college professors whose productivity stagnated more than that of primary and secondary school teachers? Probably so, though for reasons that relate to a compositional shift in college faculties. The great postwar expansion of higher education meant that the professors being paid at the end of the century were far less elite than the few who were professors and instructors back in 1910. This could cause a decline in relative pay, even if every professor were more productive than his or her counterpart a generation earlier. What happened to university faculty did not happen to some other high-paid professions, by the way, at least not in the golden age of economic growth from 1945 to 1973. In this era, physicians and dentists pulled ahead of most other professions, and engineers and accountants also

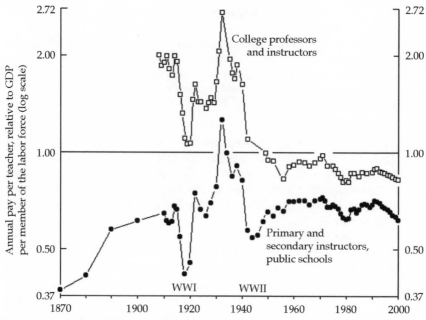

FIGURE 6.2. The Relative Pay of American Teachers since 1870.

Sources and Notes: Note three reasons why these ratios look lower than one might expect:

(1) The numerators are rates of pay per academic year, usually only about 9 months' work or less.

(2) The denominator is all of GDP per member of the labor force, not just personal income per member of the labor force. The latter, about 83 percent of GDP in 1929 and 84 percent of GDP in 2000, is a more appropriate denominator but is not available for years before World War I.

(3) The denominator is also an average income, not a median income. It therefore includes some very high personal incomes.

Elementary and secondary teachers: For 1869–1998, U.S. National Center for Education Statistics (NCES) (2000, 51, 85). For 1999 and 2000, I spliced onto this base the figures from U.S. Census Bureau (2001, 1251). The eventual base is "all instructional staff," 1869–1970, as reported by both U.S. Census (1976, 375–6) and U.S. NCES (2000, 51).

For GNP per capita, 1929–2000: http:// www.bea.doc.gov/bea/dn/nipaweb/ Table 8.7, last accessed 28 February 2003. For 1929, Balke–Gordon implies GNP/ capita = 853 vs. 857 from www.bea.doc.gov. I have used the Balke–Gordon series, un-spliced, for 1869–1929.

All college teachers, 1929–1970, U.S. Census Bureau (1976, 175–176); all faculty and Associate Professors, 1970/1 – 1997/8, U.S. NCES (2000, 276). For 1999 and 2000, I spliced on the series from U.S. Census Bureau (2001, 173), using a simple average of public and private series. For 1929–52 the series refers to large public institutions only.

Associate professors: For public universities only 1908–72, Willis L. Peterson and Joseph C. Fitzharris, "The Organization and Productivity of the Federal-state Research System in the United States," University of Minnesota, Department of Agricultural and Applied Economics, Staff Paper P74-23 (October 1974). For 1908–42, rose relative to university professors. These nonacademic professions have held onto their pay advantages since 1973.

If U.S. primary and secondary school teachers did not decline in their overall relative pay, what was the history of their pay disadvantage relative to teachers in other countries? Were they always behind or is that a recent development? Truly international clues for resolving this issue are hard to come by for any time before 1984. It might have been true that the United States was lower than most OECD countries in its relative pay for primary and secondary teachers *throughout* the twentieth century, not just in the postwar period covered by recent writings on the subject. So suggests evidence for the year 1910. Among ten countries yielding sufficient data for that year, the United States apparently ranked only about seventh in the ratio of teacher salary rates to GDP per capita.[23]

If teachers get paid relatively less in the United States, is it because they are of a lower quality than teachers in other countries? This is a difficult controversy to resolve, despite at least a century of U.S. concern and debate about a perceived decline in teacher quality. If you believe that teacher quality is proportional to absolute pay, overlooking the point made earlier about different pay equilibria in different countries, then you might think that U.S. teachers are revealed to have a higher average quality. If you judge quality according to relative pay, you get the opposite conclusion.

Setting aside pay evidence in favor of direct data on qualifications, one finds recent evidence that U.S. primary and secondary school teachers have more education credentials than teachers in most countries.[24] Perhaps that was always true. If so, we need to work out two contradictions. First, how could U.S. teachers of the same quality as in other countries be paid less in relation to national average income? Second, how can we reconcile the suggestion of no decline in teacher quality with the frequent view that U.S. teachers are declining in quality?

The first contradiction is easily resolved. Separate countries have their own separate price environments, so that a productive input of the same quality can reap different rewards. There is nothing implausible about U.S. teachers getting paid differently from teachers of the same quality in other countries – just as the same quality of land, equipment, wood, or a mineral can have different prices in different countries. As a rich, high-technology country since at least the late nineteenth century, the United States can quite plausibly have teachers that are paid more in absolute terms, but who are paid less relative to the high rewards elsewhere in this economy.

FIGURE 6.2. (*continued*) their source is George Stigler, "Employment and Compensation in Education," NBER Occasional Paper no. 33, 1950. For 1948–72, they drew from the American Association of University Professors, Bulletin, various years.

Splicing the "college teacher" series: I used the all-college-teacher series back to its beginning in 1929, then spliced the associate-professor series for public universities back to 1908 onto the 1929–2000 series.

The contradiction with others' assertions about historically declining quality in U.S. teachers is also easily resolved. First, much of the tradition of saying the United States has a teacher quality problem boils down to nothing more than a sense that we would like to raise that quality, for the sake of the children. It is not based on firm evidence of a historic decline. Even the best, most recent evidence on teachers' qualifications is historically shallow and shows only that the skills and rewards of many high-paying occupations rose strongly, especially in the 1990s. While Lakdawalla provides some indirect evidence suggesting a decline in teachers' relative education, other studies disagree. No great decline emerges with the in-depth study by the research team of Sean Corcoran, William Evans, and Robert Schwab. To find out whether the academic qualifications of those entering teaching careers were really falling over time, relative to the qualifications of others with some college education, this research team has combined data on succeeding cohorts' schooling and career development. Compared to a woman entering a teaching career around 1964, the average new female teacher around 1992 was only slightly less qualified, as judged by her test-score percentile. The slight overall decline in average test scores was driven largely by a decline in the top ranks. That is, many fewer women with top test scores entered teaching. Yet the overall net change was slight.[25] Furthermore, the trend did not worsen across the 1980s and early 1990s, as Dale Ballou and Michael Podgursky have pointed out.[26]

Finally, the history of the teaching profession reveals another way in which U.S. teachers may have been of comparable quality to teachers elsewhere despite their being paid less relative to the average occupation. In all countries, women's share of the teaching profession has long been constrained by social biases. While the barriers lasted, those women that broke through them were presumably of higher quality relative to male teachers than their annual pay revealed. North America led the world in the feminization of teaching. As of 1900, the female share of primary school teachers was already 79 percent in Canada and 70 percent in the United States, with the northeastern states having taken the lead. No European country hired women as much. Today all leading countries hire mainly women teachers, with North America only slightly more feminized than the OECD average. Yet until recently the earlier shift to hiring women was one of the secrets to North America's being able to create human capital so cheaply.[27]

SUMMING UP THE UNITED STATES' SYMPTOMS

Looking at the whole album of snapshots from the end of the twentieth century, we can see ways in which the United States does or does not stand out. Figure 6.3 depicts some of the highlights, using bar graphs that run from lowest rank to highest rank in the international league tables.

On the output side, the United States leads in quantity of schooling but not in quality. Its educational attainment is matched only by Canada's, though

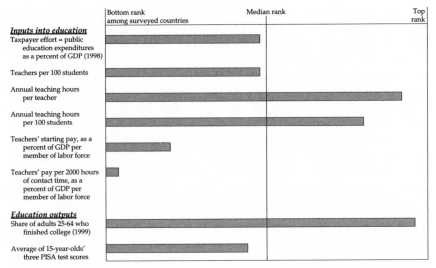

FIGURE 6.3. A Summary of the International Standing of American Primary and Secondary Education in 1999.

Sources and Notes: See Tables 6.1–6.3 and the sources cited there.

Each international ranking is summarized in bar-graph form as follows. Let N = the number of countries surveyed. Let R = the U.S. ranking among those N surveyed countries, from 1 = top rank to N = bottom. Each bar shows a ranking achievement equal to the formula $1 - ((R - 1)/(N - 1))$, so that achieving the top rank graphs as 1 and occupying the bottom (Nth) rank graphs as a zero.

Where Table 6.2 gave teaching inputs and teachers' pay for each of three levels of schooling, the one graphed here refers to elementary schooling. As Table 6.2's numbers confirm, the primary or secondary level of schooling chosen makes little difference in the international ranking of the United States.

"Finished college" here means completion of any tertiary-education program, as defined by OECD.

Note that the public expenditure share and the share of adults finishing college both refer to all three levels of education, even though they are displayed here as symptoms of primary and secondary education.

The figure for "teachers' pay per 2,000 hours of contact time, as a percent of GDP per member of the labor force" refers to teachers with 15 years of experience, the result would be essentially the same for starting teachers, however.

other countries will gain ground in the early twenty-first century. The quality dimension, however, serves some warnings about the process of primary and secondary schooling in the United States. The United States' relative test-score performance seems to drop off between age nine and age seventeen. At ages nine and ten the scores show no clear signs of any trouble in the students that will present themselves as raw material to middle schools. They ranked well enough internationally in the 1980s and 1990s, and there was no period of decline in their scores anytime since the earliest national data in the 1950s. Yet U.S. children's relative performance slipped increasingly as they advanced through middle and secondary school. Was that always the case? If one searches for an earlier time period in which the United States' teenage scores might have fallen in the world ranks, the most visible candidate would be between the twelfth-grade student cohorts of 1967 and 1980. We do not know, however, whether students in other countries also declined in their achievements in the same era.

On the input side, Figure 6.3 reminds us that the most striking contrasts relate to the teaching environment. As of 1999, U.S. primary and secondary teachers had several disadvantages to offset their being from a rich country. Each of these disadvantages relative to other OECD countries was more serious for secondary school teachers than for primary. Specifically:

- U.S. teachers worked longer contact hours than most, especially in secondary school.
- U.S. teachers had lower pay relative to the economy as a whole and to the other professions. This disadvantage was also more severe in secondary school than in primary school.

What could explain this combination of symptoms? There are too many possibilities to resolve here. We can, however, come up with some straightforward suggestions that are frugal in the sense of using only a very few systematic forces to explain this whole set of symptoms.

The search for causal explanations cannot be a pioneering one, since public debate over the quality of U.S. public schooling has already pointed fingers in different directions. The debate and the blame center on teaching, with teachers acting as plaintiffs in some accusations and as defendants in others. While the range of alleged culprits is as boundless as the human imagination, we need to look at three leading possibilities here: blame society for underrewarding teachers, blame bureaucracy and teacher unions for restricting choice and productivity, and assert that some or all of the problems are illusory.

For leaders of U.S. teachers' unions, the key symptom and the cure are both obvious. America's teachers are paid too little, they are worked too hard, and they are given too little support and authority in the classroom. So say the American Federation of Teachers (AFT) and the National Education Association, which team up to form one of the strongest lobbies in the corridors of Congress and a top contributor to election campaigns for Democrats. Not surprisingly, a study sponsored by the AFT buttressed this conclusion by citing that U.S. teachers faced longer hours and lower pay, as a percentage of GDP, than their counterparts in other countries.[28]

An alternative view blames teacher unions, collective bargaining, and bureaucracy. This view has fed the voucher movement, which continues to push for public funding of vouchers that parents can use in any public or private school, even a religious school. There is no denying that U.S. public schools are constrained by centralized rules and collective bargaining. The key empirical question is whether these institutions have dragged down student achievement. A careful study by Caroline Hoxby supports this view, blaming the strength of teacher unions and collective bargaining for accepting, and even imposing, a pay structure designed to protect mediocrity, even if it means having lower average salaries.[29] Later in this chapter we return to her U.S. evidence, and some related international evidence, on the role of unions.

Perhaps at least part of the problem is not a problem at all. Perhaps it is just a natural by-product of success in high-tech development, as the recent provocative study by Darius Lakdawalla claims.[30] While not all of his evidence is persuasive, we must take his reminder that teacher pay can look low in an economy where other careers are in demand and have shown faster growth in productivity.

THE UNDERLYING INCENTIVE ISSUES

To come to grips with this odd set of patterns, it helps to start with an economist's usual preferences for how the education industry should be managed in the best of worlds. Viewed from this ideal starting point, we can quickly see which problems were solved by the United States, which were solved by other countries, and which are not well solved by any countries.

Most economists share clear preferences about how to design institutions that give people the right incentives. We tend to advocate institutions that

- offset external costs or benefits, and
- promote competition where it has a chance to work.

To offset externalities, economists usually favor using taxes to cure the bad incentives that create external costs and using subsidies to cure the bad incentives that create external benefits.[31] We also like competition as a preferred institution for revealing what works and what doesn't. In some cases, however, we retreat to central regulation and law enforcement where competition doesn't work.

These two principles are central to the difficult social task of getting the right amount, and the right kind, of education. The first principle, that of offsetting externalities, has been applied by governments for the past two centuries, with fair success in getting the right *amount* of education. Yet we still lack any easy tax-subsidy solution to the problem of getting the best *kind* of education, as agonizing debates in the late twentieth century have shown. For this tougher task, some countries have tried to use the competition principle. In a complicated world, make school districts compete for teachers and for students. Make teachers compete for good students and good pay. Make students compete for the right to stay in school, by showing discipline. Above all, let students and their parents be sovereign consumers, choosing among schools.

Milton Friedman said that. Like Adam Smith and Thomas Jefferson, Friedman endorsed government funding of primary and secondary education, because there were external benefits, or "neighborhood effects," of providing basic education for citizenship. Like most economists, he rightly challenged the idea that the government had to provide that education itself. His famous call for vouchers envisioned government funding of both private and public schools by giving the school money to parents. The role of the government should be confined to enforcing curriculum standards and preventing the kind of religious schools that would be divisive. Friedman felt that the programs for the education of U.S. veterans after World War II illustrated his point.[32] In fact, as we shall see, he could have chosen more apt illustrations from other countries. Some of Europe's welfare states have developed school systems closer to what Friedman wanted than have the Americans.

Quantity Incentives versus Quality Incentives

An individual's schooling has a time dimension and an intensity dimension. Its time dimension is the number of years a student continues to advance in school. Its intensity dimension is the value of inputs, in teachers' paid time and supporting materials, devoted to the instruction of each student each year. The quantitative needs of schooling are easier to diagnose and easier to supply than the sources of greater quality in the schooling received by each student each year.

The sources of greater quantity of schooling time are relatively transparent. These sources have been neatly summarized by a long tradition of discussing and measuring the rates of return on extra years of education. We know that the private incentive to get extra years of education depends on the after-tax income gains the economy offers to those with the extra schooling and on the privately borne costs of getting that extra schooling. The income gains depend in turn on the economy's demand for the extra skills that schooling bestows, and the costs of getting the extra years of schooling depend mainly on how much taxpayers subsidize those extra years and how many students are allowed access to these subsidies.

The sources of extra years of schooling have historically been as transparent to governments and the general populace as they have been to scholars. Where there was a will to use tax money to keep children in school, children stayed in school longer. Chapter 5 had a fairly straightforward explanation for international differences in enrollments in the nineteenth century. The keys to success on the quantity of schooling front were relatively easy to find: Have taxpayers foot most of the bill and have the economy and society be receptive to anybody acquiring the skills that come with extra years in school. Accordingly, country after country ended up subsidizing the quantity of schooling: The more time the average child spends in schools, the greater the subsidy they received.

The twentieth century brought us face to face with a difficulty that was there all along: It is much harder to agree on the sources of the *quality* of instruction a student receives each year, largely because it is hard to measure that quality itself and to design institutions that promote higher-quality instruction. How should parents and society measure the output, the human capital gain, from different educational inputs? The traditional market solution of having consumers themselves evaluate the quality of the product, and shift their patronage to better suppliers, is quite difficult in the sector supplying primary and secondary education. At the university level, by contrast, the student consumers are mature. They have a fair idea about the usefulness of instruction, and their preferences are expressed both in teaching evaluations and in their switching from one campus to another. The same mechanisms do not work so well at lower levels of education, because it is harder for students to convey, and for parents to interpret, differences in the quality of instruction.

What kinds of institutions address this basic problem of assessing and rewarding quality of instruction? How do international differences in these incentive-relevant institutions help us unlock the puzzle of the United States' apparent shortfall in the quality of primary and secondary education at the end of the twentieth century?

Student Accountability

Critics of U.S. education performance argue that we need accountability in the form of central exams that test what students have learned from the curriculum. U.S. students are less subject to such exams than students in other OECD countries. To be sure, U.S. students do take a wide array of standardized exams. All of them take various minimum competency exams, and those seeking admission to college usually take either the Scholastic Assessment Test (SAT-1 and SAT-2) or the American College Testing (ACT) exam. Yet none of these, with the exception of the optional and underemphasized SAT-2, is a comprehensive curriculum-based achievement test or tests what a student has learned from the curriculum beyond minimum levels. Critics argue that the lack of such exams in most states has dulled learning incentives.[33]

A growing number of countries have begun to emulate the curriculum-based external exit exams (CBEEEs) taken by students around the ages of thirteen and seventeen. There is a whole spectrum of CBEEE institutions, ranging from mandatory national tests to no test at all. As of 1997, countries grouped themselves according to mathematics and science testing as shown in Table 6.4.

TABLE 6.4. *Countries Which Had Central Exams Testing Math and Science Achievement for Thirteen-Year-Olds in the 1990s*

- At least 31 countries had national curriculum-based external exit examinations (CBEEEs): Bulgaria, Czech Republic, Denmark, England, Finland, Hong Kong, Hungary, Indonesia, Iran, Ireland, Israel, Italy, Japan, Jordan, Korea, Lithuania, Malaysia, Moldova, Morocco, Netherlands, New Zealand, Russia, Scotland, Singapore, Slovak Republic, Slovenia, South Africa, Taiwan, Thailand, Tunisia, and Turkey.
- At least four countries had national tests in mathematics but not science: France, Iceland, Norway (science for 30% of students), and Romania.
- At least four countries had CBEEEs for only part of the national student body: Australia (81% of students took the CBEEEs), Canada (51%), Germany (35%), and the United States (7%).
- At least eight countries had no CBEEEs: Austria, Belgium, Chile, Colombia, Cyprus, Greece, Kuwait, Macedonia, Philippines, Portugal, Spain, Switzerland.

Sources: Woessmann (2002b, Table 1), and Bishop (1997).

The emerging international evidence says the critics are right. That is, having a regional or national curriculum exam leads to better performance on the part of both schools and students, as reflected in scores on separate international tests. So says the evidence from international math and science tests in the mid-1990s, presented in separate studies by John Bishop and Ludger Woessmann.[34] The evidence comes in several forms. The fact that some Canadian students were subject to CBEEEs in the mid-1990s and others are not allowed Bishop to estimate the effects of provincial exit exams on students' achievements, on school administrators' behavior, and on home behavior and attitudes in the mid-1990s. The effects look large enough to make a case for the central exams. Students subject to the exams had higher average scores by about four-fifths of a U.S. grade-level equivalent in mathematics and by about three-fifths of a grade level in science. They shifted their time from TV watching to educational activities. School administrators in central-exam schools took steps to sharpen teacher qualifications and to extend classroom hours in mathematics and science.

International statistical tests seemed to agree with the achievement results from Canadian provinces. Both a modest sample of fifteen nations or regions and a study of forty-one nations agree that having national exit exams raises test scores on the separate international tests of mathematics and science. While more tests should be forthcoming soon, these early results do suggest a link from national accountability to learning – and to productivity in adult careers.[35]

So far there seems to be clear sailing for the idea that centrally administered achievement exams improve student performance. The main mechanism surely works through the student, the student's parents, and the universities and employers that the student will face. National exams send clearer signals of a student's achievement than course grades alone, especially once grade inflation has destroyed much of the signaling value of course grades, as in the United States. Students and their parents apparently respond to this, improving students' average performance even at earlier ages, such as the international tests administered to thirteen-year-olds. Through this mechanism alone, there seems to be a strong case for central subject-matter achievement tests (CBEEEs).

Less certain is the current policy task of using central exams to improve the performances of schools and school districts. Having national and regional exams would be more effective if schools received the signal that students' poor performance would be costly to them. How should such a signal be sent to schools, supplementing student accountability with school accountability? One channel is through the individual student's freedom of school choice. The money could automatically follow the student migrating from district to district. If the amount of money a poor school loses with student emigration exceeds the marginal cost of retaining the extra student, the school should respond by improving its performance to retain mobile students. As we shall see shortly, this individual-student resource mechanism operates more widely in some other countries than in the United States.

An alternative mechanism works through governments' punishing poor schools directly by cutting their budget in response to poor aggregate exam scores. The latter mechanism, divorced from individual student choice, is currently in effect in some U.S. states and is mandated by the No Child Left Behind Act of 2001. Central monitoring through aggregate test scores may or may not work as well as individual student choices, however. In its favor is the fact that central monitoring doesn't force individual students or families to move in order to get better performance from their school. Yet disciplining school districts directly may be inferior to subsidizing individual choice through vouchers. There are many pitfalls in setting the formula for punishing (or rewarding) schools. The formula could fail to help those whose individual exit options were constrained by the current system, just by choosing the wrong school-grading formula between levels of test scores, changes in test scores, and either levels or changes conditioned on measures of how "disadvantaged" the student population was. Comparisons of the likely effects of different formulas suggest that the voucher approach may be better, with its discipline delivered through losses or gains in government subsidies tied to individual students' enrollment choices.[36]

Competition among Schools

Not surprisingly, concerns about the quality of U.S. education have encouraged advocacy of the school choice and voucher solution since the 1960s, among conservatives, among religious groups, and among economists. The idea of vouchers and school choice has also established a strong constituency among African-American parents trying to free their children from some of the worst of U.S. school systems.[37]

When and where has school choice really functioned and has it really improved the quality of instruction? Let us turn to four kinds of experiences: (1) The broad sweep of the United States' historical experience with varying degrees of parental freedom to choose schools, (2) careful studies of recent local U.S. experiments with limited school choice, (3) a California deviation away from school choice, (4) the greater choice offered in higher education, and (5) a surprising international perspective on where school choice operates today.

The Long Sweep of U.S. School Choice

Many might imagine that U.S. parents were given more choice over their children's schooling in the past than parents have in today's ponderous public school systems. Chapter 5 might even have nurtured that imagination, by stressing the success of decentralized schooling in the U.S. non-South. Yet the degree of school choice probably rose across the first half of the twentieth century, before declining in the second half. Back in the nineteenth century, parents could not shop freely for schools. In a less populated and less prosperous continent, our ancestors had a hard time picking up and moving from one community to another just because they disapproved of the only school in their community. That decision probably became easier for prosperous suburbanites in densely populated metropolitan areas across the twentieth century.

A subtle but apparently powerful mechanism raising choice, competition, and school efficiency in suburban United States has been the "Tiebout mechanism." As Charles Tiebout theorized in the 1950s, people choose their governments at the local level. Some prefer higher taxes that pay for better schools and other local public goods, and others do not. Thus in a major metropolitan area, with many suburbs to choose from, people vote with their feet. Those that highly value the extra tax-financed public goods gravitate toward living in the higher-budget localities, while those who are more antitax move in the opposite direction.[38]

Tiebout's story of local choice has a happy implication for efficient financing and operation of schools. Young couples that are going to move into their first house will sort themselves out among suburbs partly on the basis of their taste for spending more for schools. As William Fischel has said, in the decentralized Tiebout world of shopping for the local government you like, a good local school system makes even childless oldsters willing to pay the extra taxes for schools, because they will be compensated through their property values:

The genius of American public education at the local level provides a financial incentive for people to support the education of other people's children.... It also supplies an additional incentive for local taxpayers to monitor the performance of educators.

Capitalization of the benefits of education into individual property values makes it rational for even childless people ... to offer support for education.[39]

The high water mark for freedom of school choice for white Americans was probably reached around 1950, when young couples chose among fast-growing suburbs in the early postwar housing boom. For African Americans, that freedom rose only more slowly across the second half of the century. Yet through the entire history, U.S. school choice was limited by a constraint that we return to shortly: Public subsidies served only public schools, not private schools.

A historical force restricting the freedom of school choice has been the rise of centralization in school administration. This tendency dates back at least to the consolidations and standardization of common schools in the 1830s. It presumably derived its strength from the growing political power of the education lobby itself. Most of the centralization, however, seems to have come in the second half of the twentieth century. Its history has been gradual and hard to summarize. One fair measure for the complex centralization of rules, and the loss of parents' choice among schools, is the amalgamation of schools into fewer and fewer school districts across the land. Granted, the locus of restrictive policies does not coincide neatly with the boundaries of school districts. Yet we are probably given a fair hint about the decline of school choice by following the historical curve for the number of U.S. school districts shown in Figure 6.4. Between 1940 and 1970 the number of separate public school districts plunged about 85 percent, while the number of students soared. There has been no proliferation of districts since 1970.

The fact that it is harder and harder for a family to escape a school district would not bring much harm as long as school quality is upheld in the increasingly large districts. Yet more concentrated school districts may have combined with a second force to restrict students' school choices and dampen the productivity of educational inputs. That second force is the spread of state legislation facilitating the rise of teachers' unions. As shown in Figure 6.4, the period from 1960 to 1974 saw a jump in the share of states where laws facilitated collective bargaining and permitted teacher unions to strike under certain conditions. By 1988, when only 19 percent of the U.S. labor force was unionized, fully 75 percent of public school teachers belonged to unions.[40] It is possible that the centralization of districts contributed to the mobilization of teacher unions, as in Kenneth Galbraith's "bigness begets bigness" explanation of the earlier rise of organized labor. Standard economic reasoning would expect that the combination of local producer monopolies and union strength could raise costs to captive student consumers.

A recent study by Caroline Hoxby finds three kinds of hints of this negative interaction in school district data between 1972 and 1992. First, unions directly raised the student dropout rate, a key measure of bad performance. Second, highly concentrated school districts seem to be the ones where

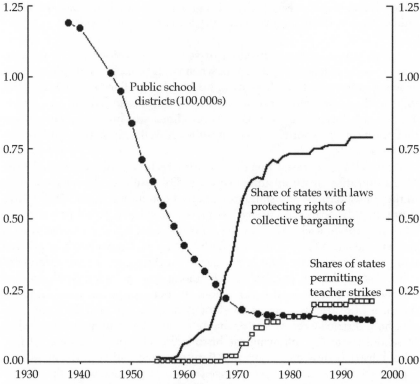

FIGURE 6.4. Public School District Consolidation and the Rise of Laws Enabling Teachers' Unions in the U.S. 1938–1996.

Sources and Notes: The number of public elementary and secondary school districts in the United States comes from U.S. National Center for Education Statistics, *Digest of Education Statistics 1999* (2000, 97).

The collective bargaining and strike variables are drawn from an update of the NBER Public Sector Collective Bargaining Law Data Set. I am indebted to Kim Rueben of the California Public Policy Institute for her supplying the updated version extending the 1955–1984 data set up through 1996. For the original data set, see www.nber.org/data/nber collection, and some further details of the variable coding in Valletta and Freeman (1988).

The collective bargaining rights variable is a transformation of the original Valletta–Freeman codes for the same variable, summed over the states and divided by fifty to create a zero-to-one range. Their "no provision" and "collective bargaining prohibited" have been coded as zero; their categories for "employer authorized but not required to bargain with union," "right to present proposals," and "right to meet and confer" are coded as 0.5; and their two "duty to bargain" categories are coded as 1.0.

The right to strike variable is also a transformation of Valletta–Freeman codes and is again summed over the states and divided by fifty. Their "no provision" and "prohibited" categories become zeroes and their "permitted (with qualifications)" becomes a 1.0.

unionization adds more to the student dropout rate. Finally, unionization seems to lower the effectiveness of other inputs (teachers per one hundred students and teacher salaries), so that union power raises the dropout rate even though it raises teacher jobs and teacher pay. The results are not over-powering statistically, but they have suggestive power. They may help to ex-plain why so many other studies found that the effectiveness of extra school inputs seemed to drop from the student cohorts that went to school before 1960 to those in school after 1960.[41] The combination of large districts and rent-seeking unions may have limited school performance and school choice. The historical timing of unionization in Iowa, for example, does slightly pre-cede the timing of the slump in Iowa test scores shown earlier in Figure 6.1.

Even if the choice-restricting effect of union power was only hinted at in Hoxby's 1972–1992 evidence, the effect seems obvious on the political front. The American Federation of Teachers and the National Education Association spend considerable resources fighting any legislation that would facilitate school choice, especially legislation that would allow parents to spend vouchers in private schools.

Analyses of Local Experience with School Choice

Detailed statistical analyses that look at both traditional competition and special policy experiments in U.S. localities seem to point in the same direc-tion. The first kind of evidence comes from traditional competition between schools, rather than a special pilot experiment. U.S. metropolitan areas differ enough in the ease of student mobility between public schools, or between public and private schools, to allow tests of the effect of school competition on reading and math scores in eighth and twelfth grades. Both kinds of tra-ditional competition, public–public and private–public, seem to raise the test scores.[42] Similarly, a study of fourth through sixth graders in Texas in the mid-1990s found that students who switched among public schools made better grade-to-grade gains on the Texas Assessment of Academic Skills, other things equal. Note that Texas in the mid-1990s was a case combining school choice and student accountability. The underlying mechanism seems to have been that competition raised teacher performance.[43]

The limited local experiments in school choice in the United States also seem to show a favorable effect on test scores when the experiment runs long enough and the analysis is able to hold the right things equal. In Michigan in the 1990s competition from charter schools seems to have improved the math and reading scores of fourth and seventh graders in Michigan's public schools. In Wisconsin between 1996 and 2000, students in the Milwaukee school voucher experiment experienced greater gains on tests in several sub-jects relative to a Wisconsin non-Milwaukee control group, other things equal.[44]

The case for greater competition among school districts thus looks quite strong at the local level. As an explanation of what happened to the whole nation, it retains some of that strength, but must compete with other causal explanations.

In particular, that visible slump in 1967–1980 may have been due in part to other forces. As noted at the start of this chapter, there is a long list of usual suspects specific to this era. In particular, we should not overlook a demographic pressure that may have affected these cohorts of students more in the United States than in other countries. This was the baby boom, which was more pronounced in the United States than in other OECD countries. The baby boomers are the famous cohort of children born 1945–1963, entering school 1950–1968, and being tested in twelfth grade in 1962–1980. In several ways, they may have received lower home inputs and lower school inputs per child than the general drift toward greater inputs per child would have implied. On the home front, for example, they were raised in larger families, which lowered the inputs of time and money they received.

In the 1950s and 1960s the baby boomers also suffered a dent in the long-run trend in the educational support ratio, measured as educational expenditures per child five to nineteen divided by income per adult. In general, that support ratio rises very elastically with the growth in income per adult. Yet its income elasticity was marked lower in the baby boom wave. If the baby boom children received below-trend inputs both at home and at school, then those twelfth graders tested in 1962 through 1980 should have had a below-trend performance on average.

The timing of the slump in test scores, from the twelfth graders of 1967 to those of 1980, fits imperfectly with either the baby boom story or the story that blames the rise of teacher unions and centralized school systems. For its part, the baby boom story does not fit so well with the fact that twelfth graders' test scores were *declining* from a 1967 peak to a 1980 trough, instead of staying uniformly low 1962–1980. It does jibe well enough, however, with the slight improvement from the 1980s through the 1990s, when the baby bust children were finishing high school. On the other hand, the story blaming unions and centralized school systems has to explain why the deterioration in performance stopped in 1980. It might be supplemented by the (unproven) hypothesis that either reforms came after 1980 or long-run trend forces continued to improve achievement scores as well as IQ scores, so that the deterioration relative to trend has remained in place ever since the 1960s. Since both the baby boom story and the story blaming unions and centralization are also supported by microeconomic evidence, I tentatively assume that both played roles in the drop in U.S. education performance from 1967 to 1980.

Deviant California

One of history's best illustrations of the Tiebout choice mechanism's effect on schooling is a case in which the mechanism was dramatically disabled. In the event, the blow was struck not by any ban on migration, but by a virtual ban on offering better than average public schools, which removed the incentive to migrate in search of better public education.

The ability of Californians to move to places where they liked the schools was dealt a serious blow by the California Supreme Court in its two Serrano judgments. In *Serrano v. Priest* 1971 (alias Serrano I), the Court prohibited the use of the local property tax as a basis for funding schools. The court deplored the fact that reliance on local property taxes gave rich Beverly Hills much better schools than Baldwin Park in impoverished East Los Angeles. In a follow-up decision of 1977 (known as Serrano II), the Court ruled that the state must administer all California schools on a fairly rigid cost-equalization formula: General-purpose spending on education must not vary by more than $100 per pupil across districts.[45] By itself, this decision would have given parents less difference in public schools and therefore less reason to move in search of better ones.

The most important consequence of the *Serrano* decisions, however, was California's famous Proposition 13 in June 1978, which was passed within a year of Serrano II. This classic taxpayer's revolt slashed the property tax permanently. Voters voted two-to-one in favor of Proposition 13 in response to three developments: their property tax assessments were soaring in the inflationary 1970s, the state government began to run a huge surplus, and the *Serrano* decisions meant that their extra property taxes could not go to their local schools. With all funds for schooling going to the state instead of to local students, why go on paying those taxes? As one California legislator sarcastically put it, "This is the revenge of wealth against the poor. 'If the schools must actually be equal,' they are saying, 'then we'll undercut them all.'"[46]

Serrano had an additional political effect that prevented any more moderate tax-and-schooling solution. The state legislature considered giving property owners some tax relief to head off the looming threat of Proposition 13, but abandoned the attempt in the face of *Serrano*. The court would have probably overruled their tax relief because it went to taxpayers in proportion to their property values, contrary to the *Serrano* decisions. Thus the egalitarian *Serrano* judgments led to a huge cut in property taxes and funds for local schools, leaving devastated local governments newly reliant on aid from the state.[47]

What were the effects of *Serrano* and Proposition 13 on California children's performance? California's inputs per student certainly fell relative to those in other states. By the 1990s California had perhaps the most crowded classrooms in the nation. Its real expenditures per pupil also were dropping through the ranks. Of the fifty states California's expenditure per pupil in average daily attendance ranked seventeenth in 1970, before *Serrano*; then twenty-second in 1980, soon after Proposition 13; then thirty-fifth in 1990; and thirty-ninth by 1996. From 1994 on, the average student in California received less support than the average student in Texas.[48]

By itself, the clear relative decline in inputs per student does not show any damage to the education of California children. If there were no evidence that this state history has led to lower test scores or more dropouts, then an antitax rebel could gleefully point to the combination of clear spending cuts and unclear effects on children as evidence that Proposition 13 merely eliminated waste.

The damage done to test scores and dropout rates seems clear from indirect evidence. California's test scores in the 1990s looked suspiciously low for one of the nation's richest states: The state ranked between forty-first and forty-seventh in eighth-grade math and science tests, usually below Texas and Arizona, which had similar immigrant proportions. The Texas – California differences in test scores have now been statistically linked to differences in school funding and class sizes.[49]

Another fair test has been offered by David Figlio. Using interstate evidence rather than evidence restricted to California, Figlio examines the effects of states' tax limitations and school equalization constraints on educational inputs and outputs in a cross-section of 6,100 schools in 1987–1991. He finds that such limitations on local freedom to supply better schools did indeed lower eighth-grade test scores in math, reading, science, and social studies. On the input side, the tax limitations lowered teacher salaries, while raising class sizes and administrative costs per student.[50] One could choose not to be persuaded by these results. It would be better to have a panel of data that actually spanned the time period in which the equalization formulae and budget limitations were imposed. Still, there is at least good *prima facie* evidence that rulings like *Serrano* and budget slashing like Proposition 13 did harm students in California and several other states, by stifling local attempts to improve schools with extra tax revenues. While parents still technically had the right to move to localities with better schools, those schools were forbidden to offer more resources per pupil.

Choice in Higher Education

Does the virtue of competition make a case for college vouchers, with taxpayers subsidizing students to attend Stanford instead of Berkeley? There are at least three reasons why competition and choice have less need for subsidy in higher education than in primary and secondary schooling. First, the individual consumers are informed adults. They gather data and shop around, with or without consulting the *U.S. News and World Report* guide to colleges. Their written evaluations of their college teachers actually affect the teachers' pay, and they frequently transfer from one institution to another in a huge market. Second, the public sector is already a much smaller share of total supply in higher education and even of the distribution of government and philanthropic aid. Much of the strength of the voucher idea for primary and secondary schools is that it helps counter the choice-stifling dominance of large, and often dysfunctional, public school districts. Large state universities have no such dominance even in their home states. Indeed, the different campuses of the same state university system compete against each other for students and for faculty. Third, the externality argument is weaker at the highest level, as Milton Friedman argued. The basic citizenship externalities that make all taxpayers want universal primary education lack urgency for adult students. Such arguments seem to have prevailed in the policies of prosperous democracies, though Third World governments have often oversubsidized higher education at the expense of primary.[51]

Subsidized School Choice in Other Countries

The United States is in fact firmer than other OECD countries in its rejection of public funding that students can take between school districts and between the public and private sectors. Other OECD countries offer students and parents more school choice, though not as a result of any bold new experiment with vouchers of the sort debated in the United States. Rather, greater school choice has evolved in some countries of continental Europe mainly through historical compromises in the long fight over schools, churches, and the state.

The parting of the ways, with the United States refusing to subsidize religious schools and some European countries allowing such subsidies, emerged from the randomness of national histories. Our Constitution and our history have placed the United States at the end of the spectrum dominated by secular public schools. The First Amendment's protection of religious freedoms has come to mean a rigidly secular public school system. Subsidies to religious schools threaten to open a Pandora's box of legal fights. Only in October 2001 did the Supreme Court signal a cautious shift in favor of using government school vouchers for religious schools. On a five-to-four vote it approved of Cleveland's voucher program for children wanting to leave badly performing schools, on the grounds that the school was being chosen by the individual family and that nonreligious schools were allowed to compete. Yet for the United States these are still uncharted waters. School choice still faces the hurdle of having to pay both school taxes and tuitions to send your child to a private school, and the American Federation of Teachers has vowed to keep fighting against voucher programs in legislatures and in the courts.

Similar battles over religion and the schools led to very different outcomes in different countries. In Belgium, France, Denmark, and the Netherlands, history ended up leading to government subsidies of ostensibly religious schools, even though religious devotion was on the wane. Let us follow the case of the Netherlands here.

The Dutch policy settlement emerged from bitter fights that flared up when schooling expanded in the nineteenth century. Catholics and orthodox Protestants, sometimes in alliance, fought against secularists over the school finance issue. As it happened, a compromise of 1917–1920 bundled generous subsidies to church schools with universal adult male suffrage. The school curriculum was centralized and allowed little religious instruction, in exchange for decentralized ownership and management of schools. In the face of the new competition, public school enrollments dropped from 55 percent in 1920 to 30 percent by 1940, a share that has been pretty steady ever since. As of 1998, with still only 30 percent of Dutch students in public schools, the government provides about 94 percent of all funding for primary and secondary education on a fairly equal per-student formula. When students and their parents choose to switch schools, the per-pupil government money moves with them.

Belgium reached a similar settlement around World War I, again helped by a bundling of the school finance issue with the suffrage issue. In the conciliatory mood right after the war, the new majority of Liberals and Socialists were willing to trade support for Catholic schools for other concessions by the Catholic party.

France has some of the same subsidized private school choice, but again the historical path has imposed constraints. By the start of World War II, a century of fights over this issue had left France in the secular mode of denying much aid to private schools. Then in November 1941 a decision was taken to allow subsidies to religious schools. Yet because that solution was taken by the Petain government under Nazi domination, the subsidies were promptly removed under communist pressure immediately after liberation. The subsidies returned only after the 1959 Loi Debré, reinforced by the more permissive Loi Guermeur in 1977. Yet the aid to private schools, with its encouragement of school choice, is still not embedded in the Constitution and could still be withdrawn in a hostile political climate.[52]

Once history has given subsidies to private religious schools in some countries and not others, does school choice really improve the efficiency of education in countries that subsidize such choice? We cannot rely on the mere fact that the Netherlands, Belgium, and France consistently score better in international tests than the United States. It is not easy to extract a clear verdict, because nations differ in many ways. Some international evidence suggests an affirmative answer, however. Comparing large samples of students and schools across several nations in the 1990s, Ludger Woessmann finds evidence that student performances on the Third International Mathematics and Science Study in 1995–1999 were enhanced by local school autonomy, as well as by the centralized exams (CBEEEs) mentioned earlier. His evidence touches the school choice issue indirectly, using local autonomy, private schools, and the absence of teacher-union influence over the curriculum as proxies for school competition. The proxies all have the effects we would expect from believing that school choice enhances test scores.[53]

The evidence suggesting that school competition enhances learning does not yet demonstrate that bold school voucher reforms will mean better schools wherever they are tried. In new experiments, as well as in history, context means a lot. Note that the supporting evidence comes from two kinds of settings that might show school competition at its best. The first consisted of long histories of well-developed local choice, as in the Netherlands or in decentralized schooling in the United States before the middle of the twentieth century. The second consisted of those new policy experiments in which the status quo ante was so bad that school choice could hardly fail, as in the voucher reforms targeted at disadvantaged students in Milwaukee, Cleveland, and other U.S. cities.

As a cautionary contrast, let us consider a case in which vouchers were suddenly sprung on a whole nation, covering both disadvantaged and advantaged students alike. It is possible that such a large-scale voucher reform would lead to sorting on the basis of social peer effects with little relationship to productivity. Perhaps schools would compete only in their ability to attract students with the right social peer groups and not in their efforts to teach more effectively. In such a case we could end up with the same average student learning and the same inequality of student learning as before.

Chile's voucher system, as decreed by Pinochet in 1981, may have given such a result. It replaced Chile's different school systems with an overall system approaching the textbook case of equal vouchers good at any school. The Chilean experiment has the further advantage that it has stayed in place for two decades, with repeated national testing of students. The initial effect was a boom in setting up new private schools. Voucher financing accounted for most of the jump in the private share of school enrollments from 20 to 40 percent in the first seven years. The growth of private schools differed enough to show how the degree of privatization related to the average level, and the inequality, of student test score performance. Studying three hundred municipalities across the 1980s and 1990s, and correcting for several potential statistical biases, Chang-Tai Hsieh and Miguel Urquiola conclude that vouchers led to a great deal of sorting, no change in school effectiveness, and no reduction in the inequality of students' test scores. The students in the new private schools came disproportionately from the better-off urban families, seeking out similar peer groups as the sorting hypothesis would predict. Yet one school's better peers are another school's worse peers if there is no tendency for schools to compete by improving their learning environments. It appears that schools have competed mainly by advertising their student peer groups. There was no clear gain in test scores on Chile's national exams, and Chile's ranking in the Third International Mathematics and Science Study (TIMSS) tests was no higher in 1999 than in 1970.[54]

Yet the presumption remains in favor of some kind of school choice. Even where its gains are hard to measure, the mere right to exercise choice is a gain in people's perceived well-being.

Rewarding Individual Teacher Performance

To give individual teachers an incentive to teach better, most of us would recommend the use of merit pay. But no OECD country's public school system does much of that. All OECD countries advance their teachers' salaries in slow locked steps with each year of service. In the pay structures from the year 1994, the percentage gain in salary from fifteen years of experience is centrally fixed at 30–40 percent in most countries. Eventually, after 16–42 years of service, the maximum allowable salary was still less than double the starting salary in every country but Portugal. As for merit bonuses in 1994, only one OECD country reported maximum bonuses for the best public school teachers as high as 18–23 percent.

That country with the highest, but still modest, bonuses for public school teachers in 1994 was the United States. By 1999, three other countries (New Zealand, Portugal, and Spain) posted higher maximum performance bonuses, but the United States' modest merit pay was still one of the highest.[55] The United States was also the only OECD country, as of 1995, where teacher salaries were determined primarily at the level of the local school or school district.[56] For all the misgivings one may have about the United States' rigid pay structure, and its failure to link teachers' pay and performance, all other OECD countries' structures are even more rigid, even those countries with the higher test scores. Apparently every leading public school system has failed to devise satisfactory institutions for appraising and compensating teachers' individual productivity.

CONCLUSIONS: WHICH EXPLANATIONS FIT THE SYMPTOMS?

To highlight the forces that seem best to account for differences in national educational outputs, it is well to begin with six common suspicions that are *not* confirmed.

(1) The quantity-over-quality character of the U.S. educational system is not an obvious defect. The United States' quantity approach reflects its better mobilization of tax funds to capture the externalities of extra years of schooling. It also gets more effort out of the average teacher. Many will seize on the mediocrity of U.S. students' test scores as evidence that a national mistake has been made. Yet there is nothing inherently wrong with excelling in quantity rather than quality. The question is what has happened to the overall gains in human skills and at what cost. By analogy, it is not wrong to expand the supply of physicians beyond the elite corps of a few super-doctors. Expanding the quantity of doctors while lowering their average quality makes sense if it saves more lives.

(2) Test-performance shortfall in the United States was probably not fully explained by differences in home environments. It is common for white native-born Americans to suspect that the United States' average

performance is dragged down more than other countries' averages by the presence of disadvantaged home environments. Yet several aspects of the evidence argue against this as an explanation. As noted earlier, every country has its disadvantaged groups, and the international test score performance of non-Hispanic whites in the United States does not rank any better relative to comparable advantaged groups in other countries than did all of the United States in the overall international ranks. Also, the fact that U.S. children test rather well at age 9–10 but more poorly thereafter has no clear link to disadvantaged home backgrounds. Furthermore, African-American children in particular are often trapped into poorer school choices by the combination of residential segregation, centralized urban school systems, and local teacher union power.

(3) The United States' schooling quality problem is not an issue of public versus private. The countries with better test performance than the United States are neither consistently more public nor consistently more private in their education than the United States.

(4) The United States' quality limitations do not deliver a one-note sermon about centralization versus decentralization. The more successful national educational systems have centralized some monitoring functions and decentralized others. Higher levels of government have a comparative advantage in setting and monitoring curricula and exams. Lower levels of government and private parents have a comparative advantage in rewarding or punishing individual schools and teachers.

(5) The United States' scorecard did not hinge on any differences in average teacher pay. The fact that U.S. teachers earn more in absolute terms but less in relation to average national income has had no obvious bearing on international school performance. Nor is there solid evidence that U.S. teachers are of lower absolute quality.

(6) The lack of merit pay rewards for individually better teachers is not guilty of worsening U.S. school performance relative to that of other countries. On the contrary, other OECD countries' pay structures seem even more rigid than that of the United States. The lack of merit pay should be tentatively indicted for worsening the school performance of *all* national school systems. There is reason to suspect that all nations could work harder at identifying the quality of an individual teacher's performance and rewarding it.

The two institutional forces that have most clearly shaped the international test-score gap, and the decline in U.S. scores, 1967–1980, seem to be student accountability in external exams and the degree of school choice.

Why did U.S. teenagers' test scores slump between the twelfth-grade cohort of 1967 and that of 1980? The first culprit is the United States' defective exam incentives, as emphasized by John Bishop. The United States has underinvested in central achievement exams. Students qualify for college on the basis of class ranking in course grades (a zero-sum competition, blurred further by grade inflation) and on the basis of tests that are still more about aptitude than about learning in the classroom. The other apparent culprit was the combination of declining school choice, especially in certain cities' increasingly concentrated districts, and the rise of teacher union power after 1960. As this combination of little choice and collective bargaining spread, test scores dropped.

Both of the United States' two institutional culprits – less accountability and less school choice – also help to explain the persistent failure of the United States' comparative international performance to match its resources.

Or so it appears from the evidence that is now gathering. Much of the underlying comparative institutional history of education remains to be written, however.

7

Explaining the Rise of Social Transfers
Since 1880

Starting around 1880, the scope of social transfers widened. No longer were social transfers just classic poor relief. Wholly new kinds of social transfer programs emerged – redistributive pension programs, unemployment compensation, accident and disability compensation, public health for the poor, and housing subsidies. More and more countries initiated each kind of transfer.

Why did the rise of social transfers happen so late in the long sweep of history, gathering momentum only late in the nineteenth century? Why did it then continue for one hundred years? What kinds of countries raised social transfers and the taxes needed to pay for it, becoming full-fledged welfare states? What forces made their political systems do this, when other countries held back? Why, after 1980, did the share of social transfers in GDP stagnate but not decline, despite the highly publicized conservative revolution led by Reagan and Thatcher?

The history of social transfers since 1880 is explained largely by the same democratization that shaped the pre-1880 history of poor relief in Chapters 3 and 4 and the rise of public education in Chapter 5 and 6. Four other starring roles were played by population aging, globalization, income growth, and shifts in the social affinities felt by middle-income voters. A supporting role was played by a shift in Catholic attitudes toward government social programs. This chapter sketches how these starring and supporting roles help us interpret the delayed and partial emergence of the welfare state.

WHO WERE THE PIONEERS BEFORE 1930?

Which countries led the way in the dawn of social transfers between 1880 and 1930? The leadership roles were not the same for social transfers as for public education. By 1930, as we saw in Chapter 5, the North Americans had taken the lead in public education, both because of Germany's troubles and because of the U.S. revolution in secondary education.[1]

Social transfers, like public education, rose in all advanced countries over that half-century. The only countries without such a rise were those low-income countries whose transfers remained at zero as late as 1930. The sequence of types of social programs tended to start with old-style poor relief (or "welfare") and health care subsidies. Pension subsidies tended to be next, followed by unemployment compensation and by housing subsidies.

Zeroes still dominated the global snapshot of social transfers in 1880. Aside from small pension subsidies in Norway and Denmark, no government paid nationwide subsidies for pensions, housing, or even unemployment. Subsidies consisted of traditional poor relief and health services such as hospitals. Even these were confined to a dozen countries. They reached 1 percent of national product only in Norway and Denmark, with Britain having fallen from earlier leadership in poor relief. From this 1880 starting point, countries followed different paths. Figure 7.1 follows the emergence of some of the leaders in social transfers as a share of GNP, first for total social transfers and then for poor relief and government pensions.

The new numbers on social transfers contradict some time-honored stories about who led the rise in safety net programs after 1880.[2] Most authors

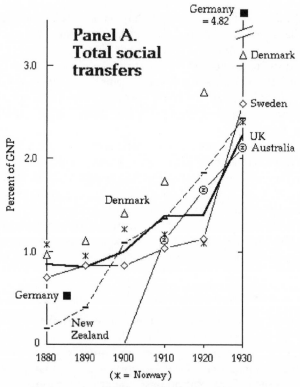

FIGURE 7.1. The Rise of Social Transfers, Leading Countries, 1880–1930.

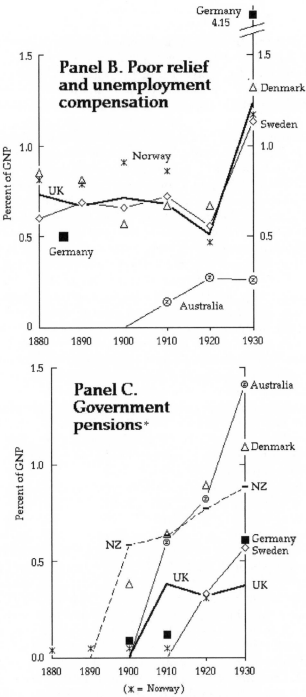

FIGURE 7.1. (*continued*)

credit Bismarck and Germany with the pioneering role in development of the welfare state. Daniel Levine puts the professional majority view succinctly and casually: "Germany is where it all began in the modern industrial world. . . . It all began in Germany in 1883. . . . [M]odern social insurance as a way of dealing with the cost of industrialization was first introduced in Germany."[3]

Yet the pioneering award for redistributive insurance programs may have been given to the wrong country. The famous Bismarckian programs insuring accidents from 1881, sickness from 1883, and old age from 1889 did not meet the modern definitions of a government redistribution or social insurance – at least not in their earliest years.[4] Unlike today, German taxpayers contributed almost nothing in the 1880s. Rather, the costs of insurance were borne by the workers themselves and by their employers. For workers' accident and sickness insurance, the subsidies were essentially zero. In the case of old-age and invalidity insurance, the state paid only 6 percent of all insurance revenues as of 1891 and still only 18 percent as late as 1908.[5] The shares of national product were tiny, even for the leading countries in Figure 7.1.

The achievement of Bismarck's famous innovations in social insurance consisted of his sweeping away most of the transactions cost of getting a settlement among hundreds of firms and millions of workers. Without his political maneuvering, there could have been long delays in setting up Germany's comprehensive insurance systems covering accidents, sickness, disability, and old age. The new insurance systems, however, did not involve much redistribution through government budgets. The only program that loomed large in prewar Germany, as shown in Figure 7.1, was traditional poor relief, which antedated the formation of the Empire. And even that spending was a smaller share of national product than in Britain and three Scandinavian countries as of the 1880s.[6]

One might counter that Germany's three insurance laws of the 1880s still involved government as a redistributive catalyst forcing business to pay for some of their workers' insurance. Even this view overrates the redistribution. True, employers were forced to pay for accident insurance, for one-third of sickness insurance, and for almost half the old-age insurance. Yet the net redistribution was muted. First, it is likely that labor demand was more elastic than labor supply in the affected industries, so that workers would have paid for over half their own insurance in the long run, as employers offered smaller wage increases than otherwise, once they were forced to make insurance contributions. Second, industrialists correctly perceived that their interests differed when it came to compulsory insurance for workers. Some saw benefit in the idea, because they had already set up company-level insurance and welcomed a law that inconvenienced their competitors. A powerful lobby in favor of the original accident-insurance bill consisted of the large heavy-industry firms of Westphalia, the Saar, and Upper Silesia. The opposition was less organized and more diffuse, consisting of firms that were smaller, more labor intensive, and more export oriented.[7] The battle between large firms favoring government regulation and small firms opposing it is reminiscent of Howard Marvel's explanation of how large firms manipulated the battle over England's Factory Acts of the 1830s.[8] It makes a fine case study in the political economy of regulatory laws, but merits only a footnote in the history of the welfare state or redistribution through government budgets.

Britain's leadership, like prewar Germany's, is diminished somewhat by Figure 7.1's new numbers. Her twentieth-century intellectual leadership was not matched by leadership in program developments after 1880. While such thinkers as Tawney, Beveridge, Marshall, and Titmuss led the way in advancing the ideology of basic social rights for all citizens, and Britain popularized the phrase "welfare state,"[9] actual practice left Britain out of the spotlight between 1880 and 1930. It is curious that Britain was a leader in welfare-type programs only much earlier, when poor relief was a regretted necessity before 1834, and not in the twentieth century, when so much social vision originated in London. In the late nineteenth century she lagged behind Denmark and Norway in total relief, old plus new programs together. Even New Zealand pulled ahead of Britain for a decade, led by its pioneering pension law of 1898, which included government subsidies to the elderly. Britain momentarily regained more of a leadership role in the prewar years of Lloyd George's social victories (1908–1914), but after the war Britain's commitment to social spending was not outstanding, though it was growing rapidly and still above average in the ranks of the main industrial countries.

Instead, the starring role in welfare-state development up to 1924 goes to Denmark. The Danes were already in the vanguard of traditional poor relief by the time the Rigsdag passed the pension law of 1891. That law called for tax-based subsidies that were four times as great a share of national product as was yielded by Germany's better-known old-age insurance law of 1889.

Starting around 1924, a new ranking of nations by their commitment to social transfers emerged. This era, not the prewar era, found Germany in the forefront. Struggling to buy social peace after defeat, hyperinflation, and putsches, the Weimar governments gave out nearly 5 percent of national product in transfer payments by 1930, far above the share redistributed through any other Western government before World War II. Another leader as of 1930 was also a republic born in strife: the Irish Free State continued and expanded the poor-relief and pension systems inherited from British rule. After Germany and Ireland came Scandinavia, Britain, and Australasia, in roughly that order. Aside from these, all other countries spent little or nothing. The international rankings for 1930 bore a moderate resemblance to the postwar rankings, with Scandinavia near the top and the United States and Japan near the bottom. There were countercurrents, however. Taxpayers in four countries – Austria, Belgium, Netherlands, and Italy – gave far less generously around 1930 than their postwar successors, who were near the top of the OECD welfare-state rankings. Conversely, three other countries – Australia, New Zealand, and Switzerland – transferred more generously, in international perspective, around 1930 than in the postwar era. Such was the spread of social transfers on the eve of the Great Depression and World War II.

SHARED FEARS FROM WORLD WARS AND THE GREAT DEPRESSION

The best-known part of the social transfer revolution came in the 1930s and 1940s. Throughout Europe, North America, Australasia, and Japan, the Great Depression of the 1930s and World War II taught people that their fortunes could sink and they needed collective insurance. The phrase "That could be me" became more a fear of getting poor than a hope of getting rich. For North America, this lesson was delivered mainly by the 1930s, where everybody saw that they could lose their jobs, lose asset values, or both. Franklin Delano Roosevelt used freedom from want and from fear as a keynote for launching aid to the unemployed and Social Security for the elderly and disabled. Britain's national memory features the dark hours of World War II as an experience that forged a national resolve to provide for all when the war was over. Late in 1942, the Beveridge Report captured the imagination of the majority with its vision of national insurance.[10] For Sweden the revolution came when the Social Democrats swept into power and set the nation on the road to egalitarian recovery. For continental Western Europe, it was the end of World War II and the spread of communism that frightened both the Church and Christian Democratic parties into social democracy.

The political victory of new social programs was ensured by the fact that even middle class individuals shared in the fear of falling and the new sense of everybody's being in the same boat, so that "[t]he impoverished were no longer marginalized as the only ones in need."[11]

Crucial as the watershed of the 1930s and 1940s may have been, the great rise of social programs was still only half completed as late as 1960. The share of social transfers in national income rose as much in the two decades of the 1960s and the 1970s as it had risen over all previous history, and it has not declined since 1980, as Chapter 1 noted. The net result is sketched in Table 7.1's snapshot of the social transfers and public education expenditures as of 1995, which resemble the shares they had already reached in 1980. The contrast between the welfare states and the lower-spending OECD countries features public pensions and related programs. Comparing the lower spenders with those countries spending more than a fifth of national product on total social transfers – those countries above the line in Table 7.1 – reveals that about half of most differences stem from pensions alone. Thus, for example, the difference between the shares spent on public pensions,

TABLE 7.1. *Social Spending in Twenty-One OECD Countries in 1995*

Countries, Ranked by Total Social Transfers	Public Pensions, Disability, & Survivors	Unemployment Compensation	Basic Public Assistance (Welfare)	Public Health	Public Housing & Other	Total Social Transfers	Public Education
			Percentages of GDP at Current Prices				
Sweden	14.8	+2.3	+6.2	+7.5	+2.2	=33.0	6.6
Finland	14.2	4.0	5.8	6.5	1.1	31.6	6.6
Denmark	11.6	4.6	6.0	6.2	2.4	30.9	6.5
Norway	12.4	1.1	5.1	7.8	1.1	27.6	6.8
Belgium	12.2	2.8	3.7	7.8	0.6	27.1	5.0
France	10.9	1.8	3.9	8.9	1.4	26.9	5.8
Netherlands	10.4	3.1	2.5	8.7	1.0	25.7	4.6
Germany (E + W)	10.3	2.4	3.4	8.1	0.8	24.9	4.5
Italy	15.2	0.9	1.7	6.0	0.0	23.7	4.5
U.K.	10.6	0.9	2.8	6.1	2.1	22.5	4.6
Austria	10.5	1.4	2.8	6.3	0.4	21.4	5.3
Spain	9.8	2.5	1.2	6.8	0.2	20.4	4.8

(*continued*)

177

TABLE 7.1 (continued)

Percentages of GDP at Current Prices

Countries, Ranked by Total Social Transfers	Public Pensions, Disability, & Survivors	Unemployment Compensation	Basic Public Assistance (Welfare)	Public Health	Public Housing & Other	Total Social Transfers	Public Education
Switzerland	6.7	1.1	1.5	8.2	1.3	18.9	5.5
New Zealand	6.4	1.1	2.9	7.4	0.8	18.6	5.3
Ireland	4.7	2.7	3.4	6.2	1.3	18.3	4.7
Canada	5.2	1.3	1.4	7.1	3.1	18.1	5.8
Portugal	6.7	1.0	1.8	5.6	0.1	15.2	5.4
Australia	4.1	1.3	3.4	5.8	0.3	14.8	4.5
Greece*	9.6	0.4	0.4	3.9	0.1	14.4	3.7
U.S.	5.2	0.3	0.8	6.7	0.6	13.7	5.0
Japan	5.3	0.4	0.5	5.8	0.2	12.2	3.6

Sources and Notes: The sources are OECD, *Social Expenditure Database 1980–1996* (CD-ROM), and OECD, *Education at a Glance: OECD Indicators 1998.* For detail on both social and other spending, see Tanzi and Shuknecht (2000, Chapter 2).

* 1993 for all social transfers, 1995 for public education.

   All transfers exclude benefits paid to government and military employees, on the grounds that these are contributory benefits paid directly by the employer, rather than redistribution from third parties.

   The educational expenditures consist of direct public expenditures for educational institutions.

disability, and survivor benefits in Sweden and the United States – 14.8 minus 5.2, or 9.6 percent – accounted for over half the difference in all social transfers (33.0 – 18.9, or 14.4 percent).[12] Contrary to much of the public discourse on the rise of the welfare state, payments targeted at the poor and the unemployed were both smaller than pensions and smaller as a share of the international contrasts in total social transfers.

What explains the rise of social transfers, first in that dawn before 1930 and then in the postwar boom that created true welfare states? Let us survey the roles of three main driving forces – political democracy, population aging, and social affinity.[13] The words and displays in the rest of this chapter are based in part on the statistical analysis of Chapters 16 and 17 in Volume 2. Most references to a force being a strong influence on social transfers correspond to statistical results showing that it explains a large share of the differences between countries or between years.

THE ROLE OF POLITICAL VOICE

Democracies, Elite Democracies, and Full Democracies

The key contrasts between the social budgets of nondemocracies, elite democracies, and the fuller democracies in which all classes could vote show up most clearly in historical settings where democracy had advanced fully in some countries, only partly in others, and not at all in still others. Such a setting was the period from the 1880s to the 1930s.[14]

The first contrast is between the average nondemocracy of that time (Austria, Latin America, Japan, etc.) and the elite democracies of the late nineteenth century (Britain, Netherlands, Norway, and Sweden), in which property requirements kept most men from voting. Relative to the average of the various nondemocracies, the elite-dominated democracies were less willing to set up government tax-financed pension programs, as we saw in Chapter 4.[15] It may seem odd that Britain, the Netherlands, Norway, and Sweden should appear as a group that was slow to adopt government pension programs, since in the postwar era they were leaders in this respect (until Britain's pensions were privatized under Thatcher). Yet these same leaders were laggards in extending the vote to the lower-income classes in the late nineteenth century, as Figure 7.2 illustrates for the Netherlands, Sweden, and the United Kingdom. Their nineteenth-century politics did not resemble their twentieth-century leadership in redistributive social programs. Aside from the contrast in pensions, the elite democracies and the nondemocracies were similar in the modesty of their social programs and their use of direct taxes.

Fuller democracies, however, spent much more of taxpayers' money on social transfers than did those elite democracies. Here the 1880–1930 laboratory provides an excellent test. The last prewar decades, 1880–1910, were an era in which the transition to universal adult male suffrage was still being

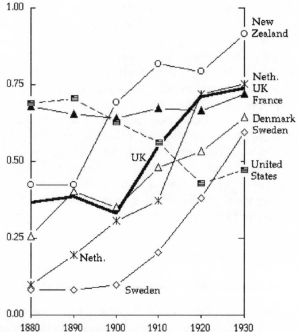

Each share is the ratio of persons actually voting in the latest previous election to the adult population in the enfranchised gender(s). Women gained their legal right to vote in 1893 in New Zealand; 1918 in Denmark, Netherlands, the United States, and (partially) in the United Kingdom (fully by 1928); in 1921 in Sweden; and in 1945 in France.

FIGURE 7.2. Voters as a Share of the Adult Population in Seven Democracies, 1880–1930.

completed throughout Europe, as Figure 7.2 also illustrates. It is not surprising that extending the vote to lower and lower income groups would tip the political scales in favor of redistributive programs. Extending the voting share from 40 percent to 70 percent raised total social transfers, public pension spending, spending on primary-school teachers, and the income tax. We would expect as much from reading the speeches of Lloyd George, Britain's leading soak-the-rich politician of the early twentieth century, and his rise to power followed soon after the extension of the vote to 70 percent of men.

Another relevance of the rates of voting is revealed by the U.S. experience shown in Figure 7.2 and by comparisons of interwar and postwar voting rates in the democracies of Western Europe. As Figure 7.2 records, the share of U.S. adults who voted actually dropped from 70 percent to less than 50 percent, a low share that persists even today. Part of this drop resulted from a loss of voting rights and part resulted from the voluntary refusal to exercise those rights. Southern blacks lost their votes involuntarily, when Southern states passed the infamous Jim Crow laws between about the late 1880s and World War I. The voluntary rise of nonvoting has been attributed to a loss of a previous social function of campaigning and voting. In a nineteenth-century world of smaller communities, participating in elections and other political events gave men a sense of belonging. The rise of cities and the arrival of immigrants eroded this social bond, especially in the Northeast, and many younger men stopped voting.[16]

The interwar period, on the other hand, exposes a hidden second relevance to the rate of voter turnout. Even though all adults could vote in eleven democracies by 1930, and all adult males could vote in two others (Belgium and France), the turnout was often low by postwar standards. In elections in the late 1920s, the turnout ranged from 46–47 percent (Finland and United States) to 92 percent (New Zealand). The incompleteness of voter participation may help resolve a puzzle about the interwar period. Why did the interwar successors to Lloyd George soak the rich so little despite the arrival of universal adult suffrage? Part of the answer, presumably, is that the interwar governments faced peculiar budgetary difficulties. Part, however, may be that the kinds of voters sympathetic to progressive taxation and (here) transfer payments were less integrated into the political process than in the postwar era.

After World War II, the same central role for the spread of democracy shows up in global samples that have varying degrees of democracy. The OECD countries studied here offered little variation on this front, however. All were electoral democracies in our sample periods, except for Greece 1967–1973. All OECD democracies recognized women's right to vote, except for Switzerland before 1972. Given this historical setting, one should expect that differences in electoral democracy take on a gentler form.

The rate of voter turnout for elections continued to have a strong positive effect on governments' social transfers and taxes, just as it did one hundred years ago. Specifically, raising the voting share from 70 to 85 percent of eligible voters significantly raises pensions, public health care, total social transfers, and educational spending. This impact resembles the impact of extra voters back in 1880–1930. Yet the postwar differences in countries' voting shares reflect differences in people's willingness to use the votes they are allowed and not differences in the right to vote. It is striking that in Switzerland and the United States fewer than half of eligible voters actually vote and that this has apparently weakened the political will of both countries to raise taxes and social transfers, relative to countries where 85 percent of eligible voters show up at the polls. One factor depressing the voting share in Switzerland and the United States is the frequency of referenda. In these two countries, particularly Switzerland, voters are faced with so many ballots and voting dates that each vote seems less important.[17]

Who are the nonvoters? U.S. information suggests that the nonvoters are not elderly on the average, since the elderly vote at least as faithfully as younger adults in all settings. Thus the bias against social transfers cannot be due to any relative absence of protransfer elderly from the polls. Rather, the nonvoting pattern that lowers social transfers is probably the heavier nonvoting by low-income and low-education voters. This is especially likely where election laws and registration practices continue to exclude, or to underrepresent, the poor.[18] Whether voluntary or not, their failure to vote serves to lower transfers they would benefit from.

Votes for Women

Women's gaining the vote in the early twentieth century seemed to be accompanied by a jump in social transfers and the introduction of progressive income taxes. At first glance, one might think that the change upon the arrival of female suffrage was a response to the demands of the new women voters. That inference was recently drawn by Lott and Kenny, who found that when states in the United States separately introduced votes for women, state government spending seemed to increase.[19]

Yet it is hard to imagine both that women's voting preferences were so different from men's and that they got politicians to do their bidding so promptly in several countries by 1920 and 1930. There is no universal wide gap in voting preferences by gender. On the contrary, a set of postwar studies finds that countries differ strikingly in their gender politics. The idea that women vote for candidates favoring more social transfers and taxes fits only two out of six major countries. In the United States since the 1960s and in Sweden (1970s–1980s), women have indeed favored the more left or Democratic parties – or, equivalently, men have favored the more conservative parties. Yet the opposite pattern held in three other countries, with women favoring conservative parties more than men do. So it has been in Germany, in Britain (especially *before* Margaret Thatcher's prime ministry), and in France from the 1960s to the late 1980s.[20] There has been no clear gender voting differential in Australia. Thus there is no easy conclusion about gender voting preferences, political parties, and social transfers.

More likely, the kinds of societies that granted women their right to vote were societies in which the whole political balance among males had also begun to shift in favor of safety net programs. A clue in favor of the broader-shift argument, not the direct role of women's own votes, comes from New Zealand's experience. In New Zealand in 1890, the Liberal Party was victorious and held power for 22 years. It carried out an extensive program of social reform, including that pioneering and eventually expensive pension program, regulation of wages and working conditions, taxes on income and land, and votes for women in 1893. The historical sequence suggests that even male voters had come to the view that it was time for social programs, and it would probably be wrong to imagine that the new programs were created by women's own votes.

The same suggestion of a broader shift in public preferences, not one confined to women, comes from the international timing of the arrival of female suffrage itself. New Zealand's pioneering was followed by the arrival of female suffrage in Finland (1906), Norway (1907), Australia (1908), and Denmark (1915). Yet the great breakthrough of votes for women at the national level came during and immediately after World War I – including Russia, Canada, and Poland in 1918 and Austria, Czechoslovakia, the Netherlands, and the United States in 1919. Britain granted voting power to some women in 1918 and to all women over twenty-one in 1928. Similarly, it was the aftermath of World War II that brought voting power for women in France (1945), Italy (1946), and Belgium (1948).[21] Even though women had been the leaders of the women's suffrage movement for decades, the eventual victories of female suffrage were part of a broader movement that led to a new sense of citizens' rights and new demand for safety nets, even among male voters.

The Rate of Turnover of the Chief Executive

The final electoral influence with at least a century of impact on social transfers is the rate of turnover of the top executive – replacing the president or prime minister with somebody who is not a direct political ally. More frequent change at the top over a ten-year span seems to raise the share of GDP spent on public pensions, on public health, and on total social transfers in the 1880–1930 era, though its effect seemed weaker in the postwar era.

At least two possible mechanisms might deliver this impact. One might be thought of as the "bread and gladiators" effect, in memory of the image of ancient Roman politicians trying to placate the masses when they felt their rule was insecure. In a high-turnover setting, incumbent office holders may try to buy votes with extra transfer payments, somehow hiding the tax cost of those transfers. The other might fit postwar Italy better than ancient Rome: perhaps countries with a high rate of turnover at the top are countries that had been fighting amongst themselves over redistributive taxes and transfers, so that a period of high turnover frequently led to a higher-spending resolution during the twentieth-century advance of political voice.

THE ROLE OF AGING: GRAY POWER?

As populations get older, the politics of social spending shifts in favor of the policies catering to the perceived needs of the elderly. So says a host of empirical studies of postwar policy patterns.[22] In fact, the pattern has been there ever since life expectancy began to accelerate in the late nineteenth century.

Let us first look at the simple positive effect of aging that is revealed by statistical analysis of the 1880–1930 period, before turning to the subtler and more self-reversing effects of further population aging after World

War II. Between 1880 and 1930, rather early in the modern trend toward older populations, the effect of population aging was clear and straightforward. Having a greater share of elderly in the population raised all kinds of social transfers.

If the age mix of the adult population is such a strong influence on social transfers, what explains that influence? How exactly did it work?

The pro-spending influence of older adults did not operate solely through their being automatically entitled recipients. In principle, it could have worked that way. If, for example, society had already set certain standards of support for the elderly, a rise in the elderly share of the population could have automatically raised the share of GDP spent on their support even without any change in policy. Such a mechanism cannot explain, however, the 1880–1930 patterns in the effects of age shares on social transfers. The clearest effect of a higher elderly share on social transfers was a rise in total social transfers per old person. Two aspects of this effect deserve emphasis. First, the effect on total transfers was stronger than the effect on programs to which the elderly were entitled to benefits. An older population favored more social transfers across the board and didn't just qualify for more age-specific benefits on a fixed formula. Second, having a greater share of the population over sixty-five raised total social transfers *per old person* between 1880 and 1930, something that no fixed entitlements formula would have produced.[23]

Probing more deeply for causes of the age effect, one might suspect that perhaps the aging of the adult population is just a proxy for the vital rates and immigration flows that caused it, and perhaps it is these flows that affect social spending. In particular, cutting off immigration might be an important force raising societal willingness to give out government transfer payments regardless of age. We might be deceived if we attributed its protransfer effect to the aging of the adult population caused by that same cutoff of immigration. Yet separate tests suggest that the aging effect remains the same whether or not one controls for life expectancy. That is, it does not seem to matter whether the source of the age effect on social transfers stems from longer life expectancy or from the other two possible causes, immigration and reductions in fertility.[24]

The best tentative explanation for the apparent age effect is that an older population tipped social sentiment and the political balance in favor of granting security of income and health. This is the "gray power" motif so familiar in recent years.

Will detailed histories support the gray power hypothesis? Statistics cannot speak for themselves, and we need a view of how the political machinery actually transmitted such an impulse. Was an older population's greater concern for security sensed so keenly by politicians that they responded more in settings where more of the adults were old? The idea does not require the assumption that politicians in any one country compared their situation to other countries or earlier times. Yet it would help to know whether older adults used their voice, getting sympathy from younger adults, and how that voice was heard.

Two preliminary indirect clues suggest the historical emergence of gray power. First, most elderly did vote, and even voted promptly when the franchise was first extended to them. Postwar evidence shows that the elderly vote as faithfully as the average adult.[25] Historical data reveal the same pattern even for people who have just gained the right to vote: The elderly voter turnout was about average among women in the interwar era and among all voters in the first election after a dictatorship ends.[26]

Second, in two high-income countries whose adult population aged dramatically between 1880 and 1900, new pension programs were started and overall transfer spending expanded. In 1880, only 2.5 percent of New Zealand adults (over twenty) and only 3.1 percent of Australian adults were over sixty-five. By 1900, both countries' elderly share had jumped to a more normal 7.3 percent. New Zealand passed the world's second noncontributory comprehensive pension law in 1898. New South Wales followed suit in 1900 and all of Australia in 1908. What is remarkable in both countries is the absence of controversy when the new pension laws were passed.[27] The testimony of silence suggests broad background pressures and an easy consensus on principle, conditions that fit a prosperous and suddenly aging democracy. Across the first half of the twentieth century, both countries showed more stability in their age distributions and faded from the top international ranks in both income and social programs. This two-country sketch, however, offers only circumstantial evidence, and we await more detailed testing of the gray-power hypothesis.

Since World War II, the elderly have become a much greater share of the adult population than before 1930, and the aging trend will continue at least up through 2050. In this more superannuated setting, countries have run up against the limits to gray power. As the population ages more and more, something has to give, as we have been warned repeatedly since the 1980s. If the elderly became, say, half the adult population someday, how much generosity of pension support could they extract from younger adults in a pay-as-you-go system of the sort that still generally prevails? If half of all adults were retired, they could receive 100 percent of a typical young adult's after-tax income only if the young were willing to work and pay a 50 percent tax rate to get no more than retirees get. At some point on the way to such an extreme, protests by the young would check the rise in pension benefits. There should be a humped relationship between a lobby's share of the population and the rate at which it gains net transfers from the rest of the polity. In other words, gray power – as measured by the generosity of public pensions per old person – should have a nonlinear rise-and-fall pattern in relationship to the elderly share of the population. The empirical literature on the aging effect needs to allow for such nonlinearities, especially as aging continues in the early twenty-first century.

As it happened, by 1980 some of the older European countries were indeed pushing against the limits of the ability of an older society to win greater pensions per person and greater social transfers in general. An older society definitely spends a greater share of GDP on public pensions and even a greater share on total social transfers, other things equal. All the historical experiences of OECD countries since 1880 agree on this, as we shall see in the next chapter. For all the pressure that a rise in retirees per worker imposes on government budgets, the political pattern so far has resisted cutting total social transfers. Pensions have also tended to increase their share of GDP at least as much as overall social transfers. What does get cut eventually is public pension support *per old person*, not pension support as a share of income.

GLOBALIZATION AND SAFETY NETS

Another force that has shaped both the dawn and the postwar boom in social transfers is the openness, or exposure, of the economy to international trade. Thanks to some recent scholarship, we are coming to understand that there is a link between a country's exposure to international trade and its reliance on social safety nets.

What is remarkable about this link is that it runs in the other direction from what recent intellectual fashion would have predicted. Many have imagined that increasing exposure to international trade and investment – alias "globalization" – would trigger a race to the bottom in social spending. If social programs were a tax burden on businesses, wouldn't businesses flee from the welfare states and head for low-tax havens? Wouldn't the welfare states have to surrender and race to cut their taxes and social transfers to compete for business? This fear is entirely plausible.

Yet the evidence from both before and after the World Wars points in the opposite direction. Greater openness to international trade (and investment) makes a country use more, not less, taxes for social transfers. Dani Rodrik raised this possibility and supported it with international evidence from the late twentieth century. Rodrik conjectured that the link runs from a small country's vulnerability to trade shocks to its choosing sturdier safety nets for those hurt by international competition.[28] The same positive effect of trade exposure on safety nets and protection of workers apparently existed even before World War I, according to recent findings by Michael Huberman and Wayne Lewchuk.[29] Surprising as it may seem, countries that have chosen to remain more open to international trade competition have also chosen to channel more taxes into social transfers.

SOCIAL AFFINITY: "THAT COULD BE ME"

There are good reasons to believe that redistributive taxing and spending should depend in part on whether median, typical, or middle-income voters feel affinity with those lower, or with those higher, in the income ranks.[30] The more a middle-income voter looks at the likely recipients of public aid and says "that could be me" (or my daughter, or my whole family), the greater that voter's willingness to vote for taxes to fund such aid. Affinity would be fostered by ethnic homogeneity between middle-income voters and the perceived recipients. Conversely, ethnic divisions would create suspicions that taxpayers' money will be turned over to "them." So would durable divisions between middle and lower income classes, because such divisions undermine the political demand for safety-net programs. In the other direction, affinity between the middle-income and rich groups, and a greater sense of upward mobility, is traditionally thought to promote the conservative view that taxes and safety nets are bad for economic growth and moral discipline.

The postwar historical information allows us to explore social affinity effects, which the tests on 1880–1930 experience had to omit for want of data. One new resource is the set of ethnographers' indexes of ethnic fractionalization for most of the world's nations in the 1960s. Using the indices from the Soviet *Atlas Narodov Mira* as fixed national attributes reveals the predicted negative effects on some, though not all, kinds of social spending. Ethnic divisions reduce spending on pensions and public health, though not on welfare-unemployment spending or on public schooling. The overall effect on total social spending is clearly negative, as expected. This accords with other studies' finding that ethnic divisions reduce all sorts of public nonmilitary spending.[31]

A second dimension of social affinity that one would expect to influence public budgets is intermobility among the income ranks. This should be a powerful force. It's not easy to measure, though. An instructive recent exercise, with a focus on children, compared the poverty persistence with poverty rates across seven countries (Britain, West Germany, Ireland, Spain, United States, Hungary, and Russia), using these countries' large panel data sets following individuals over five years or more. The United States stands out for its combination of high and persistent poverty. Among these seven countries its poverty rate was second only to that of Russia in the 1990s. It also had the most persistent poverty, meaning that it had the lowest share of children dropping into the bottom fifth of the distribution of household income and also the lowest share of the bottom fifth escaping from poverty.[32]

Thus if one imagines that perceptions about intermobility resemble the facts about intermobility, then U.S. perceptions should have resisted the notion that a middle-income person's children could sink into the poverty of the bottom fifth. In the United States that just didn't happen as often as in the other countries for which we have data on intermobility. Note a basic asymmetry in the U.S. pattern, however: While intermobility with the poverty population is lower in the United States, income mobility between the middle and the upper ranks is not necessarily lower, and geographical mobility is higher. Thus the economic evidence continues to show good reasons to expect a different ideology, a lower social affinity with the poor, in the United States.

This hunch about differences in income mobility receives indirect support from international differences in income gaps as proxies for parts of inter-mobility. It stands to reason that if middle and lower income groups tend to be separate over the generations, their human capital and their incomes should also be further apart. That same seven-country study by Bradbury and coauthors did find that the middle-versus-lower income gap was distinctly broader in the United States, correlating with the difference in intergenerational mobility. Other writings have developed a pair of income-distribution proxies that imitate the larger income-distribution skewness: the upper and lower income gaps, measured by the ratios of (top 20 percent/middle 20 percent) and (middle 20 percent over bottom 20 percent) income averages for different countries. These two income-gap variables affect social transfers in the predicted directions.[33] A wider "lower gap" between middle and bottom incomes *lowers* social transfers, particularly the welfare and unemployment compensation that target the poor most closely. Also in accord with the social affinity theory, a wider "upper gap" between rich and middle *raises* total social transfers, by raising welfare and unemployment compensation. This combination means that a middle-income group closer to the bottom and further from the top will tilt toward more income-support programs funded by taxing higher incomes. It is the kind of income skewness that fit Lloyd George's assault on England's rich a century ago, and it has been generally absent in the United States. Its absence is one reason why the United States, and to a lesser extent Australia, resists social the commitment to social transfers that has been stronger in several countries of Western Europe.

SUMMARY

We now have a clearer view of the forces that caused the initial emergence and the later boom on social transfers in the now-industrialized OECD countries. The same five leading forces help to explain the rise of social transfers and why countries differed so much in that rise. The five leaders are, again,

(1) democratization,
(2) the aging of populations,
(3) globalization,
(4) the rise of income per capita, and
(5) international differences in the social affinities felt by middle-income voters.

Which of the five was most important depended on the historical question asked. If one asks why no country transferred even 3 percent of national product before the end of the nineteenth century, the answer centers on the delayed spread of political voice or democratization. The primary reason social transfers accelerated only after 1880 is that the groups that would have pushed for such transfers lacked political voice.

That long delay in the permanent rise in social transfers may also have owed something to the delay in those other four basic forces: population aging, globalization, the rise of average incomes, and the empathy that middle-income voters felt toward the poor, the sick, and the elderly. Yet each of these other four forces seems to have helped in raising taxes and transfers only after democratization had created the political will to raise taxes and transfers. Population aging had only a delayed effect for the simple reason that there were still few elderly before 1880. Globalization did not raise transfers until the late nineteenth century because globalization had not accelerated until after the 1820s, and its translation into more transfers awaited democratic regimes willing to combine openness and safety nets. The rise of average incomes did start earlier than these other forces, but its contribution to transfers before 1930s was overshadowed by the effects of democracy and aging, as we have seen. Finally, the delay in the spread of political voice explains the delay in middle-income social affinity for the poor. In most early settings, political voice was restricted first to hereditary elites and then to a broader propertied group with low empathy for the poor. Granted there were at least some stirrings of middle-class empathy in the nineteenth century, enough to help sell such writings as *Oliver Twist* and *Les Miserables*. Yet such stirrings built few safety nets until workers and the poor had won the franchise.

To interpret the rise of transfers across the Great Depression and the postwar boom of the welfare state, one should give less emphasis to the rise of democracy, which had already made great strides by 1930, and more emphasis to other forces. Viewing the half-century 1930–80 as a whole, one sees starring roles for our other four main forces, now joined by a religious shift. The same shift of emphasis also helps to explain why some countries developed welfare states and others did not. That is, the starring roles in the 1930–1980 period went to population aging, globalization, and income growth, whether we address the fifty-year rise in average OECD social transfers or the stark international differences in the extent of that rise. In particular, the Great Depression and World War II gave middle-income voters new reasons to believe that they and their families might sink economically and might need a safety net. The new feeling was stronger in those ethnically homogeneous countries where the middle and bottom income ranks were more intermobile. The supporting role for religion was played by the Catholic Church and Catholic political parties, which shed their economic conservatism after World War II.

Finally, when we wonder why social transfers' share of GDP stopped growing, yet did not decline in the OECD countries after 1980, the answer seems to lie in the nonlinearity in the effect of aging on social transfers.

As the elderly share of the population soared, first in Scandinavia and then elsewhere, gray power was destined to weaken. The elderly could no longer win such generous public pensions, or total social transfers, once the fruits of their lobbying were spread over a large share of population. This non-linear effect of aging on transfers will be the centerpiece in Part Three's predictions.

PROSPECTS FOR SOCIAL TRANSFERS

8

The Public Pension Crisis

If the upward march of social transfers as a share of GDP has stalled since 1980, might it ever be reversed? What might cause a future reversal?

There is indeed reason to believe that the rise of public generosity will be reversed in at least one dimension and that the reversal has already begun. The direction of likely retreat points toward less support for the average pensioner. The main reason for that partial retreat is that people now live too long for the current system of pensions to be sustained, though policy history also determines which countries face the greatest budgetary problems. Specifically, I shall argue here that:

(1) The aging of national populations poses a great threat to the current rates of support for the pensioners (retirees). Other things equal, this effect is especially strong in countries that are aging faster.

(2) The budgetary pressure is especially intense in countries that moved in the wrong direction between 1960 and 1990, by encouraging early retirement.

(3) The combination of these demographic and political forces jeopardized Italy's pension system the most and also strongly threatens pensions in Austria, Belgium, Finland, France, Germany, Greece, Netherlands, and Spain. Some of these have already cut back pension generosity. Other countries faced less danger of a crisis, even though some of them have extremely old populations.

(4) The necessary adjustments, which already began late in the twentieth century, will be paid for mainly by the pensioners themselves, in the form of reduced support per pensioner. Other kinds of social transfers will probably not be cut, and taxpayers will go on paying the same, or slightly rising, shares of national income for social programs.

(5) Extra immigration has little to do with the pension crisis.

(6) The realities of intergenerational politics seem to preclude any return to funded or strictly private pensions.

Or so it appears. When it comes to forecasting economic and political trends, humility is in order. Nobody should pretend to know exactly how tax and transfer policies will behave over future decades. If the courts ever ruled that journalists, market analysts, and social scientists could be sued for malpractice whenever their forecasts were wrong, these professions would collapse. Even with the help of the systematic forces identified in Chapter 7, forecasts of social transfers can only be as good as our forecasts of changes in those forces – in aging, democracy, income, and social affinity.

Fortunately, we do have some inkling about future trends in these variables. To be sure, we have no predictive power about changes in democracy or social affinity, which we might as well set aside for now. Yet the trend in income per capita is likely to be positive over the decades ahead and that is likely to exert a gentle upward pressure on the share of GDP spent on social programs. Above all, we know that the population will get older – much older. Seizing on the inevitability of aging, this chapter will offer some conjectural forecasts that seem to be better than just flipping a coin or rolling dice.

IN AN OLDER WORLD, SOMETHING HAS TO GIVE

We can imagine an ideal world in which there is no pension crisis because everybody saves for their own old age and everybody accurately forecasts how much they need to save. For most of history, this imagination was indulged by the fact that few people lived well enough or long enough to enjoy many years of retirement. Even when countries decided that the government had to set up a social security system to keep people from undersaving, the initial form of this system was what we call a "funded" system. That is, people got back in old age the accumulated investment value of what they themselves had put away in earlier life. The only difference between private and public funded pensions was that in the public variant, or social security, you had no choice. The government forced you and your employer to set aside contributions for your old age. Thus the U.S. Social Security System, set up in 1935, was originally a funded scheme, one that would have paid for itself *if* people died on schedule and *if* politics left the system alone.[1]

This world of sufficient funded saving faded from our imaginations as people started living better and longer across the twentieth century. The downside of longer lives shows up in pension budgets. The danger of long life haunts both private and public pensions. Any pension planning can be confounded by living longer than expected and that seems to have happened to succeeding generations in an increasingly healthy world. Pensions might well run out.

The lengthening of life has also affected the political balance. As we saw in Chapter 7, older populations tend to favor more social transfers and higher taxes. In the case of public pensions, this took the form of a demand for having the current generation of working young adults pay for part of the retirement of today's elderly, instead of just paying into a fund for their own later retirement. Thus one country after another pressured its government to develop "pay-as-you-go" (PAYGO) pension schemes in which your retirement, for which you inadequately saved in earlier life, should be paid for by the younger generation of current workers. Practically every industrialized OECD country switched to PAYGO in steps across the 1960s through 1980s. The switch was especially generous to the generation reaching age sixty-five between 1960 and 1990, since they did not pay for earlier generations' retirement and got part of their own more generous retirement benefits paid for by the younger generation. One favorable effect of this shift was that many of the elderly were lifted out of poverty. In the United States, for example, fewer and fewer elderly lived below the poverty line, and the typical poor household was now headed by a young single parent, not an elderly worker with a low-wage history. Yet as elderly retirees continued to rise in numbers relative to the numbers of workers, the original calculations of retirement needs became unrealistic.

As each nation gets older in a PAYGO world, a budget crisis looms. Something has to give. To summarize the choices that have to be made, we need to look at some compelling algebra. The typical government social-transfer budget is a balance between the taxes or contributions paid into the social programs and the benefits paid out, both to the elderly and to others. That is,

$$\begin{matrix} \text{Net tax revenues} \\ \text{devoted to social transfers} \end{matrix} = \begin{matrix} \text{pension} \\ \text{benefits} \end{matrix} + \begin{matrix} \text{nonpension} \\ \text{social transfers} \end{matrix}$$

To show how population aging puts pressure on this social budget equation, let us use a few definitions:

B = benefits per elderly person
N_{young} = number of working-age adults
N_{old} = elderly population (over sixty-five, say)
r = share of the working-age population receiving nonpension benefits (public health care, welfare, unemployment compensation, etc.)
t = share of income paid in taxes (minus nontransfer government spending)
u = nonpension social benefits per recipient of working age
Y = national income per person.

If we have a pure pay-as-you-go system, with no surplus or deficit, then the net tax revenues taken from workers each year for this purpose just equal the benefits paid to both kinds of recipients.[2] So each year, out of income = $Y_{young}*N_{young}$, the government collects taxes and distributes them to the elderly and to younger recipients of transfers:

$$t * Y_{young} * N_{young} = (B * N_{old}) + (u * r * N_{young}).$$

This basic equation for the social-transfer budget can be rearranged to show that

$$(N_{old}/N_{young}) = \frac{t * Y_{young} - u * r}{B}$$

The left-hand side is sure to rise, as every national population in the world eventually gets older. How can the right-hand side rise to preserve the equality? For any given average income per person in the labor force (Y_{young}), there are *three unattractive choices:*

(1) The nation can raise the tax rate on current workers' earnings and property (t),

(2) it can cut nonpension transfers per young person ($u * r$), either by lowering the benefit payments for entitled recipients (u) or by cutting the share of young persons who are entitled to any benefit (r), or

(3) it can cut pensions per elderly person (B), either by postponing benefits to older retirement ages or by slashing pension rates across the board.

None of these options is popular, but at least one of them has to happen.

Which countries will suffer the most? Within the most-suffering countries, which of the three groups of potential victims will suffer the most – the general taxpayers, the younger recipients of nonpension transfers, or the elderly themselves?

PRESSURES IN THE OECD COUNTRIES

Other things equal, the greatest budgetary troubles regarding pensions should visit countries that either are aging fastest or have precommitted to generous public pensions. Which countries are those? Let us turn first to the fastest-aging countries and then to those whose generosity to the elderly has added to their vulnerability.[3]

Who Is Most Threatened by Population Aging?

The geography of the world's senior citizens will change by the middle of this century, according to the United Nation's "medium-variant" projections of the shares over the age of sixty-five. Before 1990, Sweden and Norway were the world's oldest countries, followed by others in Northern Europe. Yet as Table 8.1 and Figure 8.1 illustrate with the apparent trends for Sweden, this has ceased to be the case. Japan will have one of the world's oldest populations throughout the first half of this century. That this could lead to a public pension crisis will surprise those who still think that Japan has no social security system and that this is the reason why Japanese households have led the world in their private saving rate. Japan has had basic public support

TABLE 8.1. *The Rising Share of Elderly in the OECD, 1990–2020*

		The Percentage of Population that is over Age 65		
	1990	Projected to the Year	Projected Share	Net Change in the Elderly Share
(A) Shorter projections for OECD countries surpassing 20% elderly before 2020:				
Italy	14.5	2005	19.2	4.7
Japan	12.0	"	18.6	6.6
Greece	13.7	2010	19.4	5.7
Finland	13.4	2015	19.0	5.6
France	14.0	"	18.9	4.9
Spain	13.4	"	19.0	5.6
Sweden	17.8	"	20.0	2.2
Switzerland	14.3	"	18.7	4.4
(B) OECD countries still just nearing the 20% elderly share by 2020:				
Australia	11.2	2020	15.9	4.7
Austria	15.0	"	18.7	3.7
Belgium	15.1	"	20.0	4.9
Canada	11.2	"	18.1	6.9
Denmark	15.6	"	19.0	3.4
Germany	15.0	"	20.0	5.0
Ireland	11.4	"	15.9	4.5
Netherlands	12.8	"	20.1	7.3
New Zealand	11.1	"	18.2	7.1
Norway	16.3	"	18.2	1.9
Portugal	13.6	"	19.0	5.4
United Kingdom	15.7	"	19.1	3.4
United States	12.4	"	16.3	3.9

Sources and Notes: The percentages of persons over sixty-five are from United Nations, Population Division, *World Population Prospects: The 1996 Revision* (1998).

for all adults since 1961 and had made the public pension entitlements fairly generous by 1985. Japan's system is PAYGO and is under serious pressure.

Italy and several other European countries, including some in Eastern Europe, must also cope with rapid aging. For Italy, as for Japan, the aging crisis is already at hand. Already by 2005, the elderly share of the population will have soared past 20 percent, a threshold that exceeds what any country experienced in Chapter 7's OECD experience up through 1995. The same ominous threshold of 20 percent elderly will be crossed in Greece sometime soon after 2010 and soon after 2015 for six other OECD countries. Thirteen other OECD countries will approach the 20-percent threshold by 2020, as Table 8.1 shows. Here the thermometers for 2020 read fever for some patients, but not for others. Aging will have put downward pressure on the

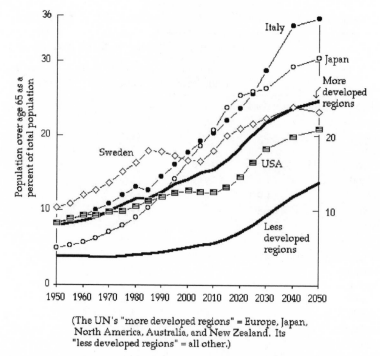

FIGURE 8.1. The Rising Share of Elderly in More Developed Countries, 1950–2050.

support for the elderly in eight European countries – Austria, Belgium, Denmark, Germany, Netherlands, Norway, Portugal, and the United Kingdom – in addition to the eight countries in Panel A. By contrast, Ireland, North America, Australia, and New Zealand will not show the key sign of budgetary pressure, because their populations will still be young enough in 2020 to avoid or postpone any crisis.

Who Is Least Prepared?

Vulnerability to a public pension crisis also depends on the generosity of over-sixty-five pensions and the generosity of early retirement schemes. Let us focus on the early retirement schemes, since these differentiate countries more than the generosity of their over-sixty-five pensions. Starting in the 1960s, several European countries invited their workers in the fifty to sixty-four age range, and especially those over sixty, to retire early. The implicit tax on staying at work peaked at the start of the 1990s.

The incentives to quit work varied. Most European countries formalized an early retirement age, the fifty-fifth birthday for Italians and the sixtieth for others. Belgium and France gave the fifty-five to sixty-four age group extra

TABLE 8.2. *Heading the Wrong Way: Employment Rates since 1980, for Men of Ages Fifty-five to Sixty-four*

Country	Percent of Men Ages 55–64 Who Were Employed in			Notes	Net Change, 1980–1999
	1980	1990	1999		
France	65.3	43.1	38.9		−26.4
Spain	71.6	57.3	52.7		−18.9
Italy (ages 50–64)	72.1	63.7	54.6		−17.6
Canada	73.3	59.0	55.9		−17.4
Germany	64.0	56.6	48.0		−16.0
Netherlands	61.0	44.2	46.0	b	−15.0
Greece	69.6	58.8	55.4	a,b	−14.2
Finland	55.1	46.5	41.1		−14.0
Belgium	47.7	34.3	35.1	a	−12.5
Ireland	72.1	59.5	61.6	c	−10.5
Sweden	77.4	74.3	67.0		−10.4
Portugal	74.2	66.3	64.5		−9.8
Australia	66.3	59.0	57.7		−8.6
Norway	79.5	70.6	73.5		−6.0
Denmark	63.4	65.7	60.1	a	−3.3
U.K.	62.6	62.4	59.4	e	−3.1
Japan	82.2	80.5	79.5		−2.7
U.S.	67.0	63.9	65.1		−1.9
New Zealand	n.a.	78.9	78.6		n.a.
Switzerland	n.a.	85.2	78.9	d	n.a.

Notes:
[a] 1980 is really 1983.
[b] 1999 is really 1998.
[c] 1980 is really 1981.
[d] 1990 is really 1991.
[e] 1980 is really 1984.
Sources: OECD, *Labour Force Statistics 1979–1999* (2000, Part 3).

unemployment and layoff benefits. The Germans up to 1982, the Italians before 1984, and the Dutch before 1995 offered especially generous disability benefits, making it easy for workers to claim that they had a job-related disability.

Such golden handshakes may be a main reason why men have been retiring earlier and earlier. Table 8.2 shows this trend for twenty countries. In 1980, when the data series begin, Belgium and Finland stood out as countries where men retired earlier. Between 1980 and 1999 men in the fifty-five to sixty-four age group cut back on work in all countries. French men were world leaders in quitting work earlier than their predecessors back in 1980, catching up to Belgium in the level of early retirement. Men in Spain, Italy,

Canada, Germany, and the Netherlands also cut back heavily on work. This shift away from older men's work, which was only partly offset by the rise in older women's work, further strained budgets in these countries.

So far, the combination of aging trends and early retirements suggests that Italy may be the country whose pension system is in the most trouble, followed by France and Belgium. The Italians seem to have realized as much in the 1990s. For Italy, public pension coverage for private employees had won great victories back in the late 1960s. It was around 1969, in response to the financial distress of postwar funded schemes, that the government gave cost-of-living protection to all pensions, tied pensions to employees' high final salaries, and set up the means-tested *pensione sociale* as a safety net for all elderly.[4] At that time, as Table 8.1 and Figure 8.1 have shown, Italy's age distribution was not unusual among the more developed countries. By the early 1990s, even politicians recognized the implications of Italy's having one of the world's lowest birth rates, excellent life expectancy, and not much immigration. Small reforms designed to improve the social security budget were passed in 1992 and 1995. Yet these limited reductions take effect only in this century, and the basic math of Italian pensions remains problematic.

Beyond Italy, the group of countries with the greatest danger might be Austria, Belgium, Finland, France, Germany, Greece, Netherlands, and Spain.[5]

How Will Budgets Be Adjusted?

If these countries face strong pressures on their pension programs, who will end up bearing the rising cost? Will young adult taxpayers simply have to sacrifice more for the politically powerful elderly? Will other social transfer programs, such as family assistance, unemployment compensation, public housing, and public health, have to be slashed to pay for the extra pensions? Or will the elderly themselves have to take a cut in the generosity of what each of them receives to keep the budget balanced? That is, in the terms of our basic equation above, will countries raise the tax rate t, cut the nonpension benefit rates ur, or cut B?

To judge an outcome that will depend as much on politics as on demography and the economy, let us use countries' behavior in the recent past as a rough guide to the future. Returning to the sample of twenty-one countries whose social transfer behavior in 1978–1995 was sketched in Chapter 7, we can extend the nonlinear relationship of social transfers to the age distribution into a near future in which populations are older.[6] We should extend our view only so far into the future, however. It seems risky to try to imagine the politics of populations that are much older than any populations in our 1978–1995 sample of historical experiences. Therefore, Figure 8.2, Table 8.3, and the underlying statistical work restrict their crystal ball to the near future in which countries approach that threshold of having 20 percent

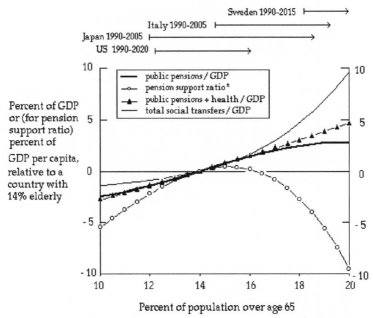

FIGURE 8.2. How Population Aging Affects Taxpayers, Pensioners, and Younger Transfer Recipients.

of their people be over the age of sixty-five, a threshold already reached by the oldest countries before 1995.[7]

As a country's population gets older than the 14 percent elderly share that was about average in 1990, the political process raises taxes, public pensions, public health benefits, and other transfers as shares of GDP. Or at least that is the tendency sketched by three of the curves in Figure 8.2. These are only rough estimates, and we cannot firmly say that the true effects on these budget shares are not zero. Still, if these curves truly do rise, then taxpayers (paying for all the transfers) lose and recipients of nonpension transfers gain from the political tendency for an older population to vote for more taxes and transfers. The pensioners themselves may also capture a rising share of GDP – yet they clearly lose from becoming so numerous. They lose because, as the fourth curve shows, having more than 15 percent of the population be elderly lowers the generosity of pensions *per elderly person*, relative to average GDP per capita. In other words, having more old people raises the total pension budget by a smaller percentage than the growth of the elderly population itself. The underlying political reason seems to be that

TABLE 8.3. Old-Age Tensions in OECD Countries: Projecting Pension Support and Social Transfers to 2020, Using the Aging Effect Alone

	Share of Total Population that is Older than 65			Predicted Changes from 1990 to 2020 due to the Rise in the Share of the Elderly (over-65s) in Total Population			
	1990	Projected to the Year	Projected Share	in Public Pensions as a % of GDP	in (Pensions/Elderly), % of (GDP/capita)	in Total Social Trans. as % of GDP	in Nonpension Transfers as % of GDP
(A) Shorter-range projections for OECD countries surpassing 20% elderly before 2020:							
Italy	14.5	2005	19.2	2.4	−6.5	7.1	4.7
Japan	12.0	"	18.6	4.0	−2.1	6.8	2.8
Greece	13.7	2010	19.4	3.0	−6.8	8.1	5.1
Finland	13.4	2015	19.0	3.1	−5.1	7.2	4.1
France	14.0	"	18.9	2.7	−5.2	6.7	4.0
Spain	13.4	"	19.0	3.1	−5.1	7.2	4.1
Sweden	17.8	"	20.0	0.4	−7.3	5.3	4.9
Switzerland	14.3	"	18.7	2.4	−4.8	6.0	3.6
(B) OECD countries still just nearing the 20% elderly share by 2020:							
Australia	11.2	2020	15.9	3.2	3.7	2.7	−0.6
Austria	15.0	"	18.7	1.9	−5.0	5.5	3.6
Belgium	15.1	"	20.0	2.0	−9.9	8.8	6.9
Canada	11.2	"	18.1	4.4	0.5	6.0	1.7

Denmark	"	15.6	19.0	1.6	−5.9	5.7	4.1
Germany	"	15.0	20.0	2.0	−9.9	8.9	6.9
Ireland	"	11.4	15.9	3.1	3.3	2.6	−0.5
Netherlands	"	12.8	20.1	3.6	−8.8	10.5	6.9
New Zealand	"	11.1	18.2	4.4	0.4	6.2	1.8
Norway	"	16.3	18.2	0.9	−3.1	3.1	2.2
Portugal	"	13.6	19.0	3.0	−5.2	7.1	4.1
United Kingdom	"	15.7	19.1	1.5	−6.2	5.8	4.3
United States	"	12.4	16.3	2.7	1.6	2.8	0.0

Sources and Notes: The percentage of persons over sixty-five are from United Nations, Population Division, *World Population Prospect: The 1996 Revision* (1998).

The age effects on pensions/GDP, the pension support ratio, and total social transfers are based on cubic functions of the elderly share, in equations like those sketched in the causal diagram. I have used twenty-one-country regressions for 1978–1995 (without full fixed effects) from Appendix E.

the more old people there are, the more dramatic the cost of giving each one of them a better deal on pensions.[8]

So in general the behavior of countries back in 1978–1995 suggests that *the elderly generally lose, per person, as they become more numerous than 15 percent of the population.*[9] In per-person terms, they are the ones who really pay for their growing numbers, more than do taxpayers. *Younger transfer recipients seem to escape* from sharing in the budget pressures from the aging process.[10] If these projections are correct, the public pension crisis will not become a general crisis for the welfare state.

Applying the curves to individual countries between 1990 and the year in which their elderly population share reaches about 20 percent gives us the predictions shown in Table 8.3. The countries' predictions differ because their age distributions differ, both in 1990 and in the trends thereafter.

Pensioners will lose in already-old countries, but not in younger countries, owing to the bend in the curve for the pension support ratio in Figure 8.2. For countries that were already old in the 1990s, political leaders must bite the bullet and actually cut the generosity of support for the elderly to keep the total pension budget from rising much. Such is Table 8.3's forecast for Italy by 2005, Sweden by 2015, and Belgium and Germany by 2020, a forecast that comes from the behavior of old-population countries like Sweden and Norway before 1995, when pensions per old person were already being trimmed. The only countries where the pattern does not predict a serious cut in pensions per old person are those that still had young populations in 1990. These young populations are the United States, Canada, Australia, and New Zealand. Here the elderly are still benefiting politically from the rise in their population share. True, the media in all four countries speak of a "social security crisis," but the clear prediction from international behavior in 1978–1995 is that the elderly will win that tug-of-war in North America and Australasia, forcing taxpayers to spend slightly higher shares of GDP on public pensions so that benefits per old person rise as fast as GDP per capita.

The politics of the aging crisis in the 1990s has already begun imitating these forecasts. Japan's aging trend, as we have seen, ranks with Italy's as the most severe in the world. By itself, this sudden aging means a major crisis for Japan's public PAYGO system. Yet Japan has some peculiarities that make a retreat to more private pensions relatively feasible. First, the country has always had the world's top or near-top rate of private household savings, which opinion polls have shown is motivated largely by a desire to provide for one's own retirement. Second, Japan has had the world's top rate of labor-force participation among men over the age of fifty-five and the second highest rate among women over fifty-five (behind Sweden), partly because the public system contains work incentives even up to age seventy. The trend toward earlier retirement already stopped in Japan around 1988, and its high labor force participation rate has been steady since then.[11] None of these peculiarities means that the public pension system will avoid a severe crisis. They do mean, though, that private mechanisms for financing retirement are already stronger in Japan than elsewhere, so that Japan's retirees will have relatively more private resources when the public-pension crisis reaches its climax.

Other countries have joined Japan in taking limited initial steps to trim retirement benefits. These involved varying mixes of slowly raising the full-benefits retirement age, trimming the formula for the cost-of-living escalator, and shifting the wage-history base back from the peak-wage years to include a longer stretch of earlier paychecks. Germany cut back benefits in 1992, soon after accepting a huge social-transfer bill as part of the national reunification. The same year also saw cutbacks in France and Italy. In 1995 Italy's Dini Reform cut benefits further, but largely by tightening the means testing, so that the poorest retirees were spared. In France that same year, however, the Juppé Plan to cut special occupational retirement benefits was defeated by protests. Japan's partial pension reform of 1994 was designed to trim some of the generosity from the system, to prepare for the tsunami of elderly that will hit Japan in this century.[12] Also in 1994, Sweden's Parliament set up a new tighter pension system, with the details to be worked out in later years. In June of 1997 Spain's Parliament shifted to less generous benefit formulae. Such reforms in the 1990s seem to announce the beginning of policy responses that Table 8.3 has predicted on the basis of earlier behavior.[13]

IMMIGRANTS AND PENSIONERS

Even though all industrialized countries talk about their own looming pension crises, some countries are fortunate enough to be facing less difficulty than others. These less threatened countries include four countries whose adult populations remain younger, largely because they continue to receive relatively large inflows of immigrants. Could it be that those four countries – United States, Canada, Australia, and New Zealand – will be spared the worst of the coming pension storm because they have more immigrants? That is possible, though we must approach the idea with care, because population changes have subtle and dynamic effects on government budgets.

To know how immigration has affected, and will affect, the pension crisis, we must look at all the effects of immigration on the overall government budget, not just the narrow direct effects of senior immigrants on pension payments. As we have already noted, anything that puts pressure on the government budget balance makes it harder to pay pensions to an aging population. Immigrants pay taxes, some of them become entitled to government transfers, and all of them eventually retire.

How does it all balance out? Do extra immigrants help relieve budget pressures or do they make them worse? Economists and demographers have studied the issue carefully and have found ways to compare the pluses and minuses. The answers depend on the question being asked. Are you curious about the effects of immigrants on government budgets this year or their effects over the whole next century?

Let's first consider the pay-as-you-go question: Are this year's fresh immigrants a net burden on the native taxpayers this year? If you are narrowly interested in the nation's pension balance, the answer is no, immigrants are actually a help this year. As far as pensions go, Italy could help relieve this year's pension crisis by admitting more young adult Albanians, and France could do the same by admitting more immigrants from West Africa. Remember, however, that in today's PAYGO world, pensions depend on the state of the overall government budget, not just on balances that carry a special "pensions" or "social security" label. So if this year's new immigrants drain any other part of the government budget, they can endanger pensions (or any other spending program). An example is the taxpayers' having to pay for public schooling for immigrants. The net result this year depends on whether immigrants' contributions to social security and other programs exceed their claims on public schooling and other programs.

Over their entire lives, immigrants affect budget balances in the opposite way from their effect this year. The pension contributions they make right away are eventually reversed by their later claims to pension benefits. It is reversed because immigrants earn less over their careers than the average native-born person, and public pension systems are designed to give a net lifetime transfer to lower-income persons. While this lifetime transfer would seem to burden native taxpayers, it is offset by an opposite reversal: Publicly schooled immigrant children give back to society when they become adults. Thus whether one asks about one year or a whole lifetime, there are offsetting effects of extra immigrants on government budgets and therefore on pensions in a PAYGO world.

How it all nets out has been calculated by demographers Ronald Lee and Timothy Miller using the United States' fiscal data and population projections across the twentieth century and beyond. They start with the immigrant mix of 1998 and follow that year's immigrants, their children, and their grandchildren through their life cycles. While the 1998 immigrants' children are still in school, their families are a net claim on U.S. government budgets. That is, the initial burden of immigrant children in school exceeds the initial tax contribution of the immigrant adults. Within sixteen years, around 2014, the 1998 immigrants' families become substantial net taxpayers, helping the government continue pensions and other spending programs. The net balance remains positive from then on, through the generations. So admitting extra immigrants for one year helps relieve government budgets and the pension crisis. Letting in the same number of immigrants year after year has the same initially negative budget effect and an eventual positive effect. In this case of repeated immigrant inflows, the initial negative phase lasts longer, up to 2030, but the eventual net tax contributions become even bigger.[14]

Thus admitting more immigrants ends up bringing net relief to government budgets. Should Italy and France use immigrants as budget bailers, thus allowing their workers to keep retiring early? The answer depends on the social as well as the economic effects of extra immigrants. It can be done, anyway.

RETURNING TO A FULLY-FUNDED SYSTEM IS UNLIKELY

The public pension budget crisis has led many to propose going back to a fully-funded system, in which each generation pays for its own retirement. That looks like an appealing way to prevent public fights over who should pay hard-earned money to other people. The return to full funding can take either a public or a private form. The public form would have people forced to pay into a social security trust fund, from which all of their later retirement benefits would be drawn. The private form has them decide for themselves how much to save. Both the public and the private form could allow the individuals to decide what assets to hold or it could constrain their choices of assets. Such issues are the stuff of lively public debate in most OECD countries.

Yet the return to full funding causes serious trouble for intergenerational politics, regardless of how public or private the new system is. To see the trouble, let us first recall what was so attractive about the initial shift from full funding to PAYGO in so many countries from the 1960s through the 1980s. Shifting part of the burden of current oldsters' retirement onto current young workers gave that first generation of PAYGO-assisted oldsters a break, one that lifted many of them out of poverty. Younger adults were not too aggrieved by this extra tax as long as the system promised to give them the help of the next generation under PAYGO. Their opposition to the shift was also cleverly mitigated by program designs that made it *look like* there was still a trust fund and a link between what you pay and what you get later in life. You'll be older too, someday, and the system looks permanent.[15]

A good reason why PAYGO might look permanent is the low probability of reverse travel, from PAYGO back to a fully-funded system in which everybody pays for their own retirement. Suppose that a country were to try reverting to a fully-funded system within one generation. This would mean that one generation of young adults would have to start paying for its own retirement while still paying for part of the previous generation's retirement. The deductions from their paychecks would be large enough to cause an outcry. Both adult generations currently alive, the working young adults and the retirees, would fear that politics would somehow make their generation pay more than its share of the transition bill.

The difficulty of the transition from PAYGO back to fully funded pensions seems to be the main reason why the public debates over switching back to a fully-funded system, or privatizing pensions, lead to little action. Britain made some moves in that direction under Margaret Thatcher, but has reverted to PAYGO. Chile's Pinochet did aspire to fully funded privatized pensions and had the political advantage of a dictatorship. Yet he also saw the political risks of switching from PAYGO to full funding and privatization, a combined reform that would have sorely taxed the current young or dispossessed many of them in their old age, or both. Pinochet's apparent solution was to have the general taxpayers raise their contributions to the current generation of public pensioners and only gradually, starting in 1981, switch toward full funding. What he decided not to do was to privatize pensions. Indeed he even accelerated government contributions to private pensions, presumably to quell protest with greater protection of private pensions against the effects of his other liberalizing reforms. There has thus been no reversion to private and fully-funded pensions by a stable government.

SUMMARY

Next to the silver lining of improved life expectancy, there is the dark cloud of increasing pressure on government budgets. The unexpected improvements in survival have pushed pension finance toward a crisis. At first, up to the 1980s, the rise of the elderly population gave the elderly more political clout in the industrialized OECD countries. The rise in their political strength was one reason why the relative generosity of pensions rose and budgets switched from fully-funded pension systems to pay-as-you-go systems, giving one lucky generation higher pensions paid for in part by the younger generation. By the 1980s, the pressure on government budgets had become acute.

From that point on, the further rise in the elderly share of the population began to undermine their political strength. True, pension budgets are not declining and are projected to rise a bit more as a share of GDP. Yet the level of pension support *per elderly person* is destined to go on dropping as a percentage of the average income of the whole population. This reversal had already begun in the Scandinavian countries in the late 1980s and 1990s.

Several countries continued to court trouble on the pension front in the 1980s and early 1990s, adding generous subsidies for earlier retirement while the ranks of the elderly continued to swell. France, Spain, Italy, Canada, Germany, and the Netherlands have generously subsidized early retirement by men in the fifty-five to sixty-four age group. They checked their drift toward generosity in the 1990s, but of these countries only the Netherlands has been bold enough to keep from being a leading candidate for serious budget showdowns in the early decades of this century. Meanwhile, the pension pressures should be less severe in other countries. Some, like Japan, Norway, and Sweden, have already begun preparing for a higher elderly share by keeping people at work past age sixty-five. Countries admitting large numbers of immigrants will also face less of a crisis, because a sustained immigrant inflow eventually supplies more tax revenues than it claims in transfers. For this reason the United States, Australia, and New Zealand are not top candidates for a serious pension crisis.

As population aging continues to build up to mid-century, the elderly themselves will probably bear most of the cost. To judge from the policy patterns of already aged societies in the 1980s and early 1990s, taxpayers will pay only a slightly higher share of GDP, and the younger recipients of nonpension transfers will be spared any great cuts. The pension budgets, while not declining as a share of GDP, will become increasingly less generous per elderly person. There is no politically viable retreat from PAYGO back to fully-funded pensions, and no OECD country has really made that switch. The main barrier to a return to full funding is that the young adults during the transition would have to pay for the retirement of the older generation while also paying for their own retirements. They will resist and democratically elected governments will not be able to force them to bear the cost of reverting to fully-funded pensions.

The pressures featured in this chapter have been budgetary, and the fight has been over which group must bear the cost of changing the tax-transfer policies to accommodate the extra elderly population. Yet, as we shall see in Part Four, this redistributive fight seems to have little effect on overall economic growth. It is a fight over who must accept less share of a pie that will keep on growing.

9

Social Transfers in the Second and
Third Worlds

What will happen to social transfers in the Second World, those countries of Eastern Europe, the former Soviet Union, and Asia that were previously under communist rule? What will happen to social transfers in the Third World if it starts to catch up to the OECD countries in living standards? What will happen to those Third World countries that will fall further behind?

Following the historical patterns of social transfers in what are now the industrialized OECD countries actually gives clear insights into the likely social transfer trends in other parts of the world. There are both reliable similarities and steady differences between the earlier history and the paths now being followed by non-OECD countries. Granted, countries and regions follow their own trajectories. Yet it turns out that there are simple consistent patterns in how today's reforming and developing economies differ from the earlier history at comparable levels of development and comparable stages of population aging. This chapter will suggest the following:

(1) The same forces featured in Chapter 7 will continue to drive global trends in social transfers for the next half-century. Countries' social transfers, like their commitment to public schooling, will depend mainly on their income growth, their population aging, and the fullness of their democracy. The Robin Hood paradox will continue to hold in the year 2050: The countries that still spend less than 10 percent of GDP on transfers, and little on schools, will be the troubled countries where poverty and inequality call most loudly for such social spending.

(2) The formerly communist transition economies of Eastern Europe and the former Soviet Union face a distinctive struggle with social transfer policies.

(3) The Third World countries that succeed in industrializing and prospering will raise their social transfers along paths that parallel, but are generally higher than, the paths toward social transfers traced by

the already industrialized countries transferred at comparable times in the past.

(4) In this respect, East Asia is not different from the earlier industrializing countries of Europe and North America. For all the talk of a separate Asian cultural approach to welfare and aging, industrializing East Asia has been following the same path traced out for each income level and age distribution by earlier experience. Rather, if there is a persistent regional departure, it is that Latin America and the Middle East have committed themselves to still higher transfer shares than those spent on the historical path followed by the OECD countries and East Asia.

(5) Several developing countries have already experienced pension crises, but not the kind of pension crisis now facing the already industrialized OECD countries. Rather, the occasional pension crises in developing countries will stem from the general breakdown of government and from public bankruptcy. The real purchasing power of public pensions, like other kinds of public spending, will be casualties of each crisis of the entire government budget, regardless of how old the population is.

THE AGING TREND IS NEARLY GLOBAL

Populations are getting older in most continents, though with very different age distributions. There will be a widening age gap between what the United Nations calls the "more developed regions" – roughly, the OECD countries – and the rest of the world, or "less developed regions," and shown by the thick lines in Figure 9.1. Outside of Europe and Japan, the oldest national populations around 2020 will be island enclaves: the predominantly Chinese communities of Hong Kong, Macao, Singapore, and Taiwan, along with Cyprus and Malta. By mid-century, however, China is projected to have a relatively old population, as an echo of the one-child policy imposed on the families of urban and eastern China since the 1970s. At the other end of the age spectrum, the youngest populations will be in the least developed countries, especially in Africa. With or without high mortality from AIDS, sub-Saharan Africa and the other poorest countries will age very little throughout the twenty-first century, according to the forecasts.

The aging of all continents other than Africa means that social transfers will rise as a share of domestic product. We know this because some statistical analyses have shown the same role of aging in social transfer policy in Asia, the Middle East, and Latin America as Chapter 7 sketched for the already industrialized countries. Population aging is the most powerful of the three most powerful predictors of social transfer policies around the world, namely aging, GDP per capita, and democracy.[1] Therefore the aging trends shown in Figure 9.1 for less developed regions suggest that social transfers should

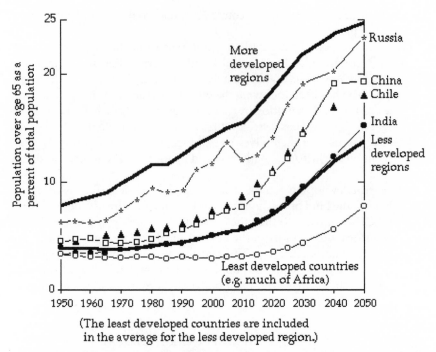

FIGURE 9.1. The Rising Shares of Elderly in Developing Countries, 1950–2050.

march upward in Asia, the Middle East, and Latin America as the population ages there.

SPECIAL PRESSURES IN TRANSITION ECONOMIES

The transition countries of Eastern Europe and Central Asia face a social policy crisis that should continue to be more severe than the pension crisis in the OECD. History has exerted three pressures that are pushing the transition countries to cut their social transfers, including their pensions. First, in the 1990s, they were emerging from a communist legacy demanding high levels of social spending. Second, their populations were almost as old as those of the average OECD country, as shown by the curve for Russia in Figure 9.1. Having a large share of elderly, just like having a communist legacy, tilts a country's policies toward supplying more safety nets at government expense. Third, these countries fell into even greater relative poverty in the disruption of the early 1990s.

It would not have been surprising to see all of them slash their social budgets and fall back to the historical path followed by OECD countries of similar income levels and elderly shares, such as Greece. Yet nothing was simple in Eastern Europe and Central Asia in the 1990s, and a counterpressure made some of them *raise* the shares of GDP spent on the elderly and the poor. The new postcommunist governments desperately needed political support, or at least acquiescence, from the general public. Since the elderly tend to be politically vocal, their demands for safety nets were not so easily suppressed. What emerged was a variety of social policy responses in different countries. As we shall see, the patterns suggested in Chapter 7 held again: Having an older population and an insecure political regime tended to raise the share of GDP spent on social programs.

The best starting point for surveying the turbulence in social policy in the 1990s is the Soviet prototype as it had evolved by the 1980s. Soviet social policy famously provided comprehensive social programs, with greater spending of resources on child care, schooling, public health, public housing, and pensions than one would have predicted of a nonsocialist country with the same income level and age distribution. In addition, jobs were so secure and so marginally productive that many received what might be called unemployment compensation on the job, as in the familiar Soviet expression "they pretend to pay us, and we pretend to work."

Pension spending may have crept slowly upward as a share of GDP in the Soviet bloc in the 1960s, around the time it was rising in the OECD countries. In the Soviet Union, collective farmers were belatedly added to the national pension scheme in 1961. With the retirement age set as low as fifty-five for women and sixty for men, the number of recipients of old-age support and privileges greatly exceeded the over-sixty-five population. In the 1970s and 1980s, budgetary pressures started to thin out this support per elderly person, even though pension spending remained a high share of national product.[2] With similar pension developments throughout the bloc, by the late 1980s cash pensions amounted to about 6–9 percent of GDP in all republics, except in the young populations of Romania and Muslim Central Asia.[3] In addition, the elderly were given housing and other aid in kind.

The collapse of the Soviet Union and the communist regimes of East Central Europe in 1989–1991 caused political turmoil and an economic slump. The new regimes reacted differently on the social transfer front. Some cut back, as one might expect in hard times and in the collapse of the whole system of taxation. So it was for pension spending in Belarus, Estonia, Kazakhstan, Moldova, and Ukraine and for nonpension cash transfers in Bulgaria, the Czech Republic, Romania, and again Estonia and Ukraine. Yet other countries moved in the opposite direction between the late 1980s and 1993–1994, raising social entitlements to unprecedented levels even as their economies slumped. Poland and Hungary stood out, raising the shares of GDP spent on both pensions and other cash transfers. Pensions also jumped as a share of GDP in Bulgaria, Romania, Slovenia, and Uzbekistan, and nonpension transfers rose in Russia. Such upward ratcheting of transfers was probably the result of both a need to buy support for new regimes and the continued rapid aging of the population. Over the rest of the 1990s there was no clear trend, to judge from the shares of social transfers in the GDP of the Czech Republic, Hungary, Poland, and Russia.[4]

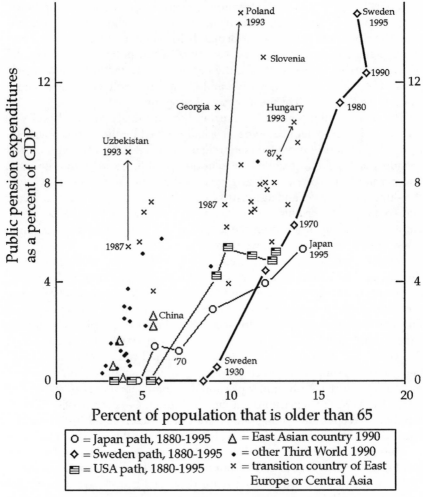

(For the data graphed here, see Appendix F in Volume 2.)

FIGURE 9.2. Old Age and Public Pensions around the World in 1990 versus Historical Paths 1880–1995.

The peculiarity of the situations in the transition countries is underlined by comparing their shares of transfers in GDP since the late 1980s with both a global view for 1990 and the longer sweep of history sketched in this book. Figures 9.2 through 9.5 set the larger regional differences into perspective. Each figure helps us focus on some national and regional oddities by projecting social transfers against either the old-age share or GDP per capita. Two diagrams offer this view for pensions alone and two offer it for total transfers.

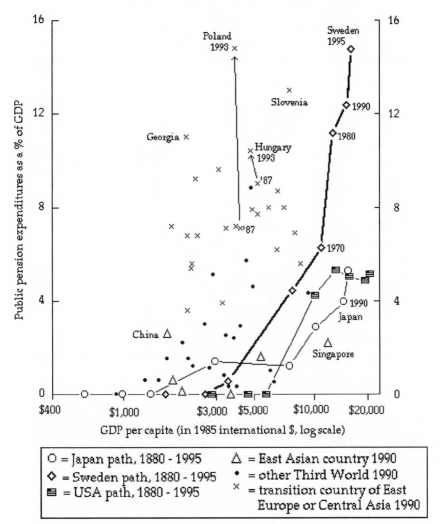

(For the data graphed here, see Appendix G in Volume 2.)

FIGURE 9.3. Income Levels and Public Pensions around the World in 1990 versus Historical Paths 1880–1995.

The same peculiarities emerge in all cases – whether one looks at pensions or at total transfers, whether one projects them against age shares or against GDP per capita, and whether one compares the transition economies to the long flow of OECD history or to Third World countries around the year 1990. To illustrate, let us turn first to Figure 9.2, comparing pensions as a share of GDP with what one would expect given the elderly share of

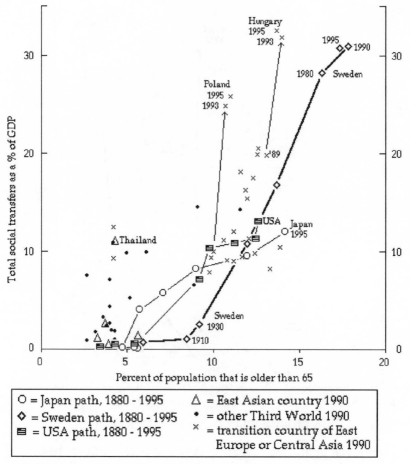

(For the data graphed here, see Appendix G in Volume 2.)

FIGURE 9.4. Age and Total Social Transfers around the World in 1990 versus Historical Paths 1880–1995.

the total population. In the lower right, we see the flow of OECD history from 1880 through 1995, for the generous pensions of welfare state Sweden and for the lower-spending United States and Japan. The countries of the former Soviet bloc clearly devote a greater share of GDP to public pensions than Sweden, the United States, Japan, or other OECD countries ever did. Their commitment to public pensions also exceeds that of East Asian countries (triangles) or other Third World countries (dark dots). What is most peculiar is the differential departure from the late-1980s norm of spending 6–9 percent on public pensions. Most of the transition economies (the x's) kept their shares from rising, as mentioned. Yet the public pension shares in Hungary and Poland had jumped by 1993 to levels that rivaled the pension

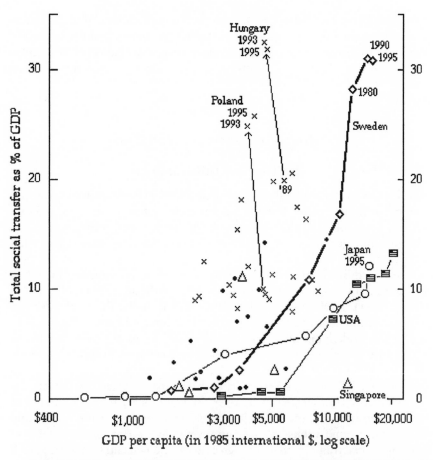

(For the data graphed here, see Appendix G in Volume 2.)

FIGURE 9.5. Income Levels and Total Social Transfers around the World in 1990 versus Historical Paths 1880–1995.

commitments of Western Europe's welfare states. Public pensions were also strikingly high in Slovenia and Uzbekistan. Similarly clear contrasts between these countries and others stand out in Figures 9.3–9.5.

Thus the transition economies of Eastern Europe and the former Soviet Union retain a stronger commitment to social transfers than other parts of the world, for any given age distribution and level of income. And within this

group Hungary and Poland stand out for the jump in their transfer shares
after the collapse of communism. Are these high commitments sustainable?
It is risky to forecast social policy trends in such unsettled political settings.
Yet our historical intuition suggests that the budgetary crisis should come
as soon in still-aging Hungary and Poland as it should in elderly Italy and
Japan.[5]

THIRD WORLD SOCIAL TRANSFERS

Are They on a Different Path?

The Third World, broadly defined as all non-OECD nontransition countries,
also has striking regional differences. These call out for explanation, so that
we can better predict what is likely to happen to social transfers globally.
Here again, Figures 9.2–9.5 help show us the regional differences and what
we might expect in the near future.

The Third World as a whole spends more on social transfers, including
pensions, than was spent in the earlier history of the advanced OECD countries at similar levels of purchasing power and at similar shares of elderly in
the population. So say either the positions of dots and lines in Figures 9.2–
9.5 or the underlying numbers.[6] To illustrate, let us compare Sweden in
1930, just before the Social Democrats first came to power, with some
developing countries around 1990. Back in 1930, Sweden spent only 2.6
percent of GDP on social transfers, at a time when it had a relatively aging population (9.2 percent were over the age of sixty-five). Compared to
the Sweden of 1930, the following developing countries were poorer and
had younger populations around 1990, yet paid a *greater* share of GDP in
taxes for social transfers than Sweden's earlier 2.6 percent: Costa Rica (10.9
percent), Panama (9.8 percent), Tunisia (7.0 percent), Sri Lanka (5.3 percent), Egypt (4.4 percent), and Bolivia (3.3 percent, by the central government only). The same was true for some other developing countries as
well.

Within the Third World, two large regions clearly spend more than two
others. Latin American and the Middle East generally spend more on the
elderly, the disabled, the unemployed, and the poor than either Africa or East
Asia. The lower social spending of Africa and the Indian subcontinent can be
explained in large part by differences in income levels and age distribution.
Yet one particular contrast stands out even after we have controlled for
income and age. East Asia – that is, Asia east of India and Bangladesh –
taxes and spends less than Latin America or the Middle East, the two regions
that dominate the set of Third World dots in Figures 9.2–9.5. The contrast
is blurred in the age perspective of Figures 9.2 and 9.4, since the East Asian
countries tend to have young populations. Yet in the income perspective
of the other two figures, the contrast comes back to us: Why should East

Asia, which is more prosperous, pay a lower average tax rate for social transfers?

If we keep the historical time-path of the OECD in view, with the help of Figures 9.2–9.5, we might consider the possibility that the peculiar regions are Latin America and the Middle East, not East Asia. After all, it is they, not the East Asians, who spend more on transfers than did the Europeans before 1930, when income levels and age distributions were comparable. Perhaps the real question is why Latin America and the Middle East departed from the historic norm by giving more transfers. Perhaps much of the story is that Islam and Roman Catholicism have adopted a pro-state-welfare culture. Recall that Chapter 7 confirmed a seismic shift in Catholic policy after World War II.

East Asia Is Not So Different

Many observers of the regional differences have brushed aside Latin America and the Middle East, however, and have imagined instead a contrast between a tougher and more virtuous East Asia and a more welfare-dependent Euro-American community. Is there a separate anti-welfare East Asian culture? How old is it? Will it last?

The imagined separate Asian culture was trumpeted in the literature on Japan as Number One, which was peaking in popularity just before Japan's asset markets crashed so resoundingly between 1989 and 1991, leading to Japan's "lost decade" of stagnation and policy stalemate in the 1990s. In the 1970s and 1980s many Japanese and foreigners thought that Japan had achieved the world's Number One Welfare State without government, by having families take care of themselves out of savings and mutual aid. The premise of high private savings was correct, of course, though Japan's data have never revealed any peculiar mutual aid or coresidence between the generations since World War II. Returning to Figures 9.2–9.5, we see that Japan's historical time-path of pensions and other social transfers was indeed near the bottom of the range of OECD paths, well below that followed by Sweden. Yet it was not far below that of the low-spending United States and Switzerland, complicating the task of distilling a historical lesson about Asian culture.

Louder and more sustained than the drumbeat on behalf of Japanese values has been the emphasis on antiwelfare Confucian values in the predominately Chinese countries. In these countries twentieth-century leaders often preached the Confucian traditional emphasis on the family as the main source of support in times of need. That was even true of the government of Mao Zedong, at most times, despite the obvious tension between elevating the family and elevating the state and the wisdom of its leader. It is true that, in the Great Leap and in other times, Mao compelled local units of work-and-government to provide for the needy. But family self-help remained preferable to government aid. As Mao warned in 1948, during the Revolution:

A sharp distinction should ... be made between the correct policy of developing production, promoting economic prosperity, giving consideration to both public and private interests and benefiting both labour and capital, and the one-sided and narrow policy of "relief," which purports to uphold workers' welfare but in fact damages industry and commerce.... [7]

Regarding old-age support, it is easy to cite cases in which Chinese culture lays primary responsibility on the family. Under Mao, a recurring theme of the newspaper *China Youth* was personal responsibility for supporting one's aging parents, both on moral grounds and as a practical relief for the government budget in a poor society:

When children fail to support their parents, they are in practice shifting this responsibility to society or the nation. In doing this, they are undoubtedly doing harm to socialist construction and will at the same time create serious social problems. [8]

According to the 1953 census, there were 64,000,000 men over sixty and women over fifty. If the government has to support all of these people even with a small sum, say ¥50 per year for each person, the total cost ... will come to ¥3,200,000,000. This sum is greater than the total 1955 expenditure for welfare and education and is more than 10 percent of the total expenditures of the nation according to the budget of 1956. If the system of state care for the aged is adopted, it will plunge the nation into deep financial troubles and cause serious interference with the development of socialist reconstruction. [9]

In Singapore, former President Lee Kuan Yew and the ruling People's Action Party (PAP) seldom pass up the opportunity to reassert the superiority of his "Asian values" over the Western disease of "welfarism." His successor, President Ong Teng Cheong repeated the PAP sermon when opening Singapore's Parliament in 1994:

Developed countries in Europe, Australia, New Zealand, and Canada once proudly called themselves welfare states. Now they have to revamp their welfare systems in order to remedy the disastrous side effects of state welfare: weakened family bonds, diminished incentives to work, and impoverishment of the country's finances.... Their problems confirm that we have chosen the right path. [10]

Britain's Prime Minister Tony Blair appears to have agreed. On taking office in 1996, he pronounced Singapore's social policies a success and hoped that Britain could use such policies to foster social cohesion as had been done in Singapore. [11]

The data have much to say about the rhetoric of a separate East Asian path. Figures 9.2–9.5 suggest that, with one exception, the East Asian experiences do not reveal any bias against government social transfers. On the contrary, the East Asian experience shows similar relationships to income and age as were shown in the earlier history of the OECD countries like Sweden and the United States. We should expect a further expansion of the welfare state as East Asia ages and prospers.[12] Thus, especially for the pension issue, there is no difference in the dynamic. The same warning is already built into Japan's path in Figures 9.2–9.5. As Japan prospered and aged, it ratcheted up its social transfers. Its social programs have already grown to the point that they exceed, as a rate of tax effort, the social transfer programs of most developing countries even in Latin America and the Middle East. Only the top welfare states of Continental Europe, including postcommunist transitional states, are far ahead of Japan in this respect. Do we really know that China, Singapore, and other East Asians will be more resistant to rising transfer budgets than Japan has been, when they approach Japan's income level and age structure? True, Singapore is trying to resist. Its 1996 Maintenance of Parents Act made it easier for elderly parents to sue their adult children for insufficient aid. Whether or not this is a Confucian or Asian way of promoting family values, it does look like an attempt by a one-party government to run for budgetary cover in advance. As a general tendency, however, we have seen that today's industrializing East Asian countries have followed a path that initially involves *more* social transfers as a share of GDP than Japan used to give when it was similarly young and poor. East Asia does not look different from the historical experience of Western Europe and North America. Rather, as already suggested, the most likely departure from European and North American experience in today's Third World is the extra strong commitment to social transfers in Latin America and the Middle East, not something different about East Asia.

A DIFFERENT KIND OF PENSION CRISIS

The Third World has had severe pension crises, but not for the same reasons as the leading OECD countries. Most pension troubles in the Third World come from political sources like those that have put so much pressure on the budgets of formerly communist countries. Most crises have been by-products of the general breakdown of government budgets, though some have been exacerbated by special inequities in pension finance. That is, instead of the usual causation running from population aging to pension crisis and general-budget crisis, as in the leading countries, pension crises in the Second and Third Worlds come as much from the larger political and budget breakdowns as they do from population aging.

The initial motivation for public pensions also differs from earlier European history, even before any crisis has built up. The driving force is less often egalitarian help to the poor and more often schemes to transfer income from the low-income taxpayers to the well-connected elite, especially in Latin America. In Brazil, for example, the pension privileges for legislators, civil servants, and military daughters had become ruinously generous by the late

1990s. A congressional representative or a career civil servant could retire in his late thirties, with lifelong pensions not far below his earlier rate of pay. In fact, he could even get a new job and still keep receiving the full pension the rest of his life. Subsequent governments have trimmed this leaky pension program, but it is still generous and low-income taxpayers have to pay a large part of the bill. We are beginning to understand that the elitist nature of many Third World public pension systems is a global phenomenon. One telltale sign of elitism in public pensions is that they do not cover agricultural laborers or casual workers. Many are specific to government officials and the relatively well-off industrial and commercial sectors.[13] The generosity of pensions for the elite is one reason why Third World public pensions seem to claim such a high share of GDP even under nondemocratic governments.[14]

GLOBAL DIVERGENCE, CONVERGENCE, AND THE ROBIN HOOD PARADOX

In the year 2050, which countries will be spending a smaller share of national product on social transfers than they do today?

The safe prediction from these last three chapters is that by 2050 most countries cutting the share of GDP spent on social transfers and public education will be troubled countries. The way to keep social spending from rising over the first half of the twenty-first century would be to have no growth in average real income, no gain in life expectancy, and no shift toward democracy.

The most likely candidates for this dubious slim-budget distinction would be countries that fall apart, like Somalia or Sierra Leone. Indeed most of sub-Sahara Africa, afflicted with rising AIDS mortality and rulers like Mugabe and Arap Moi, is the region where social transfers will remain meager. In social transfers, as in other respects, the main global divergence may be the widening gap between an expanding world and a stagnant Africa. The great divergence in social transfers and in education will probably be a widening of the gap between Africa and the rest of the world.

By contrast, there is likely to be a convergence of the shares spent on social transfers and public education in the rest of the world. The twentieth century saw a convergence of income growth and in life expectancy. The income convergence took the form of having successive waves of newly industrializing countries reform their economic institutions and catch up with the leading countries. At first the fast-growing catchers-up were European countries and Japan, followed later by the East Asian Tigers, and a few Latin American success cases. While incomes and life expectancy converged, there was also a net movement toward democracy, except in Africa and the Middle East after 1950.[15] Since we have found that the rise of social transfers and public spending on education is driven mainly by income growth, aging, and democratization, the convergence in these three factors has meant a convergence in social spending as a share of GDP. This trend is likely to continue over the first half of this century, if not longer.

The convergence in many countries' commitments to social spending, and the divergence between this good growth club and the remaining troubled countries, will continue to produce an expanded version of the Robin Hood Paradox. That paradox, as stated in Chapter 1, referred to policies toward the poor: Poverty policy within any one polity or jurisdiction actually helps the poor less, the lower the average income and the greater the income inequality. The global historical experience shows that this paradox can be extended to all other forms of social spending. Not only help to the poor, but also public pensions, public health, and public schools are less available where they are more justified by the existence of inequality and poverty. The trends that seem likely to continue through 2050 should conform to the paradox: The truly troubled countries that need safety nets and public human investments of all kinds are the countries where they probably will not happen. Conversely, the countries enjoying prosperity and long life and democracy will spend at least as high a share of GDP on social transfers and on public education as they do today. True, the elderly in the rich countries with the oldest populations will have to accept pension support that declines as a share of average incomes, as we saw in Chapter 8. Yet even in these cases the taxpayers of rich countries will go on paying a slightly rising share of GDP on social transfers and public education.

As a corollary, there is no sign of a global race to the bottom. That is, nothing in the analysis of Part Three has even faintly suggested that countries are scrambling to reduce the tax rates implied by their social budgets to compete for mobile factors of production. The free lunch puzzle introduced in Chapter 1 still stands: Nations have not been recoiling from the cost from the tax-and-transfer package. We now turn to the evidence confirming that this free-lunch puzzle is real and has a plausible explanation.

PART FOUR

WHAT EFFECTS ON ECONOMIC GROWTH?

Keys to the Free-Lunch Puzzle

It is well known that higher taxes and transfers reduce productivity. Well known – but unsupported by statistics and history. This chapter dramatizes a conflict between intuition and evidence. On the one hand, many people see strong intuitive reasons for believing that the rise of national tax-based social transfers should have reduced at least GDP, if not true well-being. On the other, the fairest statistical tests of this argument find no cost at all. Multivariate analysis leaves us with the same warnings sounded by the raw historical numbers (back in Chapter 1). A bigger tax bite to finance social spending does not correlate negatively with either the level or the growth of GDP per capita. How can that be? Why haven't countries that tax and transfer a third of national product grown any more slowly than countries that devote only a seventh of GDP to social transfers?

The conflict between intuition and evidence can be explained with better tests and a closer look at institutions. Those well-known demonstrations of the large deadweight losses from social programs have overused imagination and assumption. There are good reasons why statistical tests keep coming up with near-zero estimates of the net damage from social programs on economic growth. It's not just that the tales of deadweight losses describe peculiarly bad policies. It's also that the real-world welfare states benefit from a style of taxing and spending that is in many ways more pro-growth than the policies of most free-market countries.

The keys to the free-lunch puzzle are:

(1) For a given share of social budgets in gross domestic product, the high-budget welfare states choose *a mix of taxes that is more pro-growth* than the mix chosen in the United States and other relatively private-market OECD countries.

(2) On the recipient side, as opposed to the tax side, welfare states have adopted several devices for *minimizing young adults' incentives to avoid work and training.*

(3) *Government subsidies to early retirement* bring only a tiny reduction in GDP, partly because the more expensive early retirement systems are designed to take the least productive employees out of work, thereby raising labor productivity.

(4) Similarly, the larger *unemployment compensation programs have little effect on GDP*. They lower employment, but they raise the average productivity of those remaining at work.

(5) Social spending often has a positive effect on GDP, even after weighing the effects of the taxes that financed the spending. Not only public education spending, but even *many social transfer programs raise GDP per person*.

Once these keys are found, Chapter 11 will show how they have worked in Sweden, and Chapter 12 will suggest how the keys were fashioned by the political process.

THE FAMILIAR CAUTIONARY TALES MISS THE MARK

The intuition that taxing and giving hurts economic progress is centuries old. Since the 1970s a host of analytical supports have seemed to reinforce this intuition. This section surveys the new ramparts defending the old beliefs, noting their limitations.

Disincentives on the Blackboard

It is easy for anybody with undergraduate training in economics to believe that taxing some people to pay others who earn little will reduce national output, and cause deadweight losses of net national well-being. The effects could be drawn on the blackboard with two labor market diagrams, one diagram showing the labor market for those productive persons who pay taxes and the other showing the labor market of those low-skill persons who are poor enough to qualify for benefits.

The key insight in such a pair of diagrams is that there are costs on both sides of the tax-transfer system. In the market for productive effort, having to pay a higher tax will lower the after-tax wage rate for those supplying effort or raise what their employers must pay, tax included, or do both. Either the suppliers feel a disincentive to produce as much or their employers (or customers) feel a disincentive to pay for as much of their now-more-expensive services. There will be what economists call a "deadweight cost," here meaning the loss of something that was really worth more than it cost society to produce. The size of that cost depends on how much their production is cut, and we return to this. But clearly a new tax, to pay for transfers to somebody else, can give productive people a disincentive to produce so much.

On the recipients' side, there is also a disincentive to produce. For each extra dollar a low-skilled person earns with extra work, part or all of that dollar will be taken away from that person because he or she has less "need" for income support. Surely that too presents a disincentive to be productive. One can fiddle with the system, promising to let the recipients keep their first $x of labor earnings before starting to deduct benefits. But sooner or later the benefits must be withdrawn if the person keeps earning more and becoming more self-sufficient. And the higher the earnings threshold at which the benefits are withdrawn, the more the program drains the government budget. There are disincentives on both sides, and both must be quantified to judge the damage done by taxing the productive and supporting the poor.

The logic is persuasive, but so far the story is fiction. The deadweight costs are something we imagine, not something we derived from facts and tests.

Harold and Phyllis

The recipient side of the imagined double disincentive was persuasively dramatized in 1984 by Charles Murray's book *Losing Ground*. Murray told us a parable of a young poor couple and then added citations to economists' empirical studies that seemed to back up his case.

The parable concerns Harold and Phyllis, a fictitious poor unmarried couple who have just finished high school and lack either the family resources or the inclination to go to college. Phyllis is pregnant. Now what?

Murray offers one script for 1960 and another for 1970, after U.S. welfare policy had become more lenient. In 1960, Harold has to take a dead-end job in a laundry, because he does not yet qualify for much unemployment compensation, and Phyllis' having the baby would not give them much Aid to Families with Dependent Children (AFDC) support.[1] Phyllis considers not marrying Harold and trying to live off the higher single-parent AFDC. But she rejects having to live separately or having to risk being caught living together and losing all entitlements. Besides, she could not supplement her AFDC single-mother aid with her own labor earnings, because benefits in 1960 would be withdrawn as soon as the earnings came in, typically dollar for dollar, leaving her with no gain from working. So they get married and Harold is the sole supporter – in the 1960 scenario.

In the 1970 scenario, the incentives are changed by a wave of Great Society programs and court rulings. AFDC now pays something comparable to working at a bottom-skill job. In addition, the new "thirty-and-a-third" rule, legislated in 1967, allows Phyllis to keep the first $30 of her monthly earnings and a third of any subsequent earnings. That is better than losing 100 percent of benefits, but it is still a marginal tax rate of 67 percent, however. Worse, if they are married, anything Harold earns counts against Phyllis' support. There is less reason to get married in the 1970 scenario, however, since the Supreme Court struck down the man-in-the-house rule and welfare agencies could no longer police whether a man lived in the house of a woman receiving AFDC. "The bottom line is this: Harold can get married and work forty hours a week in a hot, tiresome job; or he can live with Phyllis and their baby without getting married, not work, and have more disposable income."[2] Under 1970 conditions, they agree on nonmarriage, living together, having more children, his seldom working, and living dependently ever after.

These first two kinds of arguments, the economist's theory on the blackboard and the parable of disincentives for the Harolds and Phyllises of the world, share the obvious limitation that they are fiction. Educated and plausible fiction, perhaps, but still not evidence from the real history of any country that tried generous social transfers. Granted, Charles Murray did choose his example with the help of historical wisdom. Writing in the early 1980s, he did seize on a historical moment when the marginal disincentive to work and to marry hit its peak. Both at the start of the 1970s and especially in the early Reagan years, welfare benefits were strictly means-tested rather than universal entitlements for the whole population. Later we shall note how this setting discouraged work more than in later years or in the true welfare states.[3]

Micro-Studies of Labor Supply

If there are disincentives on both the taxpayer and the recipient sides, how do we know whether people respond to the incentive gaps? If they don't adjust their effort or their willingness to innovate and take risks, then the disincentives to be productive would have no growth consequence. Some further kinds of analysis have been designed to argue that people will respond, leading to a loss of output.

Economists have probed deeply into a key parameter that sets the scale of losses from work disincentives. That parameter is the elasticity of labor supply, which measures the percentage change in labor supply as a share of the percentage change in after-tax wage that caused it. How big is the elasticity of labor supply relative to the net after-tax wage? That matters a great deal to the debate, since loss of labor effort is imagined to be a main vehicle taking us from the extra disincentives to the lost output and well-being.

The after-tax wage is something that we imagine could be changed either through market forces that determine the pretax wage or by changing the tax and subsidy incentives. Economists have used large data sets of individual households' labor supplies to infer how changing tax rates would cause lost employment, to which the main losses in GDP and well-being would be tied if taxes were changed. Careful econometrics has produced a range of estimates and a general understanding of the estimation difficulties.[4] Economists specializing in labor economics and public finance, surveyed in the 1990s, tended to agree that the elasticities of labor supply with respect to the after-tax wage were between zero and 0.50 for both men and women, though a few outliers believed in either elasticities above 0.50 or negative elasticities (as if people would work less in response to a higher wage). The specialists have agreed that women's labor supply is more elastic than men's labor supply. If both sexes faced a 10 percent increase in take-home wage rates, women's labor supply should respond by 3.5 percent more than men's essentially zero response.[5]

The main limitation to this literature is that most of it has been written in the wrong laboratory. Most of the studies try to use *nonpolicy* variation to infer the effects of policy changes. The large data sets consisting of surveyed households in one country, typically the United States, don't provide the real-world laboratory in which the whole national tax and benefit structure is transformed from a relatively free-market economy into a high-budget welfare state. Rather the people in the sample differed mainly in their gross wage rates, as well as their wages net of taxes and benefits, for individual reasons. It is not a fiscal policy experiment, not a test of the welfare state environment.

Part of this literature, however, does succeed in exploiting differences in policy regimes to see how people respond to changes in work incentives. Some were controlled-sample experiments in which some people were given one set of welfare and tax incentives not given to a control group, as in the U.S. "negative income tax experiments" of the 1960s and 1970s. These tended to yield rather modest elasticities of labor supply response like those just summarized.[6] Other valid policy experiments used interstate differences in welfare policies to infer the differences in labor supply. These tend to confirm that marginal rates of taxation do matter, especially when they are combined with work hours requirements.[7] Yet if this smaller group of studies confirms that more generous guarantees of a minimum income discourage work, why don't such guarantees drag down the GDP of high-budget welfare states? We return to this puzzle below.

Simulations

The next type of analysis uses computer simulation models to follow how the effects of taxes and welfare payments would reduce output and well-being. It focuses mainly on the cost of the tax side, though some exercises in this genre also allow for those productivity disincentives on the recipients' side.

Since the 1970s several economists have used basic theory and computer simulations to estimate how much, in their view, greater taxes and social spending will cost the nation as a percentage of the amounts transferred. While the reasoning would have been clear to an eighteenth-century critic of poor relief, the analytical apparatus is much more sophisticated. Our focus here is on their results, not on the details of their assumptions.

The deadweight-cost argument rests on a strong negative influence of tax-based spending on GDP, an influence that should rise with the square of the tax wedge. In an article in the *Journal of Political Economy*, Browning and Johnson argued in 1984 that each dollar redistributed to the poor not only costs taxpayers that dollar but also entails an additional $2.49 of dead-weight costs around 1976.[8] At that time the Browning–Johnson estimate was atypical both in method and in magnitude. Yet even measures based on more widely accepted welfare economics, such as Charles Stuart's estimate of $0.72 in deadweight costs on top of the dollar taken from taxpayers, also suggested substantial costs. Alternative simulations by Ballard and Triest got deadweight-cost rates like those of Stuart, such as $0.50–1.30 in certain baseline cases.[9] These are still noticeable costs.

A more recent set of simulations has raised the imagined price once again. In a 1999 article in the *Review of Economics and Statistics*, Martin Feldstein estimated the welfare losses from the income tax around 1991. His focus was limited to the tax side, with emphasis on tax-avoidance behavior other than the usually imagined withdrawal of labor and capital. Having an income tax system at all has cost us only 32 cents in welfare for each dollar collected. Expanding the marginal income tax rates by 10 percent would be worse, however, costing $2.06 for each dollar raised. And making the income tax system more progressive would bring a deadweight loss of $3.76 for every dollar of revenue.

High as these estimates may seem, they all leave out a cost we should include if we are to quantify the effects of the tax-transfer system on the level of gross national product, something easier to measure than deadweight losses or gains in well-being. The deadweight cost concept allows any loss of productive effort to be offset in part by the value of one's own extra home time (if one works fewer hours) or of one's energy. Any drop in gross domestic product is *not* offset by that personal saving of time and energy, so the resulting drops in GDP would be typically bigger in the simulations run by these studies than their deadweight-loss price tags have shown us. If these studies are correct, the GDP loss from extra taxes and social spending must be huge.

The most glaring limitation of the simulation-based estimates of the dead-weight cost per dollar redistributed is their sheer extravagance. How could countries spending a sixth of GDP on welfare alone and, taking half of GDP in taxes, defy their logic? Surely the deadweight costs should show up empirically. Consider the fact that Sweden spent 20 percent more of GDP on tax-based social transfers than the United States in 1995. If we used the simulation-based deadweight cost multipliers, Sweden's decision to have such a large welfare state must have cost Sweden anything from 10 percent (the bottom Ballard–Triest estimates) to 50 percent of GDP (Browning–Johnson), or even higher if Sweden had a progressive tax system like that Feldstein imagined. Such large figures, again, refer only to the deadweight costs, not the larger GDP costs. Such huge effects cannot be plausible unless empirical tests can somehow establish such large costs. Nor did any of the simulation studies provide the evidence, the empirical tests. Like the blackboard exercises and the parables, they are educated fiction. The computer was told to imagine a virtual reality. We await the true tests.

Global Growth Econometrics

The final kind of evidence of the growth costs of government spending takes the econometric form of a significantly negative coefficient on government consumption in recent studies that explore the determinants of 1960s–1980s growth in scores of countries around the world.[10] These studies succeed in taking many factors into account, including political instability and type of political regime. The fact that they get negative effects of government consumption suggests a cost of bigger government that stands out when other factors have been given their due.

The econometrics of economic growth in global cross-sections cannot be used to assess the cost of redistributive taxes and transfers, however. Their government consumption, which negatively affected growth, does not even refer to social spending.[11] Rather it is government purchases of goods and services other than for current national defense and education, excluding all transfers and most public education services. It therefore consists of an eclectic set of purchased services, including government payrolls.

Even as a comment on the costs of what it does measure, the government consumption measure fails to show costs relating to OECD democracies, for at least two reasons. One is that the government consumption sector is a service-producing sector for which the accepted way to measure its outputs is by measuring its inputs, mainly inputs of labor time. Therefore, by design, no productivity gains can be measured, even if those services are improving. Therefore, a larger government consumption sector automatically lowers the measured labor-productivity growth of the whole economy, regardless of its performance. A second reason for the negative effect of government consumption comes from the sample's inclusion of Third-World nondemocracies. These did indeed waste a lot of money in government consumption between the 1960s and the 1980s. In 1987, for example, such government consumption was 37 percent of GNP in Kenneth Kaunda's Zambia and 26.4 percent in Robert Mugabe's Zimbabwe. The share may have been similar in Mobutu's Zaire, though we lack specific figures. The fact that such kleptocracies were bad for economic growth tells us nothing about Europe's welfare states.

WHAT BETTER TESTS SHOW

The best laboratory for finding the harm that heavy taxation and redistribution might do to economic growth should have these attributes:

(a) Social transfers take a large share of national product on the average – large enough to show their damage to GDP per capita.

(b) Their share varies greatly over the sample.

(c) The units of observation are the polities that set policy toward taxes and social transfers.

(d) We have credible data on most of the usual leading sources of growth, not just the budgetary policies being judged.

(e) The sample is a pooled time-series and cross-sectional analysis, in order to walk the least dangerous line between the perils of time-series analysis and the perils of cross-sectional analysis.

(f) We have enough separate insights on the sources of both social transfer behavior and economic growth to identify both sides of the simultaneous system explaining both social spending and growth. Other studies have omitted this simultaneity between policy determination and the sources of growth, with possible biases in their growth results.

(g) We allow the GDP effects of social transfers to be nonlinear. Theory says they should rise nonlinearly, but authors of past empirical studies have failed to explore this crucial twist.

These attributes call for a postwar OECD sample, whether or not it is supplemented by data from non-OECD countries in the good data club. The tests are presented in Chapter 18 of Volume 2. Here I shall simply summarize two key results:

(1) The data do confirm the usual intuition if we ask about imaginary bad versions of the welfare state. For example, if a country foolishly taxed only capital or property, and taxed them so heavily as to fund a Swedish level of social transfers, then yes, there would be large costs in terms of GDP, though the deadweight costs would be smaller.

(2) The overriding fact about the cases of costly welfare states, though, is that *they never happened*. Such costs only arise when the patterns are *extrapolated beyond the sample range*, beyond the actual historical experience. Within the range of true historical experience, there is no clear net GDP cost of higher social transfers. Here the econometrics confirm the general drift of the institutional and historical facts we turn to next.

HOW CAN THAT BE TRUE?

How can the statistical evidence contradict our common belief that taxing and transferring through government will lower national product?

Institutional history can explain how econometric near-zero results are not only plausible but even likely. Knowing more of the recent history of the high-budget welfare states can stimulate fresh thinking about how program costs and benefits are handled in practice, even though we cannot offer a complete accounting of all growth effects. The keys are to be found on both the tax side and the social spending side of the welfare state. Let us turn first to the taxpayers' side, before looking at the transfer recipients' side and the pro-growth social programs.

THE WELFARE-STATE STYLE OF TAXING: PRO-GROWTH AND NOT SO PROGRESSIVE

Postwar history has brought the evolution of a different style of taxation in the countries where social transfers take a large share of GDP. Contrary to what many have assumed about redistributive welfare states, that style tends to raise GDP and inequality, relative to the tax mixtures in the lower-spending countries. In some high-tax high-budget social democracies, the taxation of capital accumulation is actually *lighter* than the taxation of labor earnings and of leisure-oriented addictive goods. That, at least, is what the latest attempts to compare tax rates across countries seem to tell us.

Measuring the growth effects of the whole tax system is at least as difficult as measuring the growth effects of government social expenditures. The first problem is to decide between marginal tax rates and average tax rates. There are advantages and drawbacks to each.

Knowing that it is marginal rates, not average rates, of taxation that govern choices about how much to work or accumulate or innovate, economists have tried to measure the growth effects of "the" marginal rate of income taxation.[12] Yet as the path-breaking authors in this line of research freely admit, marginal tax rates are not only harder to find for a large sample of countries, but hard to trust as well. There are two core problems with using marginal tax rates as quantifiable growth influences. One is that marginal rates of taxation are too numerous to summarize. Even a single income-tax code typically has a multiplicity of marginal rates, and it is not obvious how to average them into "the" marginal rate. The other core problem is that individuals find numerous ways, mostly legal, to make the effective marginal rate lower than the top official marginal rate. Many individuals switch activities or assets so as to cut the effective tax, and it is hard to measure the lower marginal incentive they actually face.

The difficulties of gathering and interpreting marginal tax rates have led other researchers to develop the "average effective tax rate" (AETR), first in a series of articles by Enrique Mendoza and coauthors and then in some OECD studies.[13] Once again the authors have been candid about the limitations of their estimates. All the usual ambiguities about the final incidence of taxes apply to the AETRs, as well as to the marginal rates. While the AETRs may

TABLE 10.1. *Marginal and Average Tax Rates 1991–1999 versus the Social Transfer Share of GDP 1995*

| | Top Marginal Tax Rate on Dividends in 1998 | Tax Wedge on the 1999 Percent Rate of Return on Capital in Manufacturing | Average Effective Tax Rates, 1991–1997 | | versus – Social Transfers in 1995, as a Percent of GDP |
			on Income of Labor	on Consumption	
Australia	48.5	1.6	22.6	11.9	14.8
Austria	25.0	1.2	41.8	20.0	21.4
Belgium	15.0	1.1	39.7	18.7	27.1
Canada	54.1	4.0	28.7	13.1	18.1
Denmark	40.0	2.3	42.8	25.7	30.9
Finland	28.0	1.3	44.5	22.7	31.6
France	61.0	4.0	40.2	18.0	26.9
Germany	55.9	1.6	35.9	15.8	24.9
Greece	0.0	0.4	24.3	18.6	14.4
Ireland	48.0	2.1	25.1	22.8	18.3
Italy	12.0	1.0	36.3	16.0	23.7
Japan	65.0	2.9	24.0	6.7	12.2
Netherlands	60.0	2.8	41.0	18.7	25.7
New Zealand	33.0	1.5	24.2	19.8	18.6

Norway	28.0	1.1	35.5	26.9	27.6
Portugal	25.0	1.1	22.7	20.5	15.2
Spain	47.6	2.3	30.4	13.7	19.0
Sweden	30.0	1.9	48.5	18.7	33.0
Switzerland	43.9	1.9	30.2	8.4	18.9
U.K.	40.0	2.3	21.0	16.9	22.5
U.S.	46.6	2.6	22.6	6.1	13.7
Simple average	38.4	2.0	32.5	17.1	21.8
Correlation with social Transfer share	−0.135	−0.045	0.882	0.615	

Sources and Notes: The marginal tax rates on top dividend income are from Carey and Tchilinguirian (2000, Table 13). The figures for the average tax rates on labor income and on general consumption are from Table 4 of the same source, though Carey and Rabesona (2002) imply somewhat different rates. The simple average of the rate-of-return wedges on retained earnings, new equity, and lending at interest refer to rates in the manufacturing sector, as estimated by Joumard (2001, Table 5). The cigarette tax rates are from http://www.drugs.indiana.edu/drug_stats/cigtax_burden, last accessed on December 12, 2000. The tax rate on alcoholic content was derived using data from *OECD Revenue Statistics 1965–1999* (OECD, 2000b); *OECD Health Data 2000* (OECD, 2000a); and United Nations (1998) *World Population Prospects, 1996 Revision.* The environmental tax shares of GDP are taken from Joumard (2001, 24). The social transfers shares are derived from OECD's CD-ROM *OECD Social Expenditure Database 1980–1996* (1999) and from World Penn Tables, version 6.0, early file as of December 2000.

The regression line slopes' confidence intervals exclude zero at the 5 percent level in all the upward-sloping cases, but not for capital and property taxes.

have the defect of not being the most incentive-relevant marginal rates, they capture in their own indirect way many of the effects of tax exemptions and tax avoidance.

Let us turn to a mixture of the two approaches. For capital incomes, let us look at two kinds of marginal rates paid by corporations and top-income households. Capital incomes have not been subject to higher rates of taxation in the welfare states than in, say, the United States. So say the top marginal tax rates on dividends and on all sources of capital invested in manufacturing.[14]

Whatever one might have thought, smaller-government countries such as Japan, the United States, and Canada tax business investors at least as heavily as the welfare states of Scandinavia or Belgium. Taken at face value, the estimates in Table 10.1 and Figures 10.1 and 10.2 imply that the taxation

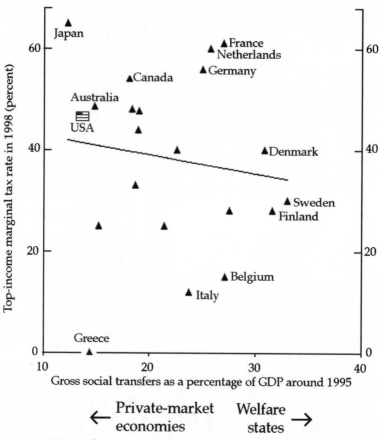

FIGURE 10.1. Marginal Tax Rate on Dividends Earned by Top Incomes 1998, versus Social Transfers 1995.

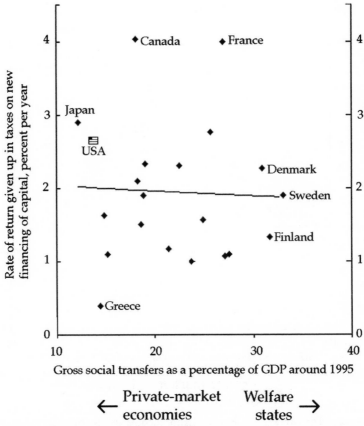

FIGURE 10.2. Marginal Tax Wedge on Capital Finance in Manufacturing 1999, versus Social Transfers 1995.

of capital and property is slightly negatively related to the social-transfer share of GDP, a proxy for welfare state democracy. One institutional mechanism underlying the burden on capital in low-spending Canada, Japan, and the United States in Figure 10.1 is their double-taxation of dividends, as both corporate income and household income. Other countries, including the welfare states, either excuse dividends from personal income tax or give it a lighter tax rate.[15] The U.S. Canadian, and Japanese taxation of business investors is also slightly higher as an average of all three sources of corporate investment funds – retained earnings, new equity, and lending to manufacturing businesses – as shown in Figure 10.2. So far, the clear conclusion is that business dividends and real investments are taxed no higher in the high-budget welfare states.

The capital-taxation issue has been explicitly debated in countries like Sweden, with attention to issues of international capital mobility as well as

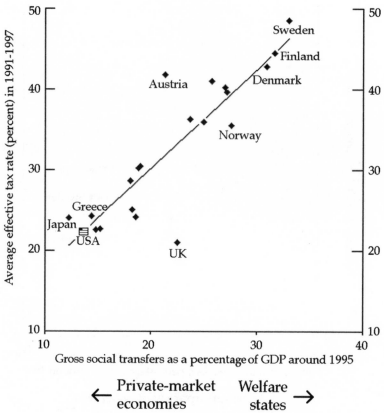

FIGURE 10.3. The Average Tax Rate on Labor Income versus Social Transfers, 1991–1997.

to issues of equity. Indeed, in Sweden in the 1980s, the effective net tax rate on personal capital income was actually negative for the top 60 percent of the income ranks, once one adjusts for the generous provisions regarding deductions of interest payments and other tax advantages. It has been estimated that the taxation of personal capital income *reduced* government tax revenues by half a percent of GDP as of 1982. Part of the tax relief on capital came from the distinction between real and nominal income in the presence of rising prices. Wealthy households got to deflate their gross capital incomes to pay on only their real incomes in prices of an earlier year. Yet they got to deduct the full nominal value of interest payments on debts incurred to pay for their capital assets. Accordingly, many wealthy households took on higher gross assets and debt than otherwise, thus avoiding virtually all taxes on capital income. As of 1982, the final effective tax rate on capital income was still positive for modest-income households but actually negative for the wealthy.[16] Thus the true average tax rates on Swedish capital and property incomes were lower than the rates shown here.

By contrast, labor incomes have been taxed more heavily in the welfare-state countries, as Figure 10.3 shows. Their preference for taxing labor rather than capital is regressive, of course. It is also pro-growth, to the extent that capital is internationally mobile and would take positive productivity effects with it when migrating. Indeed the difference here resembles a change in the tax system that U.S. public economists have favored on growth grounds, namely full replacement of all capital income taxation with labor taxation. The median U.S. specialist in public economics thinks that the shift from capital taxation to labor taxation would raise the annual growth rate of GDP by 0.2 percent.[17] The pro-growth regressive switch in tax mixture has been put into effect – in the welfare states, not in the United States.

Consumption taxes are more pro-growth than income taxes, as many conservatives have insisted. If you are subject only to a 15 percent consumption tax now and forever, with no income tax, your incentive to save is not

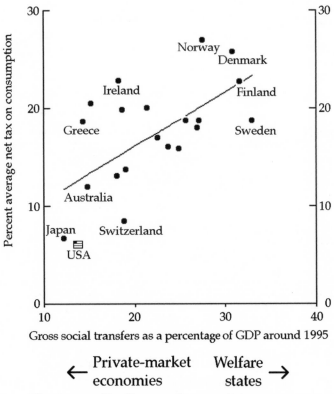

FIGURE 10.4. The Average Tax Rate on Consumption 1991–1997 versus Social Transfers 1995.

strongly affected. Either you pay the 15 percent on today's consumption or you pay the same 15 percent when consuming a future accumulation of income. As long as we discount your future taxes at the same discount rate you earn on the accumulated savings, the present value of your consumption taxes is the same whether you spend now or you save so that you and your heirs can have more to spend later.[18] Income taxes, by contrast, take from your saved income twice, both when you initially earned the income you decided to save and again when your savings earns new capital income.

As Figure 10.4 shows, the welfare-state democracies also tax consumption more heavily, just as they tax labor incomes heavily. The heaviest tax rates on general consumption tend to be those in Scandinavia (and Ireland). By contrast, this more pro-savings and pro-growth form of taxation has been less preferred in low-spending Japan, Switzerland, the United States, and Australia.

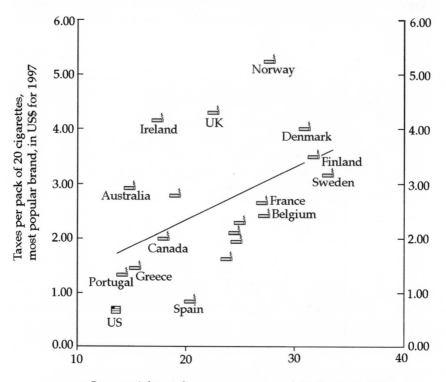

Gross social transfers as a percentage of GDP around 1995

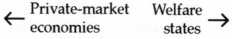

FIGURE 10.5. The Average Tax Rate on Cigarettes 1997 versus Social Transfers around 1995.

The difference even extends to the design, as well as the overall level, of consumption taxes. The consumption tax is not only higher, but *flatter* in high-budget Europe than in the low-spending countries. Food and other necessities have historically had to pay the same consumption tax rate as other goods in Denmark, Norway, and Sweden, in contrast to the practice in other settings, such as exempting foods from state sales taxes in the United States. Similarly, luxuries usually do not bear special higher tax rates in the same three Scandinavian countries or in Germany or Ireland.[19]

Another striking pattern emerges when we look at the taxation of specific types of consumption goods. To encourage work ethic, health, and a cleaner environment, one would want to shift taxation away from productive activities and toward the consumption of addictive goods that are complements to leisure or threaten health and environmental quality. To serve these social goals, one would want to lower the general tax rates on income and consumption and raise the specific tax rates on tobacco, alcohol, and gasoline – even though such a shift takes a greater percentage tax bite from lower income groups.

Which countries put the heaviest taxes on three kinds of goods with external costs is shown in Figures 10.5–10.7. The heavier the reliance on social transfers through government, the heavier the tax rates on cigarettes, alcohol,

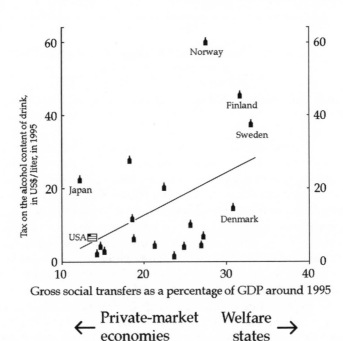

FIGURE 10.6. The Average Tax Rate on Alcohol Content of Drinks, versus Social Transfers in 1995.

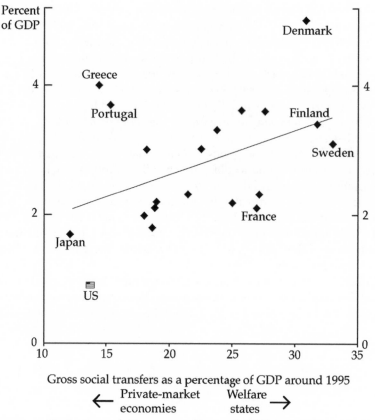

FIGURE 10.7. Environmental Taxes as a Share of GDP in 1998, versus Social Transfers.

and such environmental-cost products as gasoline. Behavior that has bad externalities ends up being punished more in welfare states. In each case, special national factors might have played a role. For cigarettes, it might be that tobacco producer interests, as in the United States and Japan, lobbied for holding down the tax and for delays in the rise of antismoking laws.[20] For alcohol, it might be that Scandinavian governments are able to exploit a less elastic demand. For gasoline and other environmental-cost goods, the correlation may be reinforced by the United States' peculiar policy taste for heavy energy consumption, which might be unrelated to budgetary fights over the welfare state. Yet the correlations with social transfer budgets remain.

Thus the welfare-state choice of a large overall tax burden to support transfers is usually accompanied by the political choice of taxes that promote growth and environmental quality – without equalizing incomes much more than in lower-spending countries.[21] This is not just a temporary condition captured in our 1995 snapshots. It has been the case over the last third of the twentieth century, with some softening of the relative taxes on capital after

1980. We are several steps closer to understanding how high shares of social transfers in GDP might not have meant any reduction in GDP per capita.

On the recipients' side, as well as on the taxpayers' side, welfare states seem to avoid huge disincentives. In some policy dimensions, recipients of transfers in high-budget countries have *more* incentive to work than their U.S. counterparts. In other policy dimensions, the higher-budget welfare states do indeed discourage more work, but with little effect on GDP.

The Poor May Face Lower Work Disincentives in the Welfare State

Just as the high-budget countries often have lower marginal tax rates at the top of the income spectrum, so too they can have lower marginal tax rates at the bottom, with high marginal tax rates only across the broad middle range of incomes. If that is true, then the debate over work incentives needs to be redirected. The net effect on labor supply and GDP may depend on something never researched, namely whether work and productivity respond more sensitively to marginal tax rates in the middle range or at the ends. If the response is greater in the middle range, then the welfare state indeed reduces work and GDP. But if conservative fears are correct in emphasizing that the supply of effort is most fragile at the two ends of the income spectrum, then it is possible that the pattern of marginal tax rates in the high-budget welfare states discourages work less than the pattern prevailing in low-budget countries.

Fortunately, we have the benefit of a long policy debate and careful research that has penetrated the jungle of marginal incentives faced by those at the bottom of the income spectrum, most of it relating to the United States and the United Kingdom. The policy under investigation is the policy toward poor lone parents – or unmarried "welfare mothers" in the U.S. parlance. A pair of studies has grappled with the whole complexity of the tax and transfer system that people face in that situation.

The United States' national policy has traditionally faced poor lone parents with high marginal tax rates, cutting off aid as soon as the recipient earns even a low-wage income.[22] The Social Security Act of 1935 set up AFDC this way. The then-small population of single mothers, mainly young widows who were expected to stay at home with the children, faced a 100-percent marginal tax rate on any earnings. Such strict "means testing" of benefits had become controversial by the 1960s, when the share of women who sought work outside the home had risen considerably. Economists Milton Friedman and James Tobin, among others, called for a change in policy that would let the poor keep much of their benefits while still earning modest amounts outside the home. In 1967 such concerns helped to shape

TABLE 10.2. *Hurdles in the Path Out of Poverty: Marginal Net Tax Rates Faced by a Lone Parent with Two Children in the United States and Britain in 2000*

Each number is a marginal net tax rate, or the change in (gross earnings − benefits), as a percentage of the change in gross earnings

| | The Change in the Parent's Work Scenario: | | | |
	From no Work to Part Time Min. Wage	From Part Time to Full Time, Min. Wage	From Min-Wage to $9/hour, Full Time	The Whole Jump, from no Work to $9/hour Full Time
If there were no Tax Credits for Low-Pay Work (no EITC in U.S., and no WFTC in U.K.)				
Median of 12 U.S. states	52	67	27	51
United Kingdom	141	83	2	60
With the Actual Tax Credits for Low-Pay Work (EITC in U.S. and WFTC in U.K.)				
Median of 12 U.S. states	12	28	65	45
United Kingdom	−2	7	69	33
Sweden 1991	<— Between 30% and 50% —>			

246

Sources and Notes: The sources are Acs et al. (1998), Brewer (2000), and Gustafsson and Klevmarken (1993).

EITC = Earned Income Tax Credit on modest wage incomes in the United States. EITC started on a modest scale in 1975 and was expanded in 1986–1994. This calculation based on October 1997 rates ignores some state supplements to the federal EITC that were being set up around 2000.

WFTC = Working Families Tax Credit in the United Kingdom, which reached its current levels in June 2000, after starting more modestly in 1971.

Part-time work = 20 hours a week, and full-time work = 35 hours a week.

Min. wage = For the United States the national minimum wage as of October 1997, or $5.15 an hour. For comparison with the United States Brewer's calculation for the United Kingdom uses £3.65 an hour as the $5.15 minimum wage and £6.50 as the $9 wage.

These calculations assume a 30-day month of 4.29 (=30/7) work weeks.

I have ignored any effect of EITC on other benefits or tax rates.

I have assumed that the U.S. parent has not yet exhausted her lifetime welfare eligibility under the U.S. welfare reform of 1996 (PRWORA). In the U.S. case, none of these work scenarios receives enough net disposable income to lift the three-person household out of poverty. Working full time at $9 an hour brings a net income of only $1351 a month, whereas the official poverty line for such a household was $1367 in 1997.

Each of these calculations ignores consumption taxes.

The twelve U.S. states analyzed by Acs et al. are Alabama, California, Colorado, Florida, Massachusetts, Michigan, Minnesota, Mississippi, New Jersey, New York, Texas, and Washington. In all twelve cases, every contrast between rates is in the same direction as described in the text.

The Swedish rates are the averages of those generally characteristic of a single adult student, a couple with children in day care, and an absent parent subject to child support, all in Stockholm 1991.

new legislation lowering the marginal tax rate to two-thirds, but in 1981 Congress and the Reagan Administration reverted to stricter means testing and raised the marginal tax rate back to 100 percent. Meanwhile, related welfare programs expanded and became more complex, so that an accurate measure of the true marginal tax rate would require an in-depth study of the combination of AFDC, Food Stamps, medical care for the poor, subsidized housing, child care subsidies, and Supplemental Security Income for groups with particular needs.

Yet the concern about heavily taxing work by the poor continued to push both the United States and Britain toward a system that lowered the marginal tax rate for those getting a low-paying job. In both countries this took the form of a tax credit for low-earning households, beginning in the 1970s but becoming a major factor only in the 1990s. In the United States, this tax credit is the Earned Income Tax Credit (EITC) started in 1975 and greatly expanded in 1993. The British counterpart is the Working Family Tax Credit (WFTC), started as the Family Income Supplement in 1971 and fully implemented in 2000. Similar employment-conditioned benefits now exist in Australia, Ireland, Canada, Finland, France, and New Zealand, most of them countries with relatively low social transfer budgets.

The 1990s drift toward EITC and WFTC lowered marginal tax rates at the bottom of the income spectrum, raising them in the "phase-out range" further up the ranks. The upper panel of Table 10.2, even though it is based on conditions in the year 2000, aptly shows the state of play before the 1990s, such as the 1970s world of Charles Murray's fictitious Harold and Phyllis. When the poor didn't get any tax credits for low-pay work, they faced very high marginal tax rates in both countries. By taking on low-paying work, a single mother could lose more than half of her earnings in withdrawn benefits, a higher marginal tax rate than is faced by most people.

What would happen if instead of tough means testing, we let poor lone parents keep much of their extra earnings? This experiment has crept into U.S. and British policy when EITC and WFTC were phased in. It's a step toward the universalist approach to family benefits in some high-budget welfare states, where you keep your benefits, still paid for by taxpayers, even if your earnings rise toward the national average. The lower panel in Table 10.2 shows us the results under this policy of tax credits for low-paid work, as practiced in these two countries plus Sweden. In the United States and Britain it lowers the tax rates from getting a job at all and from moving from part-time to full-time work at minimum wages. On the other hand, it raises the marginal tax rate higher up the ladder, as shown by the third column of numbers. Reaching that phase-out range is inevitable, since somebody somewhere up the income ranks must pay the extra taxes if the poorest people don't. Still, the final column reveals that the drift toward broader forgiveness from taxes has brought a net reduction in marginal tax rates for the whole range of options facing lone parents in the bottom income ranks.

So at the bottom of the income spectrum, as at the top end subject to taxes on capital and property income, the universalist welfare states may well have lower marginal tax rates than the lower-budget countries, which emphasize strict means testing. Table 10.2 implies that Sweden was a more universalist case, keeping the marginal tax rate below 50 percent for people below the threshold for defining poverty.[23]

If welfare states really have lower marginal tax rates at the top and bottom of the income spectrum, but higher tax rates in the middle, do they discourage work more, or less, than the low-budget governments of Japan, Switzerland, and the United States? Putting it this way shows that the net balance of work disincentives rests on something that nobody has measured yet. How do these conflicting responses net out for the labor force as a whole? We don't know yet. For now, it is time to take one step backward, away from the common implicit assumption that higher-tax countries have higher marginal tax rates up and down the income ranks.

Early Retirement: Good Riddance to Old Lemons?

The most dramatic withdrawal of people from paid work has occurred in the fifty-five to sixty-four age group, not among young single mothers or work-shirking young men. As we saw in Chapter 8, many European countries took dangerous steps to subsidize earlier retirement. This invitation to quit work earlier, combined with the rise of senior life expectancy, has hastened the crisis over pension budgets.

So surely, one might think, it is in the lavish public subsidies to earlier retirement that we finally discover a program that must have taken a large toll on gross domestic product. And the subsidies are indeed lavish in some cases. Take the case of France versus the United States. In 1995, France spent 10.9 percent of GDP on public pensions, disability, and survivors' benefits, which was more than double the U.S. share of 5.2 percent. Many of the extra French benefits went to people who were in the fifty-five to sixty-four age group, in the form of more generous pensions, more generous disability payments, and special unemployment benefits for that age group.[24] In the same year, the percentages of people in the fifty-five to sixty-four age group who were working differed as follows:

	France	United States
Both sexes	33.6	55.1
Men	38.4	63.6
Women	28.9	47.5

Doesn't France's paying people to quit work in their mid-fifties and early sixties mean dramatic losses in GDP? Hasn't the United States gained GDP by restraining the invitation to earlier retirement?

In fact, public subsidies to early retirement have only a negligible cost in terms of GDP, for three main reasons.[25] First, we must remember that the incentive to retire in the fifty-five to sixty-four age range is built into many private employers' pension plans as well as public social security programs. A world in which taxpayers decline to subsidize early retirement is still a world in which each extra year of work just before age sixty-five can still pay a tax in the form of lost retirement benefits. Private and public pension programs vary in their net retirement incentives, and the average difference is less than the public subsidy viewed alone.[26]

Second, even in the smoking-gun cases where public pension programs do kill some work incentives, and the GDP loss cannot be zero – as in Belgium, France, Germany, Italy, and the Netherlands[27] – the loss of output is still quite small. Some basic accounting guides us toward a rough answer. Here is a definitional relationship between the gross domestic product per capita, numbers of workers, and the age distribution: GDP per capita = GDP per worker *times* (total workers divided by the fifty-five to sixty-four population) *times* (fifty-five to sixty-four population divided by total population).

Converting this into rates of change and rearranging terms yields a link between the growth of GDP per capita and the amount of labor lost by subsidies to earlier retirement: The percentage change in GDP per capita induced by retirement subsidies = (A) the percentage change in productivity per worker *plus the product of these three terms*:

- (B) induced percentage change in employment for the fifty-five to sixty-four age group,
- (C) the share of those fifty-five to sixty-four who are employed (if no subsidies), and
- (D) the ratio of the fifty-five to sixty-four age group's population to total employment.

For France in 1995, the policy-induced percentage change in employment (B) might have been as great as the whole difference between the French and U.S. employment shares for the age group, or (33.6 percent minus 55.1 percent = −21.5 percent. This looks like a large number. In fact, it was larger than the percentage shortfall of France's GDP per worker below the U.S. GDP per worker in 1995, or 19 percent. But the GDP effect of the jobs given up by France's fifty-five to sixty-four year olds is smaller. Using the formula above, this induced change of −21.5 percent in employment for the fifty-five to sixty-four age group must be multiplied by the two fractions (C) and (D). One is the initial share of those in the fifty-five to sixty-four age group who would have jobs if there were no early-retirement subsidy (C). That initial share would be something below France's actual share of 0.336, but let's use the 0.336 multiplier to get a conservatively high number. The next fraction is the ratio of France's fifty-five to sixty-four population to France's total employment for all age groups. This works out to 0.259. So the policy-induced change of −21.5 percent gets multiplied by (0.336 times 0.259), which brings it down to a net GDP loss of less than 1.9 percent – *if* the same ratios applied to all women. They do not. The effects on women's work are smaller, suggesting a still lower GDP cost. The same point holds for five main smoking-gun cases of taxpayer subsidies to early retirement – Belgium, France, Germany, Italy, and the Netherlands – though it does not apply to the longer-working populations of Canada, Japan, Sweden, Norway, and the United States.

The third reason deserves the most attention here. Subsidizing early retirement probably *raises productivity* per worker. That is, it raises (A) in the simple accounting above. Those who retire early have lower-than-average productivity in their age group. Having them quit work means an even lower percentage cost in GDP than in employment.

Could early retirement have no cost at all in terms of GDP? Could the marginal productivity of a retiring senior worker be zero? Such an absolute-zero result was actually suggested by Xavier Sala-i-Martin in 1996. In what we might call his "good riddance to geezers" hypothesis, Sala-i-Martin argued that older workers could be so counterproductive in their effect on the whole work unit's output that their marginal product is in fact zero. That might be the case if senior workers have excessive power and are especially hard to get rid of once their marginal product has dropped off. He quoted the controversial remarks of Doctor William Osler in a valedictory address at Johns Hopkins University on February 22, 1905:

My...fixed idea is the uselessness of men above sixty years of age, and the incalculable benefit it would be in commercial, in political, and in professional life, if, as a matter of course, men stopped work at this age....That incalculable benefits might follow from such a scheme is apparent to any one who, like myself, is nearing that limit, and who has made a careful study of the calamities which may befall men during the seventh and eighth decades [of life]. Still more when he contemplates the many evils which they perpetuate unconsciously, and with impunity.[28]

Sala-i-Martin says that university faculties illustrate Osler's point. Faculties could still produce as much if they paid professors over, say, fifty-five to leave campus permanently. The idea deserves further investigation (by younger faculty?), even if the assumption that an extra fifty-five to sixty-four year-old adds zero to the economy seems extreme, at least to this author.

The truth, if less extreme, does point in the same direction. The productivity of the lost labor is reduced by the way in which the early-retirement incentives are structured. Countries that invite early retirement actually send a more urgent invitation to the less productive workers. The Gruber–Wise research team found a much greater early-retirement subsidy for workers earning only in the 10th salary percentile than for workers earning in the 90th. Lower-earning, and presumably less productive, workers were given much less incentive to continue work in those same five countries – Belgium, France, Germany, Italy, and the Netherlands – and also in Canada, Japan, Spain, and Sweden. Of the eleven countries studied by the Gruber–Wise research team, only the United States and Britain kept the tax on senior workers low at all salary levels up to age sixty-five.[29] There is at least some evidence that such generous exit packages were approved and manipulated by employers as a way of getting rid of less productive and more problematic workers.[30]

There is indirect evidence that less productive senior workers do respond more strongly, given the stronger invitation, relative to more productive seniors. The OECD found a definite relationship between educational level and the employment shares at different age groups.[31] Those who stay on the job tend to be more educated in any age group, but especially in the fifty-five to sixty-four age group. For French men in 1995, with generous early-retirement subsidies in effect, there was a particularly strong educational twist in the age–employment profile. The share of men with a university education who were still at work in the fifty-five to sixty-four age group was 30 percentage points greater than if they had retired as fast as the less educated. This pattern, combined with the biased retirement incentives we have just noted, suggests that early-retirement policies deliberately and successfully culled out the less productive and kept the more productive at work.

Does the Dole Also Harvest Lemons?

Thus far my listing of work incentive studies has given only light treatment to a core kind of transfer payment: classic unemployment compensation, or what British history has called "the dole." Doesn't this kind of subsidy to not working (for a while) lower job-taking? The answer is yes, it does lower employment, according to both past writings and new results aired in Volume 2.[32] But here a puzzle arises: If the dole clearly cuts employment, why does it not visibly reduce GDP?

The resolution to this part of the puzzle is twofold. First, the true effect of unemployment compensation on GDP could be negative, but small enough to hide within the broad confidence intervals in statistical tests. Second, jobs may be lost with very little reduction of GDP if the more generous unemployment compensation widely practiced in Europe actually raises the average productivity of those who continue to work. This might occur because European governments use unemployment compensation as a way to get the least productive workers out of their jobs, to leave a more productive labor force at work, just as we saw them doing with early retirement policies. That is, the dole may be so implemented in practice that it casts out "lemon" workers, those with the lowest contribution to overall labor productivity. Indeed, Chapter 19 in Volume 2 revises the econometrics of European job markets to show that more generous unemployment compensation goes with higher productivity per worker or per labor hour, other things equal.

SOME GROWTH BENEFITS OF HIGH SOCIAL TRANSFERS

Thus far, we have established that the GDP costs of early retirement and unemployment compensation are close to zero, even closer than their effects on labor time would imply. From these costs should be subtracted any small gains in work and earnings coming from the fact that higher-budget welfare states may impose a lower marginal tax rate on poor lone parents. The deadweight effects on well-being are smaller still, because the reduction in labor time means a gain in valuable home time. Were we to switch focus from GDP costs to true well-being, then the extra leisure and vacation time of the European welfare states would loom large enough to erase any net loss at all. Yet if we stick with the GDP focus of the free-lunch puzzle, there is still a bit more work to do. As long as there is a net reduction of work from the welfare-state package, we should still presume that the GDP loss is close to zero, but not zero.

The next step is to note that some kinds of social transfers have positive effects on the level and growth of GDP. Many types of social transfers are in fact pro-growth, and the growth benefits they provide tend to be greater in the higher-spending countries. If we set aside the clear productivity gains from extra public education, which are not defined as "social transfers" here and were covered in Chapter 6, what kinds of social transfers are most likely to have a positive GDP impact that has not been confronted yet?

Active Labor Market Policies: Not Much There

We start on the downbeat, with a social transfer that should have raised GDP, but probably brings very little net gain at best. Support for the unemployed often includes sizable expenditures on "active labor market policies" (ALMP), a rubric that covers public subsidies to job search, job retraining, and public sector jobs for those who are hard to employ.

Studies of the ALMP bundle of pro-job interventions suggest only modest payoff in improved job-holding and earnings and therefore a near-zero rate of return. The modesty and fragility of the gains show up in all three main parts of the ALMP bundle – job search assistance, retraining, and public sector jobs for the least qualified. The return is particularly low for males and not so bad for females, perhaps because females' prior disruption of training was less rooted in an aversion to school.[33]

Such sobering limitations to the payoff of active labor market policies seem to square with three other kinds of findings by labor economists. First, detailed studies have found that ALMP has often been used as a way to pad and extend ordinary passive unemployment benefits. Second, the vast research on interventions to improve the lot of disadvantaged youth has concluded that the earlier the intervention in the life cycle, the better. Interventions in prenatal, infant, and preschool care and training have achieved high returns, especially under certain program designs. Yet programs to set teenagers back on track have shown only weaker returns, unless one counts just keeping them off the streets and out of prison as a major social gain.[34] This earlier-is-better pattern squares with the low returns to retraining and public employment for young adults. Finally, economists are gravitating toward the belief that the greatest gains from public supports for work and earnings come from a mixture of carrots and sticks. For carrots, the emphasis increasingly favors tax credits for earnings such as the United States' EITC or Britain's WFTC, with only a very limited role for retraining programs.[35] On the stick side, work requirements are as effective as retraining programs for part of the population receiving public aid and tax credits. It seems likely that the ALMP policy bundle has not been sufficient to erase even the small net loss of jobs from the same countries' generous unemployment compensation. Yet, as Chapter 19 in Volume 2 shows, ALMP does not significantly change GDP because it raises the productivity of those at work by enough to cancel its negative effect on jobs.

Child Care Support and Career Investment in Mothers

Greater returns appear to have come from the welfare states' stronger support for career continuity for women, especially for mothers. The more modern and skilled-based the economy, the more our human capital is built up on the job. At least as important as extra schooling beyond secondary school is continuity of career development during employment. Whatever interrupts employment and makes one reenter the labor force later is doubly costly. Not only are earnings lost during the time spent out of work, but in a skill-based world one has to prove oneself again and catch up on job skills upon reentering. That people get paid less when reentering work reflects the loss of their productivity in employers' eyes as a result of their career interruption.

The gains from career continuity, and the losses from interrupting it, weigh more heavily on women who have children than they do on either men or childless women. Having a child necessitates at least some work stoppage for mothers, and the work time losses are still very unequally shared between mothers and fathers. How much this costs mothers in lifetime earnings potential depends on how long they are compelled to stay out of work and how much less employers pay and promote women who are perceived as shorter-term employees not riding the career escalator.

We have some hints that the lifetime pay disadvantage of mothers grows in settings where their child care demands are met only in private markets. First, in the United States between 1960 and 1986, the pay disadvantage

TABLE 10.3. *Parental Leave and Child Care Provisions in Sixteen OECD Countries, 1994*

Countries Ranked by Social-Transfer Share of GDP in 1995	Leave Provisions (Weeks)		Gov't Payments for Formal Infant Care as % of GDP
	Parental Leave	Separate Maternal Leave	
Countries with high social-transfer budgets			
Sweden	62		1.36
Finland	26 to 156	17.5	1.08
Denmark	10 to 52	18	1.21
Norway	52		0.91
Belgium	130	15	0.08
France	0 to 156	16	0.24
Countries with intermediate transfer budgets			
W. Germany	156	14	0.27
Italy	26	22	0.10
United Kingdom	(none)	14 to 40	0.35
Austria	112	16	n.a.
Countries with low transfer budgets			
Switzerland 1988	8 to 12	8 to 12	n.a.
New Zealand	52		0.04
Canada	10	17	0
Australia	52	52	0.19
United States	(unpaid) 12		0.01
Japan	52	14	0

Notes and Sources: The infant care subsidies, from all levels of government, consist mainly of formal day care, excluding kindergartens. Some of these percentages refer to earlier years because of reporting changes: The France percentage is for 1989, and those for Italy and West Germany are for 1990. The care facilities used in Britain and the United States were primarily privately run.

The sources on family leave provisions and the family cost of infant care are Waldfogel (1998, 141) and Joshi et al. (1998, 10). The shares of infant care subsidies as percentages of GDP are from the OECD's CD-ROM (1999).

of married women relative to unmarried women widened for all ages up to about forty-six.[36] That disadvantage of married women was presumably a muted reflection of the disadvantage of mothers relative to all childless women. More concretely, the pay-path disadvantage of mothers is estimated to have grown in Britain between 1980 and 1991.[37] Both countries lacked any major government or legal support for women's reclaiming their old jobs after a childbirth interval or any major subsidy for formal child care.

Other countries, however, do have government and legal support for parental leave without job loss plus government support for infant care. The extent of such support is a hidden correlate of social transfers and a hidden source of their growth benefits. Table 10.3 shows which countries those are.

On the whole, countries that support women's careers with parental leave laws and with affordability of child care tend to be those with an overall commitment to social transfer spending. The countries offering new parents the least support are the United States, Britain, Canada, and Switzerland.

The first two columns of Table 10.3 summarize the number of weeks of legally mandated parental leave, sometimes with a separate maternal leave length. For those numbers of weeks, one or both parents can take time off work while retaining their right to return to the same job. Who pays for the leave differs from country to country. For some of the longer-leave countries, the burden is on the taxpayers and the government, especially in Scandinavian countries where the government is the dominant employer of women. In some, it is on the employer, which means that the employer and their employees in the aggregate implicitly pay for some cost of childbirth and infancy. In the United States, the parents must take unpaid leave. Only in 1993 was a national family medical leave act passed guaranteeing the right to reclaim one's job after twelve weeks of parental leave, but those twelve weeks were still without pay.

Government subsidies to the care of infants are more noticeable in Scandinavia and Finland than in other OECD countries. The family therefore shoulders less of a burden to buy infant care than in Britain, the United States, or New Zealand. Accordingly, Scandinavia and Finland also have low pay shortfalls for mothers relative to childless adults of the same age and the highest median wage rates for all women relative to the male median wage.[38] There seems to be a positive return on government investments in infant day care, though the rates of return have not yet been quantified.

Thus government financial and legal support for working mothers appears to be an underlying pro-growth feature of welfare states. It seems likely that this return can be cumulative over decades and generations. A major barrier to women's being promoted to more productive and higher-paying jobs has been "statistical discrimination." A common form of this discrimination is employers' perceptions that there is less need to invest in the intrafirm careers of young women because childbearing may take those women back out of the labor force.[39] The more continuity there is in women's careers, helped by subsidies and laws cutting the private cost of motherhood, the more the perception of a gender difference in job commitment will erode, allowing women more on-the-job accumulation of skills.

While the gains in women's work and in GDP from such career supports are hard to quantify, the hints at strong gains agree with other tendencies we have already noted. First, women tend to have a more elastic labor supply than men, so that a given percentage incentive should yield more extra work and earnings if aimed at women than if it is aimed at the same number of men. A supporting hint of such likely gains from this difference in elasticities comes from the fact that women's pay is already closer to men's in several European countries than in the United States, Canada, or Japan. Second, as noted in the previous section, the payoff from job retraining and other active labor market policies looks more hopeful for women, because the women who qualify as needing such programs are less unreceptive to extra schooling and training than the corresponding group of men. Even though specific numbers still elude us, it makes sense that the more committed welfare states' career supports for mothers are likely to have a strong payoff in jobs and GDP.

Public Health Care

People are healthier and live longer in those democracies with a more public and more centralized approach to health care – and the superiority of comprehensive public health care explains part, though only part, of this difference. Here we have an abundance of evidence. To illustrate the possible pro-growth aspect of a public approach, this section focuses on the longevity issue, even though better health raises GDP *per person* only indirectly and modestly.

With life saving as with economic growth, a simple frontal view shows a positive correlation between such social benefits and the welfare state. Figure 10.8 hints that social transfers correlated negatively with male and female mortality in OECD countries in 1995. Both for males and for females, premature mortality looks lower in the higher-budget countries, such as Sweden. The correlation is not very strong, of course. Among low-social-budget countries, the United States stands out as being peculiarly unhealthy, and Japan stands out as being peculiarly healthy.

How could general social transfers be linked to the length of life? To move beyond crude correlations like that in Figure 10.8, we need some systematic way of separating the effects of public health care spending, the part of social spending most directly relevant to longevity, from the many other influences that we know will make nations differ in their average length of life.

One statistical study is particularly convenient for our present purpose of comparing nations' health. Using the new OECD standardized measures of premature mortality and a pooled cross-section approach, Zeynap Or finds that a greater public-expenditure share, for given total expenditures, significantly reduces mortality, especially among men, among OECD countries since 1980.[40] Table 10.4 reports some of the cross-sectional part of the results. In the mortality-change perspective, where minus signs are good, some familiar factors lower mortality down toward the world-best Japanese standard. Those factors include higher income, white-collar occupations, cleaner air, abstention from bad consumption habits, and greater total spending on health care. On balance, though, a more public approach to the same health care expenditures also helps significantly. It explains a small part of the United States' greater mortality. Even beyond this public–private contrast, however, the United States is a high-mortality outlier. Firearms are probably an unmeasured factor, as are cheeseburgers, fries, donuts, and lack of

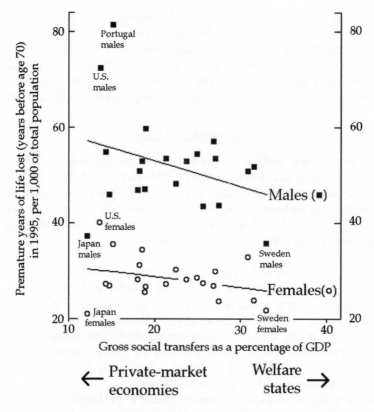

Sources for Figure 10.8: OECD Health Policy Unit, which kindly
supplied the mortality data used in Or (2000), and the
OECD's CD-Rom for social expenditures and GDP.

FIGURE 10.8. The Rate of Early Death in 1992 versus Social Transfers 1995.

exercise. Similarly, Uwe Reinhardt, citing a Germany–U.S. comparison for
1990, decomposes the extra U.S. health cost per capita (PPP$) into higher
U.S. administrative costs, higher U.S. prices, less real use of inputs in U.S.,
and so forth.[41]

One of the mechanisms linking the average length of life to the public–
private institutional choice is the mixture of types of care. Any medical system
mixes basic care for the entire population, including hygiene assistance and
other preventative care, with high-budget items designed to lengthen life for
those middle-age and elderly populations who can afford it. In this difficult
trade-off between broad basic care and sophisticated high-cost care, two
conclusions seem inescapable: (1) any health delivery system must choose to
let somebody die earlier, but (2) those systems that tilt more toward basic
and preventative care seem to achieve longer average life expectancy.

Public health care systems, like private and nonprofit health care providers, must make life-and-death choices. While it is conceivable that an efficient public health system could bring net mortality reductions on all fronts, it does not work out that way in practice. So difficult are the choices that in practice the public health systems, like private medicine, must choose to let some kinds of patients die sooner. That does happen, and there seems to be a pattern to the differences in how public and private systems ration life. The public systems provide less of the highest-budget life-extending services and more of the basic health services protecting mothers, children, and the poor. For example, experiences with overinvestment in CAT scanners and in (in-hospital) renal dialysis has forced U.S. authorities to retreat toward rationing a lesser supply of the relevant equipment, much as the nationalized health systems of Britain, France, and Sweden have done.[42] By contrast, the evidence on basic ground-level health care, featuring preventative medicine through public clinics, has continued to have such a high return as to suggest underinvestment in such care in the more private health care systems.[43]

Still, the efficiency of public health care, and indeed the whole set of factors entertained by Or (2000), can explain only part of the differences in health and life expectancy between the welfare state populations and the most market-oriented populations.[44]

Another part of the explanation may lie in the differences in income gaps. Even for a given kind of health care system, the poor die younger. The relationship between income and wealth is strongly nonlinear. Health status and mortality have been more sensitive to income in the bottom income ranks than across the rest of society. Poverty shortens life through at least three channels: The poor are given less access to health care at public expense, they cannot afford to buy as much health care in private markets, and they take poorer care of themselves. The nonlinear relationship is such that redirecting health care away from those in the bottom fifth of the family-income ranks will lower the average health status and life expectancy of the whole nation.[45]

Historical studies suggest that income inequality, if accompanied by the private approach to national health, shortens life expectancy, both for the poor population and for the entire population. So says historical experience since the late nineteenth century, especially in the United States and Britain.[46] Careful international comparisons of today's health care systems agree, whether they are in-depth comparisons for two countries or broader statistical comparisons of many countries. The verdict is the same whether one is comparing high-income OECD countries, low-income developing countries, or both.[47]

A defender of free-market health might seek to retain the belief that the poor die younger because they do not take care of themselves. Historical and analytical studies do allow a little retreat in this direction, but only a little. It is true that for any given health system, even a free public system, the poor

TABLE 10.4. *Health Care Systems and other Determinants of Life Saving, Selected Countries versus Japan in 1992*

Explaining premature years of life lost (PYLL) per 100,000 persons living in 1992 relative to Japan, both sexes (Negative = better life-saving relative to Japan)

	France	Netherlands	Sweden	U.K.	U.S.	OECD Average
Actual excess mortality (PYLL) relative to Japan	34.7	19.3	6.0	28.2	61.3	31.1
Amount of excess PYLL due to differences in:						
Income and occupations	−5.9	−8.6	−9.9	−4.5	−18.7	4.9
Pollution	6.3	8.8	10.4	9.9	14.5	8.5
Four bad consumption habits	25.9	14.9	6.7	15.0	12.7	13.5
Total health expenditures per capita	0.3	4.1	5.2	5.7	0.9	5.3
Public share of total health expenditures	−0.9	−1.3	−3.1	−2.8	8.5	−0.6
Not explained by any of these forces	8.9	1.4	−3.3	4.8	43.6	−0.5

Sources and Notes: All estimates are from Or (2000/1), with displays results for twenty-one countries, 1970–1992.

PYLL = Premature years of life lost before age 70, per 100,000 of population. An infant death counts as a loss of 70 years, and a death at age 65 counts as 5 years lost. Thus the United States excess of 61.3 relative to Japan in 1992 is equivalent to 6.13 excess U.S. deaths at age 60 per 100,000 of population where the corresponding Japanese would have survived to age 70. Alternatively, the 61.3 is equivalent to almost one (61.3/70) extra infant death per year per 100,000 of population.

Income and occupations = the sum of two products of (regression coefficients* the differentials or changes) in two independent variables.

The two are real GDP per capita in 1990 international dollars and the share of white collar workers in the total labor force.

Pollution = the contribution to PYLL from NO_x emissions per capita, in kilograms per year

Four bad consumption habits = the contributions to premature mortality made by

(1) liters of alcoholic beverages per person over 15;

(2) consumption expenditure on tobacco per person over 15, U.S.$ at 1990 price levels and PPPs for tobacco consumption;

(3) butter consumption per capita, in kg per year; and

(4) sugar consumption per capita, in kg per year.

Total health expenditures per capita is measured in U.S.$ at 1990 price levels and PPPs for medical consumption.

Public share of total expenditures = the share of public expenditure in total health expenditure.

Not explained by these = the sum of the residual, or prediction error, plus (for Panel(A)), the fixed effect for that country.

fail to consult physicians as often and they indulge more in such unhealthy habits as smoking and alcohol.[48] This self-care factor has commanded attention among bothered observers of British health history. Why should an increasingly egalitarian health system encounter such persistent social gaps in life expectancy, with both the lowest occupational groups and their children dying sooner?[49] Part of the answer has to lie in those differences in pursuing one's own health. Yet the same studies make it clear that a large part of the difference lies in the inequality of access to health service. The systematic results in Table 10.4 have already agreed: By holding occupation and bad health habits as constant as possible, that OECD study still found a significant health difference by type of delivery system.

We also know that health care supply, rather than personal health care demand, dominated mortality differences across the twentieth century from studies of regional inequality in health care services and in mortality outcomes in the United States and Britain. The United States' supplies of physicians and of nurses, like its mortality rates, have been more unequal across regions than Britain's since 1890. Differences in personal habits of the poor could not have played as great a role as these clear differences in health care delivery to different parts of the same country. That the supply of physicians and nurses did matter is also suggested by the downtrend in those regional inequalities of both the supply of doctors and nurses and the mortality outcomes between 1890 and 1970.[50]

The more general point behind such historical experiences seems clear enough. Whatever role might have been played by poor families taking less care of themselves, their behavior was not an exogenous force that differed widely over time and space. Rather their lower use of health care, like their earlier deaths, must have been due to the only relevant traits that poor families shared over so many decades, regions, countries, and cultures – their poverty itself and the related denial of low-cost health care. Income inequality, combined with private and decentralized health care, has shortened life outside the welfare states.

Thus public health care contributes to longer average life expectancy. The fact that public health spending, which has been counted here in social transfers, lengthens people's lives does not directly add to GDP per person. Yet the odds are that such spending does help raise productivity per person, especially if it is spent on basic and preventive care for the young and the poor.[51] Reducing sickness and morbidity enhances later productivity. By contrast, the extra expenditures on high-budget items to extend the lives of the rich and elderly do not raise GDP per capita. This combination of the favorable average productivity effect of health investments and the greater productivity enhancement from basic and preventative care than from high-budget repairs seems to help explain how a large part of social transfers – here, the public health budget – has been pro-growth.

WHY THESE KEYS?

So far, we have found that the net GDP cost of high tax-financed social spending is near zero, and we have found some reasons why.

If in one dimension after another, the high-budget welfare states seem to have designed their budgetary policies so as to preserve economic growth and not soak the rich too heavily, how does it work out that way? How could the notoriously messy process of political democracy yield such a design? It is hard to believe that it was smoothly planned.

Subsequent chapters suggest answers. First, Chapter 11 takes a closer look at how it worked in one country. Then Chapter 12 suggests a political economy of rich democracies that offers systematic reasons why high social budgets should have been virtually free of any net cost in terms of GDP growth. Chapter 18 and Appendix E in Volume 2 deliver the underlying statistical evidence.

On the Well-Known Demise of the Swedish Welfare State

The case for acquitting social programs from the charge of retarding economic growth has thus far relied on newly available comparative evidence that sweeps across a score of OECD countries. Powerful as the comparative overview may be, we need a closer look at the specific policies and institutions of individual countries. Some of the needed country studies have already been written. Only one single-country chapter is ventured here, to complement the comparative analysis of Chapters 10 and 12.

In choosing that country, one might prefer Denmark, Germany, or the Netherlands for their pioneering roles and the extremes to which some of their labor-market institutions were pushed before being repaired in the 1990s. But the overwhelming choices of the English-language literature on the welfare state are Britain and Sweden. Revisiting British experience here is less valuable than a look at Sweden, however, since Britain's status as a welfare state has always been less clear, despite the traditional bows to Beveridge.[1] For a welfare state prototype – either as the "third way" champion or as a socialist democracy run amok – the press has usually turned to Sweden. So Sweden it is.

The usual rhetoric about a "demise" or "crisis" of the welfare state misses the mark for Sweden, as well as for other countries. Sweden did have a set of economic crises between the mid-1970s and the mid-1990s and fell behind some other countries. Policy errors were indeed to blame for much of Sweden's difficulties. But the errors had little to do with the tax-based social transfers at the core of the welfare state. The core social programs did not malfunction, nor did they shrink or become unpopular.

WHO PROCLAIMED IT AND HOW

That Sweden's economy was falling behind and that its welfare state was to blame were repeated themes in the Anglo-American press in the period 1977–1998. The editorial page of the *Wall Street Journal* took the lead around

1977, and soon the negative view of Sweden had spread to its staff of reporters and to the other leader U.S. papers.[2]

So insistent was the U.S. criticism by 1990 that Sweden's top Social Democrat, Prime Minister Ingvar Carlsson, felt the need to write a letter to the *Washington Post* assuring its readers that "The 'Swedish Model' Doesn't Need Fixing."[3] At that time, his argument could hardly have been persuasive, since he and his party were about to be voted out of office and Sweden was soon plunging into its worst recession since the 1930s. The negative tone continued to prevail in the U.S. press until mid-1998.[4]

In Sweden's darkest postwar hour, the London-based *Economist* joined the leading U.S. newspapers in pronouncing the Swedish model a failure, in a string of articles in the 1990–1994 era.[5] Its tone seemed less insistently ideological than that of the *Wall Street Journal*'s editors, but the *Economist* overcame that moderation by gloating about the demise of a model that had been used to criticize British performance for so long. Late in 1992, as Sweden's recession deepened, the *Economist* handed down the full set of three indictments: Sweden's economy was sinking, the welfare-state third way model was at fault, and the Swedes themselves had just abandoned that model:

If recession-hit Britons want to cheer themselves up, they need look no further than Sweden...[and look at] the famous, but now abandoned, Swedish model....But since the model was scrapped in the past few years, Sweden has had its deepest recession since the 1930s. Was it wrong to dump its old policies?...High taxes and benefits destroyed the incentive to work, and Sweden's growth rate suffered: Once one of the richest countries, today its income per head is below the OECD average....The third way, if it ever really existed, is no longer there.[6]

The mood continued as Sweden went through the worst of that recession. Late in 1994, the *Economist* was still gloating over the demise for the Swedish model:

It is hard for the outsider not to feel a touch of *Schadenfreude* when contemplating Sweden. Its past century has been so glorious; its immediate past, catastrophic....Now the economy looks a pale shadow of its former self....

In this case, however, with Sweden having just voted Ingvar Carlsson and the Social Democrats back into power, the *Economist* rightly noted that the Swedes somehow just didn't get the message:

Swedes find it hard to imagine a fall in living standards, and yet that is the prospect that faces them over the next decade....It is not at all clear that Swedes realize how big a problem their country has.[7]

By 1998, however, Sweden's economic recovery was obvious. The death announcements had all but stopped, having gone the way of those 1980s journalistic proclamations that the United States could not possibly compete against Japan and the East Asian tigers – or, back in the 1960s, that Europe could not possibly compete against IBM and Boeing and "the American challenge." In Sweden's case, as in those earlier cases, the actual movements in real productivity eventually forced the press to change its view of where the world was heading. By July 2000, with Sweden's technology boom in full swing, even the *Wall Street Journal* was reporting that Sweden was combining prosperity with an apparently permanent welfare state.[8]

For all their excessive mood swings, the journalists were not alone in criticizing Sweden between 1977 and 1998. Rising above the caricatures that dominate ideological debates, many scholars have studied Sweden's institutions more carefully and objectively. There is a rich literature to draw on, and the Swedish government itself has made repeated use of expert studies to reevaluate its past political choices. This careful empirical literature also found much to criticize in Swedish's policies and institutions, including the taxes and transfers at the core of the welfare state. We draw on these studies in what follows.

One particular study stands out, for the wisdom of its recommendations and the serious public attention it commanded in Sweden. On December 10, 1992, the Swedish government appointed the Economics Commission (*Ekonomikommissionen*) of seven independent academics to analyze the economic crisis in Sweden and suggest ways to solve it. The commission, headed by Assar Lindbeck of Stockholm University, was asked to deal with short-term as well as medium-term problems. Its two-hundred-page final report, often called the Lindbeck report, was presented three months later, on March 9, 1993. An extended version was published in English the following year.[9]

As if to play the role of an IMF mission to Sweden, the Lindbeck report proposed reducing the budget deficit at all levels of government. In the dark fiscal year 1993–1994 the overall government budget deficits were in the range of 14–16 percent of GDP, far above the 3 percent Sweden would have to get under if it was to comply with the Maastricht Treaty's formula for members of the European Union. The Lindbeck report called for cutting the deficit by 7–9 percent of GDP, mostly by expenditure reductions rather than by tax increases. The cuts in social transfers were to be on the order of 2 percent of GDP, achieved by dismantling the annual allowance per child and by cutting the "replacement rates" on pensions and health insurance and unemployment insurance to 70 percent of pay. Note that the commissioners implied that cuts in social transfers should do only about a quarter of the deficit-cutting work (2 percent out of the 7–9 percent of GDP), even though they were a little over half of all government expenditure at the time. By implication, they must have felt that the public would not perceive larger cuts in social transfers to be a fair way out of the budget crisis.

When speaking or writing alone, Assar Lindbeck gave sterner warnings about the welfare state than did the Lindbeck report. Even at the time he walked into a 1993 press conference to present his report, Lindbeck was heard to mutter "Only the devil knows whether the country can be saved."[10] His book *The Swedish Experiment* (1997), written during the country's recovery, continued to feature warnings about the welfare state as well as about macroeconomic policy. Lindbeck clearly acknowledges that his compatriots continue to tolerate, or even like, a system that has impressively reduced poverty and insecurity. Yet he continues to see serious distortions of incentives as some of the defects in the system and worries that reforms may stall and may not continue to pull Sweden back from the excesses of the welfare state:

What then are the future prospects of the Swedish economy? To the extent that the poor economic performance since about 1970 is due to factors such as distorted incentives, regulated markets and weak competition, recent reforms [of the 1990s] are likely to improve the performance in the future.... The general trend... implies that Sweden has become a more "normal" West European country again – as it was prior to the radical experiments starting in the mid-1960s and early 1970s. Membership in the EU as of 1995 is likely to accentuate this development. If recent developments... continue, the Swedish model... will turn out to have been a brief historical episode – an interlude lasting no more than three decades, from the mid-1960s to the late 1990s.

Yet history never ends.... We know from a number of opinion studies that the support among voters of many government spending programs is very strong.... Several interest groups, including labor unions, have also pledged a return to previous institutions, rules, and policies.... Furthermore, about 65 percent of the electorate receive (nearly) all their income from the public sector.... Is this 'a point of no return?'[11]

One person persuaded by Lindbeck's warnings was Robert Solow: "Lindbeck has found good reasons to believe that in Sweden the welfare state had expanded to the point where it - along with other special characteristics - had become a significant drag on economic performance.... Sweden was an extreme case."[12]

Are they right?

SWEDEN'S GROWTH AND SOCIAL SPENDING SINCE 1950

What was Sweden's actual performance record? Were the critics right about Sweden's first rising and then falling in the international income ranks? Did the social transfers at the core of the welfare state follow a time-path that was correlated, positively or negatively, with Sweden's growth performance? When did Sweden abandon its commitment to a high share of tax-financed social transfers in national product?

There was a definite rise and fall of Sweden relative to the United States and other leading countries over the second half of the twentieth century. At mid-century Sweden already occupied a respectably high rank among nations. The credit for this might in small part be due to Sweden's having kept up its capital formation, its employment, and its incomes during the

1930s, when other countries were depressed. More important, however, was Sweden's escaping major damage in the two World Wars. Starting from mid-century prosperity, Sweden seemed to outperform many other countries over the next quarter-century, as shown in Table 11.1 and Figure 11.1. This was the performance that spawned the literature admiring Sweden's successful "third way."

Since 1975, Sweden's position has declined. Countries that had their own problems of decelerating productivity growth nonetheless overtook Sweden. Some of them were countries not committed to the welfare state. The most dramatic overtaking of Sweden was achieved by Japan – but Japan, of course, grew faster than *everybody* between 1950 and 1990. As best we can judge from the tricky international comparisons of purchasing-power-parity-adjusted figures on GDP per capita, Sweden was also slightly overtaken by Australia, a low-spending country.[13] The available estimates say that Denmark, Norway, and the Netherlands also overtook Sweden, and Finland has nearly caught up to Sweden since 1975. That these countries also commit large shares of GDP in taxes for social transfers means that whatever held Sweden back after 1975 might have been specific to Sweden and not a simple by-product of welfare-state policies.

While Sweden's position in the international income ranks was slipping after 1975, the share of its income devoted to social transfers held steady. Figure 11.2 traces the path of social transfers since 1980, the first year covered by the OECD's new data series. Public health spending did drop somewhat as a share of GDP. One reason was that some health care and disability subsidies were in fact cut from 1991 on, and another reason is that the health-care-intensive elderly population began to decline as a share of the total population after 1985. Public pensions held firm, however. In fact, they rose slightly as a share of GDP. Given the slight drop in the elderly share of the population, the pension support ratio – or (public pensions/person over sixty-five) as a percentage of GDP per capita – rose even more noticeably after 1985. Sweden has not yet had a pension crisis, and Chapter 8 has argued that it is not one of the countries most likely to have a pension crisis by 2020. The two most cyclical kinds of social transfers, welfare and unemployment compensation, rose considerably in the recession of the early 1990s before falling back to earlier levels. Thus around the time of the tax reform of 1991, that moment in which the country was trying hardest to trim the welfare state, social transfers actually peaked as a share of GDP. This anomaly resembled the curious jump in Britain's social transfers in the early 1980s, when Margaret Thatcher's insistent attack on the welfare state was temporarily overpowered by the rise of unemployment.

Sweden did cut some things after the reforms of 1991. An excess-profits tax was revoked. A socialistic "wage-earners fund" tax started in the 1970s was dropped by the center-right coalition, and dropping it was upheld by the Social Democrats after they returned to power in 1994. The rates of

TABLE 11.1. *Real GDP per Capita, Sweden and Other Countries, 1900–1998 (Relative to USA = 100 for the same year)*

	Low-Social-Transfer Countries						High-Social-Transfer Countries				
Year	Sweden	U.K.	Japan	Switzerland	Canada	Australia	Denmark	Finland	Norway	Japan	Netherlands
From Maddison (1995, Table D1-a):											
1900	62.5	112.1	27.7	86.2	67.3	105.0	70.8	39.6	43.0	69.6	86.3
1913	58.3	94.8	25.1	79.3	79.4	103.7	70.9	38.6	42.9	65.0	74.4
1929	56.0	76.1	28.2	90.4	69.5	73.8	70.7	38.2	45.7	67.6	80.4
1950	70.4	71.5	19.6	93.4	73.6	75.4	69.8	43.2	51.9	54.5	61.1
From Penn World Tables 6.0:											
1950	66.4	67.6	19.5	98.4	82.0	81.5	71.0	44.5	59.4	50.2	61.1
1951	69.7	70.3	20.8	100.1	79.8	77.1	64.6	46.5	56.5	50.1	57.4
1955	77.8	74.9	24.9	105.3	80.4	78.1	65.6	51.0	61.5	52.6	64.0
1960	81.6	70.9	34.7	118.7	81.2	81.9	80.0	58.3	64.8	62.6	71.1
1965	85.0	70.3	44.0	117.2	81.9	79.2	83.8	60.0	65.5	66.0	71.2
1970	87.7	71.2	65.5	121.5	82.4	85.1	85.7	67.5	67.0	74.4	78.1
1975	80.2	67.8	70.0	114.5	89.4	84.4	84.8	73.3	75.3	78.3	80.5
1980	77.8	65.9	72.9	110.7	88.9	81.0	82.7	73.3	81.6	78.2	77.2
1985	76.0	68.8	74.1	103.4	86.0	77.7	84.6	72.0	83.0	72.3	71.1
1990	69.6	66.0	81.4	101.3	83.3	73.3	81.5	74.1	79.7	74.6	72.2
1993	74.2	68.1	83.0	95.0	79.2	75.2	81.7	63.1	84.1	71.6	72.6
1995	72.2	66.5	79.5	85.8	79.9	78.7	83.0	67.3	87.0	71.7	73.5
1998			74.1	79.4	77.4	74.0	75.8	70.8	85.5	68.5	72.7

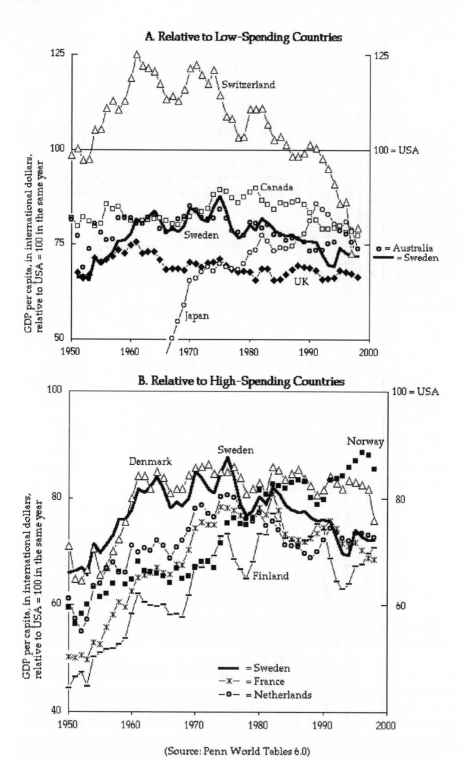

FIGURE 11.1. Sweden's GDP per Capita, Relative to Other Countries, 1950–1998.

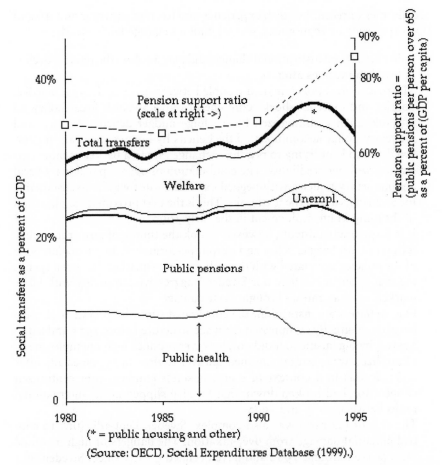

(* = public housing and other)

(Source: OECD, Social Expenditures Database (1999).)

FIGURE 11.2. Sweden's Social Transfers as Shares of GDP, 1980–1995.

support (replacement rates) were lowered on some forms of social insurance, especially sickness and dental insurance.[14] On the other hand, some tax rates were notched up slightly, and the tax base grew faster than GDP during the recovery because the tax system was still somewhat progressive. Yet Figure 11.2 still delivers the main verdict on social transfer spending: It has not dropped as a share of GDP, despite all the public debate.

WHAT WENT WRONG AFTER THE 1970S?

To understand the decline of Sweden's relative income position after 1975, we must identify its sources and their relationship to the package of policies known as the welfare state. Within the welfare state package, we must separate out the roles of social spending from the roles played by other policies and institutions usually associated with the welfare state. Thanks to the peculiarities of recent Swedish experience and to an extensive monitoring of that experience by economists, several findings emerge fairly clearly:

- Policy errors and institutional changes did play a role in the relative decline of Swedish incomes after 1975.
- Macroeconomic policy invited trouble between 1976 and 1992. Swedish politics and external shocks combined to give Swedish fiscal policy an unstable quality, dramatized by the huge budget deficits of 1983, and monetary policy accommodated the deficits by buying government debt. Sweden also kept trying to peg the exchange rate to a basket of other currencies, without credibility. The combination of over-expansionary fiscal and monetary policies with pegged exchange rates was as unsustainable for Sweden as it is in the textbooks. This is the best proximate explanation of the jump in unemployment in the early 1990s.
- It is surprisingly difficult, however, to link the timing of any other policy mistakes with Sweden's job and output performance. In particular, none of the policies associated with the welfare state – neither the social spending that is our focus here nor Sweden's aggressive tampering with labor markets and tax rates – brought clear damage.
- One welfare state institution, the corporatist centralized system of wage bargaining, greatly compressed the wage structure before 1975 and led to a revolt by big business. It did not, however produce high unemployment. Centralized wage bargaining then unraveled after 1975, especially after 1983. It was in a context of union–business conflict, after centralized cooperation had broken down, that Sweden slipped in the international ranks between 1975 and 1992.
- The role of tax rates was also complex. Sweden kept adjusting to control potential damage from over-taxation. The dangers of high marginal rates peaked around 1982 and have declined greatly since. Sweden thus fits Chapter 10's pattern that high-transfer states choose a tax mix that reduces any damage to economic growth.
- Social spending – the core of the welfare state and the topic of this book – did not deliver any net damage to Sweden's GDP, either before or after 1975. Partly this is because Sweden invested strongly in women's human capital. Partly it is because the country was one of the better performers in terms of education and retraining. And partly it was because Sweden's pension policies have actually produced some of the world's highest rates of employment for those over the age of fifty-five.

Macroeconomic Policy

Swedish macroeconomic policy was defective from the 1970s through 1993, causing bouts of inflation and currency devaluation and one round of high unemployment.

A key failing was Sweden's attempt to maintain an adjustable peg exchange rate of the sort that prevailed under the Bretton Woods system of 1944–1971.[15] The adjustable peg policy calls for a fixed exchange rate that should be defended only up to a point. If too much pressure builds up, in the form of speculators' selling off its currency, then the adjustable peg policy calls for a sharp devaluation, followed by trying to defend the new lower value of the national currency. International economists have reached general agreement that the adjustable peg policy is costly and unsustainable. A fixed exchange rate can be defended only if the country's government and central bank are credibly committed to keeping that rate fixed forever, even if fixing it means some unemployment or inflation. The slightest sign that the country is not willing to make such sacrifices causes speculators to bet that it will devalue as soon as inflation within the country starts to make its goods look too expensive on international markets. Soon there is a foreign-exchange crisis in which officials swear they will defend the national currency and speculators do not believe them. The speculators engage in the infamous one-way gamble, selling off this country's currency to the hapless officials. Sooner or later the country, low on reserves, gives up and devalues. It has lost money in the process and speculators have gained by attacking its currency. Later on, the cycle is repeated.

In accordance with this judgment by international economists, the Lindbeck report insisted that Sweden drop its adjustable peg system. Specifically, the report called the central bank (the Riksbank) and the government to target the domestic rate of price inflation, keeping it at a low rate like 2 percent a year, instead of pegging the exchange rate. Its recommendation has been followed since then. The report also rightly called for new laws making the Riksbank more independent of the elected government, so that it could fix its policies on the goal of price stability, as has been done by the central banks of Switzerland and Germany.[16] This has not been done, and Sweden's joining the European Monetary Union complicated the issue in the early 1990s.

The flaw of having the wrong exchange-rate regime gets exposed when some other force makes the adjustable peg unsustainable. In Sweden's case, that destructive force arose from time to time from the country's domestic policies. For example, a storm began to brew in the mid-1970s when wage rates were allowed to rise much faster than labor productivity. For the rest of the decade, fiscal policy defended those wage rates and Swedish jobs with a rapid expansion of government spending, causing greater budget deficits. The central bank in turn accommodated the government by buying much of its extra debt – in effect, creating new money and worsening the tendency for inflation.

Sweden's way out of the inflation, relative to other countries' prices, was to devalue the currency (the krona) sharply in 1981 and 1982. That bought time by making Sweden's goods look cheaper when priced in other currencies. Sweden kept inflating the domestic economy and running large government

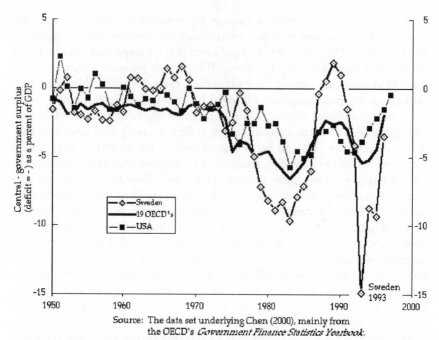

FIGURE 11.3. Central Government Budget Balance as a Percentage of GDP, Sweden and Other Countries, 1950–1997.

budget deficits. Figure 11.3 shows the depth of those deficits and how much they exceeded other countries' deficits as a share of GDP. If Sweden had run only the deficits run by the average OECD country (the thick line) by spending less or taxing more, it would have had less price inflation and the krona could perhaps have stayed pegged. Had Sweden followed that thick line, we might have said that the country was only riding out the oil-shock crises in the same way as other countries, smoothing out their taxes by borrowing extra for a while. Yet Figure 11.3 shows something Swedish observers felt keenly: Between 1978 and 1986, Sweden's budget was out of line with general practice. Like Italy, Sweden ran excessive deficits, raising the nation's debt burden relative to GDP. Sooner or later, this stood a good chance of bringing new speculative attacks on the already cheapened krona.

The new crisis came in the early 1990s, when Sweden was hit by high global interest rates and renewed competition from foreign manufactures. This time, instead of devaluing or just letting the exchange rate float, Sweden tried to commit to fixing the krona to the German mark and the emerging European Union currency (ecu). Finland made the same mistake at the same time. Swedish and Finnish goods were priced out of international markets, and speculators abandoned the krona. While the government held on to the fixed exchange rate, the country sank into a sharp depression. The year 1993 brought the biggest Swedish deficits of all time and the most unemployment since the 1930s. In November 1992, Sweden finally gave up on the fixed value of the krona and let the exchange rate float.

The upshot of the macroeconomic policy mistakes is that Swedish policy did indeed make major policy errors in the welfare-state era – but these were macro-policy mistakes and had nothing to do with the welfare state's social transfers.

The Demise of Swedish Corporatism

Sweden had been known as one of the most corporatist countries, the ones that negotiate wage rates and job policy through centralized bargaining between labor and management organizations, often with government participating as a third party at the bargaining table.[17] The usual impression does not quite fit Swedish experience, however. For one thing, there was never an age in which organized labor, organized business, and the government fashioned trilateral agreements to hold down wage costs, keep businesses competitive, and ensure full employment. Such happy macroeconomic outcomes did occur – but the three parties never reached centralized agreements for consecutive years.

Instead, the postwar history of wage bargaining has been constantly changing its form, in a way that *should have* brought worse results than we actually see. Let us focus on two main periods, pre-1983 and post-1983, even though there were changes within each period.

The pre-1983 era saw the rise of centralized bargaining between the powerful blue-collar union Landsorganisationen (or LO) and the large-employers' organization Svenska Arbetsgivareföreningen (or SAF). As with the history of most innovations, this rise is traditionally dated from an initial announcement that came long before it really took effect. The traditional starting date is the Saltsjöbadsavtalet, or the Basic Agreement, of 1938 between the LO and SAF. It soon became associated with a solidarity wage policy promoted by LO economists Gösta Rehn and Rudolf Meidner. The solidarity wage policy called for an "equal pay for equal work" principle that came to be interpreted both as a rejection of separate wages based on separate firms' profitability and as a general call to compress wages between regions, sexes, and even occupations. Yet economy-wide centralized bargaining between LO and SAF really gathered momentum only in the 1950s.[18] Peak-level agreements between LO and SAF continued annually from 1956 through 1982.

From the 1950s to 1983 the solidarity wage policy was accompanied by extreme compression of all wage differentials – differentials by region, by sex, by age, and by occupational group. At the low point in wage differences around 1978–1983, Sweden's wage structure was probably the most compressed of any OECD country. We would expect such extreme compression to have strained the private market sector of Sweden's economy in three ways:

1. The wage compression should have lowered the incentive to get higher education.
2. If the wage compression was really imposed on labor markets by centralized bargaining and the solidarity wage policy, it should also have caused widespread unemployment of low-skilled labor.
3. It should have caused discontent among higher-skilled workers and those who want to hire them and give them flexible wage incentives. We would expect some of these groups to have defected from the LO–SAF bargains.

Economists' best guess seems to be that the severe wage compression did have the first and third effects, but not the second.

The rate of return on getting extra education was indeed depressed up to the mid-1980s in Sweden. The percentage pay gain from having a university education instead of finishing with a gymnasium education was cut nearly in half between 1967 and 1983. The net rate of return on university education, a measure that takes the cost of education into account, dropped even more over the same period. People responded at the margin with a temporary stall in the rise of university education across the 1980s, a change that left the country shorter of the skills needed in the post-1993 recovery.[19]

The compression of wages did not lead to mass unemployment of lower-skilled workers, however. Why not, if it was truly imposed from above by LO–SAF bargaining? Those who have written directly on this question (in English) sense that the observed wage compression could have been due to ordinary demand and supply forces, not to the solidarity policy. From the 1950s to the early 1980s, the educational attainment of Sweden's labor force rose impressively, possibly glutting the market for skills (before the post-1993 tech boom) and withdrawing the relative supply of low-skilled workers. Similarly, the supply of younger, less experienced workers also contracted as Sweden continued to lead the world in population aging. Low-skilled industries went into decline and more skilled sectors continued to take a larger share of employment and national product. Perhaps there was virtually full employment (up to the early 1990s) because of market forces. Perhaps centralized bargaining played no real role.[20]

If centralized wage setting really did shape the wage structure, then we should expect opposition to arise among skilled workers and the firms that want to hire them and give them more flexible incentive-rich pay scales. That did indeed happen, whether or not the later economists were correct in believing that demand and supply really caused the wage compression. The first conspicuous opposition arose among employers in large engineering firms. As early as 1969 their Association of Engineering Employers (Verkstadsföreningen, or VF, until 1992) was outspoken against corporatism.

Other trends were also causing the larger SAF to become more negative on continued annual bargaining rounds after about 1975. One was the underlying drift toward higher-skill, higher-discretion jobs, for which a more flexible reward system made more sense. The same drift toward skills slowly eroded the LO's share of all workers, in favor of new white-collar and professional unions.

The employers were particularly alienated by a power grab on the part of the LO and its main defenders with the Social Democratic party. In the early 1970s the LO began to push for national legislation giving workers more managerial power within firms. It also called for taxes on profits to support a new wage earners' fund, by which the unions could buy majority ownership of the largest firms. While the wage-earner fund idea was eventually defeated in the political arena, it lasted long enough to spark a new employer offensive against peak-level bargaining. Finally, in 1983, the VF and SAF were able to walk away from further peak-level negotiations. They adamantly refused to return to the centralized bargaining table thereafter.[21]

Since 1983, the central government has made efforts to forge a few agreements, but without SAF cooperation, and with intermittent battles between government and the powerful but fading LO. Within this longer period, the recession of 1991–1993 was a special case in which the government successfully pressured all parties into a short-term incomes policy designed to make the sudden deflation more acceptable.

An important thing about this timing is that corporatism was on the decline after 1983 and arguably even since the 1970s. The devaluations and budget deficits of the 1980s and early 1990s were not the result of any upward push on real wages under corporatist institutions. They came when those institutions were unraveling, and no clear link between centralized bargaining and the degree of wage push has ever been established.[22]

WHAT ROLE FOR SWEDEN'S HIGH TAX RATES?

It is hard to quantify the effect of tax rates on overall GDP. Many have tried, of course, but we saw in Chapter 10 that such attempts either retreat to fiction (computer simulations, general equilibrium models, etc.) or conduct econometric tests that cannot reject the argument that the true effect is zero. Even for the purpose of fictitious exercises about the effect of a tax rate, economists know that they must answer these key conjectural questions: This tax rate relative to what other rate? And what happened to the revenue from this tax? For the latter question, one must choose among these answers:

a. Assume that the tax revenues just disappear into thin air.
b. Assume that they go to other people in some way that has no effect on their behavior other than their consuming the full amount transferred to them (the "lump sum" assumption).

c. Assume that some other tax rate is cut, perhaps with favorable side effects.
d. Assume that nonsocial expenditures are raised by the amount of the extra revenue.
e. Assume that social expenditures are raised by the amount of the extra revenue.

For our purposes, assumption (e) would be most appropriate. But the analysis delivered by experts in the field typically makes the lump-sum assumption (b) instead. This could make the literature on the growth effects of Sweden's taxes not only complex, but also rather inappropriate for present purposes.

Fortunately, there is a set of simpler points to make about Sweden's tax system. Instead of pursuing the elusive causal links between taxes and economic results, we can improve our understanding just by noticing some features of Sweden's tax system that few would have imagined. What people usually hear about Sweden's tax system is that the government taxes away more than 50 percent of people's incomes. Given Sweden's insistent egalitarianism, most outside observers also presume that Sweden's tax system is highly progressive, taking over 70 percent of income from rich people at the margin and giving it to the poor. Sweden's actual tax practice is so far from these natural perceptions that we can gain a great deal of insight just by describing features of the system, without trying to quantify its growth effects.

To see how far the often-cited tax rates exceed the average taxes that the wealthy Swedes pay, and the marginal tax incentives they face, requires some reckoning of the many deductions that allow them to pay less than the statutory tax rates. There is much to reckon with here. Even the Lindbeck report, which wanted to stress that Sweden's tax burdens are excessive, cautioned its readers that "[t]he size of public-sector spending [and taxation] in Sweden is not strictly comparable to that of many other countries, because several types of transfers in Sweden are taxed, while in many other countries they are not."[23] This "clawback" effect goes only part of the way toward a more realistic estimation of the tax burden (and transfer benefits) in Sweden.

Many deductions and complications have effectively lowered tax rates, especially the taxes on corporate and personal capital, and especially before the 1991 tax reform. By the early 1980s, Sweden had achieved a complex tax system, for better and for worse. For better, because Sweden had kept corporate and personal capital from fleeing the country by devising numerous special tax breaks. For worse, because the system of taxes and breaks was complicated and struck some as unfair. What the 1991 reform delivered was more uniformity and simplicity, along with some convergence of the higher tax rates on labor earnings down toward the lower rates on capital incomes.[24]

One set of estimates that hints at the departure of the oft-quoted statutory tax rates from the rates really paid is summarized in Table 11.2. The departure is clearest for taxes on corporate income. Ostensibly, they were above

TABLE 11.2. *Tax Rates in Sweden: Statutory Marginal Rates versus More Typical Rates 1965–1995* (*Percentage rates*)

	1965	1970	1975	1980	1985	1990	1991	1992	1993	1994	1995
Statutory versus average marginal effective tax rates paid on corporate incomes											
Statutory corporate tax rate (including profit-sharing tax)	50.3	52.6	55.1	57.4	61.6	52.0	30.0	30.0	30.0	30.0	30.0
Average marginal effective tax rate (METR)				2.0	17.0	18.1	3.6	3.6	3.6	11.6	4.9
Statutory versus average tax rates paid on capital incomes (personal and corporate together)											
Top marginal rate	71.0	72.4	82.2	85.0	80.0	66.2	30.0	30.0	30.0		
Average marginal rate	42.2	47.4	53.4	56.8	50.2	52.1	30.0	30.0	30.0		
Average rate paid	19.4	17.7	15.0	8.8	15.2	28.3	33.4	22.0			
Statutory versus average tax rates paid on labor incomes (including social security contributions and consumptions taxes)											
Top marginal rate	71.0	72.4	82.2	85.0	80.0	66.2	51.2	51.0	51.0		
Average marginal rate	42.2	47.4	53.4	56.8	50.2	52.1	39.0	39.0	39.0		
Average rate paid	40.3	45.3	48.5	52.0	55.0	57.6	51.2	53.5			

Sources and Notes: Normann and McLure (1997).

50 percent until Sweden's tax reform cut them to 30 percent in 1991. Yet, as already noted in the last chapter, Sweden's tax system allowed so many deductions that the effect of capital taxes on total tax revenues may not have been positive. Corporate income gains from real investments, especially in machinery, could pay negative taxes if they were financed by borrowing in time of inflation, as happened in the 1980s. This is one reason why the Norrman–McLure estimates of corporate tax rates show so much less being paid on the average than the statutory marginal rates would have led us to expect.[25] The discrepancy between the visible and publicized statutory rates and the average rates actually paid is equally glaring in the history of the tax rates on all capital income, personal as well as corporate.

Labor incomes were given less of a break in Sweden's pre-1991 tax system, just as in most other welfare states.[26] Table 11.2 shows that the average rate paid on labor incomes had drifted above 50 percent by 1990, on the eve of the tax reform. That is a high average rate in world perspective. Note, however, that this rate includes "taxes" that would not have been included as taxes in other countries. Most importantly, it includes the social security deductions from one's paycheck as if they were income taxes *and* it includes all consumption taxes as if they were a tax on labor income. Such procedures have not been followed elsewhere, either in the estimates of Sweden's capital incomes or in the estimates of other countries' labor income taxes.

Overall, then, Sweden's tax system had these features, especially before the 1991 tax reform:

- Labor incomes paid high taxes by world standards.
- Capital incomes, both corporate and personal, paid lower taxes than labor incomes.
- Both kinds of income paid lower net tax rates – either average or marginal, and either on labor incomes or on capital incomes – than we are usually told.

If Sweden taxed capital less than many have imagined, is Sweden's tax system really regressive in the sense that it takes a larger share of income from low-income groups than from high-income groups? Economists specializing in public finance have learned to be humble and cautious about estimates of the incidence of taxes across income classes, in view of the uncertainties about the full ramifications of taxes once their revenues have been spent and all markets have adjusted. We do have estimates of tax incidence by income class for Sweden, for the United Kingdom, and for the United States in the year 1985.[27] Our comparison of these is constrained by the fact that the Swedish estimates refer to the personal income tax alone and omit Sweden's regressive consumption taxes. Even with this constraint, Sweden's income tax looks about as progressive as Britain's entire tax system. If consumption taxes were reckoned in, Sweden's tax system would probably have looked a bit more regressive than Britain's in 1985, though still not to the point of neutrality. The United States approximated that neutrality, with the tax system neither clearly progressive nor clearly regressive in 1985. That is, in the U.S. tax system taxes' share of pretax income was not clearly different between top and bottom groups. Thus, when we look at the tax side alone – temporarily ignoring the great progressivity of Sweden's distribution of social expenditures – Sweden's tax system does not look extraordinarily progressive. And, as Chapter 10 has already implied, its heavy taxation of alcohol and cigarettes and its light taxation of capital income probably make Sweden's tax system more pro-growth than the systems of many countries preferring lower budgets.

WHAT SURVIVED: PRO-GROWTH SOCIAL SPENDING

Every argument about the productive side of social spending applies as fully to Sweden as it does to the average OECD country. Thus the arguments of Chapter 10 still apply here. Expanding public health care seems to have positive marginal effects on longevity and probably on productivity. Public education still has a positive marginal return in Sweden, as elsewhere. Expenditures on labor-market programs have limited costs. What need emphasis here are the peculiarities of Sweden's transfer programs.

Relative to other OECD countries, Sweden's institutions seem to produce greater employment, especially jobs held by women and the elderly, with positive effects on GDP. Table 11.3 underlines this point by contrasting Sweden's basic employment ratios with those of the United States and the relatively welfare-state countries of the European Union in 1995:[28] Looking at the overall employment ratios, for both sexes and for the whole fifteen to sixty-four age range, one would single out the United States, not Sweden, as the country most oriented toward paid work. Yet as soon as we look at the patterns by sex and age, we see what is special about Sweden. First, Sweden has the highest rate of *women's* employment for any age range and therefore over the entire fifteen to sixty-four age range as well. Second, what made the United States look like a more heavily employed country than Sweden was really the peculiarly high rates of employment recorded for the young fifteen to twenty-four age group in the United States. Focusing on the broad mid-career age range twenty-five to fifty-four reveals that Swedes are more heavily employed than Americans overall, though not among males. Finally, in the elderly fifty-five to sixty-four age group, Swedish and American men tend to have the same employment ratios, but Swedish women work more. Sweden's extra employment stands out more clearly when the comparison is with the European Union average rather than with the United States. The patterns thus set us off on three searches. First, why are Swedish women so heavily employed? Second, do Sweden's expensive retraining programs for young and mid-career adults dampen the overall work rate? Finally, why do elderly Swedes stay employed longer than their counterparts in other countries?

TABLE 11.3. *Employment Ratios by Age and Sex in 1995: Sweden versus the United States and European Union (Employment/population, as percentages)*

			Sweden	United States	European Union
Entire work-age range	Ages 15–64	Both sexes	72.2	72.5	60.1
		Men	73.5	79.5	70.3
		Women	70.8	65.8	49.8
Young	Ages 15–24	Both sexes	42.3	58.3	37.7
		Men	41.8	61.5	41.3
		Women	42.9	55.1	34.0
Mid-career	Ages 25–54	Both sexes	82.6	79.7	73.2
		Men	84.0	87.6	85.2
		Women	81.1	72.2	61.2
Elderly	Ages 55–64	Both sexes	61.9	55.1	36.2
		Men	64.4	63.6	47.3
		Women	59.5	47.5	25.7

Source: OECD (1998d, 191–202).

Investing in Women's Work and in Child Care

Virtually all of Sweden's employment growth between the 1960s and the early 1990s consisted of jobs for women. This change suggests that some policy change relating to women's work must account for the high employment rates reached by Swedish women in the 1990s. The causes of this change, and the reasons why the share of women working became so high by the 1990s, seem to lie on the demand side of the labor market, not on the supply side. There is probably nothing distinctive about Swedish women's willingness to supply labor, once one understands all the differences in the conditions women face in Sweden's workplaces.

To see that the reasons for the high employment rate among Swedish women lie on the demand side, it helps to recall one fact already noted and to introduce a new one. Back in Chapter 10 we noted that the rich microeconomic literature estimating how labor supply responds to differences in the after-tax wage rate found that *women have a more elastic labor supply than men.* That is, any given percentage increase in everybody's take-home wage would cause a significant rise in the percentage of women working, but not in the percentage of men working. So if a society opens more doors for women, there will be a rise in the share of the whole adult population working, even if the opening of doors to women meant an equal drop in the demand for male labor.

The new fact that needs to be introduced here is that *Sweden's women get better pay relative to men than in any other OECD country.* Figure 11.4

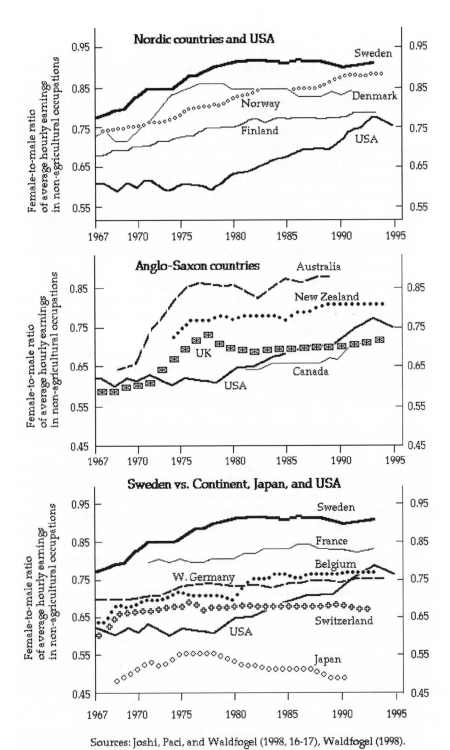

Sources: Joshi, Paci, and Waldfogel (1998, 16-17), Waldfogel (1998).

FIGURE 11.4. Female-to-Male Wage Ratios, Sweden versus Other Countries, 1967–1995.

suggests as much, by showing that the average female hourly wage rate was a greater share of the average male wage in Sweden than in any other leading country, with Australia coming closet to Sweden in this respect. Given this better relative female wage, and given that Sweden's women are more heavily employed than women in other countries, something in Sweden's economy, probably something relating to government policy, must have shifted the demand curve in favor of female labor relative to male labor.

To understand what lies behind this strong relative demand for women in Sweden, consider these forces that might raise the female/male wage ratio:

1. Firmer enforcement of institutions that prevent pay discrimination
2. A sectoral demand pattern favoring sectors that hire more women
3. Better in-career investments in women's continued work and in their advancement
4. Better education for women, relative to men
5. If women's pay rates still fall below men's, then any force reducing overall pay inequality between occupations would raise women's wage rates toward men's

At least four of these five forces played a role in giving women a positive work incentive in Sweden. The one that is in doubt is (1), better enforcement of nondiscrimination in wages. True, Sweden does have equal-pay laws and tries to enforce them. Yet it is hard to quantify international differences in this respect, and other countries, such as the United States and Italy, have a longer history of such laws and enforcement than Sweden.[29] So let us concentrate on the other four forces.

A special feature of Sweden's gender economics combines forces (2) and (3). The Swedish pattern of sectoral labor demand favors the hiring of women in a way that also helps other women continue their career progress. Over three-quarters of the national job creation between the 1960s and the 1990s consisted of the hiring of women in the local-government sector alone. About half of this local-government hiring was in the health and education sectors, and perhaps one-seventh of it consisted of infant day-care jobs.[30] Thus the employment of women is closely tied to Sweden's having the world's seventh highest share spent on public health services, the world's second highest share spent on public education, and the world's highest share of GDP spent on public infant care.[31]

How was the growth of GDP affected by the extra spending that hired so many women in these human-services sectors? Even without the benefit of specialized studies of the rate of return on health and education expenditures in Sweden, we can tentatively presume that the rates have been positive, both through the short-run services provided and through the favorable long-run human-capital effects of women's job experience.

Couldn't Sweden's local governments have gone too far, investing too much in the social services provided mainly by women in the public sector?

In particular, could they have overdone the allocation of taxpayers' money to the public supply of infant care? Here we have the benefit of a thoughtful study by the late Sherwin Rosen on Sweden's heavy commitment to public day care. Rosen provided an articulate case for suspecting that Sweden's local governments have over-invested in day care, yet also provided information allowing us to see that even the marginal net return on the last bit of public day care has probably been positive. Let us begin with his core suspicion that using taxes to pay women to mind others' children brings a net deadweight loss:

> In Sweden, a large fraction of women work in the public sector to take care of the children of other women who work in the public sector to take care of the parents of the women who are looking after their children. If Swedish women take care of each other's parents in exchange for taking care of each other's children, how much additional real output comes of it?
>
> Large estimated efficiency losses are practically inevitable, given the relatively large empirical estimates of female labor supply responses to wage incentives and the enormous tax burdens in Sweden today.... By reducing the linkages between personal contributions to production and claims on social output, the welfare state encourages people to produce utility in ways that do not have to be shared with others. The real household sector in Sweden is too large on both counts. The monetization of subsidized household services provided through the subsidized state bureaucracy increases the demand for publicly provided services and the size of the public sector but reduces the value of social output and living standards in the overall economy. Total output is smaller than it would have been if household services had been paid for privately and transacted through the market.[32]

As far as simple GDP accounting goes, Rosen was correct in doubting that we have added anything productive just by exchange through the public sector what we would have provided within homes anyway. And if it takes taxpayers' money to pay for the public exchange, the higher tax rates might discourage somebody else's productive effort.

The bad tax effects depend on our starting point. Rosen rightly pointed out that there could be what economists call a "second-best" argument in favor of subsidizing day care. Suppose that we start by taking Sweden's high tax rates as given and start off with no public day care. As he noted, we would be starting from a (second-best) situation in which something is already wrong with the incentives facing parents, especially women.[33] With high tax rates on extra labor income, people have too much incentive to stay home and provide their own family with tax-free care. Subsidizing public child care could draw them back out into paid employment while somebody else looks after the children, correcting some of the initial work deficiency. This gain could be positive even if extra taxes were raised to subsidize the day care. Beyond some high point of generous subsidy, however, Sweden will be overdoing its tax-based public care. Rosen suspected that Sweden has moved into that range of excessive day care. Specifically, his illustrative calculations suggest that a 10-percent reduction from its current 90 percent of the cost of day care to 80 percent, "would reduce the deadweight loss, whatever it is, by about 10 percent" (Rosen 1997, 101). So Sweden, in his view, has overdone its public care services.

Even at this outer Swedish margin of public day care funded by local taxes, however, the net returns are probably quite positive. To see how, we should first note the tiny magnitude of Rosen's calculated deadweight costs. As a share of GDP, they work out to be the product of two fractions: (deadweight costs as a share of the amounts spent on public day care) and (amounts spent on public day care as a share of GDP). For 1993 that worked out to 0.18 percent of GDP, which hardly begins to explain any shortfall in Sweden's overall growth performance.

Yet there are unmistakable positive returns to public day care, as we saw in the last chapter. One is the extra pay that women are capable of earning if their careers are not greatly interrupted by having children. Using a 1984 Swedish household survey, Gustafsson and Stafford find that "high quality public day care in Sweden encourages labor market activity of women with preschoolers even when the spouse's income is high, and that when spaces are not rationed, a lower price encourages use."[34] The outward signs certainly suggest that this gain in lifetime productivity is big for the women of Sweden. They have the highest ratio of female to male wage rates, as we saw in Table 11.2, and almost the highest rate of female employment[35] of any OECD country.

Parental leave and public infant care might also improve the children's skill development. The gains or losses for children depend on (a) the quality of infant care in three settings – parental care at home, private care by non-parents, and public care; (b) how much each of these receives public support; and (c) how much impact such early interventions have on children's later development. Sweden's strong support of parental leave almost surely brings positive gains in child development. For infants in the one to five age range, the issue is how the developmental benefits of publicly subsidized, and largely publicly supplied, infant care compare with the benefits from the alternative of mixing more parental care with unsubsidized private care. Ten careful U.S. studies find that early intervention programs have high returns, especially for children of low-income parents, as we noted in Chapter 10.[36] This resolves the question of whether early interventions in child development have a high payoff. Indeed they do, both privately and socially.

In Sweden's case, the net gains from publicly subsidized and provided care depend on how two differences balance out. On the one hand, children aged one to five receive better at-home care in Sweden than in the disadvantaged homes covered by the U.S. programs, suggesting a low return to public provision and subsidization of infant care in Sweden. On the other hand, the quality of Sweden's public caregivers is reportedly higher than the average public provider in the United States, raising the return to public provision in Sweden relative to past U.S. experience.

The other two forces that promoted women's work, and thereby raised GDP, are (d) the relative education of women, and (e) the dependence of women's pay on the overall occupational pay gaps. At first glance, these might seem like forces that could only elevate women relative to men, with no implication for the productivity of the whole economy. Yet even if either of these forces depressed men's pay by the same percentage as it raised women's pay – which seems unlikely – a positive effect on total work and GDP would still follow from a key fact we have already noted about elasticities of labor supply. Women have a more elastic labor supply than men, and that converts gender gaps into effects on total work and GDP.

Sweden ranks high among countries in terms of the relative educational attainment of women, as well as in the education of the adult population as a whole. Sweden had one of the highest shares of women among the postsecondary graduates, and for university degrees, Sweden's share is in fact the highest of all. Again, the cause seems to lie on the demand side of women's career markets, which strongly influenced women's demand for postsecondary degrees. Sweden's strong demand for employees in the public health and education sectors has probably played a role in getting women to pursue higher education, raising their relative pay, their employment, and – again because of the gender difference in labor supply elasticities – national output.

Finally, the pay prospects for women have also depended on the overall inequality of pay by occupation, to the extent that women still have not achieved parity in ascending the occupational ladder. One force raising the relative pay of women closer to gender parity in Sweden than in other countries is the fact that the entire distribution of earning power is more compressed for Sweden than for other countries. The more equal are the incomes at different percentile ranks of the overall income distribution, the closer to the middle income will be any group with below-average job qualifications in the eyes of employers. As far as higher education and job experience are concerned, women in the twenty-five to sixty-four age range have still not achieved parity in any country.[37] Therefore whatever raises the relative position of the lower-paid job categories raises the relative wage of women. That has happened in Sweden. By contrast, U.S. women have had to "swim upstream" in job markets since the 1970s. They have been rising toward educational parity and pay parity too, like their Swedish counterparts, but their gains have come against a strong current of widening pay gaps between more skilled and less skilled workers in the United States.[38] This final effect, the dependence on the overall income distribution, helps explain why Sweden's women have come the closest to achieving pay parity.

Education and Retraining

How well has Sweden done in the core human-development policies of ed-ucation and retraining? It would appear that Sweden's overall educational policy has been successful, though not exceptionally so, and the retraining and reemployment policies for which Sweden is famous have actually yielded little if any contribution to growth.

On the broad educational front, Sweden's position in the higher-education ranks is respectable. Aside from its leadership in higher education for women, however, it does not stand out in measures of adult attainment of higher degrees, in math test scores, or in expenditures as a share of GDP. Sweden's educational ranking today resembles its ranking in schooling before World War I, reported in Chapter 5: respectable, not outstanding.

A kind of human capital policy that many associate with Sweden is active labor market policy, an umbrella concept that covers different kinds of policy targeted at getting the unemployed into paid work: public-sector relief jobs, retraining, and job-search brokering. On some definitions, it also can cover subsidies to payrolls and employment to reduce entry into unemployment.

Sweden does indeed stand out in its commitment to these policies, relative to the rest of the OECD.[39] Its ALMP cost per unemployed person looks very high in comparisons with the United States. If you seek to cast doubt on the wisdom of such expenditures, you could correctly point out that an unemployed person in Sweden gets, in unemployment compensation plus training subsidies, as much as tuition, room, and board at Harvard. If you are of the opposite persuasion, you could point out that what Sweden spends on each covered unemployed person roughly matches what the United States spends per inmate in a high-security prison.[40]

How effective have Sweden's active labor market policies been? The quick summary of experts' judgment that ALMP has modest returns is neither a great cost nor a great solution. Rather, its magnitude and its rate of return seem modest. The public-sector relief work brings only a modest gain at best, partly because it displaces some private-sector jobs that would have been created otherwise. The retraining and job-search services have also had only modest returns. Flanagan's early judgment was that "[t]here is disappointingly little evidence that these expenditures have improved the productivity of the Swedish work force" (Flanagan 1987), and Forslund and Krueger reached the same conclusion a decade later, after surveying several studies on both Swedish and U.S. data.[41]

One other kind of active labor market policy can still have positive returns, especially in a second best world in which several government interventions are already in place. Subsidizing new hires and continued employment, as part of Swedish ALMP does, can bring social gains by avoiding unemploy-ment that might have been caused by Sweden's own artificial wage-propping and generous unemployment compensation.[42] Of course, this is only a very constrained argument for ALMP. It only says that one aspect of it can help to undo damages caused by its other aspects. Still, there is no *damage* to economic growth from Sweden's ALMP, if the alternative is simply to pay unemployment compensation or to leave people unsupported.

The best tentative conclusion is that Sweden has not reaped any net gains from its well-known active labor market policies. Rather, the pro-growth side of its labor market policies is one less advertised: The gains through aid to mothers' careers just discussed and the incentives delaying retirement, to which we now turn.

Late Retirement

One might expect that a country guaranteeing generous support from cradle to grave would use generous public subsidies to induce people to retire early. Doing so would serve the egalitarian goal of providing fuller employment for young and middle-age workers. Knowing that Sweden has generally had a low rate of unemployment, one is prepared for the news that Sweden helped that rate look low by removing older workers from the labor force.

Yet the opposite is true of Sweden. Swedish men work to later average retirement ages than men in any other core OECD country except Japan, Norway, and Switzerland.[43] Swedish women work to later average retirement ages than women anywhere else in the world. Continuing work at advanced ages is one of the ways in which Sweden achieves higher GDP per capita.

What makes retirement come so late in Sweden is that the country has for some time worked out a set of incentives that keep most persons from retiring in the fifty-five to sixty-four age range where retirement looks so attractive in other countries. This is probably more a comment on those other countries than on Sweden. As we saw in Chapter 8, population aging is going to put greater stress on some other countries' government budgets than on Sweden's. Perhaps this owes something to Sweden's having had such an old population for so long and having stopped the aging trend temporarily between 1985 and 1995.

Policies toward early retirement certainly do differ between Sweden and some other countries. Sweden's position contrasts strongly with those five prominent subsidizers of early retirement – Belgium, France, Germany, Italy, and the Netherlands. By any measures for the early 1990s, for men or for women, a smaller share of people in the fifty-five to sixty-four age range has left employment in Sweden than in the other five countries. The contrast in average retirement ages is not due to differences in the official age of optional early retirement, which is sixty for Sweden as for many other OECD countries. Rather the difference lies in the share of one's income one could receive by retiring early.

Sweden has gone on to revise its pension system in a way that further fine-tunes some incentives to work and save, while changing the structure of macroeconomic risk. A set of principles enunciated in 1994, and enacted by Parliament as the pension reform of June 1998, created what has been called a "notional defined contribution system." The new system involves three changes of mechanism:

(1) In place of the old mixture of a flat basic pension and one in proportion to individual earnings over the individual's fifteen best years of earnings, the new system averages over the whole working career.
(2) It continues to be predominantly a pay-as-you-go system, with only a touch of funded privatized pensions.
(3) Instead of indexing pension benefits to consumer prices, it now indexes them to national income.

Each year the employee and employer contribute 18.5 percent of the employee's gross pensionable income. Of the 18.5 percent, 16.0 percent is a pay-as-you-go contribution to this year's retirees, continuing the pay-as-you-go principle. The imputed nominal value of this large share of pensions rises with nominal national income, not with a price index. The remaining 2.5 percent goes into a mandatory retirement account, which the individual can privately allocate among securities. To this extent, Sweden's pension system has been partly privatized.

Three motives underlay the pension reform:

(1) The reformers and Parliament wanted stability in pensions' share of GDP. Something like this has been achieved. Sweden's pensioners are now more akin to landlords "on shares," with active workers playing the part of sharecroppers. Thus retirees and workers split the risks of fluctuations in national income. For pensions this means more fluctuations in their nominal benefits. For the nation as a whole, it should dampen those sharp swings in government budget deficits we saw in Figure 11.3, at the cost of dampening the macroeconomy's automatic stabilizers.
(2) By making a greater share of an individual's pension rights proportional to current earnings over the entire career cycle, the reformers hoped to strengthen work incentives. (In the process, they have further reduced the progressivity of the pension system.)
(3) They also hoped to strengthen the incentive to save, though it is hard to see how a small but mandatory privatized part of the pension could achieve that goal.

Thus Sweden, the largest spender on pensions and other social transfers as a share of GDP, has nonetheless devised a public pension system in which people have a relatively strong incentive to work to age sixty-five. As it is now designed, the pension system should also keep pension payments stable as a share of GDP.[44]

CONCLUSIONS: WHY NO DEMISE

Postwar Swedish experience has revealed a number of fairly clear results regarding how economic growth relates to the country's welfare state and other policies.

(1) The first clear result is that *Swedes have not abandoned their social-transfer policies*, for all the criticism from within and without. Social transfers have not been cut back as a share of GDP, except in the hypothetical sense that they have been prevented from rising in ways that one could have imagined.

(2) The stabilization of the social-transfer share seems to reflect a *democratic balance of opinion*, one that has drifted toward the welfare state, but without dramatic reversals over time. Every country has its balance of opinions, and Sweden seems to have found its own equilibrium. Should policy err either on the side of excessive or insufficient social programs and other government intervention, Sweden's voters seem prepared to switch governments.

We have good evidence on voters' views of these core economic issues, thanks to repeated public-opinion surveys, as well as to the electoral and policy results themselves. Table 11.4 captures the spirit of Swedish opinions between 1967 and 1984. Sweden's public officials, and even the tax collectors, enjoy secure legitimacy in the public eye. In 1968, in 1974, and again in 1981 Swedish citizens were asked "Have you once been treated wrongly or unjustly by the [public authorities]?" In all cases, the shares answering "Agree" are low. Not even in 1981, at the height of tax rates, of government intervention, and of inflation, was there widespread grievance against any public agency. The top "once ... treated wrongly" group were the tax authorities, at 16.1 percent. No other agency had delivered a single perceived offense to as many as 6 percent of the respondents. Not even the police.

When asked about the wisdom of extra government spending and taxes in the troubled 1980s, Swedish respondents showed the kind of balance typical of interviewees in other countries. Most agreed, when asked, that taxes are too high. Most agreed, when asked, that more government benefits would be a good thing, especially if they could be achieved by making government more "efficient" – that is, if they cost the general public nothing. In other words, people approve of a free lunch. The payoff questions are those that really ask the public if the country has achieved the right balance, given both costs and benefits, Questions (f) and (g) within the rectangle in Table 11.4. Here the opinions are evenly divided – at a high level of taxes and spending.

There seems to be a political balancing act in which Sweden's political tides ebb and flow around a relatively stable welfare state position. Democratic

TABLE 11.4. *Swedish Attitudes toward Government and the Welfare State, 1967–1984*

Questions (ranked from Yes = Right to Yes = Left)		In 1967 or 1968	In 1973 or 1974	In 1978 or 1979	In 1981	In 1984
(a) "The State has become increasingly despotic at the expense of individual rights."	Agree					18
	Disagree					15
	Don't know					4
(b) "Have you once been treated wrongly or unjustly by the tax authorities?"	Agree	10	14		16	
(c) "Tax pressure today is so high that the individual doesn't feel inclined to work."	Agree					72
	Disagree					27
	Don't know					1
(d) "Social reforms have gone so far in this country that . . . the gov't ought to reduce rather than increase allowance and assistance."	Agree	42	60	67	47*	
	Disagree	51	33	27	38*	
	Don't know	7	7	6	15*	
(e) "The public sector is too costly and a threat to the national economy."	Agree					52
	Disagree					43
	Don't know					5

(f) "Do you think that our current social programs are too expensive and therefore ought to be reduced?"	Agree	34	39
	Disagree	50	47
	Don't' know	16	14
(g) "Sweden can afford as large a public sector as at present."	Agree	48	
	Disagree	44	
	Don't know	9	
(h) "The public sector must be retained at its present level and even expanded."	Agree	62	
	Disagree	35	
	Don't know	3	
(i) "The state is needed to equalize injustices that reproduce themselves in a society like ours."	Agree	75	
	Disagree	19	
	Don't know	7	

Source and Notes:
* The wording of Question (d) changed in 1981.
Flora (1986, 93–98).

mechanisms seem to keep both the Social Democrats and the center-right opposition fairly close together in their stances toward social programs. Democratic mechanisms have also kept the Social Democrats from having a secure grip on office. Despite their international renown as a party that has dominated since 1932, the Social Democrats have been out of office for two appreciable lengths of time and remain vulnerable. When their militant flank, led by the LO, overstepped by trying to finance worker control of manufacturing firms with a confiscatory profits tax – that infamous wage earners fund" – they were eventually forced to drop the tax and the plans for enhanced union power. Conversely, the clarion call for rolling back taxes and transfers, climaxing in the early 1990s, brought some defensible fine-tuning, but no crisis of the welfare state.

(3) *Why is Sweden's political balance more welfare-statist* than the balances achieved in other high-income democracies? Assar Lindbeck, whose work looms so large in studies of the Swedish economy, has himself given a set of reasons that seem persuasive. They are reasons that also fit the explanations offered by the model of Chapter 13 in Volume 2, and by the comparative international evidence we surveyed in Chapter 7. He points, first, to the "relatively early [postwar] aging of the population." Second, the universality of the social programs helped them capture the support of the median income ranks. This capture of center ground is one reason the policies hardly changed when the center-right coalitions were in power in 1976–1982 and 1991–1994.[45] Lindbeck also credited social affinity and its link to the kind of mobility between income ranks that promotes the feeling that "that could be me." His made this point in mirror image. Whereas our emphasis on median voters would have us emphasize just how easily people could drop from the middle income ranks toward the bottom, he noted how easily Swedes could move from the bottom ranks to the middle:

As in most other developed countries, income mobility is rather high in Sweden.... Income mobility seems to be even higher for individuals with initially very low incomes (less than 50 percent of median income).... Temporarily very low income is, in fact, often mainly a liquidity problem, sometimes reflecting periods of investment in human capital, with the returns appearing later on.[46]

His model of the low-income Swede is a young person still in school or somebody getting retraining to find a new job. Granted, his emphasis appears to have been on how little lifetime inequality there is in Sweden between the middle and the bottom ranks. Yet it is easy to draw the corollary that more middle-income people in Sweden than elsewhere can identify with someone in the bottom ranks, someone who is often like they were at a different phase of the life cycle.

(4) Whatever the median Swedish mood about the workability of their system, *does economic analysis show that their preference has cost them in terms of growth?* This chapter has found Swedish polices that have worked

badly, policies that succeed in minimizing any cost of the country's large taxes and public spending, and social policies that definitely raise Sweden's productivity.

(4a) Sweden had *defective macroeconomic policies*, at least between 1976 and 1992. The government and the Riksbank should have abandoned the adjustable peg policy on the exchange-rate front and should have floated the krona from 1971 on. The peg proved especially costly at the start of the 1990s, when Sweden tried in vain to fix the krona to the emerging European Union currency.

(4b) Sweden's *tax policies have not harmed growth* relative to the policies followed in other OECD countries. Past opinion on Sweden's taxes has paid too much attention to the high gross tax take and the high statutory rates on top incomes. By the start of the 1980s Sweden had already modified the income tax schedules with deductions and exemptions that produced low effective taxes on capital. Sweden's tax mix also emphasizes taxes on consumption, rather than on income.

(4c) Sweden's well-known *active labor market policies have had no visible growth effect*.

(4d) Finally, Sweden has *promoted work by women and the elderly*. Thanks to a whole range of policies, women's relative earning power and their work are as high in Sweden as anywhere in the developed world, and both men and women stay at work to later ages, easing the pressure on the pension system.

12

How the Keys Were Made: Democracy and Cost Control

Many have cast welfare states as nations that just don't see, or feel that the rich should bear, the soaring national costs of taxes and transfers. Yet the danger of such naive pessimism about public programs should be obvious by now. The case against social transfers can't be that simple, especially in the face of the evidence suggesting no significant net cost.

Chapters 10 and 11 have surveyed some institutional keys to the puzzle of how social transfer programs may not harm economic growth and well-being. The list of keys is eclectic and incomplete. We now have a better understanding of the tax mix practiced in welfare states and the limits on the damage done through work disincentives, both for young adults and for the elderly. These findings can only be suggestive, and we are a long way from an overall quantitative accounting.

Two main principles seem to have shaped this eclectic set of institutional keys:

(1) The budget-stakes principle: While any economic system has lapses from peak performance, higher-budget countries are more aware of the need to choose efficient designs for their tax-transfer systems because the stakes are higher. The greater the share of taxes and transfers in GDP, the greater the marginal cost of choosing the wrong program design. There is evidence that the democratic political process was partly guided by this principle en route to those high welfare-state budgets.

(2) The principle that universalism probably cuts costs. Over the centuries surveyed in this book, prosperity and democracy have allowed countries to economize on administrative and incentive costs by shifting from narrow and expensive taxes and transfers to broad taxes and broad entitlements.

DEMOCRACY, BUDGET SIZE, AND BUDGET BLUNDERS

Big Budget, High Stakes

The eclectic set of clues and examples may largely reflect a fundamental mechanism guiding welfare states toward an assortment of devices that avoid damaging their economic growth.

The mechanism is this *budget-stakes principle*: *The higher the budget, the higher the marginal cost of choosing the wrong fiscal design*, both economically and politically. To see how, suppose that expanding a budget has a deadweight-cost multiplier of 0.40 under Policy A but only 0.10 under Policy B. So, for example, expanding the budget by 10 percent with Tax-Transfer Policy A would bring a deadweight cost of 4 percent of the initial budget. The same expansion by 10 percent of the budget using an alternative Tax-Transfer Policy B would bring a deadweight cost of only 1 percent, we assume, while still delivering the same public benefits. Do we have any assurances that the political process would choose B, saving the nation an unnecessary extra cost? Not if the initial budget was, say, only 1 percent of GDP, so that the expansion of 10 percent of the budget only raises it to 1.1 percent of GDP. The deadweight costs would be only 0.04 percent of GDP under Policy A and 0.01 percent of GDP under Policy B. A small net return may not overcome the fixed cost of investigating and campaigning against the more costly choice. There is so much sand in the policy machinery that the public might have no way to react to such small magnitudes. The nation may stumble on with the wrong choice, suffering a loss of 0.03 percent of GDP without paying attention.

Suppose, by contrast, that the initial budget were already 25 percent of GDP. In this second case, people should weigh and debate the same 10-percent choice more seriously. The deadweight cost would be 1.0 percent of GDP from A and 0.25 percent of GDP from B. Getting it wrong means a net national cost of 0.75 percent of GDP.

To take a more ominous third case, if the whole earlier expansion of the budget from 1 percent of GDP to 25 percent of GDP had wrongly followed Policy A, the nation would already be staggering under the burden of a net mistake of 24 percent $\times$ (.40 − .10) = 7.2 percent of GDP. We should expect an outcry from those bearing all of this cost − or bearing more than all of it, if others favoring the costly choice actually benefit by it.

These numerical examples have in fact *understated* the tendency of the economic stake to rise with the share of taxes and transfers in GDP. They understated because they kept applying the same deadweight cost multipliers − 0.40 for Policy A and 0.10 for Policy B − at all budget levels. Yet we know from conventional economic analysis, and from the political economy of deadweight costs, that these deadweight cost multipliers rise with the amount taxed and transferred. People should be much more sensitive to possible extra deadweight costs when budgets are already bigger.

In a democracy, *the extra economic costs become political costs*, as the companion volume argues in the spirit of the Becker model of pressure-group competition.[1] The larger the budget, the greater the political risk that large groups will notice and take action against those who advocate, or implement, the wrong choice. Such a rising "shadow price" of a wrong policy suggests a reason why it is the high-budget welfare states that got certain things right. While a low-budget United States could get locked (and still is partially locked) into the double taxation of dividends, a higher-budget government would run greater economic and political risks by magnifying the same mix of taxes.

Does the political process really work that way in democracies? We have a few clear examples, even though most of the detailed budgetary histories remain to be written. Let us turn first to a case in which the democratic political process correctly foresaw the need to base giant social budgets largely on a pro-growth consumption tax and then to a few cases in which mistakes were followed by corrections.

The need to base huge increases in the social budget on relatively pro-growth hikes in the consumption tax was grasped by Sweden's political process after World War II, as its social transfers rose from under 10 percent to 33 percent of GDP.[2] The wisdom of this choice was imposed not by any major political party or lobby, but by the competitive political *process*. Right after the war, nobody wanted the sales tax that later became Sweden's huge value added tax (VAT). The dominant Social Democratic Party (SAP) and the dominant blue collar labor union (the LO) did not want it. Their coalition allies, the Communists, hated any kind of sales tax, which fell heavily on workers. The bourgeois parties to the right also opposed the sales tax, or any tax for that matter, and were not persuaded by promises that it would make cuts in the income tax possible.

Yet the money had to be raised somehow, if the popular safety nets and pensions were to be provided. Two LO economists broke ranks early, calling for a sales tax in 1948, at the same time that their union was winning its temporary repeal. By the end of the 1950s Finance Minister Sträng had come to agree, and the Social Democrats began to waver, realizing that raising taxes on capital incomes would risk capital flight from Sweden. They needed coalition partners to stay in power, however. In the end SAP leaders correctly guessed that the Communists would not dare to vote no and risk dissolving the government at a time when they were unpopular. The Communists abstained, and the sale tax was reinstated. Once in place, it became an escalator that the Social Democrats rode to ever-higher social budgets. In 1969, as the share of social transfers in GDP was reaching 16 percent of GDP, the sales tax was transformed into the VAT, which avoided double-taxing intermediate products. Meanwhile, the income tax rates had also crept up, but a rising tide of complaint won exemptions in the late 1970s and across the 1980s, as described in Chapter 11. Sweden's postwar tax history seems to show the process of considering and rejecting bad designs for an expanded budget in favor of a wiser tax mix, one that no separate interest group championed.

To spotlight the link between Sweden's correct tough choice and the size of the budget, consider the fate of the value added tax, or flat consumption tax, in the United States. The efficiency of switching to a flat tax has often been emphasized by economists, especially by those leaning toward the Republican Party.[3] Yet state sales taxes remain limited, and the idea of a federal consumption tax has been shot down every time it has been launched as a trial balloon, either by a Republican or by a Democrat. If it is proposed by a Republican, it looks like a transparent Republican call for redistributing from the poor to the rich, and Democrats would win any political fight over such a proposal. It was actually proposed once by a Democrat, Congressman Al Ullman of the House Ways and Means Committee. Ullman's stillborn Tax Restructuring Act of 1979 offered a 10 percent VAT as a replacement for social security taxes and for complicated loophole-ridden income taxes. Other Democrats denounced the shift as regressive, just like their Swedish counterparts. Tax-revolt conservatives denounced it just because it was a tax proposed by a Democrat, and any Swedish-style expansion of the welfare state was unthinkable. The bill died, and Ullman was defeated in the election of 1980.[4]

A strong influence on this political outcome is the size of the proposed social budget. At lower budget levels, the efficiency gains from the right tax design are much lower. As long as smaller government is both a reality and their wish, U.S. conservatives cannot claim that the efficiency gains from switching to the consumption tax are great enough to cover up the redistribution from poor to rich. As in our hypothetical examples above, the gains from switching to a better tax design seem much greater in a high-budget context like Sweden than in the United States.

Illustrative Tax-Transfer Blunders

The logic of democratic cost control also shows up in the cases where policy blunders are committed. We expect policy errors from government and the political process, and our expectations have been met. To repeat a reminder from Albert Hirschman, every kind of organization commits lapses from best performance.

The cost of lapses from best performance will depend on the power of the dissatisfied to exit or to speak up.[5] The threat of exit pressures governments to moderate their taxes on mobile capital. Voices raised in opposition can also curtail extreme waste in government.

How does voice work as a cost control when it comes to the tax and transfer policies that are the subject of this book? In earlier chapters, we have seen high-budget policies get out of hand, with politicians scrambling to undo them later. In Chapters 8 and 9, we saw that politicians would eventually incur some political costs to curb excessively generous public pensions in Italy and in Brazil. In Chapter 11, we saw Sweden's Social Democrats and the powerful LO labor union try to confiscate capital in the 1970s, especially with the class-war "wage earners fund," and get forced into retreat. Here let us add three other tax-transfer blunders, a high-budget blunder in the Netherlands and two blunders in moderate-budget Britain, to illustrate the rough but positive influence of voice in limiting deadweight and social costs.

Dutch Disability Policy

A well-balanced policy toward disabled workers would provide disability payments for those workers who were clearly disabled or were especially responsive to rehabilitation. It would offer such disability pay fairly and broadly, avoiding excessive stinginess, which would trigger costly litigation. It would not, however, be over-generous by granting disability pay to everybody who wanted an excuse to retire or not work, fobbing off the authorities with vague complaints about psychological stress or back pain. Harold Wilensky has argued that Germany and Sweden have achieved the right balance of coverage and cost control and that the United States and Britain have been too stingy, sparking costly litigation.[6]

The case that is most instructive here, however, is the Dutch case of clearly excessive disability payments up to 1993. Between 1967 and 1993, the Netherlands increasingly allowed disability status to be a form of subsidized unemployment. As a result, in 1993 a million Dutch workers – nearly one adult out of seven – drew disability payments amounting to 5 percent of GDP. This implies that disability pay added about a third of an average worker's income to whatever other compensation an unemployed person received, which should have reduced the incentive to work.

The issue of disability abuse became political, forcing the passage of a series of reforms. Reforms of March 1992 and August 1993 tightened up the qualifications necessary to receive disability pay and the level of benefits that qualified recipients would receive. The Dutch disability and unemployment rates started dropping significantly, so that by the end of the century the media were talking about the "Dutch miracle" of low unemployment. Yet as late as 1996, the Netherlands was still an outlier in its disability population.[7] The case of Dutch disability policy thus illustrates both a prolonged policy failure and a noteworthy correction after the amounts had become clearly excessive. Not a smooth or prompt correction, but a correction.

Labour's Selective Employment Tax of 1966–1970

Britain's Labour Party government under Harold Wilson offered an example of choosing the wrong tax base for a steady expansion of government spending. The Selective Employment Tax (SET) of 1966, while it served as a way to help fund the steady rise of social programs, was actually undertaken as a misguided attempt to improve productivity growth and the balance of payments. The brainchild of economist Nicholas Kaldor, it taxed jobs in the service sector, in the belief that the manufacturing sector gave off more external benefits for the growth process than did the service sector. This premise seems to have been based on faulty numbers, since the true productivity gains in services are often immeasurable. Most economists disagreed with Kaldor.

Still, the SET remained intact until Edward Heath and the Conservatives won a surprise election victory in 1970. The SET was repealed that year, and after some shuffling it was replaced with the broader and more pro-growth value added tax in 1973. In the event, one motivation for switching to the VAT lies outside our story: Britain joined the European Union that year and needed the VAT to harmonize with the tax systems of other members. Yet the underlying debate gave the basic correct argument for a VAT: To pay the rising bill for pensions and other social programs, it is better to use a relatively flat consumption tax, and the voting public of 1970 saw no benefits from the Selective Employment Tax.[8]

The Thatcher Poll Tax of 1989–1992

As suggested in this and earlier chapters, most economists tend to think that economic growth is well promoted by combining a broad consumption tax with a "poll subsidy," a fixed schedule of cash grants to all households. That way, everybody has at least a bearable minimum living standard, and government is funded by a tax that does not discriminate against capital accumulation.

Margaret Thatcher decided to move in an opposing direction at the close of the 1980s. Instead of offering a fixed entitlement as a safety net and social pacifier, she decided to levy a fixed tax on each adult in the population – a poll tax, not a poll subsidy. The underlying arguments say more about a particular conservative mood in 1989 than about any economic logic. Thatcher and some leading Conservative thinkers saw inefficiencies in local government and considered a poll tax as a wake-up call for those governments. But the poll tax, or "community charge," brought losses to many more people than it benefited, and there is no evidence that it improved local government efficiency or brought relief from other taxes. Her popularity took a dive, and in 1992 the Conservative Party leadership dropped both Thatcher and the poll tax. The whole episode cost Britain about £1.5 million wasted in setting up, administering, and replacing the poll tax. But that cost was only temporary and limited, thanks to the political opposition the poll tax sparked.[9]

UNIVERSALISM MAY COST LESS

The basic link between bigger budgets and greater care in tax design, by itself, should only have contained, not eliminated, the deadweight costs of welfare states. Leaving the matter there might have sufficed. Yet the choices of tax-transfer design are not so costly that one must choose between expensive evils.

There is a second unifying principle that emerges from the history we have surveyed, a principle that reveals further cost savings from the high-budget welfare state. As a guide to low-cost policy in a complicated "second-best" world, it is generally better to have broader and flatter taxes and entitlements. We distort economic signals less if we tax all alternatives at a similar rate and make people's basic guarantees independent of their specific life choices. This is the principle of *univeralism* in public finance: More uniform rules and rates, applied to all, are less costly to administer, less distorting in their effects on private behavior, fairer, and more transparent. The principle does not do away with all fiscal complexity. One must still decide such issues as whether the safety net should be held higher for those who have earned more while working. But the univeralism principle does emerge as a rough guide to efficiency and equity. It suggests, cautiously, that the most efficient tax-transfer world is one in which everybody is entitled to similar basic income support and basic services, while facing the same tax rate on all consumption.

Throughout this volume, the cost-saving merits of universalism have appeared, for both earlier centuries and today and on both the tax and the expenditure sides. Let us develop these points further, to appreciate the strength of the proposition that universalism probably costs less and has probably helped account for the free-lunch puzzle.

On the Tax Side

The rise of rich democracies has brought a gradual march from narrow and expensive taxes toward broader, more efficient taxes like the general consumption tax. We have already caught glimpses of the later part of that march from more complex income taxes toward the simpler, broader VAT in postwar welfare states. Earlier centuries saw two earlier shifts, from inefficient arbitrary tax gouging to more stable and less corrupt customs duties and excise taxes, and then from the latter to those direct income and wealth taxes that the VAT has overtaken in today's high budget countries.

The earliest tax shift was one in which rulers' arbitrary exactions were replaced by relatively stable and honest customs and excise taxes. It was a transition that took centuries in Europe and has still not taken place in many Third World kleptocracies. Where monarchs were finally forced to grant new freedoms and predictable taxes, there was a flourishing of cities, merchants, and industry. This first phase of the transition culminated in Britain's development of an efficient customs and excise system in the eighteenth century. That system helped Britain defeat France's ancien regime, which depended on a less efficient and more corrupt tax system.[10]

The development of efficient customs and excise regimes, shaped by the rise of new economic elites, improved the overall efficiency of the tax system, but it still had a high deadweight cost ratio. An underappreciated development in the rich and democratizing countries across the 1815–1914 century was the replacement of this system with lower-cost direct taxation. Both administrative costs and incentive costs fell as shares of the amounts being collected. The administrative costs of tax collection fell because increasingly efficient governments found cheaper ways to collect taxes. One way was by shifting from such indirect taxes as customs and excise to new direct taxes on income and wealth. In addition, within both the indirect-tax and the direct-tax categories, administrative costs fell as a share of the revenue collected. Figure 12.1 charts this decline for Britain and the United States. Britain's tax-collection system, which was already a recognized model of efficiency by 1780, became increasingly cheap to administer, per pound collected, across the nineteenth and early twentieth centuries. So did the U.S. customs service and the Internal Revenue Service. These cost savings implicitly reduced the cost of any programs the tax revenues were spent on, such as the social programs that are our focus here.

Like administrative costs, the incentive cost of social programs probably also came down on the tax-collecting side. The prevailing historical shift in tax collections was the same one we observe when scanning from lower-income to higher-income countries in today's global cross-section – a shift from border taxes on foreign trade to direct taxation on income and wealth. The famous incentive effects of today's direct taxation on the supply of labor and other factors are tied to elasticities that tend to be lower than the elasticities of foreign trade and other behavior subject to the older kinds of taxes. Lower elasticities of the taxed activity mean lower deadweight costs per dollar transferred, at least under most realistic initial conditions. While this point cannot be quantified here, it seems likely that the incentive costs of the rising social programs have declined relative to the amounts spent, in view of the shift toward taxes that had lower deadweight-cost ratios.

The rich democracies achieved the shift from customs and excise to direct taxation by the early twentieth century both because they got rich and because they became fuller democracies. Poorer countries had relied on customs and excise, so that an underdeveloped government sector could just set up customs collections at the borders and tax visible excise commodities as a cheap way to raise revenue without a highly literate population. The early customs and excises also reflected narrow protectionist interests, which eventually had to yield ground as others gained political voice.

Yet the shift to direct taxation is not the final step toward efficient taxation and universalism. Rather the final step is the shift toward broad consumption taxes, with few exemptions, as a major supplement to direct taxes on income and wealth. What made this shift toward a relatively universal consumption tax occur, and why did the welfare states push the consumption tax strategy further than low-budget countries? Detailed histories would help here. Even without them, however, we can see a tendency that emerged in the evidence of Chapter 10 and in the story of Sweden's turning toward consumption taxes

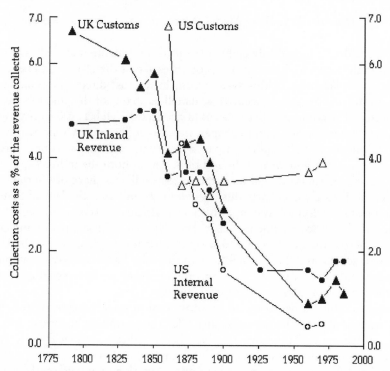

FIGURE 12.1. The Long-Run Decline in Tax Collection Costs as a Percentage of the Amounts Collected in Britain and America.

Sources: United Kingdom, main revenue services: Figures for years before World War I divide the official estimates of collection costs by gross receipts, while those after World War I divide it by what are called "net receipts." The change in official convention matters little, since adding the collection costs to the denominator would change the ratio by only about 1 percent of itself.

For *1787–1796*: The figures are calculated from The Fourth Report of Great Britain, Select Committee on Finance, July 19, 1797. The collection costs are described only as the "charges of management" on the "collection of revenues," and are compared to gross receipts. For *1830–1860*: The main source is a special return in House of Commons, *Sessional Papers*, 1862, vol. xxx, 601. Each figure from this source refers to the single fiscal year starting in the year listed. However, the customs percentages for 1840, 1850 and 1860 are five-year averages centered on that same fiscal year. For *1873–1900*: Annual Reports of the Commissioners of Customs and Inland Revenue. The figures for Inland Revenue are again single-year figures for fiscal years starting April 1, and those for the Customs service are five-year averages centered on that year. The customs figures for years between 1855/6 and 1876/7 had to adjusted upward, to correct for the temporary exclusion of the Coast Guard costs. For *1926–1986*: Single-year figures are calculated from the Annual Reports of the Customs Commissioner and the Commissioner of Inland Revenue.

United States, two main revenue agencies: All cost percentages are five-year averages calculated from the annual reports of the U.S. Secretary of the Treasury. The underlying data series on costs were discontinued in 1980.

and the VAT across the postwar decades. The rise of relatively pro-growth consumption taxes was facilitated by their being combined with generous universal safety nets. It was to raise pensions and other social transfers that Sweden's Social Democratic leadership pushed through those consumption taxes over the objections of the LO and the Communists. There is an implicit political deal: To have the transfers they wanted, they needed to choose an efficient and pro-growth tax structure, one that the workers largely paid for by themselves.

Stated this way, the link between safety nets and efficient taxes may sound like a restatement of the budget stakes principle just discussed. Yet viewed in mirror image, it shows an advantage of universalism in the building of safety nets: The Left will fight against such tax reforms as shifting to a consumption tax or relieving investors from the double taxation of dividends if these pro-growth reforms seem to be blatant redistributions from poor to rich. But if the less progressive system is being used to finance generous safety nets, class warfare recedes and efficiency has a better chance. This tax-side advantage of universalism showed itself again in 2003, when President Bush proposed that the United States stop double taxing dividends. This reasonable, and partially successful, pro-growth proposal looked like naked stroke-the-rich politics coming from Republicans that rejected most universal entitlements, even in health care.

The Expenditure Side

The historical growth of social transfers was also accompanied by a decline in administrative and incentive costs as a share of the amounts transferred. We have caught parts of this long trend when looking at different developments over the last three centuries.

Since the eighteenth century, administrative costs have declined as a share of the total amounts transferred to the poor, the sick, and the elderly. This cost-saving was already described in Chapter 3. The main kind of program before 1880 was classic poor relief. Societies intent on forcing all the able–bodied to work tried to emphasize "indoor relief" in which one was kept in a poorhouse or workhouse. They never succeeded in getting such indoor relief to account for half of their budget or for half of the recipients covered, as we have seen.[11] Still, to the extent that relief was given indoors, its administrative costs were a high share, often a quarter, of the total amount spent. The reason was simply that the poor had to be policed and completely provided

FIGURE 12.1. (*continued*) Figure 12.1 graphs a Customs series and an Inland Revenue series for the United Kingdom as if they were consistently defined throughout. That is, the figure ignores the fact that excises were shifted from the Inland Revenue series to the Customs (and Excise) series between the 1900 data point and the 1926 data point.

for. By contrast, once democracy and prosperity and other changes made society more willing to give aid to people in their own homes, with minimal supervision, the administrative costs fell as a share of the amount spent. Stricter regimes are more bureaucratic and more costly.

By the postwar era, administrative costs had fallen to almost-negligible levels in the high-income OECD countries. So say not only data on programs for the poor, but also data on pension programs. International data on pension support programs show that administrative costs are less than 3 percent of the pension-program budget in all high-income countries, and often below 1 percent. The same efficiency is not shown in all Third-World pension programs, however, some of which have administrative cost shares of up to the 7 percent recorded for Burundi and Tanzania in the late 1980s.[12]

Like the administrative costs, the likely incentive costs of transfers to the poor have also dropped as the benefits became less means-tested and more universal.[13] Strict means testing entails not only those high bureaucratic costs, but also a strong work disincentive. As we saw in Chapter 10, shifting from tough means testing to more universal entitlements cuts the marginal tax rate on work by a poor person, say a single mother. The United States and Britain finally took a step toward universalism when they gave significant low-income tax credits in 1993 (for the United States' EITC) and 2000 (for Britain's WFTC).

Finally, the gains from offering universal benefits, instead of tight means testing, are most obvious in the realm of public health and health insurance. As we saw in Chapter 10, the more privatized U.S. health system is more bureaucratic, plagued by incentive problems, more unequally distributed, and less successful in saving lives. Here is perhaps the only crisis, other than another Great Depression, that might lead the United States toward a more universalist fiscal system. If a breakdown on the health front made the United States switch to a national health system for all, it might also universalize efficiently on the tax side, switching from employment-based taxes to consumption taxes to cover the public costs while saving even more on private costs.

HENCE NO RETREAT

The pieces of the free-lunch puzzle are thus coming together, first in the detailed discoveries of Chapters 10 and 11 and then in this chapter's two principles – the budget stakes principle and the economizing side of universalism in taxes and transfers.

These insights make it easier to understand why the media coverage has been so wrong about the welfare state since 1980. For all the pronouncements to the contrary, there has been no "crisis" or "demise" of the welfare state since that dawn of the Reagan–Thatcher era. In fact, there has not even been a "rollback" or "retreat" or "retrenchment" or "scaling back," except in a few categories in a few countries. Since 1980, out of the twenty-one leading OECD countries, only three have cut the share of GDP spent on public health care, only two have cut the share spent on public pensions, only four have cut the share spent on welfare, and only three have cut the share spent on unemployment. Overall, only two of the twenty-one countries (Spain and Portugal) have cut the shares spent on total social transfers.[14] Nobody has retreated from public funding for education. Like Mark Twain's "early death," the reports of the downfall of the welfare state have been grossly exaggerated. Why be surprised that the political systems in the high budget countries never abandoned their welfare state if it has no clear net national cost?

If high-budget welfare states have achieved much the same growth with greater equality, why haven't the lower-spending countries crossed over? The shorthand answer is "history and ideology." Recent surveys confirm what we have long known. The separate historical paths followed by the low-budget countries of the English-speaking world and by Switzerland have shaped a political ideology that will remain firmly opposed to a universalist welfare state for the foreseeable future.[15] The keys to the free-lunch puzzle serve to explain why the opposite is also true: There is no compelling economic reason to expect any great retreat from the welfare state.

Endnotes

Chapter 1

1. In public-opinion surveys, as in voting behavior, taxing the rich to give transfers to the poor is consistently favored more by lower-income persons than by higher-income persons. Even though people do express a more general public-good rationale for redistributing income, their opinions are better explained by the actual and perceived differences in their direct economic self-interest than by differences in their views about the collective good.

2. It is desirable to exclude contributory pensions in this book, that is, the amounts paid by one's self or one's employer. They are not a controversial redistribution of resources, but rather just part of one's employment contract. Therefore it is desirable to exclude government-employee and military pensions from the measures used here. That proved possible in Chapter 7's data for 1880–1930 and for the OECD data series for 1980–1995. It was not possible, however, in the OECD pension data for 1960–1981, which unavoidably included public-employee pensions.

3. Both here and in Chapter 3's evidence, this conclusion excludes certain kinds of giving as self-help rather than as charity or redistribution toward others. In particular, it excludes any transfers within families or any benefits paid out by mutual aid societies and fraternal aid associations.

4. Some government officials received retirement incomes, of course, and these could be called "public" in the sense that they flowed through the government sector. Yet we should continue to set these aside as merely part of the pay package negotiated between employer and employee, not as a redistributive kind of support for the elderly.

5. In particular, see the stimulating article by David Thomson (1984). Yet Thomson's conjecture that the elderly received a higher benefit/wage ratio than in the 1980s was based on the assumption that all the elderly poor received the assistance that was the recorded norm for some, and on Thomson's switch in the kinds of wage rates with which their benefits were compared. Since the switch was from lower-paid farm workers to higher-paid industrial workers around 1870, the effect is to ratchet downward the apparent relative ratio of post-1870 support.

6. Here is a rough numerical illustration of the likely ratio of support per elderly pauper recipient (note that these were only part of the population of the elderly poor, who were only part of all elderly). In England and Wales in 1802–1803 persons over sixty were about 8 percent of the population versus about 55 percent for all adults under sixty, or they were $8/55 = 14.5$ percent of all adults or 17 percent $(8/(55–8))$ of all adults under sixty.

   All pauper recipients received 2.15 percent of national income in 1802–1803. This translated into a support ratio of 16.7 percent, which is the ratio (benefits/recipient)/(income/adult) (see Lindert 1998, Table 2). How did the support per elderly recipient compare to this support ratio? If the average elderly recipient, often a widow, got fully 2.5 times the support ratio of the average pauper recipient of any age, then the average elderly recipient could have received 41.75 percent of an average income per adult. That is low by today's standards. Furthermore, that support would have to be spread among all of the poor elderly or among all of the elderly, not all of whom received relief. The generosity per total elderly poor or per total elderly population would have fallen below that 41.75 percent-of-an-average-income that a recipient pauper received. It was not a typical public pension support for an OECD country today.

7. Smith (1776, 413, 443). Edwin G. West (1970, 98–99) denies that Smith favored "elaborate provision of universal education by the state." Taken literally and narrowly, West's denial is correct. Smith did not seek government aid to education that was *elaborate*, or necessarily a *direct* provision by government schools or run by the *central* government. As West points out, Smith hoped that in some cases the externalities could be so local that the tax-based, or even philanthropy-based, aid to education could be done at a very local level, approaching the private end of the spectrum. Yet Smith was clear that local taxes must be called upon in general, as West seems to acknowledge. As we shall see later in this chapter and at length in Chapter 6, every educationally leading country followed the same formula of launching its rise of mass schooling primarily with local taxes.

8. Smith (1776, 130–134, 420–434, 443).

9. Butts (1978, 26–28).

10. Virginia did not adopt a statewide school system until 1870, in the Reconstruction era (Kaestle 1983, 8–9 and 198–199).

    Not all of the American founding fathers shared Jefferson's espousal of tax-based primary schooling. Benjamin Franklin favored subsidies for universities, but was not interested in subsidized education for the poor (Alexander 1980, 143).

11. For a breakdown of pre-1930 social transfers into poor relief, unemployment compensation, public pensions, public health support, and public housing subsidies, see Lindert (1994, Table 1). These separate spending categories are analyzed for the postwar era in Chapter 7.

12. Imperial Germany is not viewed as a leader here. As argued in Chapter 7 and in Lindert (1994), Bismarck's famous social-insurance programs were largely self-insurance by the workers themselves and thus not a large social transfer between income classes. The high spending figure for Germany in 1930 refers to the Weimar Republic, not to Imperial Germany.

13. United Nations Development Program (1994, 196).

14. "Pre-fisc income" is shorthand for the longer phrase "income before this year's taxes have been deducted and net transfer payments from government have been added in." "Post-fisc" income therefore would mean take-home pay, or what economists call "disposable income."
15. Killingsworth (1983), Burtless (1987), Triest (1990), Moffitt (1992, 2002b).
16. Some initial hints of a significant labor-supply effect through mortality and migration can be found in Mokyr (1983, 261–274, esp. 272–273).
17. Boyer (1989).
18. The absence of a negative relationship is even starker after we make two other adjustments that correlate social transfers positively with the level of income per person:

  (1) We should shift from the conventional use of GDP per capita to GDP per labor hour, picking up the fact that West Europeans work fewer hours per year. This adjustment makes sense if you value people's free time positively. It shows what you get if you value each hour of a person's time at that person's wage rate. With free time thus valued, the level of adjusted full-time purchasing power per person would be raised more for the higher-spending economies.

  (2) We should correct the GDP figures to include incomes earned in the shadow, or underground, economy. While numbers are hard to get on the underground economy, they probably would add more GDP in the higher-taxing, higher-spending economies. For one set of clues see the 1960–1995 results for Sweden, Denmark, Norway, Germany, United States, Austria, and Switzerland in Schneider and Enste (2000, 81). The underground share of GDP grew 11–17% in the first four countries, and only 5.7–6.5% in the last three. Despite the inclusion of Austria in the second group, the first group has a higher average share of social transfers in GDP. Therefore the adjustment would tend to add a positive element to the correlation in the first column of Table 1.3.

19. Crafts (1997).
20. OECD (1998d, Table F).
21. This paragraph has defined generosity of social transfers in two ways: transfers out of state and local funds as a share of state product, and state and local transfers per recipient as a percentage of state product per capita. Total transfers, including aid from the federal government, would have had a more negative relationship to the level and growth of income per person. This negative relationship, however, would reflect only the fact that lower income attracts federal aid, not an effect of state and local aid on state income.
22. These contrasts relate to democracies and nontotalitarian dictatorship, not to totalitarian dictatorships, which are not the focus of this book.

Chapter 2

1. Between 1980 and 2000, there were at least fifteen English-language books with "crisis of the welfare state" or "welfare state in crisis" or "waning of the welfare state" in their titles. Fifteen books should offer ample coverage for an event that

did not happen. I am not the first to doubt proclamations of the crisis or demise of the welfare state. See Wilensky (2002: 221–222).

2. See, for example, Peltzman (1980), Meltzer and Richard (1981), Alesina and Rodrik (1994), and Persson and Tabellini (1994).

3. See Kakwani (1980), and the Deininger–Squire data base available on the World Bank web site.

4. See Boyer (1990).

5. The passage of the 1834 Poor Law Reform was not a simple direct result of the shift toward urban votes in the 1832 Reform Act, however. As past authors have rightly stressed, and as Chapter 5 notes, the early 1830s had brought a shift in the aristocracy's own attitude toward poor relief. Instead of thinking of it as an investment in preventing sedition, as in the stormy French War era, they came to view poor relief as an instigator of riot, as in the Swing riots of 1830–1831.

6. Toughness here means tight residency requirements for relief, not low aid per recipient. The urban centers and the Northwest denied aid to many poor, especially recent migrants, but were not particularly stingy in the levels of aid to those who qualified to receive it.

7. Aging has also been a featured influence in the quantitative sociological literature on welfare states. Pampel and Williamson (1989); Hicks and Misra (1993); Hicks (1999, Chapters 6–7).

8. Kristov et al. (1992).

9. Easterly and Levine (1997); Alesina et al. (1999).

10. Tanzi and Schuknecht (2000, 253).

11. See, for example, Koester and Kormendi (1989), Easterly and Rebelo (1993), Slemrod (1995), Commander et al. (1997), Mendoza et al. (1997), and the survey of other studies given in Atkinson (1999, Chapter 2). Chapter 18 in Volume 2 elaborates.

12. Rodrik (1997), Kuo (1999).

13. Waldfogel (1998).

14. Or (2000).

15. Bean (1994), Nickell (1997), OECD (1994b, 1994c), Scarpetta (1996), Martin (1996). See also Chapter 19 in Volume 2.

16. Flanagan (1988), Buechtmann (1993), Bean (1994), OECD (1994b, 1994c), Scarpetta (1996), Siebert (1997), Nickell (1997), Blanchard and Wolfers (1999).

17. See, for example, Bruno and Sachs (1985), Nickell (1997), Flanagan (1999), Hicks (1999), and Chapter 19 of Volume 2.

Chapter 3

1. Didn't family members help each other out in hard times in those days? They did, but there are three good reasons to set aside this tradition of imagining that in a bygone era people helped their relatives out in a way that is now lost. First, there is no convincing quantitative evidence that the rate of intrafamily giving has declined as a share of income. Second, even if that rate was once higher, aid-giving within the family does little to alleviate poverty since whole families tend to be poor (or rich) together. The third reason is definitional. The family, even the extended family, is essentially an individual in this book's exploration of how income is redistributed between truly separate groups. A

transfer from an uncle in time of need is viewed as self-insurance, not a redistributive transfer.

2. For further supporting evidence, see Chapters 14–17 in Volume 2.

3. The other pioneering country fits the main pattern, posing less of a puzzle than the English case. It is not surprising that the Netherlands, especially Amsterdam and other Dutch cities, gave over 1 percent of national income to the poor late in the eighteenth century. The Dutch, like the English, led the world in national-average income. That the Netherlands cut back on poor relief after about 1800 is also not surprising, given the collapse of the Dutch Republic and the country's defeat and budgetary strain in the French Wars.

4. The first two parts of this chapter draw heavily on Lindert (1998).

5. Woolf (1986, p. 32).

6. On early modern charities see, among others, Jordan (1959, 1960, 1962), Owen (1964), Fairchilds (1976), Forrest (1981), Jones (1982), Martz (1983), Norberg (1985), Lis (1986, Ch. 11), Woolf (1986), Mitchell (1991), Weindling (1991), Humphreys (1992), Cavallo (1995), Gouda (1995, Ch. 6), McCants (1997), and Van Leeuwen (2000).

7. Slack (1990, p. 55).

8. P.J. Elout, 'Iets over de armbedeeling' (1846), as translated by Gouda (1995, p. 173).

9. Emminghaus (1873, pp. 2, 5, 7, 10).

10. Loch (1898, pp. 308–324).

11. Owen (1964, pp. 175–176).

12. de Vries and van der Woude (1997).

13. France, *Annuaire Statistique* (1882, pp. 172–3); Weiss (1983).

14. Woolf (1986, p. 83). Some hints for nineteenth-century Belgium and Portugal underline the same conclusion. See Lindert (1998, fn 8).

   It is possible that church relief was more generous back in the middle ages. Some indirect evidence recently presented by Gary Richardson (2000) suggests as much.

15. Adema (2000, 194).

16. Another kind of support ratio measure, not used here, shares the same dangers but offers additional strengths. The "replacement ratio," popular in the literature on twentieth-century unemployment compensation, measures benefits per recipient as a share of the wage rate the recipient might have earned if employed. Symbolically, the replacement ratio is $Rw = (B/Nr)/w$, where w is the wage rate.

   On the negative side, Rw is sensitive to the difficulties of choosing the right wage rate. It is also sensitive, as is the R measure here, to getting Nr right and remembering that benefits per recipient are closely tied to who the recipients are. For example, poor relief given only to those least able to work, such as the elderly, may look like a high share of the wage rate, yet the high Rw may deceive if very few elderly actually got such support and if the wage rate is inappropriate to them. Difficulties like these complicate David Thomson's (1984) argument that the elderly got more generous support before 1870 than in the postwar welfare state, as E.H. Hunt (1990) has pointed out. On the one hand, what Thomson calls the "standard" poor-relief pension before 1870 could be a high share of certain wage rates, as he says. On the other, the elderly were a very small share of the population then, making even a high replacement ratio look cheap for the taxpayer, and we still do not know what share of the elderly received the "standard" support.

On the positive side, Marco Van Leeuwen (2000) has shown two strengths of the replacement ratio Rw that are not shared by any of the measures used here. First, the seasonality of wages can be used to show how much lower was Rw in summer than in winter, a tendency that stands out in Dutch and English data. Second, Van Leeuwen has used the low levels of Rw (and of B/wNr) in the eighteenth and nineteenth centuries to underline the likelihood that poor relief could not have been a great disincentive to work.

17. In the case of England, the classic writing of the history of poor relief from laws rather than from measures of what was actually given, and to whom, is the Webbs' two-volume *English Poor Law History* (1927 and 1929). The best pre-1980 exception, rewriting the whole history of the Old Poor Law by turning to the quantitative facts, is Blaug (1963, 1964).

18. Baugh (1975), Boyer (1990, Ch. 1), Lees (1998, Ch. 1–3).

19. Digby (1975), MacKinnon (1986), Boyer (1990), Lees (1998, Ch. 4–6).

20. Switzerland's data are mysterious, both for this period and for the 1880–1930 period covered in an earlier study (Lindert 1994). The Swiss returns sent from Berne to Britain's Poor Law Commission in the early 1830s are hard to interpret. Mulhall (1880, p. 96) implies that in the late 1870s their poor relief amounted to 88d/capita (£0.367 per capita, putting Switzerland's relief above his U.K. figure of 72d (£0.300 per capita). Was Switzerland really the secret champion of generous poor relief, as Mulhall implies?

21. The rise of private charity to Table 3.1's meager 1816–1837 peak of 0.40 percent of GDP might have come only in that era itself, lagging behind the rise of official relief. One hint of lower relief at the start of the century is that the charitable donations of money and lands reported in the 1802/3 survey were only 6.3 percent of official relief, or only 0.13 percent of GDP (Marshall 1833, p. 33). Another is that in Oxfordshire in 1813–1815 only 3.4 percent of all expenditures on the poor were derived from charitable sources (Eastwood 1994, p. 123), though this was a parish of higher-than-average official relief.

22. On the eleventh-century discussions of work incentives and the deserving poor, see the work by Brian Tierney cited in Smith (1984, 422).

23. Boyer (1990, 16–23).

24. Gouda (1995, 217–219, 232–235).

25. Porter (1851, 116–118).

26. Forsell, in his "Swedish Statistics," 1833, reprinted in Great Britain, Poor Law Commission (1834), Appendix F, p. 378F.

27. Boyer (1990), de Vries and van der Woude (1997, 661–662).

28. Woolf (1986, 31–32).

29. The data show that French hospices administered a greater share of relief than the indoor institutions of England or the Netherlands. It might be, however, that this indoor share in France includes some outdoor relief administered through hospices and reported in their accounts.

30. Porter and Hirst (1912), Digby (1975), Rose (1981), MacKinnon (1986, 1987), Humphreys (1995, 21–49).

31. Brundage (1978, 184).

32. Porter and Hirst (1912, p. 69).
33. The 2–3 percent estimate refers to U.S. social security programs in the 1980s (Estrin 1988). Taking all social security and safety-net transfers together for the United States in 1978, Robert Lampman (1984, 108–111) estimates that administrative and enforcement costs could have amounted to 5 percent of the transfers on the expenditure side, though the evidence he cites suggests lower percentages. These estimates do not include administrative costs on the tax-collecting side, which Lampman thinks could have added another 5 percent.
34. Williams (1981, 232).
35. As translated in Gouda (1995, 231).
36. Emminghaus (1873, 209), France, *Annuaire Statistique* (1878–1913), Great Britain, Local Government Board (1875, LXV, 132).
37. Sweden, *Statistisk Arsbok* (1913, 137), Porter and Hirst (1912, 85).
38. Williams (1981, 231).
39. Similar rural–urban contrasts are showing up in Clark and Page (2001).
40. On urban British poverty and poor relief more generally, see Treble (1979), Rose (1985), and Boyer (1990, Chapter 8).
41. Solar (1995, 1997).
42. Porter (1851, 110–114).
43. Belgium, Statistique Générale (1852, 260–263); Sweden, *Statistisk Tidskrift* and *Statistisk Arsbok,* various years; Emminghaus (1873, 64–65, 194–195).
44. Woolf (1986, 19–22).
45. Nash (1976), Alexander (1980), Clement (1985), David and Solar (1977), Hannon (1984, 1986, 1997).
46. This conversion of English relief levels into 1900 dollars was performed in two steps. First, the expenditures per capita (from Williams (1981, Table 4.6) and Mitchell (1975)) were deflated into constant English prices using the cost of living for the poorest 40 percent of the population as described in Hoffman et al. 2002. Then this was set at 1900 = 1.000, and converted into dollars at $4.86656 per pound.
47. On the share-of-GNP measure, U.S. tax-based relief in 1929–1930 ranked behind the shares in Australia, Austria, Denmark, Finland, France, Germany, Ireland, Netherlands, New Zealand, Norway, Poland, Sweden, Switzerland, or the United Kingdom. The U.S. share was about the same as that of Belgium, and the United States paid a higher share than Canada, Italy, or Japan. See the estimates in Lindert (1998, Table 1B).
48. Roberts (1984).
49. As cited by Joan Hannon (1997, 427–428). Lowell called for very heavy monitoring and work requirements. Since she felt that local authorities were incapable of providing these, then relief should be privatized into organizations such as the Charity Organization Society.
50. Nathaniel Ware, as cited in Klebaner (1976, 54).
51. Klebaner (1976, 34–38).
52. This despite the persistent efforts of Matthew Carey (1833, 1836) to publicize the plight of single mothers, children, and widows in Philadelphia and elsewhere.
53. Mohl (1971), Cray (1988).
54. Hannon (1997).
55. Hannon (1997).

Chapter 4

1. For the best current survey of all English poor relief since 1700, see Lees (1998).
2. Lindert (1986, 1987).
3. Lindert and Williamson (1985a), Snell (1985), Feinstein (1998), Clark (2002).
4. Boyer (1990).
5. Brundage (1978, pp. 5–6), Eastwood (1994, Ch. 2, 5).
6. A graduated local franchise, giving more power to the landlords owning the most land and hiring the most labor, promoted local poor relief only under the conditions featured by the Boyer model, conditions most applicable in the rural southeast before the 1834 Poor Law reform. The reform actually perpetuated the graduated franchise in favor of large landlords, but only under conditions where they would not provide as much support. The reform, as the text notes, forced them into larger multiparish Poor Law Unions, constrained by the re-form's strictures about what relief may be given. In addition, the rural riots of the early 1830s convinced landlords that relief would no longer buy deference. See, for example, Daunton (2002a, 262–265).
7. Lindert (1991, 47–50 and 61–62).
8. Mandeville, as cited in Eastwood (1994, 101).
9. Ramsey (1927), Atkinson and Stiglitz (1980, 366–393).
10. See Brundage (1978), Dunkley (1982), and Mandler (1987).
11. Sidney and Beatrice Webb (1927 and 1929).
12. Flora (1983, Vol. 1).
13. Another piece of legislation following in the wake of the Reform Act of 1832 might seem to contradict the association of policy outcomes with new votes for the less landed, more urban, upper-middle classes. The Factory Acts of 1833 restricted the ability of industrial employers to employ women and children for long hours. Yet Howard Marvel (1977) has persuasively argued that the legisla-tion helped, and was supported by, owners of larger-scale industrial enterprises. Being able to afford larger-scale plants operating on steam power year-round, they would be less inconvenienced by the new rules than their smaller-firm com-petitors. The latter had to make greater seasonal use of water power, necessitat-ing longer hours in the high-water season.
14. Irwin (1989).
15. See Peter Solar (1997).
16. Van Leeuwen (2000, 73–75).
17. Boyer (1990, Ch. 8 and p. 259).
18. Lindert (1987), Soltow and van Zanden (1998), Morrisson (2000).
19. Hovde (1948), Baldwin (1990, Ch. 1).
20. Hovde (1948, 589–616).
21. Hovde (1948, 570).
22. Flora (1983, 104), Baldwin (1990, Ch. 1).
23. For a recent quantitative treatment of grain protection in Europe in the later nine-teenth century, made famous by Alexander Gerschenkron and Charles Kindle-berger, see O'Rourke (1997).
24. Hovde (1948, 525–572), Flora (1983).
25. To anticipate Chapter 5's survey of mass schooling let us briefly note how its political economy fit the text's point about power and the poor. Public schooling

made better progress in Sweden than in Denmark, but was less advanced than we sometimes hear on the basis of literacy rates among Sweden's military recruits. Sweden was far more literate than educated. The throne, the church, and landlords preferred a bare literacy to promote Bible reading. Beyond that, the educational system remained tilted toward the useless and classical until the battle for a bifurcated system, allowing a more scientific track, was won in mid-century. (Hovde 1948, 589–616).

26. Hovde (1948, 605–606, 641–642).
27. See Volume 2, Chapter 16 and Appendix D. The twenty-one countries in the sample are Argentina, Australia, Austria-Hungary (then Austria for 1920 and 1930), Belgium, Brazil, Canada, Denmark, Finland, France, Greece, Italy, Japan, Mexico, Netherlands, New Zealand, Norway, Portugal, Spain, Sweden, United Kingdom, and United States.
28. Banks (1971). Chapters 5 and 7 and Appendix D list the criteria for distinguishing democracies from nondemocracies. As Chapter 5 will note, there are some difficult borderline cases, especially where the chief executive is a nonelected monarch with partial powers, as in prewar Italy and Belgium.
29. Here the use of the phrase "least likely to have any" is chosen to reflect that fact that in this early era the main differentiator was whether the country had any program at all, rather than low versus high levels of program spending. In econometric terms, this same prevalence of zero values necessitated using tobit regressions, as shown in Appendix D.
30. Brown and Oates (1987).
31. On this local resistance in favor of maintaining the old level of relief, again see Digby (1975), MacKinnon (1986), and Boyer (1990).
32. The phrase "already settled there" has a specific meaning here. Before the late nineteenth century, the countries in question all had settlements laws, allowing local communities to deny relief and other local services to newcomers. One effect of the settlements laws was to make it easier for localities to offer more generous support to their longtime local poor without fear of attracting many immigrants. This barrier is one that the model of Brown and Oates (1987) assumed away, because that model was designed to fit twentieth-century experience.
33. Thus the twentieth-century resistance of southern politicians to federal welfare programs in the United States, well described and explained by Alston and Ferrie (1998), fits the later phase of the drift toward tax-based public programs, the one in which the resisting region is outvoted nationally.

Chapter 5

1. For example, Richard Easterlin's (1981) presidential address to the Economic History Association on "Why Isn't the Whole World Developed?" rightly focused on differences in the provision of primary and secondary schooling.
2. For the dawn of mass education, and of data on education, one could have used literacy rates to trace the early history of this fundamental skill, without focusing on political determinants of educational outcomes. This has been done usefully by Cipolla (1969) and others.
   This chapter makes little use of literacy rates, however. There are two main reasons for this choice. First, literacy approaches its 100-percent limit earlier

than do other educational attainments, so that it stops offering useful contrasts sooner. Second, literacy is less related to our topic of government educational policy than are the expenditure and enrollment rates followed here.

International differences in the content and curriculum of primary education are given little mention in what follows, except in reference to the battles over classical and religious education and the hypotheses about social control.

3. The many pitfalls in measuring either enrollments or attendance comparably across different settings are catalogued helpfully by Kaestle and Vinovskis (1980, pp. 28–33) and also noted by Goldin (1998). The pitfalls are serious enough that the present chapter dwells only on the widest inequalities in measured rates.

4. Goldin and Katz (1997), Goldin (1998), Hansen (1998).

5. It has been conjectured that these visits helped shape educational policies in France and the United States. Impressions about Prussia may have affected the design of the Guizot law on French education (1833), and possibly the educational legislation of a few American states (Pattison in U.K. Education Commission 1861, pp. 166–167; Nipperdey 1977, p. 156). The links are not yet clear, however. Cousin himself believed that education should be expanded for the middle classes but not for the masses, and Guizot defended classical education (Moody 1978, pp. 33–39). France's real catch-up to Prussia in mass education did not come until 1872–1882, in the wake of military defeat.

6. Less officially, there was a wave of enthusiastic English visits to, and correspondence with, Horace Mann and his common school movement in Massachusetts in the late 1830s and 1840s.

7. Barkin (1983, p. 48).

8. See Levasseur (1897) and U.S. Commissioner of Education (various years). Levasseur drew some of his material from the U.S. reports. By 1900 the U.S. Commissioner of Education had published over eighty articles on the educational systems of central Europe (as listed in U.S. Commissioner of Education 1899–1900, pp. 721–723).

9. Hayhoe and Bastid (1987, Chapters 1, 4), Bastid (1988, Ch. I–II and Text 6), and Sukehiro and Wakabayashi (1989).

10. The terms "private" and "public" are meant to distinguish between funds paid directly from private parties and funds paid from taxes. This is not necessarily the distinction being made in the data, as noted again below.

Another measurement caveat is that there was, and is, a blurry borderline separating primary schooling from pre-primary, middle, or secondary schooling. Germany and Norway in particular had a tendency to track children into middle schools and other channels before they reached what the U.S. system would consider the end of primary schooling. The sources cited in Table 5.1 provide the needed warnings, and this paper tries to avoid leaning too hard on contrasts that could be artifacts of noncomparable measures.

11. "North America," not "United States," since Canadian rates were close to those of the United States. Just as the U.S. non-Southern states had high enrollments even before the 1830s (Fishlow 1996a), so did Upper Canada (Lewis and Urquhart 1999).

Similarly, one must allow for the possibility that New Zealand and Switzerland were world leaders in primary school even earlier than their arrival in the top ranks with the first available data for these two countries.

Some authors have implied that the United States led in enrollments in the early nineteenth century. Thus Richard Rubinson (1986, p. 521) thought that "[o]nly Prussia approached the high rates of early-nineteenth-century primary schooling characteristic of the United States." Perhaps he was looking at raw ratios of primary-school students to total population. That would give the wrong impression both because children of school age were a higher share of the population in the United States than in Prussia, and because many Prussian children made the move from primary school to middle schools at an earlier grade level than in the United States.

12. A caution is in order here, however. British enrollment statistics before about 1890 were defective. Appendix B in Volume 2 explains my attempt to reduce the flaws in the available series. It may be that the rates shown in Table 5.1 slightly overstate British enrollments 1851–1871 and understate them for 1881.

13. The only recent data presentation that I have seen showing France's supremacy in the age-adjusted enrollment rate is Schneider (1982), as reproduced without comment on this in Rubinson (1986, p. 522).

14. Readers wishing to see the conventional ratio of primary enrollments to total population for 1830–1910 can find them in Appendix A.

15. Levasseur (1897, pp. 560–561), U.S. Commissioner of Education (1893–1894 and 1900–1901), and Barro and Lee (1993a).

16. In what follows we refer to GDP because this is today's convention. Most of the national-product measures now available for the pre-1914 era are in fact gross national product, and a few are net national product (NNP) or national income, as explained in the notes to Appendix C.

17. The tables giving five different kinds of education expenditure shares in GDP appear in Appendix C of Volume 2.

18. Albert Fishlow (1966b, p. 433) has suspected that the German educational expenditures from Hoffman (1965) are overstated and that their relative share of national product is inflated by the use of net national product as the denominator. The latter point is surely correct, though the magnitude of any bias could only be the share of depreciation in GNP, too small a share to affect the qualitative conclusions suggested here. As for a possible overstatement of expenditures, the issue remains unresolved. The text assumes that the bias is not big enough to drop Germany's educational spending shares below those of other countries.

19. As quoted in Hammond and Hammond (1917, p. 55).

20. Michael Sanderson (1999, 29) similarly sees a turning point in 1890: "1870–1890 was the dangerous period when we risked falling behind and it was the last phase when we had modestly good growth rates (1.2 percent GDP per man year) compared with our competitors, yet with a poor educational system."

21. Kaestle (1976, pp. 179–180).

22. As cited in Cobbett's *Parliamentary Debates* [Hansard], 1807, vol. IX, pp. 798–799.

23. Another early-nineteenth-century English statement of the same argument that labor needs to stay in its traditional place is John Weyland's *A Letter to a Country Gentleman on the Education of the Lower Orders* (London, 1808), p. 5, as cited in Kaestle (1976, 179): "[Since] every step in the scale of society is already full, the temporal condition of the lower orders cannot be exalted, but at the expense of the higher."

The same static hierarchy was affirmed in one of the original verses of Cecil Frances Alexander's hymn "All Things Bright and Beautiful" in 1848:

> The rich man in his castle,
> The poor man at his gate,
> God made them high or lowly,
> And ordered their estate....

Corresponding views from the Southern United States are quoted in Kaestle (1976) and in Margo (1990, 48).

24. As quoted in Epstein (1966, 78).
25. As quoted in Epstein (1966, 79).
26. Kaestle (1976, pp. 184–6).
27. For example, Bowles and Gintis (1976, Chapters 6, 7), Katz (1968, 1987).
28. For tests of the hypothesis that a capitalist desire for social control drove the educational reforms of Massachusetts, see Field (1979) and Kaestle and Vinovskis (1980).
29. McGuire and Olson (1996).
30. Melton (1988), Green (1990).
31. West (1970, 1975), Lott (1990); and Lott and Kenny (1999).
32. West (1970, 1975).
33. Hovde (1948, vol. II, pp. 589, 605, 609).
34. We examine enrollments, rather than some measure of tax-based public expenditure, simply because enrollments data are more available. For the available expenditure data, see Appendix C in Volume 2.

    Why public, rather than total enrollments? There is a logical reason and a pragmatic one. The logical reason is that I am attempting to explain what forces raised or lowered the commitment of taxpayers and government, not the commitment of parents or philanthropists, to children's schooling. The pragmatic reason is that the data on private enrollments are less reliable than those on public enrollments.
35. In the enfranchised gender(s), that is. For most of the sample the reference is to the population of males over twenty. Where women's right to vote had become law, as in many countries in the 1920 and 1930 parts of the sample, the relevant population is the total adult population.
36. Chapter 7 will find that women's suffrage raised countries' tax rates and social transfers, though the evidence cannot distinguish the separate effect of women's own voting and activism in these countries in the 1920 and 1930 part of the sample.

    As for education, the regressions in Appendix D show mixed effects of female suffrage, again in 1920 and 1930. The relevant coefficient was negative for primary education, near zero for secondary, but more clearly positive for university education. The interpretation of the negative effect on primary schooling enrollments is not obvious. It is not due to any outlier case or to missing nonlinearities among the women-vote contexts, where primary education is pressing against the ceiling. And even the related equation for the determinants of the numbers of teachers hired shows a positive effect of female suffrage.
37. The prewar Belgian and Italian monarchies were also classified as nondemocracies, following Banks's (1971, Segment 1) judgment that their nonelected kings

held true power. Reversing this judgment and including prewar Belgium and Italy as democracies had no effect on the points made here.

38. Engerman, Mariscal, and Sokoloff (1998).

39. Carry (1999). The data in Figure 5.5 refer to public primary schools, where "public" is broadly defined to include all private schools in the official system of reporting and inspection. Figures on the total costs of all private schools are elusive, especially for want of valuations of the teaching labors of unsalaried priests and nuns.

    According to Grew and Harrigan (1991, 217–218), around half of the expenditures by communes (local governments) were tuition charged to parents rather than taxes. But Carry's figures, employed in Figure 5.5, seem to have been adjusted for this and can be viewed as reasonably accurate source-of-revenue shares for the reporting schools.

40. Napoleon's speech is quoted in Anderson (1975, 137). For general coverage of French nineteenth-century educational history, see also Weber (1976, 303–338), Moody (1978), Price (1987, 307–356), and Grew and Harrigan (1991).

41. Grew and Harrigan (1991). Earlier, between the tenth and the seventeenth centuries, the same line from St. Malo to Geneva had the reverse meaning. It divided a *less* literate northeast from a *more* literate southwest (Cipolla 1969, 41 and 61).

42. Cipolla (1969, 61–63), Schofield (1973), Houston (1985, 84–109), Graff (1987, 182–258, 265–371). Swedish literacy was also high in the seventeenth century, but it consisted more of the ability to read, and less of the ability to write, than in other countries.

43. Sturt (1967), West (1970), Sutherland (1973), Wardle (1976), Jones (1977), and Mitch (1992).

44. Jones (1977, 48–67).

45. Sutherland (1973, 263–347).

46. Prest (1990, 1–17). Even worse for school resources was the requirement that schools had to pay poor rates. See "Copy of Memorial addresses to the Local Government Board by the City of Manchester School Board, praying for an Alteration in the system of Assessment of Elementary Schools to the Poor Rates," House of Commons, *Sessional Papers*, May 23, 1878, 363–364.

47. This section owes a great debt to Rolf Dumke, who kindly supplied ideas, clarifications, and Prussian data. He does not necessarily agree with my interpretations, however.

48. Barkin (1983, 45).

49. Suval (1985), Hallerberg (1996, 1999), Nipperdey (1996), and Fairbairn (1997).

50. On the forcing of so much of German history into the explanation of Wilhelmine military might and the rise of Hitler, see Hagen (1991). For an insistent shaping of Prussian, German, and Hapsburg educational history around the theme of "absolutism," again see Melton (1988) and Green (1990).

51. Anderson (1970), Nipperdey (1977), Barkin (1983).

52. Barkin (1983, 31). This is not to say that German education mixed the classes evenly at all levels. At the secondary and university levels, elitism was as evident in Germany as in Britain (Sanderson 1999, 34). A related caveat is that I here accept Germany's leadership in the quantity of education, without a judgment about its relative quality.

53. As quoted in Schleunes (1989, 48). For other official announcements in which Frederick William III imposed the same conservative case against mass schooling, see Epstein (1966, 460–461).

54. Schleunes (1989, 118).

55. See, for example, the tirade attributed to Frederick Wilhelm IV, as quoted in Nipperdey (1977, p. 155). Karl Schleunes questions whether the emperor ever said that, but agrees that such an outburst did fit his reactionary tendencies (Schleunes 1989, 129–130).

56. Anderson (1970, 271), Schleunes (1989, 50–158), and Hansen (1998).

57. Gawthorp and Strauss (1984).

58. For a chronology of the political battles over Prussian educational reform and reaction, see Schleunes (1989, 50–127).

59. Nipperdey (1996, 409–410).

60. Anderson (1970, 264–270).

61. Daunton (2002a), 373–377.

62. Herrfurth (1878). The tilt of national subsidies toward the east was partly the result of a national concern for Germanizing the Poles (Schleunes 1989, 99–127, especially 100 and 119).

63. Nipperdey (1996, 409–410).

64. Upper Canada here means all provinces from Ontario through Alberta, thus excluding the Maritimes, Quebec, British Columbia, and the Northwest Territories. Upper Canada thus defined tended to have higher enrollment rates and expenditures than the rest of the country. The geography is not clear-cut, however. Enrollment rates for 1900 show that Quebec and Prince Edward Island were not lagging behind Upper Canada. Expenditure data tend to favor Upper Canada, but expenditures in Quebec could be seriously understated by the unpaid status of the clergy, who did much of the teaching. See U.S. Commissioner of Education (1903); Canada, Dominion Bureau of Statistics (1921); Leacy et al. (1983); Urquhart (1993); and Lewis and Urquhart (1999).

65. The Canadian data begin only in the middle of the nineteenth century. While Canadian schooling before mid-century is assumed to have lagged behind the United States, we lack specific early dates for the emergence of Canada's schools.

66. Cities had a harder time dealing with their diverse and transient populations, and enrollment rates were a bit lower there than in the northeastern countryside. See Butts (1978, Chapters 2–5), Kaestle and Vinovskis (1980), Kaestle (1983, Chapters 2–3), Parkerson and Parkerson (1998, 2–3), and the sources cited there.

67. Fishlow (1966a), Kaestle (1983).

68. The state-level expenditure data for 1902 are from the Legler–Sylla–Wallis data set, and the income and population estimates are those from the Census and Richard Easterlin (1960, 1961) for 1899/1900.

69. Claudia Goldin and Larry Katz (1997, and Goldin 1998, 2001) have also stressed the role of decentralized control over secondary-school funding in the United States. What they have shown for the case of secondary-school funding can be interpreted as another early-rise era for the emergence of public secondary schools, one in which decentralization allowed the areas of strongest demand to forge ahead.

70. Margo (1990).

71. Margo (1990, Chapters 2–5).
72. James Gerber (1986) has found that states where large labor-hiring plantations dominated also tended to have less schooling for the average white, other things equal, despite their also having greater discrimination in favor of whites when it came to school expenditures.
73. Ransom and Sutch (1977), Wright (1986).

Chapter 6

1. Goldin (1998, 2001). This paragraph's statements about the relative standing of North America are based on three sets of source materials. The first consists of the primary and secondary enrollments for 1830–1930 in Volume 2's Appendix A, summarized in Chapter 5. The second are male–female averages of schooling years attained in 1960–1985, from the Barro–Lee global data set on educational attainment (downloaded from www.nber.org in 2002). The third consists of the shares of adults aged twenty-five to sixty-four having completed secondary school and university as of 1999, as shown in Table 6.1.
2. Bishop (1989, 1990).
3. In addition to the results in Table 6.2, Postlethwaite and Wiley (1992) report that on algebra for seventeen-year-olds, and physics, chemistry, and biology for eighteen-year-olds, the United States was maybe average for physics, but near the bottom for the other three tests. U.S. thirteen-year-olds placed fifth out of nine countries' students in geography proficiency (U.S. National Center for Education Statistics 1999, 456).
4. Wolf (1977, 34–41). The same point applies to the smaller-scale tests of math and science in 1964–1965, not reported here. Then, too, the United States scored low, but the sampling limitations probably understated the relative position of the United States.
5. Boys have slightly better mathematics averages, but the difference is statistically significant in only half the surveyed countries. There are no gender differences in science literacy.
6. The rough calculation uses data from the U.S. national report for the PISA 2000 project (nces.ed.gov/pubs2002/2002115b.pdf, printed January 2003)(OECD PISA, 2001). It starts by equating the average non-Hispanic white test scores with weighted averages of the twenty-fifth and seventy-fifth percentiles in the whole U.S. test score distribution. The formulas that fit the white to the overall spectrum are

- for mathematics scores, white average $= 530 = .24$ (national twenty-fifth percentile score) $+ .76$ (seventy-fifth percentile);
- for reading scores, white average $= 538 = .276$ (national twenty-fifth percentile) $+ .724$ (national seventy-fifth percentile);
- for science scores, white average $= 535 = .255$ (national twenty-fifth percentile) $+ .745$ (national seventy-fifth percentile).

These white averages are then compared with synthetic averages for an advantaged group "like U.S. whites" in each other country. The averages for these advantaged comparison groups are computed from each country's twenty-fifth and seventy-fifth percentile scores using these three formulae.

If one had access to the full PISA data set, one could sharpen the comparison of advantaged groups. It would be possible to find the non-Hispanic white shares of every percentile of the overall U.S. distribution for each subject's tests scores and to apply these shares to other countries' national distributions to get advantage-equivalent distributions for comparison with U.S. whites.

7. Flynn (1984, 1987, 2000).

8. Bishop (1989, 194).

9. At least not starting from 1971, the earliest national test score averages available by race. There was also no decline in Hispanic students' test scores from 1973 on in mathematics and from 1975 on in reading, but these series start too late for any inferences about the overall 1967–1980 trends for Hispanic test score averages (U.S. National Center for Education Statistics 1999, 130, 139).

10. Margo (1990) and Donoghue and Heckman (1991).

11. See the figures for 1998 in Appendix Table C.6 in Volume 2's Appendix C.

12. Appendix Table C.6 in Volume 2 shows this near-median ranking for 1880–1910 and 1960–1975. The same might have been true in the intervening 1910–1960 period, but we don't have enough other countries' expenditure ratios for this period.

13. For a recent survey of the "does money matter?" debate, see Burtless (1996).

14. Hanushek and Luque (2002).

15. The first practical reason for this choice is simply that teachers are the dominant input, in that their pay is well over half the expense of any student's education. The second is that we lack reliable price deflators for non–teaching inputs.

16. See Appendix Tables A.1 and A.2 in Volume 2, Appendix A for enrollments and teachers 1830–1930. There are also some figures for secondary students and teachers in Appendix Tables A.3 and A.4, but the figures cover too few countries for a reliable international ranking.

17. Lakdawalla (2001, 3).

18. Cohn and Geske (1990, 247); Lakdawalla (2001); Hoxby (1996, 2003); Temin (2002).

19. For example, consider the Cohn-Geske finding that (pay per teacher)/(personal income per capita) dropped from 2.17 in 1960 to 1.61 in 1980, with a slight rebound to 1.71 in 1987. The better measure, (pay per teacher)/(personal income per member of the labor force), dropped only from 0.87 in 1960 to 0.77 in 1980 and rebounded to 0.86 in 1987, yielding no clear net change over the 27 years.

There is a similar difficulty with Lakdawalla's (2001, 2–3) indirect proxy for (pay per teacher)/(GDP per capita) in ten non-U.S. countries between 1965 and 1994. He found large declines in this measure of relative pay in nine of the ten countries, the exception being Japan. Yet one must correct his figures for the rise in the share of the population that was in the labor force. Doing so leaves large declines in teacher relative pay only for Denmark, Finland, Sweden, and the United Kingdom. It erases much of the decline in other countries and doubles the rise in teachers' relative pay in Japan. There may also be problems with Lakdawalla's numerator, which does not directly measure current expenditures for teacher pay. Indeed, had his figures been correct about the net change from 1965 to 1994, he would have posed a new puzzle on which he offered no comment: If U.S. teachers are paid so low in 1994 and today, compared with teachers in other countries, then his figures imply that their disadvantage was even much greater back in 1965. Why would that be true?

20. George S. Davis, in a report to the National Education Association, as quoted in Weaver (1983, 7).

21. Weaver (1983, 5–6).

22. Tracing the U.S. history of teachers' relative pay back even further, to the 1840s, would again show no general decline over the long run. We have separate pay series for urban and rural teachers, and for men and women separately in both settings, back to 1841. Of the four groups of teachers, only urban males had a decline in relative pay. Their relative pay was cut in half between the 1890s and World War I, much like the later decline for associate professors. Yet female teachers and rural male teachers held, or slightly improved, their relative pay position from the 1840s on.

   This note is based on a comparison of W. Randolph Burgess' (1920, 32–33) series on the weekly pay of schoolteachers with GDP per member of the labor force. For the latter I used *Historical Statistics of the United States* and Balke and Gordon (1989) back to 1869, and the Gallman estimates from the 1870s back to the 1840s.

23. This tentative result uses the identity that (pay per teacher)/(GDP per capita) = (the share of teacher pay in GDP)/(teachers as a share of the total population). I added the assumption that teacher pay was the same share of total educational expenditures in all countries. It was also necessary to divide all public educational expenditures, even those on higher education, by the number of primary and secondary teachers alone, omitting faculty in higher education. Subject to these drawbacks, the ratios suggest that the United States ranked seventh or lower, behind Germany, the Netherlands, Canada, Sweden, Italy, and France, but ahead of Norway, Spain, and the United Kingdom. See Appendices A and C for the underlying figures.

   Using employment or labor force as a better denominator population than the total population would not have affected this ranking greatly for 1910.

24. Hanushek and Luque (2002, Table 3).

25. Corcoran et al. (2002). They find that the average qualifications of new male teachers actually rose from the 1964 cohort to the 1992 cohort, but their samples of male teachers were too small for firm conclusions about the male trend.

26. Ballou and Podgursky (1997, 16–21).

27. For the history of U.S. women's entry into teaching, see Perlmann and Margo (2001). The shares of women in various countries' teaching forces in 1900 and 1999 can be found in the U.S. Commissioner of Education's *Annual Report* (1900) and OECD *Education at a Glance* (2001).

28. Nelson and O'Brien (1993).

29. Hoxby (1996). For broader attacks on bureaucracy, teacher unions, and all other non-market forces in the education sector, see West (1970) and Coulson (1999).

30. Lakdawalla (2001).

31. In some cases, economists eschew the tax and subsidy approach in favor of a property-rights approach that uses law enforcement. For example, instead of having the government tax pollution, one could assign strict private property rights to the environment. If a river belonged either to the paper mill upstream

or to the downstream beneficiaries of clean water, then one party would have to pay the other the right amount of bribe to have the river be used their way. This is the Coasian approach to making institutions efficient, which is often a valid alternative to the Pigovian approach of using taxes and subsidies. We follow only the Pigovian tax-subsidy line here, however, since it is more appropriate to the task of getting educational incentives right.

32. Friedman (1962, Chapter 6, especially 86–89).
33. Bishop (1996). The emphasis here is national exams taken by all students, not on exams given only to a random sample or in one state.
34. Bishop (1997) and Woessmann (2002).
35. On the link to productivity in adult careers, again see Bishop (1989, 1990). In the near future it would be good to have similar tests run on the PISA 2000 and PISA 2003 scores, which tested reading literacy results in addition to mathematics and science.
36. Figlio and Page (2003).
37. For an extensive analysis of the support for vouchers in opinion polls, see Moe (2001).
38. Tiebout (1956).
39. Fischel (1996, 620).
40. Ballou and Podgursky (1997, 86).
41. Hoxby (1996).
42. Hoxby (2003, final chapter on "Rising Tide").
43. Hanushek and Rivkin (2003).
44. Hoxby (2003, final chapter).
45. State school equalization formulae were also mandated by courts in six other states: New Jersey 1973, Connecticut 1976, Washington 1978, West Virginia 1979, Wyoming 1980, and Arkansas 1983. By contrast, eleven other states' top courts ruled against the imposition of equalization. These were Arizona, Colorado, Georgia, Idaho, Illinois, Maryland, Michigan, New York, Ohio, Oregon, and Pennsylvania.
46. As quoted in Kozol (1991, 220).
47. Fischel (1996).
48. U.S. National Center for Education Statistics, *Digest of Education Statistics*, various years.
49. Grissmer et al. (2000, 67–83).
50. Figlio (1997).
51. For evidence on how elitism in political voice seems to have caused India and other countries to oversubsidize higher education at the expense of basic literacy, see Lindert (2003).
52. De Kwaasteniet (1990).
53. Woessmann (2002).
54. Hsieh and Urquiola (2003). For a similar warning that peer sorting can swamp any productivity effect of having school choice, using U.S. data, see Rothstein (2003).
55. OECD, *Education at a Glance* (1996, 149; 2001, 203–205).
56. So said the school responses to the TIMSS in 1995, according to TIMSS data kindly supplied to this author by Ludger Woessmann.

Chapter 7

1. Goldin and Katz (1997), Goldin (1998).
2. For a much fuller presentation of the magnitudes of social transfers, and the details of their estimation, see Lindert (1994, especially Table 1).
3. Levine (1988, pp. 5, 39).
4. Great Britain, Royal Commission (1910); U.S. Commissioner of Labor (1910); Tampke (1981); Ullmann (1981).
5. U.S. Commissioner of Labor (1911, p. 1409).
6. Some German scholars have claimed high shares of social spending in Germany as of 1913. Peter Flora (in Mommsen (ed.) 1981, 359), citing earlier estimates by Andic and Veverka, claims that Germany spent 2.6 percent of GNP on social insurance and poor relief, 0.7 percent on health, and 2.7 percent on education. Five years later, in a volume edited by Flora (1986, 7), Jens Alber said all public "outlays on social insurance and social assistance together" were 2.25 percent of GNP, versus the 3.3 percent implied by Flora. The Alber estimates are not explained, and the Andic–Ververka estimates cited by Flora are not trusted for use here. Given that the social insurance laws of the 1880s caused only about 0.12 percent of GNP in government subsidies as of 1908, even Alber's lower estimate could only be correct if over 2 percent of GNP was old-style poor relief plus general health-sector support (e.g., public hospitals, infirmaries, vaccination services). The point remains that no significant subsidies were channeled through the insurance programs set up in the 1880s.
7. Ullmann (1981, 136–143).
8. Marvel (1977).
9. Beveridge himself was embarrassed by the phrase "welfare state." He avoided using it because of its "Santa Claus" and "brave new world" connotations, preferring the phrase "social service state" (Flora and Heidenheimer 1981, 20, citing José Harris' biography of Beveridge).
10. Baldwin (1990, 116–134, 232–247); Johnson (1994).
11. Baldwin (1990, 111–112).
12. Most of the category "public pensions, disability, and survivor benefits" consists of pension-type benefits for the elderly alone. In Sweden in 1995, for example, these were 12.34 percent of GDP, even when we exclude pension benefits paid to veterans and former civil servants. Disability and survivor benefits made up only 2.42 percent of GDP.
13. This chapter passes over five other forces that are leading candidates as influences on taxes, transfers, and the size of government.

    The first of the five deferred forces is the reliable influence of GDP per capita. Its positive influence on government spending in general, often known as "Wagner's Law," emerges from most regression tests, including most of the tests in Chapters 16 and 17 and in Appendices D and E. It is omitted here, because there is little to add. For this one reliable influence, there are numerous possible explanations, all indistinguishable from each other in predicting the same positive income effect.

    Four other forces deferred to Chapters 16 and 17 in Volume 2 are religion, a country's openness to foreign trade, its military spending, and the momentum from the past buildup of the same social programs.

The balance of power between left and right parties and the power of labor unions are passed over by both volumes of this book. These are intermediate variables governed largely by the forces already listed here, as explained and documented in Chapter 14 of Volume 2.

14. For the full statistical analysis of twenty-one countries' behavior in 1880–1930, see Chapter 16 and Appendix D in Volume 2. For the corresponding analysis of behavior in 1962/65–1978/81 and 1978/80–1993/95, see Chapter 17 and Appendix E.

15. See Figure 4.2's curves for the effects of electoral democracy on pensions, poor relief, and other transfers in this 1880–1930 period.
    The present results imply that there is no significant difference between the pension spending of the average democracy and the average nondemocracy, as found in a sample of developing countries after World War II by Mulligan et al. (2002).

16. Kleppner (1982), Kornbluh (2000).

17. Jackman and Miller (forthcoming, Chapter 5).

18. Wolfinger and Rosenstone (1980), Teixeira (1987), Jackman (1987), and Jackman and Miller (forthcoming, Chapter 5).

19. Lott and Kenny (1999).

20. Lovenduski and Norris (1993). Opinion-poll studies from the 1960s–1980s surveyed by Franklin et al. (1992) show the gender differences for a wider range of countries. Controlling for occupation and age, women tended to be consistently more conservative than men in Belgium, France, Italy, and the pre-Thatcher United Kingdom. Women consistently favored Social Democratic parties more in Canada, Norway, and Sweden. In general, females' voting preferences shifted left (or males' shifted right) in the 1970s–1980, relative to their preferences in the 1960s.

21. Switzerland did not follow suit until 1971–1972.

22. Age effects took center stage in Wilensky (1975), Pampel and Williamson (1989), Hicks and Misra (1993), Lindert (1996), Hicks (1999, Ch. 6), and Kuo (1999). Their role is confirmed in Mulligan et al. (2002).

23. The effects of aging on transfers per old person are quantified in Chapters 16 and 17, Appendix D, and Appendix E.

24. Mulligan et al. (2002).

25. In the postwar data voter turnout rises with age if one holds education constant, or is U-shaped with a peak in middle age if one does not (Wolfinger and Rosenstone 1980, 59; Niemi et al. 1984; Teixeira 1989, 51).

26. Niemi et al. (1984).

27. Hanson (1980, 11–21); Kewley (1980, 6–9, 13–21); M.A. Jones (1983, 19–26); Castles (1985, 12–21).

28. Rodrik (1997, 1998). My own tests yield an even clearer positive effect of trade openness than did Rodrik's tests. True to Rodrik's interpretation, exposure to international trade seems to have a clearer positive effect on those safety nets that are more related to current income shocks, such as unemployment compensation, than to pensions. See Volume 2's Chapter 17 and Appendix E.

29. Huberman and Lewchuk (2002).

30. This prediction is latent in most models in which a median voter determines redistributive policies. Three examples from the economics side of the

literature are Peltzman (1980), Meltzer and Richard (1981), and Kristov et al. (1992).

31. Easterly and Levine (1997); Alesina et al. (1999).
32. Bradbury et al. (2000, 11–30).
33. See Kristov et al. (1992) and Lindert (1996).

Chapter 8

1. Miron and Weil (1998), Diamond and Gruber (1999).
2. If one could pay for pensions and other social transfers out of government debt, and out of the reserves of the pension system, then the left-hand side of the equation should be modified to include payments of taxes in earlier and later years, not just the current year. Yet they have to be paid sooner or later, and the problem remains essentially as stated in this pure same-year version of PAYGO.

    Note another simplification here: This chapter ignores nontransfer spending, such as national defense, highway construction, and basic government payrolls. Taxation here refers only to those taxes that are spent on pensions and other social transfers.
3. The comparative literature on the history of public pension policy is vast. For a nonquantitative political history of the rise of generosity in Scandinavia, Britain, France, and Germany, see Baldwin (1990). For a comprehensive quantitative accounting for trends and prospects since 1960 in 11 countries, see Gruber and Wise (1999). For a readable globalization of the basic problem, see World Bank (1994).
4. Brugiavini (1999).
5. So says a combination of the OECD employment ratios for 1998/1999 in Table 8.2 and the studies by Blöndal and Scarpetta (1999) and Gruber and Wise (1999).
6. For the underlying statistical work, again see Chapter 17 and Appendix E in Volume 2.
7. See Appendices E and F in Volume 2.
8. The elderly probably also lose in the amount of health care they receive per person of given physical condition, but this likelihood cannot be quantified because of a lack of sufficient data on who receives how much medical care.
9. Note again that the measure used here is pension support per elderly person, not pension support per pension recipient. To capture coverage effects as well as the generosity of the annual payments, I have chosen the population-group denominator. This means, among other things, that postponing the official retirement age would reduce the pension support ratio even if the annual payment for full-benefit retirees stayed the same. Indeed, the kinds of cuts in pension support that are most likely politically would take the form of delaying coverage, not an outright slashing of annual benefits.
10. I prefer the present extrapolations to those recently offered by Gruber and Wise (2001). Their somewhat different results seem to depend on their using a simple linear term for the elderly population share. With some slight differences in the use of fixed effects, their result is a special case allowed for, but not favored, by my nonlinear age effects, which capture some of the political and budgetary twists of having extremely large elderly shares.

Alternative estimates by Razin et al. (2001) agree that aging will cut the overall generosity of social transfers, despite the increased political clout of the elderly population. Their study is hard to interpret, however. It ignores simultaneity between social policy and growth, it leaves some data series undefined, and it uses a dependency ratio that does not separate the elderly from children.

11. Yashiro and Oshio (1999).
12. Takayama (1992), Yashiro and Oshio (1999).
13. Gruber and Wise (1999). For an update, see *Economist*, September 27, 2003, 69–71.
14. Lee and Miller (2000).
15. For a political-economic interpretation of how social security programs are designed, see Mulligan and Sala-i-Martin (1999, especially 41–42).

Chapter 9

1. Mulligan *et al.* (2002) found that social security expenditures were driven mainly by the population's age distribution and income. Democracy was not a significant determinant.

   Somewhat similar results were obtained by Kuo (1999, Tables C1–C7 and pp. 27–30), from a sample of fifty-three nations (of which nineteen were OECD members) for four years (1975, 1980, 1985, and 1990). Kuo used a simultaneous estimation of income per capita and the separate social spending shares of GDP, following the same procedure followed in Chapters 16 and 17 of Volume 2 here. Kou found that aging was the most reliable predictor of social transfers as a share of GDP, followed by the economy's openness to international trade. Democracy promoted unemployment compensation, but had no clear effect on other social transfers.

2. McAuley (1979, 260–301); Connor (1997); Kramer (1997).
3. Subbarao et al. (1997, 40).
4. This statement rests on shares of GDP taken by government expenditures on health, social security, and welfare at the central and local levels, as reported by the IMF in *Government Finance Statistics Yearbook* and *International Financial Statistics Yearbook*. There was no clear trend for Poland (1993–1996) or Russia (1994–1998). The share jumped by about 2 percent in the Czech Republic between 1996 and 1997, but dropped about 2 percent in Hungary between 1994 and 1996.
5. All the pressures that seem likely for Hungary and Poland have already manifested for East Germany. The government of reunified Germany has paid a high social-budget price, and reunification will continue to heighten both the budgetary pressure for cuts and the political resistance to them.
6. See Appendix F in Volume 2.
7. February 27, 1948, as cited from his *Selected Works*, Volume 4 (1961 Foreign Language edition, 203), by Dixon (1981, 6).
8. *China Youth*, (December 16, 1956).
9. As quoted from *China Youth* by Dixon (1981, 247–248).
10. As cited in Tremewan (1998, 78).
11. More specifically, Prime Minister Blair was pronouncing Singapore's government-managed Central Provident Fund a success in mobilizing forced

private savings without a drain on government budgets (Goodman et al. 1998, 33). As Huck-ju Kwon points out in the same source, Singapore's Central Provident Fund (CPF) was set up by the British in 1953, before independence. While this does remove some of its Asian look, the fact remains that the PAP government has shaped the CPF as it wished for over a third of a century since independence.

12. As Goodman et al. (1998) have warned.
13. On Brazil's runaway public-sector pensions, see *Wall Street Journal*, September 9, 1999, 1. On the restrictive coverage of public pensions around the globe, see Sala-i-Martin (1996, 281–6).
14. Mulligan et al. (2002).
15. Ferguson (2001, 360).

Chapter 10

1. The federal program AFDC was later called Temporary Assistance for Needy Families (TANF).
2. Murray (1984, 160).
3. Murray may also have incorrectly used the results from two of the policy experiments to support his tale of Harold and Phyllis. In Denver and Seattle, Murray found, more lenient provisions did cause the poor to work and earn considerably less. Unfortunately for his purpose, it happens that the Denver and Seattle experiments had a bias toward greater underreporting of true earnings by those receiving the experimental aid, relative to the control group (Greenberg and Halsey 1983), and the true loss of labor was considerably less. Other experimental results, for example from New Jersey, found more positive effects on the recipients' willingness and ability to find new jobs (Watts and Rees 1977, vol. II; Meyer 1995).
4. For surveys of the pre-1995 U.S. literature, see Killingsworth (1983), Burtless (1987), Triest (1990), and Meyer (1995). For updates featuring the switch to new U.S. welfare rules, see Moffitt (2002a, 2002b).
5. The median economist opinions were 0.00–0.05 for the Marshallian labor supply elasticity for men, 0.18–0.20 for men's Hicks elasticity, 0.30 for women's Marshall elasticity, and 0.43 for women's Hicks elasticity (Fuchs et al. 1998, 1392).
6. As noted in footnote 3 above, Charles Murray's dramatization of the high elasticity of labor supply from the Seattle and Denver experiments was based on experiments that gave the highest, but also upward-biased, elasticities.
7. Moffitt (2002a, 2002b).
8. In a follow-up article published by the *American Economic Review*, Browning (1987) again plumbed for high estimates.
9. Charles Stuart (1984), Ballard (1988), and Triest (1994).
10. Barro and Lee (1993b), Easterly and Rebelo (1993), Barro (1997), Padovano and Galli (2001).
11. Barro and Lee (1993b, 279) calculate government consumption by subtracting the available data on national defense and noncapital educational spending from total government purchases of goods and services (with some difficulties about price deflators that do not need attention here). Apparently, the only kinds of social expenditures that could have remained in the measure of government

consumption are purchases of health care services and building of public-education and public-housing structures.

12. Easterly (1995).

13. Mendoza et al. (1994, 1997), Mendoza and Tesar (1998), Carey and Tchilinguirian (2000), Joumard (2001), and Carey and Rabesona (2002).

14. As an alternative to the marginal tax rates on capital shown in Table 10.1 and Figures 10.1 and 10.2, I have also examined the AETRs on capital income and on property income. The rates shown for these categories by Carey and Tchilinguirian (2000, Table 4 and annexes) give capital tax rates like those shown here. While the assumptions of the Carey and Tchilinguirian estimates seem reasonable, the subsequent paper by Carey and Rabesona (2002) shows that the figures are sensitive to such technical factors as depreciation, the taxation of social security, or how one divides self-employment income between capital income and labor income. These later estimates show somewhat higher average tax rates on capital income in the welfare states than in the low-budget countries. Yet the preponderance of evidence supports the text's finding that the average or marginal tax rates on capital are not higher in the welfare states than in the low-social-budget countries.

15. McLure (1990, 283), Carey and Tchilinguarian (2000, 39–40), and Joumard (2001).

16. Hansson and Stuart (1990, 135–137). Chapter 11 expands on Sweden's hidden deductions.

17. Fuchs et al. (1998, 1392–1394).

18. In this case of a permanent constant rate of consumption tax, the usual charge that flat consumption taxes are regressive is not correct. They take the same percentage of your income sooner or later, and the fact that the poor save less does not affect the eventual tax bite as a percentage of income. While calling the consumption tax regressive might seem to fit the text's general line of argument, it are not necessarily regressive relative to no tax at all, as this example is meant to show.

19. Steinmo (1993, 213–214).

20. The advance of antismoking campaigns does not correlate easily with the rate of tobacco taxation. Among the heavy taxers, Sweden was a pioneer in antismoking laws and campaigns, but Denmark and Norway have lagged in cutting down smoking. Among the countries with lower tobacco tax rates, Canada and the United States were relatively advanced in cutting down on smoking across the 1980s, while Japan was not (Wilensky 2002, 565–573).

21. Taxes in the welfare states are still more "progressive" than in the countries that pay less in transfers. That is, they still take a somewhat higher share of pretax income from high-income groups than they do from low-income groups. But their extra progressivity is less than many would expect. Chapter 11 offers a specific comparison of Sweden's tax incidence with that of the United Kingdom and the United States.

22. For a good summary chronology of U.S. welfare policy since 1935, see Moffitt (2002a).

23. The comparison with Sweden calls for two caveats. One is that the Swedish tax rates omit the consumption tax. Including it would require reading something like "60 percent" for "50 percent" in this paragraph. The other is that a study of

Denmark in the same Atkinson–Mogensen volume implies very high marginal tax rates, such as 90 percent. Yet the rates may not be comparable, and the Danish study goes on to note that labor supply did not seem to respond to the extremely high tax rate. Either the Danes have discovered secret improvements in program design or the Danish marginal tax rate is well below that 90 percent figure.

24. Blöndal and Scarpetta (1998), Gruber and Wise (1999), and Wilensky (2002, 550–558).

25. The deadweight welfare cost of earlier retirement is even smaller than the GDP cost, for reasons we note elsewhere. If subsidies to early retirement induce people to quit work when they otherwise would have worked, this means that they were close to a decisionmaking margin about whether or not to keep working for pay. Therefore the value of their free time must have been worth something close to their rate of pay. If a subsidy makes them retire earlier, we must value their gain in free time at something close to the wage they passed up. This adds a benefit to the retirement subsidy, one that is missed by GDP calculations.

26. See, for example, Gruber and Wise (1999, 9) and the sources cited there.

27. These five countries are singled out here as smoking-gun cases of heavy subsidy to early retirement because they stand out in that respect among the eleven countries studied by the Gruber–Wise research team. Less in-depth analysis covering more countries (Blöndal and Scarpetta 1999) suggests that Austria, Finland, Portugal, and Spain also qualify as dangerously heavy subsidizers of early work. Alternatively, if we took as our clue to early retirement generosity all those countries employing fewer than 40 percent of their men and women fifty-five to sixty-four in 1999, then we would get a list of ten top suspects that excluded Portugal but included Greece and Canada. See Chapter 8 for comparisons over the broader range of countries.

28. As quoted in Sala-i-Martin (1996, 277).

29. Gruber and Wise(1999, pp. 58–64, 94–97, 124–129, 218–220, 259–262, 284–293, 340–342, 385–389, 422–425, and 456–460).

30. See Gruber and Wise (1999, p. 277) on the popularity of disability insurance with Dutch employers.

31. OECD (1998d, 133–141 and 203–205).

32. See Chapter 19 by Gayle Allard and Peter H. Lindert, in Volume 2.

33. See OECD (1994a, 1994b) and the sources cited by Forslund and Krueger (1997). In Chapter 19 of Volume 2, Gayle Allard and I also find no clear stimulus to jobs from ALMP.

34. Heckman and Lochner (2000).

35. See Blank (2000, 2002) and the whole Volume 31 of *OECD Economic Studies* (2000/2) devoted to the theme of "making work pay."

36. Fuchs (1988, 59).

37. Joshi et al. (1998).

38. Waldfogel (1998), Joshi et al. (1998).

39. Goldin (1990).

40. Or (2000).

41. Reinhardt (2000, 77).

42. Hollingsworth et al. (1990, 141–146).

43. World Bank (1993), Mehrotra and Delamonica (forthcoming).

44. Where the contrast is between welfare states and the United States, one should note again that peculiarly U.S. conditions raise mortality, as the huge positive residual for the United States in Table 10.4 implies. One possible source of the extra U.S. mortality is lack of exercise and bad diet, which is not captured by Or's use of butter consumption to represent all fat consumption. Another is the United States' higher homicide rate, which is partly related to its extra firearms, as noted in the text.

45. Angus Deaton (2001) has criticized much of the evidence that income inequality causes health inequality in large samples of individuals, other things equal. His critique does not seem to apply to the present evidence, which does not hold other things equal and emphasizes the income-related inequalities in access to health care.

46. See Hollingsworth (1986, 188–216); Hollingsworth et al. (1990); Preston and Haines (1991); and Steckel (1995). Before the late nineteenth century, however, the poor did not always die younger. If one started as far back as the early eighteenth century in England, there may have been no difference in the life expectancy of the aristocracy and the whole nation. Such a gap did open up in mid-eighteenth century Britain, and by the twentieth century it became a general occupational split. Yet the social patterns across the nineteenth century were complicated by the fact that the cities were more deadly places to live. Thus urban professionals were often at greater risk than farm laborers. It is only when basic sanitation improvements had cut urban deaths by infectious disease in the late nineteenth century that the more familiar pattern of death by class emerged. Joseph Ferrie (2001) has found that in mid-nineteenth century United States, the modern pattern had already emerged both in cities and in the countryside: In both areas, men with lower-status occupations died younger.

47. Hollingsworth and Hollingsworth (1994); Kawachi and Kennedy (1997); Rodgers (1997); Kennedy et al. (1998); World Health Organization (1999); Reinhardt (2000); Ross et al. (2000); Mehrotra and Delamonica, forthcoming.

48. On the differences in physician visits by patients' income class across the twentieth century, see Hollingsworth (1986, 192–195).

49. Hollingsworth (1986); Hollingsworth et al. (1990).

50. Hollingsworth et al. (1990).

51. Again, there is strong evidence from developing countries linking basic health care for the poor with productivity gains. Also strong is the evidence that investing in women's basic schooling promotes their own and their children's health and productivity. See World Bank (1993) and Mehrotra and Delamonica (forthcoming) for surveys of that evidence.

Chapter 11

1. For recent surveys of British social programs and their economic impact, see Flora (1986, Volume I), Atkinson and Mogensen (1993, Chapters 4, 5), Johnson (1994), and OECD (1998a).

2. Before 1977, The *Wall Street Journal*'s editors had already expressed doubts about Sweden's economic wisdom, but less frequently. See the editorial on Sweden's problems in paying for its advanced public welfare systems, August 12, 1960; "New Swedish Budget Would Increase Taxes, Impose Other Burdens,"

January 12, 1967; and "Unrest in Utopia: Lavish Welfare Isn't Enough for Advocates of 'Equality'" January 2, 1970.

3. *Washington Post,* June 25, 1990, A23.

4. See, for example, "Sweden's Social Model Shows Signs of Cracks," *New York Times,* February 20, 1990, A2; "Welfare Stagnation Besets Smug Sweden," *Wall Street Journal,* April 5, 1990, A19; "The 'Swedish Model' Doesn't Seem Quite So Lovely These Days," *Los Angeles Times,* June 18, 1991, H1; "Sweden's Socialist Utopia Gets a Conservative Jolt; Welfare State Slated for Radical Overhaul," *Washington Post,* May 30, 1992, A13; "Sweden Trims Vaunted Safety Net," *Christian Science Monitor,* May 5, 1993, 8; "Sweden's Socialist Economy Due for a Major Overhaul; High Unemployment May Bring Free-Market Reforms," *Christian Science Monitor,* October 27, 1994, 8; "Sweden Seeks Big Social Cuts," *Wall Street Journal,* January 11, 1995, A10; "A Socialist 'Third Way' Turns Out to be A Dead End," *Wall Street Journal,* June 17, 1998, A16.

5. In addition to the two articles quoted from in the text, see "Sweden: End of an Era?" *Economist,* September 7, 1991, 50; Sweden: Toughing It Out," *Economist,* September 19, 1992, 64; "Sweden: In Retreat," *Economist,* September 26, 1992, 53; "Sweden: Worse and Worse," *Economist,* October 9, 1993, 58.

6. "Sweat It Out, Sweden," *Economist,* November 28, 1992, 22.

7. "A Case Study in Collapse," within the survey supplement "The Nordic Countries: Heading South," *Economist,* November 5, 1994, Survey 5 – Survey 7.

8. Almar Latour, "Sweden Seeks Utopia from Tech Boom," *Wall Street Journal,* July 17, 2000, A1. For other positive coverage of Sweden's welfare state after the Social Democrats' narrow election victory in September 1998, see *New York Times,* September 21, 1998, A3; *Washington Post,* January 30, 1999, E1, on funded pensions; *New York Times,* October 8, 1999, A1; and *Wall Street Journal,* March 28, 2001, A18.

9. Lindbeck et al. (1994).

10. "Ask the Devil," *Economist* March 13, 1993, 62.

11. Lindbeck (1997, 87–89).

12. Solow (2000, 22).

13. Different international PPP comparisons give different rankings. Thus Lindbeck (1997, Table 2) cites different rankings, also citing international PPP estimates. Similarly, as Table 11.1 shows, the estimates for 1950 differ between Maddison (1995) and the Penn World Tables version 6.0. The differences reveal genuine index-number problems with the international comparisons.

14. Erieksen and Söderström (1997).

15. There were variations on Sweden's adjustable-peg policy after the United States and others abandoned adjustable pegs in 1971. From 1972 to 1977, the krona was pegged to a basket of European Union currencies. In 1977, it effectively devalued while picking a different basket of foreign currencies to peg to. This policy continued until the start of the 1990s, when Sweden pegged more rigidly to the European Union currencies.

16. Lindbeck et al. (1994, 26–45).

17. Definitions of corporatism differ. Some writers use the term to refer to bargaining that is exclusively between big business and organized labor, with the two groups also comanaging large industrial firms. This definition is usually shaped

by experience in Germany and other countries and is distinguished from the welfare state countries, where government plays a bargaining role, often offering policy concessions in the trilateral bargain. Thus Goodin et al. (1999), for example, consider Germany to be "corporatist," but the Netherlands (and Sweden, which they did not study) to be "social democratic." Here I follow the definition of corporatist as involving centralized wage setting, either just between business and labor or among business, labor, and government.

18. See Edin and Holmslund (1995), Edin and Topel (1997), Swenson and Pontusson (2000), Wallerstein and Golden (2000). The SAF actually took the initiative around 1952 in calling for binding central agreements. It is not clear whether this is because the solidarity wage policy's prohibitions on tying wage rates to firm profitability appealed to the large and successful firms that dominated the SAF.

19. Edin and Holmslund (1995, Figure 11.4 and Table 15).

20. Edin and Holmslund (1995), Edin and Topel (1997).

21. Freeman and Gibbons (1995), Lindbeck (1997), Swenson and Pontusson(2000), Wallerstein and Golden (2000).

    An Employer Association (SAF) representative voiced its continued alienation in 1990: "The centralized system is a catastrophe. LO cannot deliver wage restraint. We'll go for anything else wherever it leads." (As quoted in Freeman and Gibbons 1995, 345.)

22. The Lindbeck report (1994, 36) makes a brief attempt to suggest that having a centralized peak-level round of negotiations on top of industry-level and firm-level negotiations has added to wage inflation, "because negotiations at each level lays a floor for the next." But they present no strong evidence to support this. We still lack a solid set of measures of the effect of centralized bargaining on the wage rate either before or after the breakup of corporatist bargaining in 1983.

23. Lindbeck et al. (1994, 5).

24. How did Sweden come to make the 1991 tax reform? By its dating one might think that it followed the lead of the U.S. Tax Reform Act of 1986. But in truth the wave of tax reforms in the 1980s and early 1990s had its origins in many countries, with pressures transmitted back and forth across the Atlantic. Britain was one of the leaders in tax reform, and their example helped persuade Americans that they could afford to drop special investment incentives while lowering general rates. Sweden was another early leader in some of the discussion of tax reform. In particular, Sweden had one of the longest histories of solving the problem of the double taxation of dividends, by making them a special exemption from the taxes on personal capital income. Still, Sweden's hand was somewhat forced by the 1986 U.S. reform (Norrman and McLure 1997, 146–148).

25. Note that in the phrase "statutory marginal," the operative adjective is "statutory." The marginal rate hardly differed from the average rate of tax on corporate incomes.

26. As we noted more generally in Chapter 10. Note here that labor incomes refer to all labor earnings, even professional and managerial, and not just labor incomes in the blue collar sense.

27. See Norrman and McLure (1997, 131–132): Great Britain, Central Statistical Office, *Economic Trends*, issues in 1985–1986: and Pechman (1985, 68).

28. The year 1995 is chosen here, out of the 1990–1997 range available in the source, for special reasons. One is that we have used 1995 in many other data displays since Chapter 8. Another is that 1995 gives a fair average outcome for the contrasts between Sweden and the United States. Sweden's employment ratios for the two sexes combined were either above or below the American ratios, depending on which year one chooses in the 1990–1997 range. The reason for these switches is that the data series kept changing in definition, causing anomalous jumps and drops in one series or the other. A later footnote reports the same problem for comparing women's employment ratios between Sweden and Norway.

29. Blau and Kahn (1995, 110–114).

30. Rosen (1997, 83–89).

31. These, at least, were Sweden's rankings among OECD countries in such social expenditures as a share of GDP in 1995. See Tables 8.1 and 10.3.

32. Rosen (1997, 82 and 102–105).

33. "Especially women" here, because the labor-supply studies typically find that women have more elastic labor supplies. Therefore any given percentage change in the incentive to work would evoke a greater response in women's work time than in men's.

34. Gustafsson and Stafford (1992).

35. Almost, because for the fifteen to sixty-four age group in 1990–1997, Iceland had the highest female employment ratio, and Norway and Sweden traded places with each other as the data series were revised from year to year (OECD 1998d, 193).

36. Heckman and Lochner (2000, 58–64).

37. Note that this statement refers to the attainment of higher education among persons between twenty-five and sixty-four, not to the current flow of university and technical-school graduates. In fact, females have already become the majority of university graduates, for example, in the United States since 1980. Yet it still takes time for the older cohorts to retire and be replaced by the more female mix of new university graduates.

38. Blau and Kahn (1995).

39. OECD (1999).

40. Forslund and Krueger (1997, 274–275).

41. Forslund and Krueger (1997, 280–283, 296).

42. Forslund and Krueger (1997, 275–277).

43. Men in two other OECD countries, Iceland and Korea, also work to later ages than men in Sweden. Our focus in Part Four of the book, however, is on the twenty-one core OECD countries, ignoring Luxembourg and Iceland, as well as the more recent OECD entrants.

44. Ackerby (1998).

45. Lindbeck (1997, 20–28). Another reason for the maintenance of high social spending levels in these center-right interludes was that they both happened during recessions.

46. Lindbeck (1997, 25–26).

Chapter 12

1. Becker (1983, 1985), and Becker and Mulligan (1998).
2. See Steinmo (1993, especially 126–35), and Wilensky (2002, 384–5). Daunton (2002b, Chapter 10) describes and explains Britain's similar reluctant shift to VAT in 1973, after much debate and with conservative initiative. On the multi-country shift from "visible" direct taxes toward VAT in the 1970s and 1980s, see Wilensky (2002, 378–83).
3. For a leading example, see Hall and Rabushka (1985).
4. Steinmo (1993, 142–144).
5. Hirschman (1970).
6. Wilensky (2002, 554–557).
7. Gruber and Wise (1999, Chapter 7), Wilensky (2002, 550–558), and OECD (1998e, 77–107).
8. Daunton (2002b, 293–326).
9. Daunton (2002b, 356–359), Wilensky (2002, 383–384).
10. DeLong and Shleifer (1993), North and Weingast (1989), Acemoglu et al. (2002). The part of the story emphasizing the efficiency of eighteenth- and nineteenth-century century Britain's tax system is found in O'Brien (1988), Brewer (1989), and Schultz and Weingast (1998).
11. See Chapter 4, especially Table 4.3.
12. Estrin (1988); World Bank (1994, 370).
13. Note that this paragraph focuses on programs targeted at the poor, not on public pension programs. The work disincentives of public pension programs might have become more negative as a share of extra pension transfers. It is hard to say, since those programs were so small in earlier settings in which few lived to retirement age.
14. The data source is the OECD data set on social expenditures the period 1978/80–1993/95. The countries cutting their transfer shares of GDP are Denmark, Ireland, and Sweden for public health; Netherlands and New Zealand for public pensions; Portugal, Spain, United Kingdom, and United States for welfare; Portugal, Spain, and Netherlands for unemployment compensation; and Portugal and Spain for total social transfers.

    More up-to-date figures would show a different set of countries with cuts since 1978/80, but the overall numbers would still be small.
15. Alesina et al. (2001a); Alesina et al. (2001b).

Bibliography

Acemoglu, Daron, Simon Johnson, and James A. Robinson. 2002. "The Rise of Europe: Institutional Change and Economic Growth." Draft.

Acemoglu, Daron, and James A. Robinson. 2000. "Why Did the West Extend the Franchise? Democracy, Inequality, and Growth in Historical Perspective." *Quarterly Journal of Economics* 115, 4 (November): 1167–1200.

Ackerby, Stefan. 1998. "Sweden's Pension Reform – An Example for Others?" *Unitas* 70, 4: 26–29.

Acs, Gregory, Norma Coe, Keith Watson, and Robert I. Lerman. 1998. "Does Work Pay? An Analysis of the Work Incentives under TANF." The Urban Institute, Occasional Paper Number 9 (July).

Adams, Francis. 1875. *The Free School System of the United States*. London: Chapman Hall.

Adema, Willem. 2000. "Revisiting Real Social Spending Across Countries: A Brief Note." *OECD Economic Studies* 30, 1: 191–197.

Alesina, Alberto, Reza Baqir, and William Easterly. 1999. "Public Goods and Ethnic Divisions." *Quarterly Journal of Economics* 114, 4 (November): 1243–1284.

Alesina, Alberto, Rafael DiTella, and Robert MacCulloch. 2001a. "Inequality and Happiness: Are Europeans and Americans Different?" NBER Working Paper 8198 (April).

Alesina, Alberto, Edward Glaeser, and Bruce Sacerdote. 2001b. "Why Doesn't the U.S. Have a European-Style Welfare System?" NBER Working Paper 8524 (October).

Alesina, Alberto and Dani Rodrik. 1994. "Distribution, Politics, and Economic Growth." *Quarterly Journal of Economics* 109, 2 (May): 465–490.

Alexander, John K. 1980. *Render Them Submissive: Responses to Poverty in Philadelphia, 1760–1800*. Amherst: University of Massachusetts Press.

Alston, Lee and Joseph Ferrie. 1998. *Southern Paternalism and the American Welfare State: Economics, Politics, and Institutions in the South 1865–1965*. New York: Cambridge University Press.

Anderson, Eugene N. 1970. "The Prussian Volksschule in the Nineteenth Century." In Gerhard A. Ritter (ed.), *Entstehung und Wandel der modernen Gesellschaft*. Berlin: Walter de Gruyter, 261–279.

Anderson, R.D. 1975. *Education in France, 1848–1870*. Oxford: Clarendon.

Atkinson, A.B. 1999. *The Economic Consequences of Rolling Back the Welfare State*. Cambridge, MA: MIT Press.

Atkinson, A.B. and Gunnar Viby Mogenson. 1993. *Welfare and Work Incentives: A North European Perspective*. New York: Oxford University Press.

Atkinson, A.B. and J.E. Stiglitz. 1980. *Lectures on Public Economics*. New York: McGraw-Hill.

Baldwin, Peter. 1990. *The Politics of Social Solidarity and the Bourgeois Basis of the European Welfare State, 1875–1975*. Cambridge, UK: Cambridge University Press.

Balke, Nathan and Robert J. Gordon. 1989. "The Estimation of Prewar National Product: Methodology and New Evidence." *Journal of Political Economy* 97, 1 (February), 38–92.

Ballard, Charles L. 1988. "The Marginal Efficiency Cost of Redistribution." *American Economic Review* 78, 5 (December): 1019–1033.

Ballou, Dale and Michael Podgursky. 1997. *Teacher Pay and Teacher Quality*. Kalamazoo: W.E. Upjohn Institute.

Banks, Arthur S. 1971. *Cross-Polity Time-Series Data*. Cambridge, MA: MIT Press.

Barkin, Kenneth. 1983. "Social Control and the Volksschule in Vormärz Prussia." *Central European History* 16, 1 (March): 31–52.

Barro, Robert J. 1997. *Determinants of Economic Growth: A Cross-Country Empirical Study*. Cambridge, MA: MIT Press.

Barro, Robert J. and Jong-Wha Lee. 1993a. "International Comparisons of Educational Attainment." *Journal of Monetary Economics* 32, 3 (December): 363–394.

Barro, Robert J. and Jong-Wha Lee. 1993b. "Winners and Losers in Economic Growth." *Proceedings of the World Bank Annual Conference on Development Economics*. Washington, DC: World Bank, pp. 267–314.

Barro, Steven M. and Larry Suter. 1988. *International comparison of Teachers' Salaries: An Exploratory Study*. U.S. National Center for Education Statistics Survey Report, July.

Bastid, Marianne. 1988. *Educational Reform in Early Twentieth-Century China*. Translated by Paul J. Bailey. Ann Arbor: Center for Chinese Studies, University of Michigan.

Baugh, Daniel A. 1975. "The Cost of Poor Relief in South-East England, 1790–1834." *Economic History Review* 28, 1 (February): 50–68.

Bean, Charles. 1994. "European Unemployment: A Survey." *Journal of Economic Literature*, June.

Beaton, Albert E., Ina V.S. Mullis, Michael O. Martin, Eugenio J. Gonzalez, Dana L. Smith, and Theresa A. Smith. 1996a. *Mathematics Achievement in the Middle School Years: IEA's Third International Mathematics and Science Study*. Chestnut Hill, MA: International Association for the Evaluation of Educational Achievement, TIMSS International Study Center, Boston College.

Beaton, Albert E., Ina V.S. Mullis, Michael O. Martin, Eugenio J. Gonzalez, Dana L. Smith, and Theresa A. Smith. 1996b. *Science Achievement in the Middle School Years: IEA's Third International Mathematics and Science Study*. Chestnut Hill, MA: International Association for the Evaluation of Educational Achievement, TIMSS International Study Center, Boston College.

Becker, Gary S. 1983. "A Theory of Competition among Pressure Groups for Political Influence." *Quarterly Journal of Economics* 98, 3 (August): 371–400.

1985. "Public Policies, Pressure Groups, and Dead Weight Costs," *Journal of Public Economics*, 28, 3 (December): 329–48.

Becker, Gary S. and Casey B. Mulligan. 1998. "Deadweight Costs and the Size of Government." NBER Working Paper 6789 (November).

Belgium, Statistique Générale. 1852. *Exposé de la Situation du Royaume . . . 1841–1850*. Bruxelles: Th. Lesigne.

Bishop, John H. 1989. "Is the Test Score Decline Responsible for the Productivity Growth Decline?" *American Economic Review* 79, 1 (March): 178–197.

1990. "The Productivity Consequences of What is Learned in High School." *Journal of Curriculum Studies* 22, 2: 101–126.

1996. "Signaling, Incentives, and School Organization in France, the Netherlands, Britain, and the United States." In Eric A. Hanushek and Dale W. Jorgenson (eds.), *Improving America's Schools: The Role of Incentives*. Washington, D.C.: National Academy Press, 111–145.

1997. "The Effect of National Standards and Curriculum-Based Exams on Achievement." *American Economic Review* 87, 2 (May): 260–4.

Blank, Rebecca M. 2000. "Fighting Poverty: Lessons from Recent U.S. History." *Journal of Economic Perspectives* 14, 2 (Spring): 3–19.

2002. "U.S. Welfare Reform: What's Relevant for Europe?" *CESifo Economic Studies* 49, 1: 49–74.

Blau, Francine D. and Lawrence M. Kahn. 1995. "The Gender Earnings Gap: Some International Evidence." In Richard B. Freeman and Lawrence F. Katz (eds.), *Differences and Changes in Wage Structures*. Chicago: University of Chicago Press, 145–174.

Blaug, Mark. 1963. "The Myth of the Old Poor Law and the Making of the New." *Journal of Economic History* 23, 2 (June): 151–184.

Blaug, Mark. 1964. "The Poor Law Report Re-examined." *Journal of Economic History* 24, 2 (June): 229–245.

Blöndal, Sveinbjörn and Stefano Scarpetta. 1997. "Early Retirement in OECD Countries: The Role of Social Security Systems." *OECD Economic Studies* 29, 2.

Bowles, Samuel and Herbert Gintis. 1976. *Schooling in Capitalist America*. New York: Basic Books.

Boyer, G.R. 1989. "Malthus Was Right After All: Poor Relief and Birth Rates in Southeastern England." *Journal of Political Economy* 97, 1 (February): 93–114.

1990. *An Economic History of the English Poor Law, 1750–1850*. Cambridge, UK: Cambridge University Press.

Bradbury, Bruce, Stephen Jenkins, and John Micklewright. 2000. "Child Poverty Dynamics in Seven Nations." UNICEF Innocenti Working Paper no. 78 (June).

Branch, William T., Jr. 2000. "The Ethics of Caring and Medical Education." *Academic Medicine* 75 (2): 127–32.

Brewer, John. 1989. *The Sinews of Power: Money, War, and the English State, 1688–1783*. Boston: Unwin.

Brewer, Mike. 2000. "Comparing In-Work Benefits and Financial Work Incentives for Low-Income Families in the U.S. and the U.K." Institute for Fiscal Studies, WP 00/16 (September).

Brown, Charles C. and Wallace E. Oates. 1987. "Assistance to the Poor in a Federal System." *Journal of Public Economics* 32: 307–330.

Browning, Edgar K. 1987. "General Equilibrium Computations of the Marginal Welfare Costs of Taxes in the United States." *American Economic Review* 77, 1 (March): 11–23.

Browning, Edgar K. and William R. Johnson. 1984. "The Trade-Off between Equality and Efficiency." *Journal of Political Economy* 92, 175–202.

Brugiavini, Agar. 1999. "Social Security and Retirement in Italy." In Jonathan Gruber and David Wise (eds.), *Social Security Programs and Retirement around the World*. Chicago: University of Chicago Press, pp. 181–238.

Brundage, Anthony. 1978. *The Making of the New Poor Law: The Politics of Inquiry, Enactment, and Implementation, 1832–39*. New Brunswick, NJ: Rutgers University Press.

Bruno, Michael and Jeffrey Sachs. 1985. *Economics of Worldwide Stagflation*. Cambridge, MA: Harvard University Press.

Buechtmann, Christoph (ed.). 1993. *Employment Security and Labor Market Behavior:...International Evidence*. Ithaca, NY: ILR Press.

Bullock, Milton L., et al. 2002. "A large randomized placebo controlled study of auricular acupuncture for alcohol dependence." *Journal of Substance Abuse Treatment* 22 (2): 71–7.

Burgess, W. Randolph. 1920. *Trends in Schools Costs*. New York: Russell Sage Foundation.

Burtless, Gary. 1987. "The Work Response to a Guaranteed Income: A Survey of Experimental Evidence." In Alicia H. Munnell (ed.), *Lessons from the Income Maintenance Experiments*, Federal Reserve Bank of Boston Conference Series No. 30, 22–52.

Burtless, Gary (ed.). 1996. *Does Money Matter? The Effect of School Resources on Student Achievement and Adult Success*. Washington, DC: The Brookings Institution.

Butts, R. Freeman. 1978. *Public Education in the United States from Revolution to Reform*. New York: Holt Rinehart and Winston.

Cahalin, Lawrence P., et al. 2002. "Efficacy of diaphragmatic breathing in persons with chronic obstructive pulmonary disease: a review of the literature." *Journal of Cardiopulmonary Rehabilitation* 22 (1): 7–21.

Canada, Dominion Bureau of Statistics. 1921. *Historical Statistical Survey of Education in Canada*. Ottawa: Thomas Mulvey.

Carey, David and Josette Rabesona. 2002. "Tax Ratios on Labour and Capital Income and on Consumption." *OECD Economic Studies* 35 (2002/II).

Carey, David and Harry Tchilinguirian. 2000. "Average Effective Tax Rates on Capital Labour, and Consumption." OECD Economics Department Working Paper no. 258. October.

Carey, Mathew. 1833. *An Appeal to the Wealthy of the Land....* Second edition. Philadelphia.

1836. *A Plea for the Poor....* Third edition. Philadelphia.

Carry, Alain. 1999. *Le compte satellite rétrospectif de l'éducation en France (1820–1996)*. *Économies et sociétés*, Cahier de l'ISMÉA, Série AF, no. 25 (Fev–Mar).

Castles, Francis G. 1985. *The Working Class and Welfare: Reflections on the Political Development of the Welfare State in Australia and New Zealand, 1890–1980*. London: Allen and Unwin, Port Nicholson Press.

Cavallo, Sandra. 1995. *Charity and Power in Early Modern Italy: Benefactors and their Motives in Turin, 1541–1789*. New York: Cambridge University Press.

Chen, Derek Hung Chiat. 2000. "Inter-temporal Excess Burdens, Bequest Motives, Informal Support, and the Budget Deficit." Doctoral dissertation, University of California, Davis.

Cipolla, Carlo M. 1969. *Literacy and Development in the West*. Harmondsworth: Penguin.

Clark, Gregory. 2002. Clark, "Shelter from the Storm: House Rents and Housing Quality in England in the Industrial Revolution, 1550–1869." *Journal of Economic History*, 62, 2 (June).

Clark, Gregory and Marianne Page. 2001. "Is There Profit in Reforming the Poor? The English Poor Law 1830–1842." Paper presented at the Cliometrics Society Sessions of the Allied Social Sciences Association Meetings, New Orleans, January 6th.

Clement, Priscilla Ferguson. 1985. *Welfare and the Poor in the Nineteenth-Century City: Philadelphia, 1800–1854*. Rutherford, NJ: Farleigh Dickinson University Press.

Cohn, Elchanan and Terry G. Geske. 1990. *The Economics of Education*. Third edition. New York: Pergamon Press.

Commander, Simon, Hamid R. Davoodi, and Une J. Lee. 1997. "The Causes of Government and the Consequences for Growth and Well-Being." World Bank Policy Research Working Paper 1785. World Bank, June.

Conner, Walter D. 1997. "Social Policy under Communism." In Ethan B. Kapstein and Michael Mandelbaum (eds.). 1997. *Sustaining the Transition: The Social Safety Net in Postcommunist Europe*." New York: Council on Foreign Relations, 10–45.

Coulson, Andrew J. 1999. *Market Education: The Unknown History*. New Brunswick, NJ: Transaction Publishers.

Crafts, N.F.R. 1997. "Economic Growth in East Asia and Western Europe since 1950: Implications for Living Standards." *National Institute Economic Review* 162 (October): 75–84.

Cray, Robert E. 1988. *Paupers and Poor Relief in New York City and its Rural Environs, 1700–1830*. Philadelphia: Temple University Press.

Daunton, Martin. 2002a. *Trusting Leviathan: The Politics of Taxation in Britain, 1799–1914*. Cambridge, UK: Cambridge University Press.

2002b. *Just Taxes: The Politics of Taxation in Britain 1914–1979*. Cambridge, UK: Cambridge University Press.

David, Paul A. and Peter Solar. 1977. "A Bicentenary Contribution to the History of the Cost of Living in America." *Research in Economic History* 2: 1–80.

Deaton, Angus. 2001. "Inequalities in Income and Inequalities in Health." In Finis Welch (ed.), *The Causes and Consequences of Increasing Inequality*. Chicago: University of Chicago Press, 285–314.

de Kwaasteniet, Marjanne. 1990. *Denomination and Primary Education in the Netherlands (1870–1984)*. Amsterdam: Instituut voor Sociale Geografie, Universiteit van Amsterdam.

DeLong, J. Bradford and Andrei Shleifer. 1993. "Princes and Merchants: City Growth Before the Industrial Revolution." *Journal of Law and Economics* 36 (October): 671–702.

de Vries, Jan and Ad van der Woude (1997). *The First Modern Economy: Success, Failure, and Perseverance of the Dutch Economy, 1500–1815*. Cambridge, UK: Cambridge University Press.

Diamond, Peter and Jonathan Gruber. 1999. "Social Security and Retirement in the United States." In Jonathan Gruber and David Wise (eds.), *Social Security Programs and Retirement around the World*. Chicago: University of Chicago Press, pp. 437–474.

Digby, Anne. 1975. "The Labour Market and the Continuity of Social Policy after 1834: The Case of the Eastern Counties." *Economic History Review* 28, 1 (February): 69–83.

Dixon, John. 1981. *The Chinese Welfare System, 1949–1979*. New York: Praeger.

Donoghue, John and James Heckman. 1991. "Continuous versus Episodic Change: The Impact of Civil Rights Policy on the Economic Status of Blacks." *Journal of Economic Literature* 29, 4 (December): 1603–1643.

Dunkley, Peter. 1982. *The Crisis of the Old Poor Law in England, 1795–1834: An Interpretive Essay*. New York: Garland.

Easterlin, Richard A. 1960. "Interregional Differences in Per Capita Income, Population, and Total Income, 1840–1950." In William N. Parker (ed.), *Trends in the American Economy in the Nineteenth Century*. Princeton, NJ: Princeton University Press. NBER Studies in Income and Wealth, vol. 24, pp. 73–140.

1961. "Regional Income Trends, 1840–1950." In Seymour E. Harris (ed.), *American Economic History*. New York: McGraw-Hill, pp. 525–548.

1981. "Why Isn't the Whole World Developed?" *Journal of Economic History* 41, 1 (March): 1–17.

Easterly, William. 1995. Comment on "What Do Cross-Country Studies Teach about Government Involvement, Prosperity, and Economic Growth?" *Brookings Papers in Economic Activity* 2, 419–424.

Easterly, William and Ross Levine. 1997. "Africa's Growth Tragedy: Policies and Ethnic Divisions." *Quarterly Journal of Economics* 112, 44 (November), 1203–50.

Easterly, William and Sergio Rebelo. 1993. "Fiscal Policy and Economic Growth." *Journal of Monetary Economics* 32, 417–458.

Eastwood, David. 1994. *Governing Rural England: Tradition and Transformation in Local Government, 1780–1840*. Oxford: Clarendon Press.

Edin, Per-Anders and Bertil Holmslund. 1995. "The Swedish Wage Structure: The Rise and Fall of Solidarity Wage Policy?" In Richard B. Freeman and Lawrence F. Katz (eds.), 1995. *Differences and Changes in Wage Structures*. Chicago: University of Chicago Press.

Edin, Per-Anders and Robert Topel. 1997. "Wage Policy and Restructuring: The Swedish Labor Market since 1960." In Richard B. Freeman, Robert Topel, and Birgitta Swedenborg (eds.), *The Welfare State in Transition: Reforming the Swedish Model*. Chicago: University of Chicago Press, 155–202.

Eisenberg, David M. 1997. "Advising patients who seek alternative medical therapies." *Annals of Internal Medicine* 127 (1): 61–9.

Ellis, Christopher G. and Jeffrey S. Levin. 1998. "The Religion–Health connection: Evidence, theory, and future directions." *Health Education and Behavior* 25 (6): 700–20.

Emminghaus, Arwed. 1873. *Poor Relief in Different Parts of Europe.* London: Edward Stanford.

Engerman, Stanley L., Elisa Mariscal, and Kenneth L. Sokoloff. 1998. "Schooling, Suffrage, and the Persistence of Inequality in the Americas, 1800–1945." Manuscript, October.

Epstein, Klaus. 1966. *The Genesis of German Conservatism.* Princeton, NJ: Princeton University Press.

Eriksen, Tor E. and Lars Söderström. 1998. "Dimensions of Privatisation: The Swedish Welfare State in Transition." In Peter Flora, Philip R. de Jong, Jun-Young Kim and Julian Le Grand (eds.), *The State of Social Welfare, 1997.* Aldershot: Ashgate, 265–282.

Estrin, Alexander, 1988. "Administrative Costs for Social Security Programs in Selected Countries," *Social Security Bulletin* 51, 88: 29–31.

Fairbairn, Brett. 1997. *Democracy in the Undemocratic State: The German Reichstag Elections of 1898 and 1903.* Toronto: University of Toronto Press.

Fairchilds, C.C. 1976. *Poverty and Charity in Aix-en-Provence, 1670–1789.* Baltimore: Johns Hopkins University Press.

Feinstein, C.H. 1998. "Pessimism Perpetuated: Real Wages and the Standard of Living in Britain during and after the Industrial Revolution." *Journal of Economic History* 58 (3): 625–658.

Feldstein, Martin. 1999. "Tax Avoidance and the Deadweight Loss of the Income Tax." *Review of Economics and Statistics* 81, 4 (November): 674–680.

Ferguson, Niall. 2001. *The Cash Nexus: Money and Power in the Modern World 1700–2000.* New York: Basic Books.

Ferrie, Joseph P. 2001. "The Poor and the Dead: Socioeconomic Status and Mortality in the U.S., 1850–1860." NBER Working Paper No. h0135 (August).

Field, Alexander J. 1979. "Economic and Demographic Determinants of Educational Commitment." *Journal of Economic History* 39 (2): 439–459.

Figlio, David N. 1997. "Did the 'Tax Revolt' Reduce School Performance?" *Journal of Public Economics* 65 (1997): 245–269.

Figlio, David N. and Marianne E. Page. 2003. "Can School Choice and School Accountability Successfully Coexist?" In Caroline M. Hoxby (ed.), *The Economics of School Choice.* Chicago: University of Chicago Press for the NBER.

Finland. 1912. *Statistisk Arsbok.* Helsinki.

Fischel, William. 1996. "How *Serrano* Caused Proposition 13." *Journal of Law and Politics* 12, 4 (Fall): 607–636.

Fishlow, Albert. 1966a. "The Common School Revival: Fact or Fancy?" In Henry Rosovsky (ed.), *Industrialization in Two Systems.* New York: Wiley, 1966.

1966b. "Levels of Nineteenth-Century American Investment in Education." *Journal of Economic History* 26, 4 (December): pp. 418–436.

Flanagan, Robert J. 1987. "Efficiency and Equality in Swedish Labor Markets." In Barry Bosworth and Alice Rivlin (eds.), *The Swedish Economy.* Washington, DC: The Brookings Institution.

1988. "Unemployment as a Hiring Problem." *OECD Economic Studies* 11 (Autumn): 123–154.

1999. "Macroeconomic Performance and Collective Bargaining: An International Perspective." *Journal of Economic Literature* 37, 3 (September): 1150–1175.

Flora, Peter. (ed.). 1986. *Growth to Limits*. Three volumes. New York: Walder de Gruyter.

Flora, Peter 1983. *State, Economy, and Society in Western Europe, 1815–1975*. Frankfurt: Campus Verlag.

Flora, Peter and Arnold J. Heidenheimer (eds.). 1981. *The Development of Welfare States in Europe and America*. London: Transaction Books.

Flynn, James R. 1984. "The Mean IQ of Americans: Massive Gains 1932 to 1978." *Psychological Bulletin* 95, 1 (January): 29–51.

1987. "Massive IQ Gains in 14 Nations: What IQ Tests Really Measure." *Psychological Bulletin* 101, 2 (March): 171–191.

2000. "IQ Trends over Time: Intelligence, Race, and Meritocracy." In K.A. Arrow, S. Bowles, and S. Derlauf (eds.), *Meritocracy and Economic Inequality*. Princeton, NJ: Princeton University Press, 35–60.

Forrest, Alan. 1981. *The French Revolution and the Poor*. Oxford: Basil Blackwell.

Forslund, A. and A. Krueger. 1997. "An Evaluation of the Swedish Active Labor Market Policy: New and Received Wisdom." In Richard B. Freeman, Robert Topel, and Birgitta Swedenborg (eds.), *The Welfare State in Transition: Reforming the Swedish Model*. Chicago: University of Chicago Press, 267–98.

France, Ministère du Commerce. Various years. *Annuaire Statistique de la France*. Paris.

Fraser, Rev. James. 1866. *Report* [to H.M. Schools Commissions] . . . *on the Common School System of the United States and the Provinces of Upper and Lower Canada*. London: HMSO.

Freeman, Richard B. 1972. "Black-White Economic Differences: Why Did They Last So Long?" Paper presented at the Cliometrics Conference, Madison, Wisconsin, April 1972.

Freeman, Richard B. and Robert S. Gibbons. 1995. "Getting Together and Breaking Apart: The Decline of Centralized Collective Bargaining." In Richard B. Freeman and Lawrence F. Katz (eds.), *Differences and Changes in Wage Structures*. Chicago: University of Chicago Press, 345–370.

Friedman, Milton. 1962. *Capitalism and Freedom*. Chicago: University of Chicago Press.

Fuchs, Victor R. 1988. *Women's Quest for Economic Equality*. Cambridge, MA: Harvard University Press.

Fuchs, Victor R., Alan B. Krueger, and James M. Poterba. 1998. "Economists' Views about Parameters, Values, and Policies: Survey Results in Labor and Public Economics." *Journal of Economic Literature* 36, 3 (September): 1387–1425.

Gallo, Joseph J., et al. 2002. "Do family physicians and internists differ in knowledge, attitudes, and self-reported approaches for depression?" *International Journal of Psychiatry in Medicine* 32 (1): 1–20.

Garfinkel, Marian and H. Ralph Schumacher, Jr. 2000. "Yoga." *Rheumatic Diseases Clinics of North America* 26 (1): 125–32.

Gawthorp, Richard and Gerald Strauss. 1984. "Protestantism and Literacy in Early Modern Germany." *Past and Present* 104 (August): 31–55.

Gerber, James B. 1986. "Southern White Schooling, 1880–1940." Doctoral dissertation, University of California, Davis.

Goldin, Claudia. 1990. *Understanding the Gender Gap*. New York: Oxford University Press.

1998. "America's Graduation from High School: The Evolution and Spread of Secondary Schooling in the Twentieth Century." *Journal of Economic History* 58, 2 (June): 345–374.

2001. "The Human Capital Century and American Leadership: Virtues of the Past." *Journal of Economic History* 61, 2 (June): 263–292.

Goldin, Claudia and Lawrence F. Katz. 1997. "Why the United States Led in Education: Lessons from Secondary School Expansion, 1910 to 1940." National Bureau of Economic Research Working Paper 6144, August.

Goodin, Robert E., Bruce Headley, Ruud Muffels, and Henk-Jan Dirven. 1999. *The Real Worlds of Welfare Capitalism*. Cambridge, UK: Cambridge University Press.

Goodman, R., G. White, and H. Kwon (eds.). 1998. *The East Asian Welfare Model: Welfare Orientalism and the State*. London: Routledge.

Gouda, Frances. 1995. *Poverty and Political Culture: The Rhetoric of Social Welfare in the Netherlands and France, 1815–1914*. Lanham, MD: Rowman & Littlefield.

Graff, Harvey J. 1987. *The Legacies of Literacy*. Bloomington: Indiana University Press.

Great Britain, Central Statistical Office. 1986–1987. *Economic Trends*. London: HMSO.

Great Britain, Local Government Board. 1875. "Poor Laws in Foreign Countries." In House of Commons, *Sessional Papers* (1875) LXV.

Great Britain, Poor Law Commission. 1834. *First Report of the Poor Law Commissioners*, Appendix F.

Great Britain, Royal Commission on Poor Laws and Relief of Distress. 1910. *Royal Commission on Poor Laws and Relief of Distress 1909, Report, Appendix XXXIII*. In House of Commons, *Sessional Papers*, 1910, vol. LV.

Green, Andy. 1990. *Education and State Formation: The Rise of Education Systems in England, France and the USA*. New York: St. Martin's Press.

Greenberg, David and Harlan Halsey. 1983. "Systematic Misreporting and Effects of Income Maintenance Experiments on Work Effort: Evidence from the Seattle-Denver Experiment." *Journal of Labor Economics* 1, 4 (October): 380–407.

Grew, Raymond and Patrick J. Harrigan. 1991. *School, State, and Society: The Growth of Elementary Schooling in Nineteenth-Century France*. Ann Arbor: University of Michigan Press.

Grissmer, David, Ann Flanagan, Jennifer Kawata, and Stephenie Williamson. 2000. *Improving Student Achievement: What State NAEP Test Scores Tell Us*. Santa Monica, CA: RAND Corporation.

Grubb, David. 2000. "Eligibility Criteria for Unemployment Benefits." *OECD Economic Studies* no. 31, 147–181.

Gruber, Jonathan and David Wise (eds.). 1999. *Social Security Programs and Retirement around the World*. Chicago: University of Chicago Press.

2001. "An International Perspective on Policies for an Aging Society." NBER Working Paper 8103 (January).

Gustafsson, Björn and N. Anders Klevmarken. 1993. "Taxes and Transfers in Sweden: Incentive Effects on Labour Supply." In A.B. Atkinson and Gunnar Viby

Mogenson (eds.), *Welfare and Work Incentives: A North European Perspective.*
New York: Oxford University Press, 50–134.

Gustafsson, Siv and Frank Stafford. 1992. "Child Care Subsidies and Labor Supply
in Sweden." *Journal of Human Resources* 27, 1 (Winter 1992): 204–230.

Hagen, William W. 1991. "Descent of the *Sonderweg*: Hans Rosenberg's History of
Old-Regime Prussia." *Central European History* 24: 24–50.

Hall, Robert E. and Alvin Rabushka. 1985. *The Flat Tax.* Stanford: Hoover Institution.

Hallerberg, Mark. 1996. "Tax Competition in Wilhelmine Germany and Its Implications for the European Union." *World Politics* (April), pp. 324–357.

    1999. "The Political Economy of Taxation in Prussia, 1871–1914." Paper pre-
sented at the First Conference on German Cliometrics, University of Toronto,
September 26–29.

Hammond, J.L. and Barbara Hammond. 1917, reprinted 1967. *The Town Labourer
1760–1832.* New York: Augustus M. Kelley.

Hannon, Joan Underhill. 1984. "The Generosity of Antebellum Poor Relief." *Journal
of Economic History.*

    1986. "Dollars, Morals and Markets: The Shaping of Nineteenth Century Poor
Relief Policy." Paper prepared for the All-University of California Conference
on Poverty, Old Age, and Dependency in the Nineteenth Century, Laguna Beach,
1986.

    1997. "Shutting Down Welfare: Two Cases from America's Past." *Quarterly Re-
view of Economics and Finance* 37, 2 (Summer): 419–438.

Hansen, Hal E. 1998. "Caps and Gowns: Historical Reflections on the Institutions
that Shaped Learning for and Work in Germany and the United States, 1800–
1945." Doctoral dissertation, University of Wisconsin.

Hanson, Elizabeth. 1980. *The Politics of Social Security: The 1938 Act and Some
Later Developments.* Auckland: Auckland University Press.

Hansson, Ingemar and Charles Stuart. 1990. "Sweden: Tax Reform in a High-Tax
Environment." In Michael J. Boskin and Charles E. McLure, Jr. (eds.), *World Tax
Reform: Case Studies of Developed and Developing Countries.* San Francisco:
ICS Press.

Hanushek, Eric A. and Javier A. Luque. 2002. "Efficiency and Equity in Schools
around the World." NBER Working Paper 8949 (May).

Hanushek, Eric A. and Steven G. Rivkin. 2003. "Does Public School Competition
Affect Teacher Quality?" In Caroline M. Hoxby (ed.), *The Economics of School
Choice.* Chicago: University of Chicago Press for the NBER.

Harrington, Michael. 1962. *The Other America.* New York: Macmillan.

Hayhoe, Ruth, and Marianne Bastid (eds.) 1987. *China's Education and the Industrialized World: Studies in Cultural Transfer.* Armonk, NY: M.E. Sharpe.

Heckman, James J. and Lance Lochner. 2000. "Rethinking Education and Training
Policy: Understanding the Sources of Skills Formation in a Modern Economy."
In Sheldon Danziger and Jane Waldfogel (eds.), *Securing the Future: Investing
in Children from Birth to College.* New York: Russell Sage Foundation, 47–86.

Herrfurth, L. 1878. "Übersicht über die Aufwendungen für Volksschulzwecke und
über die Beschaftung der dazu erforderlichen." *Zeitschrift des Königlich Preussischen Statistischen Bureaus.*

Heston, Alan, Robert Summers and Bettina Aten. 2002. Penn World Table Version
6.1, Center for International Comparisons at the University of Pennsylvania

(CICUP), October 2002. http://www.pwt.econ.upenn.edu. Last accessed November 2003.

Hicks, Alexander. 1999. *Social Democracy and Welfare Capitalism: A Century of Income Security Politics.* Ithaca, NY: Cornell University Press.

Hicks, Alexander, and Joya Misra. 1993. "Political Resources and the Growth of Welfare in Affluent Capitalist Democracies, 1960–1982." *American Journal of Sociology* 99, 3 (November), 668–710.

Hirschman, Albert O. 1970. *Exit, Voice, and Loyalty: Responses to Decline in Firms, Organizations, and States.* Cambridge, MA: Harvard University Press.

Hoffman, Philip T., David S. Jacks, Patricia A. Levin, and Peter H. Lindert. 2002. "Prices and Real Inequality in Europe since 1500." *Journal of Economic History* 62 (2): 322–355.

Hoffmann, W.G. 1965. *Das Wachstum der deutschen Wirtschaft seit der Mitte des 19 Jahrhunderts.* Berlin.

Hojat, Mohammadreza et al. 2000. "Physicians' perceptions of the changing health care system: Comparisons by gender and specialities." *Journal of Community Health* 25 (6): 455–71.

Hollingsworth, J. Rogers. 1986. *A Political Economy of Medicine: Great Britain and the United States.* Baltimore: Johns Hopkins University Press.

Hollingsworth, J. Rogers, Jerald Hage, and Robert A. Hanneman. 1990. *State Intervention in Medical Care: Consequences for Britain, France, Sweden, and the United States 1890–1970.* Baltimore: Johns Hopkins University Press.

Hollingsworth, J. Rogers and Ellen Jane Hollingsworth. 1994. *Care for the Chronically and Severely Ill: Comparative Social Policies.* New York: Aldine de Gruyter.

Houston, Robert Allan. 1985. *Scottish Literacy and the Scottish Identity.* Cambridge, UK: Cambridge University Press.

Hovde, B.J. 1948. *The Scandinavian Countries, 1720–1865: The Rise of the Middle Class.* Two volumes. Ithaca, NY: Cornell University Press.

Hoxby, Caroline. 1996. "How Teachers' Unions Affect Education Production." *Quarterly Journal of Economics* 111, 3 (August): 671–718.

Hoxby, Caroline. 2003. *The Economics of School Choice.* Chicago: University of Chicago Press for the NBER.

Hsieh, Chang-Tai and Miguel Urquiola. 2003. "When Schools Compete, How Do They Compete? An Assessment of Chile's Nationwide School Voucher System." NBER Working Paper No. 10008 (October 2003).

Huberman, Michael and Wayne Lewchuk. 2002. "European Economic Integration and the Social Compact, 1850–1913." Cirano (University of Montreal) Scientific Series, paper 2002s–34 (April).

Hunt, E.H. 1990. "Paupers and Pensioners: Past and Present." *Ageing and Society* 9: 407–430.

Humphreys, Robert. 1992. "Much Ado about Little: The Aims and Achievements of Charity Organisation Societies in Provincial England, 1870–1890." London School of Economics and Political Science, Working Paper in Economic History no. 10/92.

1995. *Sin, Organized Charity, and the Poor Law in Victorian England.* New York: St. Martin's Press.

Irwin, Douglas A. 1989. "Political Economy and Peel's Repeal of the Corn Laws." *Economics and Politics* 1, 1 (Spring 1989): 41–59.

Italy, Ministero de Agricoltura, Industria e Commercio. 1881. *Annuario Statistico Italiano, Anno 1881.* Roma: Eredi Botta.

Jackman, Robert W. 1987. "Political Institutions and Voter Turnout in the Industrial Democracies." *American Political Science Review* 81, 2 (June).

Jackman, Robert W. and Ross A. Miller. Forthcoming. *Culture, Institutions, and Political Behavior.* Ann Arbor: University of Michigan Press.

Johnson, Paul. 1994. "The Welfare State." In Roderick Floud and D.N. McCloskey (eds.), *The Economic History of Britain since 1700. Volume 3: 1939–1992.* Second edition. Cambridge, UK: Cambridge University Press, 284–317.

Jones, Colin. 1982. *Charity and Bienfaisance: The Treatment of the Poor in the Montpellier Region, 1740–1815.* Cambridge, UK: Cambridge University Press.

Jones, Donald K. 1977. *The Making of the Educational System 1851–81.* London: Routledge & Kegan Paul.

Jones, Michael A. 1983. *The Australian Welfare State: Growth, Crisis, and Change.* London: Allen and Unwin.

Jordan, Wilbur Kitchener. 1959. *Philanthropy in England, 1480–1660.* New York: Russell Sage Foundation.

1960. *The Charities of London, 1480–1660.* New York: Russell Sage Foundation.

1962. *The Charities of Rural England, 1480–1660.* New York: Russell Sage Foundation.

Joshi, Heather and Pierella Paci, with Gerald Makepeace and Jane Waldfogel. 1998. *Unequal Pay for Women and Men: Evidence from the British Birth Cohort Studies.* Cambridge, MA: MIT Press.

Joumard, Isabelle. 2001. "Tax Systems in European Union Countries." OECD, Economics Department Working Paper No. 301 (June).

Kaestle, Carl. 1976. "'Between the Scylla of Brutal Ignorance and the Charybdis of a Literary Education': Elite Attitudes toward Mass Schooling in Early Industrial England and America." In Lawrence Stone (ed.), *Schooling and Society: Studies in the History of Education.* Baltimore: Johns Hopkins University Press, 177–191.

1983. *Pillars of the Republic: Common Schools and American Society, 1780–1860.* New York: Hill & Wang.

Kaestle, Carl and Maris Vinovskis. 1980. *Education and Social Change in Nineteenth-Century Massachusetts.* New York: Cambridge University Press.

Kakwani, Nanak C. 1980. *Income Inequality and Poverty.* New York: Oxford University Press for the World Bank.

Kassirer, Jerome P. 1992. "Clinical Problem-Solving – A New Feature in the Journal." *The New England Journal of Medicine* 326 (1): 60–1.

Katz, Michael B. 1968. *The Irony of Early School Reform.* Cambridge, MA: Harvard University Press.

1987. *Reconstructing American Education.* Cambridge, MA: Harvard University Press.

Kawachi, Ichiro and Bruce P. Kennedy. 1997. "The Relationship of Income Inequality to Mortality: Does the Choice of Indicator Matter?" *Social Science and Medicine* 45, 7 (October: 1121–1127).

Kennedy, Bruce P. Ichiro Kawachi, Roberta Glass, and Deborah Prothrow-Stith. 1998. "Income Distribution, Socioeconomic Status, and Self-Rated Health in the

United States: Multilevel Analysis." *British Medical Journal* 317, 7163 (October 3): 917–921.

Kessler, Ronald C., et al. 2001. "Long-term trends in the use of complementary and alternative medical therapies in the United States." *Annals of Internal Medicine* 135 (4): 262–8.

Kewley, Thomas H. 1980. *Australian Social Security Today: Major Developments from 1900 to 1978.* Sydney: Sydney University Press.

Killingsworth, Mark R. 1983. *Labor Supply.* Cambridge, UK: Cambridge University Press.

King, D.E. and B. Bushwick. 1994. "Beliefs and attitudes of hospital in patients about faith healing and prayer." *Journal of Family Practice* 39 (4): 349–52.

Klebaner, Benjamin Joseph. 1951. "Public Poor Relief in America, 1790–1860." Ph.D. dissertation, Columbia University. Reprinted by Arno Press, New York, 1976.

Kleppner, Paul. 1982. *Who Voted? The Dynamics of Electoral Turnout, 1870–1980.* New York: Praeger.

Koester, R.B. and R.C. Kormendi. 1989. "Taxation, Aggregate Activity, and Economic Growth: Cross-Country Evidence on Some Supply Side Hypotheses." *Economic Inquiry* 27: 367–387.

Kornbluh, Mark L. 2000. *Why America Stopped Voting: The Decline of Participatory Democracy and the Emergence of Modern American Politics.* New York: New York University Press.

Kozol, Jonathan. 1991. *Savage Inequalities: Children in America's Schools.* New York: Crown Publishers.

Kramer, Mark. 1997. "Social Protection Policies and Safety Netts in East-Central Europe: Dilemmas of the Postcommunist Transformation." In Ethan B. Kapstein and Michael Mandelbaum (eds.), *Sustaining the Transition: The Social Safety Net in Postcommunist Europe.*" New York: Council on Foreign Relations, 46–123.

Kristov, Lorenzo, Peter Lindert, and Robert McClelland. 1992. "Pressure Groups and Redistribution." *Journal of Public Economics* 48, 2 (June): 135–163.

Kuo, Chun Chien. 1999. "The Determinants and Sustainability of Social Insurance Spending: A Cross-Country Examination." Doctoral dissertation in Economics, University of California, Davis.

Lakdawalla, Darius. 2001. "The Declining Quality of Teachers." NBER Working Paper 8263 (April).

Lampman, Robert J. 1984. *Social Welfare Spending: Accounting for Changes from 1950 to 1978.* New York: Academic Press.

Lang, Forest, Kevin Everett, R. McGowen, and Bruce Bennard. 2000. "Faculty development in communication skills instruction: Insights from a longitudinal program with 'real-time feedback.'" *Academic Medicine* 75 (12): 1222–8.

Larimore, Walter L. 2001. "Providing basic spiritual care for patients: Should it be the exclusive domain of pastoral professionals?" *American Family Physician* 63 (1): 36, 38–40.

Leacy, F.H. 1983. *Historical Statistics of Canada*, second edition. Ottawa: Canadian Government Pub Center.

Lee, Ronald D. and Timothy Miller. 2000. "Immigration, Social Security, and Broader Fiscal Impacts." *American Economic Review* 90, 2 (May): 350–4.

Bibliography

Lees, Lynn Hollen. 1998. *The Solidarities of Strangers: The English Poor Laws and the People, 1700–1948.* Cambridge, UK: Cambridge University Press.

Levasseur, E. 1897. *L'Enseignement primaire dans les pays civilisés.* Paris: Berger-Levrault.

Levine, Daniel. 1988. *Poverty and Society: The Growth of the American Welfare State in International Comparison.* New Brunswick, NJ: Rutgers University Press.

Lewis, Frank and M.C. Urquhart. 1999. "Growth and the Standard of Living in a Pioneer Economy: Upper Canada, 1826 to 1851." *William and Mary Quarterly,* 3rd series, 56, 1 (January), 151–179.

Lindbeck, Assar. 1997. "The Swedish Experiment." *Journal of Economic Literature* 35, 3 (September), 1273–1319. Expanded version: *The Swedish Experiment.* Stockholm: SNS Förlag, 1997.

Lindbeck, Assar, Per Molander, Torsten Persson, Olof Petersson, Agnar Sandmo, Brigitta Swedenborg, and Niels Thygesen. 1994. *Turning Sweden Around.* Cambridge, MA: MIT Press.

Lindert, P.H. 1978. *Fertility and Scarcity in America.* Princeton, NJ: Princeton University Press.

1986. "Unequal English Wealth since 1670." *Journal of Political Economy* 94, 6 (December): 1127–1162.

1987. "Who Owned Victorian England? The Debate over Landed Wealth and Inequality." *Agricultural History* 61, 4 (Fall): 25–51.

1991. "Historical Patterns of Agricultural Policy." In C. Peter Timmer (ed.), *Agriculture and the State.* Ithaca: Cornell University Press, 29–83.

1994. "The Rise of Social Spending, 1880–1930." *Explorations in Economic History* 31, 1 (January): 1–37.

1996. "What Limits Social Spending?" *Explorations in Economic History* 33, 1 (January): 1–34.

1998. "Poor Relief before the Welfare State: Britain versus the Continent, 1780–1880." *European Review of Economic History* 2 (August): 101–140.

2001. "Democracy, Decentralization, and Mass Schooling before 1914." University of California, Agricultural History Center, Working Papers 104 (main text) and 105 (appendices), April.

2003. "Voice and Growth: Was Churchill Right?" *Journal of Economic History* 63, 2 (June): 315–50.

Lindert, P.H., and Jeffrey G. Williamson. 1982. "Revising England's Social Tables, 1688–1812," *Explorations in Economic History* 19, 4 (October): 385–408.

1983. "Reinterpreting Britain's Social Tables, 1688–1913." *Explorations in Economic History,* 20, 1 (January): 94–109.

1985a. "English Workers' Wages: A Reply to Crafts." *Journal of Economic History* 45, 1 (March): 145–153.

1985b. "Growth, Equality and History." *Explorations in Economic History* 22, 3 (August): 341–377.

Lis, Catherina. 1986. *Social Change and the Labouring Poor: Antwerp, 1770–1860.* New Haven and London: Yale University Press.

Loch, C.S. 1898, reprinted 1976. *Poor Relief in Scotland: Its Statistics and Development 1791–1891.* New York: Arno Press.

Lott, John R., Jr. 1990. "An Explanation for Public Provision of Schooling: The Importance of Indoctrination." *Journal of Law and Economics* 38 (2).

Lott, John R. Jr. and Lawrence W. Kenny. 1999. "Did Women's Suffrage Change the Size and Scope of Government?" *Journal of Political Economy* 107, 6, Part I (December): 1163–1198.

Lovenduski, Joni and Pippa Norris. 1993. *Gender and Party Politics*. London: Sage.

MacKinnon, Mary. 1986. "Poor Law Policy, Unemployment, and Pauperism," *Explorations in Economic History* 23, 2, 299–336.

    1987. "English Poor Law Policy and the Crusade against Outrelief." *Journal of Economic History* 47, 3 (September): 603–625.

Maddison, Angus. 1995. *Monitoring the World Economy 1820–1992*. Paris: OECD.

Maestri, Pietro. 1868. *L'Italia Economica nel 1868*. Firenze: G. Civelli.

Mandler, P. 1987. "The Making of the New Poor Law *Redivisus*." *Past and Present* 117: 131–57.

Marcus, Donald M. 2001. "How should alternative medicine be taught to medical students and physicians?" *Academic Medicine* 76 (3): 224–9.

Margo, Robert A. 1990. *Race and Schooling in the South, 1880–1950*. Chicago: University of Chicago Press.

Margolin, Arthur, et al. 2002. "Acupuncture for the treatment of cocaine addiction: A randomized controlled trial." *The Journal of the American Medical Association* 287 (1): 55–63.

Marshall, J. 1833. *Digest of All the Accounts . . . of the United Kingdom. . . .* London: J. Haddon.

Martin, John P. 1996. "Measures of Replacement Rates for the Purpose of International Comparisons: A Note." *OECD Economic Studies* 26, 1: 99–116.

Martz, Linda. 1983. *Poverty and Welfare in Habsburg Spain: The Example of Toledo*. Cambridge, UK: Cambridge University Press.

Marvel, Howard. 1977. "Factory Regulation: A Reinterpretation of Early English Experiences." *Journal of Law and Economics* (October): 379–402.

McAuley, Alastair. 1979. *Economic Welfare in the Soviet Union: Poverty, Living Standards, and Inequality*. Madison: University of Wisconsin Press.

McCants, Anne E.C. 1997. *Civic Charity in a Golden Age: Orphan Care in Early Modern Amsterdam*. Urbana: University of Illinois Press.

McGuire, Martin C. and Mancur Olson, Jr. 1996. "The Economics of Autocracy and Majority Rule: The Invisible Hand and the Use of Force." *Journal of Economic Literature* 34, 1 (March): 72–96.

McLure, Charles E., Jr. 1990. "Appraising Tax Reform." In Michael J. Boskin and Charles E. McLure, Jr. *World Tax Reform: Case Studies of Developed and Developing Countries*. San Francisco: ICS Press, 279–288.

Meeker, William C. and Scott Haldeman. 2002. "Chiropractic: A profession at the crossroads of mainstream and alternative medicine." *Annals of Internal Medicine* 136 (3) 216–27.

Mehrotra, Santosh, and P. Buckland. 1998. "Managing Teacher Costs for Access and Quality." New York: UNICEF. Evaluation, Policy, and Planning Working Paper no. 4.

Mehrotra, Santosh and Enrique Delamonica. Forthcoming. *Public Spending for the Poor. Basic Services to Enhance Capabilities and Promote Growth*. Submitted for publication.

Melton, J. Van Horn. 1988. *Absolutism and the Eighteenth-Century Origins of Compulsory Schooling in Prussia and Austria.* Cambridge, UK: Cambridge University Press.

Meltzer, Allan H. and Scott F. Richard. 1981. "A Rational Theory of the Size of Government." *Journal of Political Economy,* 89, 5 (October): 914–27.

Mendoza, Enrique G., Gian Maria Milesi-Ferretti, and Patrick Asea. 1997. "On the Ineffectiveness of Tax Policy in Altering Long-Run Growth: Harberger's Superneutrality Conjecture." *Journal of Public Economics* 66, 1 (October 1997): 99–126.

Mendoza, Enrique G., Assaf Razin, and Linda L. Tesar. 1994. "Effective Tax Rates in Macroeconomics: Cross-Country Estimates of Tax Rates on Factor Incomes and Consumption." *Journal of Monetary Economics* 34: 297–323.

Mendoza, Enrique G. and Linda L. Tesar. 1998. "The International Ramifications of Tax Reforms: Supply-Side Economics in a Global Economy." *American Economic Review* 88, 1 (March): 226–245.

Meyer, B.D. 1995. "Lessons from the U.S. Unemployment Insurance Experiments." *Journal of Economic Literature* 33, 1 (March).

Miron, J.A. and D.N. Weil. 1998. "The Genesis and Evolution of Social Security." In M. Bordo, C. Goldin, and E. White (eds.), *The Defining Moment: The Great Depression and the American Economy in the Twentieth Century.* Chicago: University of Chicago Press, pp. 297–322.

Mishler, Elliot George. 1984. *The Discourse of Medicine: Dialectics in Medical Interviews.* Norwood, NJ: Ablex Publishing Corporation.

Mitch, David F. 1992. *The Rise of Popular Literacy in Victorian England: The Influence of Private Choice and Public Policy.* Philadelphia: University of Pennsylvania Press.

Mitchell, Allan. 1991. "The Function and Malfunction of Mutual Aid Societies in Nineteenth-Century France." In Jonathan Barry and Colin Jones (eds.), *Medicine and Charity before the Welfare State.* New York: Routledge, 172–189.

Mitchell, Brian R. (ed.) 1975. *European Historical Statistics, 1750–1970.* Cambridge, UK: Cambridge University Press.

Moe, Terry. 2001. *Schools, Vouchers, and the American Public.* Washington, DC: The Brookings Institution.

Moffitt, Robert A. 2002a. "The Temporary Assistance for Needy Families Program." NBER Working Paper 8749 (February), forthcoming as a chapter in Moffitt (ed.), *Means-Tested Programs in the United States.* Chicago: University of Chicago Press.

2002b. "Welfare Programs and Labor Supply." NBER Working Paper 9168 (September), forthcoming in a volume of *Handbook in Public Economics.*

Mohl, Raymond A. 1971. *Poverty in New York, 1783–1825.* New York: Oxford University Press.

Mokyr, Joel. 1983. *Why Ireland Starved.* London: Allen and Unwin.

Mommsen, W.J. (ed.). 1981. *The Emergence of the Welfare State in Britain and Germany 1850–1950.* London: Croom Helm.

Moody, Joseph N. 1978. *French Education since Napoleon.* Syracuse: Syracuse University Press.

Morrisson, Christian. 2000. "Historical Perspectives on Income Distribution: The Case of Europe." In A.B. Atkinson and François Bourguignon (eds.), *Handbook of Income Distribution*. Amsterdam: Elsevier Science, 217–260.

Mulhall, Michael G. 1880. *The Progress of the World...since the Beginning of the Nineteenth Century*. London: MacGlinchy. Irish University Press reprint, Shannon, 1971.

Mulligan, Casey and Xavier Sala-i-Martin. 1999. "Gerontocracy, Retirement, and Social Security." NBER Working Paper 7117 (May).

Mulligan, Casey, Ricard Gil, and Xavier Sala-i-Martin. 2002. "Social Security and Democracy." NBER Working Paper 8958 (May).

Murray, Charles. 1984. *Losing Ground: American Social Policy, 1950–1980*. New York: Basic Books.

Musgrave, R.A. and J.M. Culbertson. 1953. "The Growth of Public Expenditures in the United States," *National Tax Journal* 6, 2, 97–115.

Nash, Gary B. 1976. "Poverty and Poor Relief in Pre-Revolutionary Philadelphia." *The William and Mary Quarterly* 33, 1, pp. 3–30.

Nelson, H. and T. O'Brien. 1993. *How U.S. Teachers Measure Up Internationally: A Comparative Study of Teacher Pay, Training, and Conditions of Service*. Washington, DC: American Federation of Teachers.

Nickell, Stephen. 1997. "Unemployment and Labor Market Rigidities: Europe versus North America." *Journal of Economic Perspectives* 11, 3 (Summer), 55–74.

Niemi, Richard G., Harold W. Stanley, and C. Lawrence Evans. 1984. "Age and Turnout Among the Newly Enfranchised: Life Cycle versus Experience Effects." *European Journal of Political Research* 12, 4, 371–386.

Nipperdey, Thomas. 1977. "Mass Education and Modernization: The Case of Germany 1780–1850." *Transactions of the Royal Historical Society*, 5th series, 27, pp. 155–172.

1996. *Germany from Napoleon to Bismarck: 1800 to 1866*. Princeton, NJ: Princeton University Press.

Norberg, Kathryn. 1985. *Rich and Poor in Grenoble, 1600–1814*. Berkeley: University of California Press.

Norrman, Erik and Charles McLure Jr. 1997. "Tax Policy in Sweden." In Richard B. Freeman, Robert Topel, and Birgitta Swedenborg. *The Welfare State in Transition: Reforming the Swedish Model*. Chicago: University of Chicago Press.

North, Douglass C. and Barry Weingast. 1989. "Constitutions and Commitment: The Evolution of Institutions Governing Public Choice in Seventeenth-Century England." *Journal of Economic History* 49 (3): 803–832.

O'Brien, Patrick K. 1988. "The Political Economy of British Taxation, 1660–1815." *Economic History Review*, Second Series, 41, 1 (February): 1–32.

Olfson, Mark, Steven C. Marcus, Benjamin Druss, and Harold Alan Pincus. 2002. "National Trends in the Use of Outpatient Psychotherapy." *American Journal of Psychiatry* 159 (11): 1914–20.

Or, Zeynap. 2000. "Determinants of Health Outcomes in Industrialised Countries: A Pooled, Cross-Country, Time-Series Analysis." *OECD Economic Studies* 30, 1: 53–77.

Organisation for Economic Cooperation and Development (OECD). 1985. *Social Expenditure 1960–1990*. Paris: OECD.

1992. *Education at a Glance 1992*. Paris: OECD.

1994a. *The OECD Jobs Study: Facts, Analysis, Strategies*. Paris: OECD.

1994b. *The OECD Jobs Study: Evidence and Explanations*. Two volumes. Paris: OECD.

1996. *Education at a Glance: OECD Indicators 1996*. Paris: OECD.

1998a. *The Battle against Exclusion: Social Assistance in Australia, Finland, Sweden, and the United Kingdom*. Paris: OECD.

1998b. *The Battle against Exclusion, Volume 2: Social Assistance in Belgium, the Czech Republic, the Netherlands, and Norway*. Paris: OECD.

1998c. *Education at a Glance: OECD Indicators 1998*. Paris: OECD.

1998d. *Employment Outlook* (June). Paris: OECD.

1998e. *OECD Economic Surveys: Netherlands*. Paris: OECD.

1999. *Social Expenditure Database, 1980–1996*. Paris: OECD.

2000a. *OECD Health Data*. Paris: OECD.

2000b. *Revenue Statistics 1965–1999*. Paris: OECD.

2001. *Education at a Glance 2001*. Paris: OECD.

OECD, Programme for International Student Assessment (PISA). 2001. *Knowledge and Skills for Life: First Results from the.... (PISA) 2000*. Paris: OECD. Printed from the pdf file at www.pisa.oecd.org, March 8, 2002.

O'Rourke, Kevin H. 1997. "The European Grain Invasion, 1870–1913." *Journal of Economic History* 58 (3): 775–801.

Owen, David. 1964. *English Philanthropy, 1660–1960*. Cambridge, MA: Belknap.

Padovano, Fabio and Emma Galli. 2001. "Tax Rates and Economic Growth in the OECD Countries (1950–1990)." *Economic Inquiry* 39, 1 (January): 44–57.

Pampel, Fred C. and John B. Williamson. 1989. *Age, Class, Politics, and the Welfare State*. Cambridge, UK: Cambridge University Press.

Parkerson, Donald H. and Jo Ann Parkerson. 1998. *The Emergence of the Common School in the U.S. Countryside*. Lewiston: Edwin Mellon.

Pechman, Joseph A. 1985. *Who Paid the Taxes, 1966–1985?* Washington, DC: The Brookings Institution.

Peltzman, Sam. 1980. "The Growth of Government." *Journal of Law and Economics* 23, 2 (October): 209–88.

Perlmann, Joel and Robert A. Margo. 2001. *Women's Work? American Schoolteachers, 1650–1920*. Chicago: University of Chicago Press.

Persson, Torsten and Guido Tabellini. 1994. "Is Inequality Harmful for Growth?" *American Economic Review* 84, 3 (June): 600–621.

Petersilie, A. 1906. *Preussische Statistik, v. 209: Das gesamte niedere Schulwesen im Preussischen Staate im Jahre 1906*. Berlin: Statistischen Landesamt.

Peterson, Wills L. and Joseph C. Fitzhams. 1974. *The Organization and Productivity of the Federal-State Research System in the United States*. University of Minnesota, Department of Agricultural and Applied Economics, Staff Paper p7, 4–23.

Pirard, Joseph. 1985. *Le pouvoir central Belge et ses comptes economiques 1830–1913*. Brussels: Palais des Académies.

Porter, G.R. 1851. *The Progress of the Nation....* London: John Murray.

Porter, G.R. and F. Hirst. 1912. *The Progress of the Nation....*

Postlethwaite, T. Neville and D.E. Wiley. 1992. *The IEA Study of Science II: Science Achievement in Twenty-Three Countries*. London: Pergammon Press.

Prest, John. 1990. *Liberality and Locality: Parliament, Permissive Legislation, and Ratepayers' Democracies in the Nineteenth Century*. Oxford: Clarendon Press.

Preston, Samuel, and Michael R. Haines. 1991. *Fatal Years: Child Mortality in Late Nineteenth Century America*. Princeton, NJ: Princeton University Press.

Price, Roger. 1987. *A Social History of Nineteenth-Century France*. London: Hutchinson.

Ramsey, Frank P. 1927. "A Contribution to the Theory of Taxation." *Economic Journal* 37, 47–61.

Ransom, Roger and Richard Sutch. 1977. *One Kind of Freedom*. Cambridge, UK: Cambridge University Press.

Razin, Assaf, Ephraim Sadka, and Phillip Swagel. 2001. "The Aging Population and the Size of the Welfare State." NBER Working Paper no. 8405 (July).

Reinhardt, Uwe E. 2000. "Health Care for the Aging Baby Boom: Lessons from Abroad." *Journal of Economic Perspectives* 14, 2 (Spring): 71–84.

Richardson, Gary. 2000. "The Prudent Village: A Corroboration of Kimball's Conjecture." Manuscript, University of California, Irvine.

Roberts, Russell D. 1984. "A Positive Model of Private Charity and Public Transfers." *Journal of Political Economy* 92, 1 (February): 136–148.

Rodgers, G.B. 1997. "Income and Inequality as Determinants of Mortality: An International Cross-Section Analysis." *Population Studies* 33, 2: 343–51.

Rodrik, Dani. 1997. *Has Globalization Gone too Far?* Washington, DC: Institute for International Economics.

1998. "Why Do More Open Economies Have Bigger Governments?" *Journal of Political Economy* 106, 5 (October): 997–1032.

Rose, Michael E. 1981. "The Crisis of Poor Relief in England 1860–1890." In W.J. Mommsen (ed.), *The Emergence of the Welfare State in Britain and Germany, 1850–1950*. London: Croom Helm.

Rose, Michael E. (ed.). 1985. *The Poor and the City: The English Poor Law in its Urban Context, 1834–1914*. Leicester, UK: Leicester University Press.

Rosen, Sherwin. 1997. "Public Employment, Taxes, and the Welfare State in Sweden," In Richard B. Freeman, Robert Topel, and Birgitta Swedenborg (eds.), *The Welfare State in Transition: Reforming the Swedish Model*. Chicago: University of Chicago Press, 79–108.

Ross, Nancy A. Michael C. Wolfson, James R. Dunn, Jan-Marie Berthelot, George A. Kaplan, and John W. Lynch. 2000. "Relation between Income Inequality and Mortality in Canada and in the United States: Cross-Sectional Assessment Using Census Data and Vital Statistics." *British Medical Journal* 320, 7239 (April 1): 898ff.

Rothstein, Jesse. 2003. "Good Principals or Good Peers? Parental Valuations of School Characteristics, Tiebout Equilibrium, and the Incentive Effects of Competition among Jurisdictions." Job market paper, Berkeley: CA (January).

Rowell, Donna M. and David J. Kroll. 1998. "Complementary and alternative medicine education in United States pharmacy schools." *American Journal of Pharmaceutical Education* 62 (4): 412–9.

Rubinson, Richard. 1986. "Class Formation, Politics, and Institutions: Schooling in the United States." *American Journal of Sociology* 92, 3 (November).

Sala-i-Martin, Xavier. 1996. "A Positive Theory of Social Security." *Journal of Economic Growth* 1, 2 (June), 277–304.

Sackett, David L. et al. 1996. "Evidence based medicine: What it is and what it isn't." *British Medical Journal* 312 (7023): 71–2.

Sampson, Wallace. 2001. "The need for educational reform in teaching about Alternative therapies." *Academic Medicine* 76 (3): 248–50.

Sanderson, Michael. 1999. *Education and Economic Decline in Britain, 1870 to the 1990s.* Cambridge, UK: Cambridge University Press.

Scarpetta, Stefano. 1996. "Assessing the Role of Labour Market Policies and Institutional Settings on Unemployment: A Cross-Country Study." *OECD Economic Studies* 26, 1: 43–98.

Schleunes, Karl A. 1989. *Schooling and Society: The Politics of Education in Prussia and Bavaria 1750–1900.* New York: Berg and St. Martin's Press.

Schneider, Friedrich and Dominik H. Enste. 2000. "Shadow Economies: Size, Causes, and Consequences." *Journal of Economic Literature* 38 (1): 77–114.

Schneider, Reinhart. 1982. "Die Bildungsentwicklung in den West-europaischen Staaten 1870–1975." *Zeitschrift für Soziologie* 11, 207–226.

Schofield, Roger S. 1973. "Dimensions of Illiteracy, 1750–1850." *Explorations in Economic History* 10, 4(Summer): 437–454.

Schultz, Kenneth A. and Barry R. Weingast. 1998. "Limited Governments, Powerful States." In Randolph M. Siverson (ed.), *Strategic Politicians, Institutions, and Foreign Policy.* Ann Arbor: University of Michigan Press, 15–49.

Siebert, Horst. 1997. "Labor Market Rigidities: At the Root of Unemployment in Europe." *Journal of Economic Perspectives* 11 (3): 37–54.

Slack, Paul. 1990. *The English Poor Law, 1531–1782.* Basingstoke: Macmillan.

Slemrod, Joel. 1995. "What Do Cross-Country Studies Teach about Government Involvement, Prosperity, and Economic Growth?" *Brookings Papers in Economic Activity* 2, 373–431.

Smith, Adam. 1993 (1776). *An Inquiry into the Nature and Causes of the Wealth of Nations.* Edited by Kathryn Sutherland. NewYork: Oxford University Press.

Smith Michael J. and Alan C. Logan. 2002. "Naturopathy." *Medical Clinics of North America* 86 (1): 173–84.

Smith, Richard M. 1984. "The Structured Dependence of the Elderly as a Recent Development: Some Sceptical Historical Thoughts." *Ageing and Society* 4, 4 (December): 409–428.

Smith, Richard. 1991. "Where is the wisdom...?" *British Medical Journal* 303 (6806): 798–9.

Snell, K.D.M. 1985. *Annals of the Labouring Poor.* Cambridge, UK: Cambridge University Press.

Solar, Peter. 1995. "Poor Relief and English Economic Development before the Industrial Revolution." *Economic History Review* 48, 1, 1–22.

1997. "Poor Relief and English Economic Development: A Renewed Plea for Comparative History." *Economic History Review* 50, 2, 369–374.

Solow, Robert M. 2000. "Welfare: The Cheapest Country." *New York Review of Books,* 47, 5 (March 23), 20–23.

Soltow, Lee and Jan Luiten van Zanden (eds.). 1998. *Income and Wealth Inequality in the Netherlands 16th–20th Century.* Amsterdam: Het Spinhuis.

Steckel, Richard H. 1995. "Stature and the Standard of Living." *Journal of Economic Literature* 33, 4 (December): 1903–1940.

Steinmo, Sven. 1993. *Taxation and Democracy: Swedish, British and American Approaches to Financing the Modern State*. New Haven: Yale University Press.

Stuart, Charles. 1984. "Welfare Costs per Dollar of Additional Tax Revenue in the United States." *American Economic Review* 74, 3 (June): 352–362.

Sturt, Mary. 1967. *The Education of the People: A History of Primary Education in England and Wales in the Nineteenth Century*. London: Routledge and Kegan Paul.

Subbarao, K., Aniruddha Bonnerjee, Jeanine Braithwaite, Soniya Carvalho, Kene Ezemenari, Carol Graham, and Alan Thompson. 1997. *Safety Net Programs and Poverty Reduction: Lessons from Cross-Country Experience*. Washington, DC: World Bank.

Sukehiro, Hirakawa and Bob Tadashi Wakabayashi. 1989. "Japan's Turn to the West." In Marius B. Jansen (ed.), *The Cambridge History of Japan*, volume 5. Cambridge, UK: Cambridge University Press, 435–498.

Sutherland, Gillian. 1973. *Policy-Making in Elementary Education 1870–1895*. Oxford: Oxford University Press.

Suval, Stanley. 1985. *Electoral Politics in Wilhelmine Germany*. Chapel Hill: University of North Carolina Press.

Sweden. Various years. *Statistisk Arsbok* and *Statistisk Tidskrift*.

Swenson, Peter and Jonas Pontusson. 2000. "The Swedish Employer Offensive against Centralized Wage Bargaining." In Torben Iversen, Jonas Pontusson, and David Soskice (eds.). 2000. *Unions, Employers, and Central Banks: Macroeconomic Coordination and Institutional Change in Social Market Economies*. Cambridge, UK: Cambridge University Press, 77–106.

Takayama, Noriyuki. 1992. *The Greying of Japan: An Economic Perspective on Public Pensions*. Tokyo: Kinokuniya.

Tampke, Jurgen. 1981. "Bismarck's Social Legislation: A Genuine Breakthrough?" In W.J. Mommsen (ed.). *The Emergence of the Welfare State in Britain and Germany, 1850–1950*, London: Croom Helm.

Tanzi, Vito and Ludger Schuknecht. 2000. *Public Spending in the 20th Century*. Cambridge, UK: Cambridge University Press.

Teixeira, Ruy A. 1987. *Why Americans Don't Vote: Turnout Decline in the United States*. New York: Greenwood Press.

Temin, Peter. 2002. "Teacher Quality and the Future of America." NBER Working Paper 8898 (April).

Thomson, David. 1984. "The Decline of Social Welfare: Falling State Support for the Elderly since Early Victorian Times." *Ageing and Society* 4, 451–482.

Tiebout, Charles M. 1956. "A Pure Theory of Local Expenditures." *Journal of Political Economy* 64, 5 (October): 416–424.

Toutain, Jean-Claude. 1987. *Le produit intérieur brut de la France de 1789 a 1982*. *Economies et Sociétés*. Cahiers de l'I.S.M.E.A., Série Histoire quantitative de l'Économie française, no. 15.

Treble, James H. 1979. *Urban Poverty in Britain, 1830–1914*. London: Batsford.

Tremewan, Christopher. 1998. "Welfare and Governance: Public Housing under Singapore's Party-State." In R. Goodman, G. White, and H. Kwon (eds.). 1998. *The East Asian Welfare Model: Welfare Orientalism and the State*. London: Routledge, 77–105.

Triest, Robert K. 1990. "The Effect of Income Taxation on Labor Supply in the United States." *Journal of Human Resources* 25, 3 (Summer), 491–516.

Triest, Robert K. 1994. "The Efficiency Cost of Increased Progressivity." In Joel Slemrod (ed.), *Tax Progressivity and Income Inequality*. New York: Columbia University Press, 137–169.

Ullman, Hans-Peter. 1981. "German Industry and Bismarck's Social Security System." In W.J. Mommsen (ed.). *The Emergence of the Welfare State in Britain and Germany, 1850–1950*. London: Croom Helm.

United Kingdom, Education Commission. 1861. *Reports . . . to Inquire into the State of Population Education in Continental Europe. . . .* London: HMSO.

United Nations, Department of Economic and Social Affairs. 1998. *World Population Prospects: The 1996 Revision*. New York: United Nations.

United Nations Development Program. 1994. *Human Development Report 1994*. New York: United Nations.

United Nations Educational, Scientific, and Cultural Organization (UNESCO). 1991–1998. *World Education Report*. New York: UNESCO.

U.S. Census Bureau. 1976. *Historical Statistics of the United States from Colonial Times to 1970*. Two volumes. Washington, DC: GPO.

2001. *Statistical Abstract of the United States 2001*. Washington, DC: GPO.

U.S. Commissioner of Education. 1873–1903. *Reports*. Washington, DC: GPO.

U.S. Commissioner of Labor. 1911. *Twenty-Fourth Annual Report . . . 1909: Workmen's Insurance and Compensation Systems in Europe*. Two volumes. Washington, DC: GPO.

U.S. Department of Education, National Center for Education Statistics. 1997. *Pursuing Excellence: A Study of U.S. Fourth-Grade Mathematics and Science Achievement in International Context*. Washington, DC: NCES.

U.S. Department of Education, National Center for Education Statistics. 1998. *Pursuing Excellence: A Study of U.S. Twelfth-Grade Mathematics and Science Achievement in International Context*. Washington, DC: NCES.

U.S. National Center for Education Statistics. 2000. *Digest of Education Statistics 1999*. Washington, DC: GPO.

U.S. Superintendent of the Census. 1872. *Compendium of the Ninth Census*. Washington, DC: GPO.

Urquhart, M.C. 1993. *Gross National Product, Canada, 1870–1926: The Derivation of the Estimates*. Kingston: McGill-Queen's University Press.

Valletta, Robert G. and Richard B. Freeman. 1988. "Appendix B. The NBER Public Sector Collective Bargaining Law Data Set." In Richard B. Freeman and Casey Ichniowski (eds.), *When Public Sector Workers Unionize*. Chicago: University of Chicago Press, 399–420.

Vanderford, Marsha L., Terry Stein, Robert Sheeler, and Susan Skochelak. 2001. "Communication challenges for experienced clinicians: topics for an advanced communication curriculum." Health Communication 13 (3): 261–84.

Van Leeuwen, Marco H.D. 2000. *The Logic of Charity: Amsterdam, 1800–1850*. Translation of his *Bijstand in Amsterdam, ca. 1800–1850* by Arnold J. Basingstoke. Hampshire: Macmillan.

Waldfogel, Jane. 1998. "Understanding the 'Family Gap' in Pay for Women and Children." *Journal of Economic Perspectives* 12, 1 (Winter), 137–156.

Wallerstein, Michael and Miriam Golden. 2000. "The Fragmentation of the Bargaining Society: Changes in the Centralization of Wage-Setting in the Nordic

Countries, 1950–1992." In Torben Iversen, Jonas Pontusson, and David Soskice (eds.), *Unions, Employers, and Central Banks: Macroeconomic Coordination and Institutional Change in Social Market Economies*. Cambridge, UK: Cambridge University Press, 107–137.

Wardle, David. 1976. *English Popular Education 1780–1975*. Cambridge, UK: Cambridge University Press.

Watts, Harold W. and Albert Rees. 1977. *The New Jersey Income-Maintenance Experiment, Volume II, Labor-Supply Responses*. New York: Academic Press.

Weaver, W. Timothy. 1983. *America's Teacher Quality Problem: Alternatives for Reform*. New York: Praeger.

Weber, Eugen. 1976. *Peasants into Frenchmen: The Modernization of Rural France, 1870–1914*. Stanford: Stanford University Press.

Webb, Sidney and Beatrice Webb. 1927 and 1929. *English Poor Law History: Part I: The Old Poor Law*, and *Part II, the Last Hundred Years*. Two volumes. London: Longmans.

Weindling, Paul. 1991. "The Modernization of Charity in Nineteenth-Century France and Germany." In Jonathan Barry and Colin Jones (eds.), *Medicine and Charity before the Welfare State*. New York: Routledge, 190–206.

Weiss, John H. 1983. "Origins of the French Welfare State: Poor Relief in the Third Republic, 1871–1914." *French Historical Studies* 13 (1): 47–77.

West, E.G. 1970. *Education and the State*, second edition. London: Institute of Economic Affairs.

West, E.G. 1975. "Educational Slowdown and Public Intervention in 19th-Century England: A Study in the Economics of Bureaucracy." *Explorations in Economic History* 12, 1 (January): 61–87.

Wilensky, Harold. 1975. *The Welfare State and Equality*. Berkeley: University of California Press.

Wilensky, Harold. 2002. *Rich Democracies: Political Economy, Public Policy, and Performance*. Berkeley: University of California Press, 2002.

Williams, Karel. 1981. *From Pauperism to Poverty*. London: Routledge & Kegan Paul.

Woessmann (Wößmann), Ludger. 2002. *Schooling and the Quality of Human Capital*. Berlin: Springer-Verlag.

Wolf, Richard M. 1977. *Achievement in America: National Report of the United States for the International Education Achievement Project*. New York: Teachers College Press.

Wolfinger, Raymond E. and Steven J. Rosenstone. 1980. *Who Votes?* New Haven: Yale University Press.

Woolf, Stuart. 1986. *The Poor in Western Europe in the Eighteenth and Nineteenth Centuries*. New York: Methuen.

World Bank. 1993. *World Development Report 1993*. Washington, DC: World Bank. 1994. *Averting the Old Age Crisis*. New York: Oxford University Press.

World Health Organization. 1999. *World Health Report*. Geneva: WHO.

Wright, Gavin. 1986. *Old South, New South*. New York: W.W. Norton.

Yashiro, Naohiro and Takashi Oshio. 1999. "Social Security and Retirement in Japan." In Jonathan Gruber and David Wise (eds.), *Social Security Programs and Retirement around the World*. Chicago: University of Chicago Press, 239–268.

Acknowledgments

When you write on a topic everybody knows something about, and cares about, you get a lot of good help.

Much of the helpful advice on earlier drafts took the form of demands that I eliminate whole passages. Among those whose help takes this invisible form was Larry Neal, whose blunt warnings greatly improved the presentation of the whole book. In his editorial role Larry had also improved my articles in *Explorations in Economic History*, which have helped to shape Chapters 7 and 16–18. Similarly, Jeffrey Williamson offered warnings that have streamlined the early chapters, along with his usual wide-ranging valuable economic insights.

Some helped by being co-authors, directly or almost directly. Gayle Allard, as noted below, co-authored Chapter 19 in Volume 2, which also draws heavily on her doctoral thesis. Lorenzo Kristov and Rob McClelland were my co-authors for an article in the *Journal of Public Economics* used heavily in Chapter 13 of Volume 2.

For their comments and suggestions I also thank the following: Daron Acemoglu, Lee Alston, George Boyer, Colin Cameron, Greg Clark, Jan DeVries, Rolf Dumke, Barry Eichengreen, Jeffry Frieden, Timothy Guinnane, Irv Garfinkel, Joan U. Hannon, Philip Hoffman, Michael Huberman, Ethan Kapstein, Frank Lewis, Anne McCants, David Mitch, Alan L. Olmstead, Marianne Page, James A. Robinson, Peter Solar, Richard Sutch, Vito Tanzi, John Wallis, Harold Wilensky, and Stanley Winer. Whole Groups offered reactions and criticisms at the All-UC Group in Economic History, the Allied Social Sciences Association meetings, Arizona, Autonoma (Barcelona), UC Berkeley, UC Davis, UC Riverside, Carlos III, the Cliometrics Conference, the European University Institute, the European Historical Economics Society conference at Montecatini, Harvard, Illinois, Indiana-Purdue at Indianapolis, Moscow State, Queens University, Toronto, Stanford, U.S. Central Intelligence Agency (Virginia), Washington Area Economic History

Seminar, Washington University (St. Louis), World Bank, and the University of Zaragoza.

Others helped with data sources. Jan de Vries, Stanley L. Engerman, Frances Gouda, and Jan Luiten van Zanden provided materials, source references, and ideas for my coverage of the Netherlands and France in Chapters 3 and 4. Rolf Dumke supplied some key German sources for Chapter 5, and John H. Bishop and Ludger Wößmann supplied hard-to-get materials for Chapter 6.

Valuable research assistance was provided by Maite Cabeza-Gutés, Lindsay Crawford, Erick Eschker, Patricia A. Levin, Brian Rosario, Bernardo Santo Domingo, Mark Siegler, and Francesca Zaccheo.

For research funding, I thank UC Davis for supporting the Agricultural History Center, and the U.S. National Science Foundation for earlier grants contributing to the British and American material.

The greatest individual research help of all was that provided by Mary V. Davis, my co-worker at the Agricultural History Center, who solved software problems, kept me supplied with materials, and distributed my earlier drafts.

Index